Iceland's Financial Crisis

Being the first casualty of the international financial crisis, Iceland was, in many ways, turned into a laboratory when it came to responding to one of the largest corporate failures on record.

This edited volume offers the most wide-ranging treatment of the Icelandic financial crisis and its political, economic, social, and constitutional consequences. Interdisciplinary, with contributions from historians, economists, sociologists, legal scholars, political scientists, and philosophers, it also compares and contrasts the Icelandic experience with other national and global crises. It examines the economic magnitude of the crisis, the social and political responses, and the unique transitional justice mechanisms used to deal with it. It studies both backward-looking elements, including a societal and legal reckoning—which included the indictment of a prime minister and jailing of leading bankers for their part in the financial crisis—and forward-looking features, such as an attempt to rewrite the Icelandic constitution. Throughout, it underscores the contemporary relevance of the Icelandic case. While the Icelandic economic recovery has been much quicker than expected, it shows that public faith in political elites has not been restored. A case in point was the sudden resignation of the Icelandic Prime Minister following mass protests in the spring of 2016. It resulted from a revelation—stemming from the "Panama Papers" leaks—that he had owned an offshore company with his wife, with large claims on the collapsed Icelandic banks.

This text will be of key interest to scholars, policy-makers, and students of the financial crisis in such fields as European politics, international political economy, comparative politics, sociology, economics, contemporary history, and more broadly the social sciences and humanities.

Valur Ingimundarson is Professor of Contemporary History at the University of Iceland and the chair of the Board of the EDDA—Center of Excellence.

Philippe Urfalino is a senior researcher at the French Centre National de la Recherche Scientifique (CNRS) and professor at the École des Hautes Etudes en Sciences Sociales (EHESS), France.

Irma Erlingsdóttir is Associate Professor of French Contemporary Literature at the University of Iceland and director of EDDA—Center of Excellence; the United Nations University Gender Equality Studies and Training Programme (UNU-GEST); and Institute for Gender, Equality and Difference (RIKK), University of Iceland.

Routledge Advances in European Politics

116 The Diplomatic System of the European Union
Evolution, Change and Challenges
Edited by Michael Smith, Stephan Keukeleire and Sophie Vanhoonacker

117 European Union Enlargement
Material Interests, Community Norms and Anomie
Thomas Mehlhausen

118 The Moral Economy of EU Association with Africa
Mark Langan

119 European Space Policy
European Integration and the Final Frontier
Edited by Thomas Hörber and Paul Stephenson

120 Policy Making at the Second Tier of Local Government in Europe
What is Happening in Provinces, Counties, Départements and Landkreise in the On-going Re-scaling of Statehood?
Edited by Xavier Bertrana, Björn Egner and Hubert Heinelt

121 The Politics of Trauma and Peace-Building
Lessons from Northern Ireland
Cillian McGrattan

122 Eurozone Politics
Perception and Reality in Italy, the UK, and Germany
Philip Giurlando

123 Politics of Identity in Post-Conflict States
The Bosnian and Irish Experience
Edited by Éamonn Ó Ciardha and Gabriela Vojvoda

124 Unequal Europe
Social Divisions and Social Cohesion in an Old Continent
James Wickham

125 Clientelism and Economic Policy
Greece and the Crisis
Aris Trantidis

126 Challenges to Democracies in East-Central Europe
Edited by Jan Holzer and Miroslav Mareš

127 Iceland's Financial Crisis
The Politics of Blame, Protest, and Reconstruction
Edited by Valur Ingimundarson, Philippe Urfalino and Irma Erlingsdóttir

Iceland's Financial Crisis

The politics of blame, protest, and reconstruction

Edited by
Valur Ingimundarson,
Philippe Urfalino and
Irma Erlingsdóttir

Routledge
Taylor & Francis Group
LONDON AND NEW YORK

First published 2016
by Routledge
2 Park Square, Milton Park, Abingdon, Oxon OX14 4RN

and by Routledge
711 Third Avenue, New York, NY 10017

First issued in paperback 2018

Routledge is an imprint of the Taylor & Francis Group, an informa business

British Library Cataloguing in Publication Data
A catalogue record for this book is available from the British Library

Library of Congress Cataloging in Publication Data
Names: Valur Ingimundarson, editor. | Urfalino, Philippe, editor. |
Irma Erlingsdâottir, editor.
Title: Iceland's financial crisis : the politics of blame, protest, and reconstruction / editors, Valur Ingimundarson, Philippe Urfalino, Irma Erlingsdâottir.
Description: Abingdon, Oxon ; New York, NY : Routledge, 2016. |
Series: Routledge advances in european politics | Includes bibliographical references and index.
Identifiers: LCCN 2016002732| ISBN 9781138669741 (hardback) |
ISBN 9781315618036 (ebook)
Subjects: LCSH: Financial crises–Iceland. | Finance–Iceland–History–21st century. | Iceland–Economic policy. | Iceland–Economic conditions–21st century. | Iceland–Politics and government–21st century.
Classification: LCC HB3798 .I34 2016 | DDC 330.94912/06–dc23
LC record available at http://lccn.loc.gov/2016002732

ISBN 13: 978-1-138-59842-3 (pbk)
ISBN 13: 978-1-138-66974-1 (hbk)

Typeset in Times New Roman
by Wearset Ltd, Boldon, Tyne and Wear

Contents

Figures

Tables

Contributors

Vilhjálmur Árnason is Professor of Philosophy and chair of the Centre for Ethics at the University of Iceland. He holds a Ph.D. in Philosophy from Purdue University. He chaired the Working Group on Ethics and Governance, which worked alongside the Parliamentary Special Investigation Commission. His research interests are in the area of social and political philosophy and applied ethics. He is currently leading an interdisciplinary research project on the practices, norms, and understandings of Icelandic democracy.

Jón Gunnar Bernburg is Professor of Sociology at the University of Iceland. He holds a Ph.D. in Sociology from the State University of New York at Albany. His work has cut across several subfields of sociology, including social theory, crime and deviance, social psychology, and social movements. His most recent work is a forthcoming book on the protest wave following the 2008 bank collapse in Iceland.

Emmanuel Brunet-Jailly is Professor of Public Administration of the University of Victoria. He holds a Ph.D. in Political Science from the University of Western Ontario. He specializes in comparative and urban politics and is Jean Monnet Chair in European Urban and Border Region Policy and director of the European Studies minor and of the European Union Centre for Excellence.

Jon Elster is Robert K. Merton Professor of Social Sciences at Columbia University in New York. He holds a Ph.D. from the University of Paris. His research interests include the theory of rational choice, the theory of distributive justice, and the history of social thought. He is currently working on a comparative study of constitution-making processes from the Federal Convention to the present and on a study of retroactive justice in countries that have recently emerged from authoritarian or totalitarian rule.

Irma Erlingsdóttir is Associate Professor of French Contemporary Literature at the University of Iceland and Director of EDDA—Center of Excellence; the United Nations University Gender Equality Studies and Training Programme (UNU-GEST); and RIKK—Institute for Gender, Equality and Difference at the University of Iceland. She has a Ph.D. from Sorbonne, Paris III. She has led several large-scale academic projects in the fields of gender studies, globalization, contemporary politics, and critical theory. Her current research focuses on the emancipatory aspects of art and transformative politics as well as on cultural critique of the crisis in Iceland.

Thorvaldur Gylfason is Professor of Economics at the University of Iceland and a research fellow at CESifo in Munich. A Princeton Ph.D., he has worked at the IMF in Washington, DC, taught at Princeton, edited the *European Economic Review*, consulted for international organizations, and published some 200 scholarly articles and 20 books as well as 800 newspaper articles. He was one of 25 representatives in the Constitutional Council entrusted with revising Iceland's constitution.

Helga Kristín Hallgrímsdóttir is Associate Professor of Sociology at the University of Victoria and a research associate with the University of Victoria Centre for Global Studies. She holds a Ph.D. in Sociology from University of Western Ontario. Her research interests bridge historical-comparative sociology, the sociology of work, social movements, and political sociology.

Valur Ingimundarson is Professor of Contemporary History at the University of Iceland and the chair of the Board of the EDDA—Center of Excellence. He holds a Ph.D. in History from Columbia University in New York. He has written on contemporary geopolitics; Icelandic foreign, security, and Arctic policies; transnational politics of justice and memory; US–European relations during and after the Cold War; and post-conflict politics in the former Yugoslavia.

Gudrun Johnsen is Assistant Professor of Finance at the University of Iceland. She holds an MA in Applied Economics and Statistics from the University of Michigan. She is chair of the board of the think tank THOR—Research and Development and vice chairman of the board of directors of Arion Bank. She was a senior researcher with the Parliamentary Special Investigation Commission.

Salvör Nordal is Assistant Professor of Philosophy and the director of the Centre for Ethics at the University of Iceland. She holds a Ph.D. in Philosophy from the University of Calgary. She was a member of the Working Group on Ethics and Governance, which worked alongside the Parliamentary Special Investigation Commission, and chairwoman of the Constitutional Council.

Jón Ólafsson is Professor of Comparative Cultural Studies at the University of Iceland. He holds a Ph.D. in Philosophy from Columbia University. He chaired a governmental committee on ethical guidelines in public service, which coordinated the creation of the first code of ethics for government ministers and for ministry officials in Iceland in 2011–2012. He is the editor of *Lýðræðistilraunir* [Democratic Experiments, 2014], which deals with democratic innovation in Iceland following the economic crisis.

Stefán Ólafsson is Professor of Sociology and director of the Social Research Center at the University of Iceland. He holds a Ph.D. in Sociology from Oxford University. His research focus is on welfare, employment, incomes and taxes, poverty, and social change.

Pasquale Pasquino is a senior research fellow at the Centre National de la Recherche Scientifique—Raymond Aron Center for Sociological and Political Studies (CNRS) in Paris and Global Distinguished Professor of Politics at New York University. He holds a Ph.D. in Philosophy and Classics from the University of Naples and a Ph.D. in Political Science from Sorbonne, Paris I. He is currently writing a book entitled *The Divided Power* on the role of courts in contemporary constitutional systems.

Björg Thorarensen is Professor of Constitutional Law and International Human Rights Law in the Faculty of Law, University of Iceland. She holds a Cand. Jur. degree from the University of Iceland and an LL.M degree from the University of Edinburgh. She is the author of numerous articles and books in the field of constitutional law, international law, and human rights, including most recently a comprehensive book on constitutional law, *The Icelandic Constitutional System—Foundations and State Powers* (2015). She was a member of a Constitutional Commission in 2010–2011, which prepared for the National Forum in Iceland and the work of the Constitutional Council.

Philippe Urfalino is a senior researcher at the French National Center for Scientific Research (CNRS) and Professor of Sociology at the Institute of Advanced Studies in the Social Sciences in Paris (EHESS). He is a member of the Raymond Aron Center for Sociological and Political Studies. He holds a Ph.D. in Sociology from the Paris Institute of Political Studies, and his research focus is on collective decision-making.

Anna Soffía Víkingsdóttir is a graduate student in Sociology at the University of Iceland.

Gylfi Zoega is Professor of Macroeconomics and Labor Market Economics at the University of Iceland and Visiting Professor at Birkbeck College, University of London, where he previously worked. He holds a Ph.D. in Economics from Columbia University and has a long-standing research partnership with Nobel Prize winner Edmund S. Phelps. Zoega is a member of the Central Bank of Iceland's Monetary Policy Committee.

Preface

This edited volume deals with the political reaction to the collapse of the Icelandic banking system in 2008. As the first sovereign country to succumb to the global financial crisis, Iceland was, in many ways, turned into a "crisis laboratory" when it came to grappling with the fallout. The disaster brought the country to the verge of bankruptcy—after a period of spectacular financial excess coupled with an unsustainable banking expansion—and caused ruptures in its relations with the outside world. While an International Monetary Fund (IMF) bailout saved Iceland from insolvency, its political, economic, and social system was put under enormous stress. In terms of crisis management, the Icelandic response to the crash was characterized by a mixture of backward-looking and forward-looking elements. The former involved an emergency banking legislation, a special investigative report, the trial of a prime minister, the removal of central bankers, and the jailing of leading managers of private banks. The latter contained, among other things, an ambitious attempt—partly through "crowdsourcing"—to rewrite the Icelandic constitution, a controversial EU membership application, and internal and external debt restructuring schemes.

Since Icelanders are still going through the politics of reconstruction after a collective shock, protests, and legal reckoning, this remains an unfinished project. To be sure, there has been a speedy economic turnaround in Iceland, with a return to high growth rates and low unemployment. But the political situation remains unsettled and unpredictable. While this ambiguous state of affairs points to the incompleteness of the volume, it is also a testimony to the subject's continued salience.

The book grew out of research projects, conferences, and lecture and seminar series sponsored by the EDDA Center in Critical Contemporary Research at the University of Iceland in collaboration with other institutions, notably the École des Hautes Études en Sciences Sociales (EHESS) in Paris, from 2010 until 2015. We are grateful to all those who have supported this undertaking. A grant from the Icelandic Research Council (Rannis) has enabled EDDA to pursue various transnational research projects, including this one. The University of Iceland Research Fund also awarded grants related to the project. We would like to thank the publisher, Routledge, for agreeing to publish the manuscript, and its editors for their cooperation and bringing the task to fruition. Senior editor

Andrew Taylor guided us through the publishing stages, with much support and encouragement; we also want to express our appreciation to editorial assistant Sophie Iddamalgoda. The same goes to project manager Ashleigh Phillips at Wearset and copy editor Sue Clements, who were responsible for the production process.

The comments and criticisms by the external reviewers, as well as others who have read the manuscript, have helped us improve it. Our debt is also to friends, colleagues, and students at various academic institutions, who have contributed, in various ways, to the book. We would like to mention specifically Jón Ólafsson, Sveinn Máni Jóhannesson, Marta Birna Baldursdóttir, and Svanhildur Ástþórsdóttir. Finally, we would like to thank the authors for their active interest in the project and for their contributions.

Valur Ingimundarson
Philippe Urfalino
Irma Erlingsdóttir

Abbreviations

ALMP	active labor market policies
CA	Constitutional Assembly (Iceland)
CBI	Central Bank of Iceland
CC	Constitutional Council (Iceland)
CDO	collateralized debt obligations
CDS	credit default swap
CoP	Committee of Privatization (Iceland)
DIGF	Depositors' and Investors' Fund (Iceland)
ECB	European Central Bank
EEA	European Economic Area
EEZ	Exclusive Economic Zone
EFTA	European Free Trade Association
EMTN	European Medium Term Note
EU	European Union
Eurostat	Statistical Office of the European Communities
FDIC	Financial Services and Compensation Scheme (UK)
FME	Financial Supervisory Authority (Iceland)
FSA	Financial Service Authority (UK)
FSCS	Federal Deposit Insurance Corporations (US)
GDP	gross domestic product
IMF	International Monetary Fund
NAFTA	North American Free Trade Agreement
NATO	North Atlantic Treaty Organization
OECD	Organisation for Economic Co-operation and Development
POS	political opportunity structure
PP	Progressive Party (Iceland)
RÚV	National Broadcasting Service (Iceland)
SaNS	Alliance for a New Constitution
SDP	Social Democratic Alliance (Iceland)
SIC	Special Investigation Commission (Iceland)
ST	Social Security Administration (Iceland)
USMTN	US Medium Term Note
VC	Venice Commission
VIRK	Rehabilitation Fund of the Labor Market (Iceland)
WGE	Working Group on Ethics (Iceland)

Introduction

Valur Ingimundarson, Philippe Urfalino, and Irma Erlingsdóttir

The collapse of the Icelandic banking system during the global financial crisis of 2008 was the biggest that any country has ever suffered relative to the size of its economy. The bankruptcies of the three main Icelandic banks, with each ranking among the ten largest corporate failures in history, were rooted in a combination of domestic and international factors. The privatization of the banks—in the early 2000s—created the conditions for a spectacular business expansion abroad. As part of the European Economic Area (EEA), Iceland had full access to European and global capital markets during a period of exceptionally low interest rates for borrowers and lax lending practices by banks. Icelandic entrepreneurs—the "Vikings," as they called themselves—took full advantage of these favorable structural conditions to embark on a debt-financed acquisition spree, which lasted from 2003 until 2008.

The economic boom seemed to open up an entirely new chapter in Iceland's history. It was thought to be based on the business success of Icelanders abroad rather than on Iceland's rich fish and energy resources or its strategic position in the middle of the North Atlantic—as was the case during the Cold War. It came, therefore, as a great shock, in October 2008, when Prime Minister Geir Haarde was forced to admit, in a televised address to the nation, that Icelanders were facing national bankruptcy. Hit by the greatest slump in the history of the Icelandic Republic, the government was unable to prevent the collapse of the country's banking system. But following an International Monetary Fund (IMF) bailout, Iceland managed to stave off default on its sovereign debt.

Apart from the dramatic political fallout—mass demonstrations and the downfall of the government—the economic consequences of the crisis were quickly felt. Those homeowners, who had enjoyed highly favorable terms on mortgage loans in foreign currency due to the strong Icelandic currency (krona), found themselves owing far more than their properties were worth as a result of the currency collapse. Fierce public opposition to accepting liability for the so-called Icesave accounts—individual savings accounts of the failed Icelandic bank, Landsbanki, in the United Kingdom and Holland—complicated the government's efforts to negotiate a rescue package with the IMF and to repair relations with the outside world. Indeed, Icesave became one of the most divisive domestic political issues in the crisis. On the one hand, the argument was made that it was crucial to reach a negotiated settlement to ensure Iceland's readmission into the world of banking and finance. On the other, it was contended that it was unacceptable, legally and morally, to make the Icelandic state liable for the debts of a bankrupt private bank, whose assets the British government had frozen by invoking anti-terrorist legislation.

What brought the matter to a head was that the President of Iceland refused to sign two Icesave bills approved by Parliament, in which the liability claims of the British and the Dutch were accepted. As a result, both bills were put to national referenda and were decisively rejected. In a European Free Trade Association (EFTA) court ruling in 2013, the case for an Icelandic non-payment was eventually vindicated when it was confirmed that there was no sovereign liability in relation to the Icesave accounts in the United Kingdom and Holland. The Icesave claims are being paid out in full by the actual debtor, the estate of Landsbanki. But the British and Dutch governments will not receive remuneration from the Icelandic government in the form of interest payments for paying back the deposits of their domestic savers in 2008.

The "reconstruction process" in Iceland has proved to be much speedier than most expected. To be sure, the recapitalization of its banking system and other crisis-related expenses caused government debt to rise from 27% in 2007 to 95% of gross domestic product (GDP) by 2011. Yet, real GDP fell by a less-than-expected 6.6% in 2009 and 4.1% in 2010, before returning to growth.[1] Moreover, Iceland benefitted from several factors beyond its control: because of its inability to save the banking system, Iceland dumped a mountain of private debt on foreign creditors. A tourist boom—spurred by a drastic currency devaluation following the financial collapse—became the source of much-needed foreign currency. And a windfall, resulting from unexpected mackerel catches within Iceland's Exclusive Economic Zone (EEZ), boosted a strong and resilient fishing export sector, which had not been hit by the crisis.

What has also raised optimism is that according to a 2015 deal with the creditors of the failed Icelandic banks, they agreed to pay a combined "stability contribution" of up to $3.8 billion to avoid a 39% exit tax, equivalent to an estimated $5.1 billion. In addition, the Icelandic Central Bank has been steadily building up its foreign currency reserves. In this way, the government and Central Bank created the conditions for a managed relaxation of capital controls. Moreover, Iceland's economic growth reached 4.0% in 2015, and the unemployment rate was down to less than 3% in the spring of 2016. Yet, while the positive economic prospects have generated optimism, the overall impact of the lifting of capital controls remains uncertain. And, more important, the political situation remains volatile with the established parties still facing deep-seated public distrust as a result of the financial crisis. This was illustrated by the dramatic resignation of Prime Minister Sigmundur Davíð Gunnlaugsson in April 2016 after it was revealed that he had owned an offshore company with his wife, which held millions of dollars in claims on the three big Icelandic banks that collapsed in 2008. Thus, the Icelandic PM became the first global politician brought down by the leaks of the "Panama Papers." The revelation, which triggered mass protests in Reykjavik, also forced the center-right government to call early elections in the autumn of 2016 in an attempt to calm public anger. The episode reopened societal wounds stemming from the banking collapse and showed that Icelandic efforts "to come to terms with the past" had not brought any closure.

The different dimensions of the Icelandic experience—financial, economic, political, social, and moral—all have narratives of their own. But the political factor is arguably key to understanding the others. Iceland is certainly not sui generis in this regard. The 2008 crisis has sometimes been described as a prime example of economic globalization, with financial interests not only dominating national politics but also trumping sovereignty concerns. The underlying primacy of politics, however, should not be discounted. The choices that facilitated the preponderance of the financial sector, in the first place, and underpinned the power of business elites were political. Similarly, attempts to contain and reduce the societal effects of the crisis were initiated by political actors. Indeed, in many cases, including that of Iceland, the experience eventually strengthened government control over the economy and market forces.

The political mobilization generated by the Icelandic financial collapse brought down the government and led to the adoption of specific mechanisms, which were, in important ways, reminiscent of transitional justice processes in post-conflict states. It included an emergency legislation, an investigative "truth" report, and criminal trials—designed to confront what was perceived as an unmitigated societal disaster. Yet, despite the severity of the crisis—and the public anger sparked by it—the "politics of transition" did not produce any radical political changes. What arguably explains this, at least partly, was that Iceland was able to recover quickly from the worst economic and social aspects of the crash.

The Icelandic response to the financial crisis has gained much international attention, if for different and opposing reasons. Elite international institutions, such as the IMF, have declared Iceland's recovery program a major success in economic terms and taken credit for its implementation. The managing director of the IMF, Christine Lagarde, has used it to justify the Fund's approach toward the Greek financial crisis and bail-out program. Conversely, anti-establishment grassroots movements have viewed the Icelandic political experience as a form of "people power," as manifested in Iceland's determination to oppose the power of far stronger states and financial interests during the Icesave crisis and in the decision to involve the public in writing a new constitution. Such contradictory interpretations raise important questions about the nature of the Icelandic crisis and the reaction to it. Iceland may have been able to stage a more successful economic comeback than most of the other European countries that were particularly badly hit, such as Greece and Portugal. But the fact that it has so far failed to transform into "political normality" shows the deep and persistent societal impact of the financial collapse.

Coming to terms with crisis

In a summarized form, the most dramatic events in Iceland—from October 2008 to April 2009—unfolded as follows. The government reacted to the collapse of the banks by enacting emergency measures to impose capital controls. Finding itself in dire need of financial assistance to fulfill its internal and external obligations, it received an IMF bailout after an unexpected Russian loan offer—prompted by an Icelandic government initiative—had not materialized. The plummeting of the value of the krona and the severe contraction of the economy led to massive layoffs, with the unemployment rate rising to unprecedented levels in 2009; grassroots activism and protest movements became a powerful force, with regular demonstrations in downtown Reykjavík, calling for the resignation of the government and key officials.

Due to popular pressure, the government resigned, and new elections were held in the spring of 2009; the parties of the Left—the Social Democratic Alliance and the Left-Green Movement—came to power after winning an absolute majority for the first time in Icelandic history. What made it possible was the massive electoral defeat of the conservative, center-right Independence Party, which has traditionally been Iceland's largest party. The government—led by the Social Democratic Prime Minister Jóhanna Sigurðardóttir and the Left-Green Finance Minister Steingrímur J. Sigfússon—was able to maneuver the country from the brink of a collapse into a situation where the worst consequences of the financial meltdown had been seriously dealt with, if not solved. The economy returned to growth and the unemployment rate stabilized at a low level.

Yet, the left-wing government became increasingly unpopular during its tenure from 2009 to 2013, not only due to internal squabbling but also because of its domestic and foreign policy priorities. Criticisms of its handling of the Icesave dispute, public debt relief issues, the constitutional experiment, and Iceland's European Union (EU) membership application undermined its credibility and support. The turn to the EU—in the summer of 2009—had signified a desperate effort in the midst of the economic crisis to get some political and economic backing from abroad. Yet, while enjoying majority public support after the crash, the EU membership application was controversial from the start. The Social Democrats had made EU accession the centerpiece of their political agenda and a precondition for forming a coalition government with the Left-Greens after the parliamentary elections in the spring of 2009. Yet, while the Left-Greens, who had been against joining the EU, agreed to ensure parliamentary approval of the application, they reserved the right to vote against EU membership in a referendum. The center-right opposition parties turned against Iceland's EU accession, not least because they did not want to submit to the EU's Common Fishery Policy and weaken national control over the fishing grounds.

In the absence of a consensus on the EU application, the negotiations proceeded slowly from 2010 to 2013, without engaging the most controversial issues: fisheries and agriculture. Moreover, the diplomatic fallout of the financial crisis, especially the Icesave issue, had detrimental effects on Iceland's relations with individual EU states, such as Britain and Holland, in the early phases of the negotiations. The subsequent financial crises in countries such as Greece, Portugal, Spain, and Ireland further undermined Icelandic support for EU accession. In other words, the EU application was not the result of a domestic political consensus, but exposed deep divisions over Iceland's foreign policy orientation. When a center-right coalition government came to power in 2013, it decided to abandon the EU application process.

The Left's defeat in the parliamentary elections of 2013 was big, with the Social Democratic Alliance and the Left-Green Movement losing more than half of their seats. Its successor, a coalition government between the Progressive Party and the Independence Party, was made up of the parties most closely associated with the policies that had made Iceland so exposed in the international financial crisis of 2008, especially, the failed privatization of the banks. Yet, despite the shift to the Right and a debt relief program earmarked for the middle classes, the government has not been able to capitalize on its electoral success, and has faced popular dissatisfaction. In 2015–16, this protest vote translated into massive support for an anti-establishment party, the Pirate Party, in public opinion polls. This shows the vulnerability of the traditional political parties in Iceland—on both the Left and the Right—and the continuing impact of the financial crisis on the political party system.

The purpose of this collective work, with contributions from 15 scholars, is to approach the response to the Icelandic crisis from broad interdisciplinary perspectives. It is an attempt to present a comprehensive treatment of the political, social, economic, and legal consequences of the crash.[2] It is divided into three parts. The first part focuses on economic aspects: it puts the Icelandic financial crisis into an international and comparative historical context, analyzes the relationship between domestic political and business interests, and explores the boom and bust cycles of Iceland's economy. The second part deals with the political and societal responses to the banking collapse, including the protest movements, the restorative and retributive mechanisms used to deal with the disaster, and questions of democratic practices and accountability. The third part is a case study on the constitution-writing process in Iceland, which was an idealistic attempt to achieve "democratic renewal" and to restore faith in the political system after a perceived national trauma.

In the Western media, the recent history of Iceland has been portrayed in contrasting terms. On the one hand, Iceland was vilified—shortly prior to and after the crash—as a symbol of spectacular excesses and abuses of the financial system coupled with the impotence and complicity of a political elite driven by neoliberal ideology. On the other, the Icelandic response to the banking collapse was applauded, as noted, by many observers across the political spectrum for restoring the country's economic health and for defying powerful external financial and political interests. Iceland has also been praised for being the only country that brought those responsible for the financial crisis to justice. The Special Prosecutor initiated more than 200 criminal cases in connection with the banking collapse. In the spring of 2016, 30 individuals had been sentenced to a combined sentence of

85 years for criminal acts associated with the financial crash.[3] This number is likely to increase if the Supreme Court ratifies additional verdicts by lower courts.

True, the handling of the criminal case of the Icelandic prime minister, Geir Haarde, who was convicted on the charge of negligence, proved to be more controversial than that of bankers. Many argued that political incompetence or policy mistakes should not be conflated with criminality, or that one statesman should not have been seen as the only culprit, when other government officials were also to blame. To others, however, the fact that a prime minister was prosecuted is an example of how seriously the Icelanders dealt with the crisis and how politicians should be held accountable for failing to perform their duty. Finally, the originality of Iceland's constitutional reform process—the decision to bypass political parties, the transparency of the deliberations, the use of random selection, and the participatory approach—made a favorable impression on many foreign observers. In the case of the "crowdsourced" constitution, the Icelandic approach has even been described as a model and recommended for similar constitutional reform processes elsewhere.

It may be argued that such a description of the Icelandic crisis is flawed because it is based on a selective choice of events, focusing on issues that contrast sharply with the experience of other countries. Icelandic society is perceived as a single entity or, at most, consisting of two compact blocs—"the elite" and "the people"—a view that generates too simplistic a narrative of the crisis and its consequences. This story has clear protagonists, offering a straightforward explanation of what happened. It leaves little room for ambiguity when it comes to questions about the causes of, reaction to, and handling of the crisis.

The contributions to this volume provide a more critical and nuanced picture of the Icelandic experience. The authors—who specialize in the fields of political science, sociology, economics, business, history, philosophy, and law—draw upon a large range of methods and approaches. The chapters, however, share three general assumptions:

1. They reflect the ambivalence and uncertainty that most of the political and economic actors had to face when the crisis hit. Instead of projecting clarity, the responses to the challenges facing Icelanders were often vague and halting. Some of the questions had to do with what caused the crisis and whether it was induced by domestic or international factors. They also raised the problem of accountability and culpability. Why did relevant actors fail to act on information that should have alerted them to danger? Who was to blame? Was it the banks, a few reckless and/or dishonest entrepreneurs, the government, or the governors of the Central Bank? What about the culpability of the political parties? The answers to such backward-looking questions are no clearer than those relating to forward-looking questions involving more direct democracy and constitutional reform.
2. In Iceland, it is often difficult to come up with a consistent account of the crisis, since accounts pull in different ideological directions. Cases in point are the sudden rise and fall of the Left and the subsequent resurgence of the Right,

which is now being tested by the surge of an anti-system party challenge. The approach to reforming the constitution may have been highly original, but Parliament proved unable to transform the draft constitution it received from the Constitutional Council into a passable bill. This raises the question of whether the old constitution had anything to do with the crisis. If not, was it really necessary to embark on a radical constitutional experiment? The constitutional issue remains unsolved, and could even be revived at short notice. Yet, the contrast between the "people" and elites, on the one hand, and leftist reformers and center-right politicians, on the other, fades into gray.

3 The authors are attentive to the fact that political, economic, and legal institutions are connected to political parties and interest groups in complex and sometimes contradictory ways. This means that the development of the political situation in Iceland from 2008 cannot be interpreted merely as a confrontation between a handful of political groupings and economic blocs.

The contributions do not seek to offer an all-encompassing unified interpretation of the Icelandic crisis, but they provide a more differentiated understanding of it. The authors resist a reified narrative, celebrating Iceland's response to the crisis; they offer detailed analyses of events that thrust Iceland into an unwanted spotlight and that caught the attention of the world.

The macro- and micro-economic background

Despite the relatively quick economic recovery, the magnitude of the Icelandic crisis, when judged by international comparisons, should not be discounted or relativized. Three events paved the way for the banking collapse: a huge capital influx, an unsustainable jump in borrowing, and a rapid increase in asset value. Between 2003 and 2007, consumption and investment grew speedily, fueled by easy credit and achieved through a spectacular growth of the banking sector. The total foreign debt, which was overwhelmingly private, increased from 75% to 476% of GDP during this period.

As Gylfi Zoega points out in his macro analysis, the combined bankruptcy of the Icelandic banks represented the third biggest corporate failure on record.[4] That this could have happened in a country with a population of only 330,000—with the Central Bank having no chance to act as a lender of last resort—is, among other things, a textbook example of oversight failures. That the three cross-border Icelandic banks were also able to operate freely with toothless regulatory supervision—and embark on their explosive growth—within the European Economic Area points to major shortcomings of EU banking supervisory legislation. Finally, it is a damning testimony to the workings of the global financial system that Iceland's creditors paid little or no attention to the unsustainable creation of a colossal banking sector in what some scholars used to characterize as a microstate.[5]

While the banking collapse had many things in common with other financial crises, Zoega stresses two things that set Iceland apart from other capital recipient countries, such as Greece, Portugal, and Ireland: first, the phenomenal growth of the banking system had no historical parallel. It led to the formation of large groups of interlinked entities with no real capital and to the buying and selling of interrelated businesses to prop up accounting goodwill and to record unrealized profits from the stock market bubble. This practice, it turned out, constituted, in some cases, illegal market manipulation. Second, what divided the Icelandic banks from many of their foreign competitors was the extent of speculation in comparison to the volume of the enterprise. Combined with the size of the banks in comparison to GDP, it was simply impossible to rescue the banking system when the crisis hit.

Focusing on the micro level, Gudrun Johnsen demonstrates, in her analysis of the privatization of the Icelandic banking system and its inflated growth levels, that these interrelated processes were deeply flawed. The privatization drive was tainted by politicization and special interests, with the two main banks essentially divided between businessmen close to the center-right Independence Party and the centrist Progressive Party. She also makes clear that, apart from the irresponsible behavior of the banks, their expansion was unsustainable by any measure, not least because of poor collaterals, which even included their own listed shares. Thus, the fall of the banks was rooted in their own structural weaknesses: their risky incentive schemes, their bad loan portfolios, and their vulnerable funding strategy.

The failure of this project may also be seen in the fact that it never grew above being a purely national endeavor. No foreign bank or international group showed real interest in acquiring any of the Icelandic banks; the Icelandic investors who were allowed to buy them lacked the experience and expertise. In 2003, the three large privatized banks, Glitnir, Landsbanki, and Kaupthing, represented 85% of the Icelandic banking sector. Their owners, as well as leading managers, had very limited knowledge of international banking. Their success in the years that followed rested on the international financial bubble. For that reason, and because of weak financial regulation authority, poor practices went unexposed until conditions changed.

Stefán Ólafsson also explores how government policy shifts and financial liberalization fueled what he terms the "politics of debt and speculation." Citing Hyman Minsky's theory on the role of the banking system in creating instability in capitalist economies, he concludes that the Icelandic crisis was the result of a typical financial bubble. What was exceptional was its enormity—the boom and bust in Iceland was, in relative terms, more drastic than in the United States during the Great Depression—the extensive intermeshing of political and business interests, and lax oversight rules.

The Icelandic banks began to face serious difficulty in obtaining long-term credit as early as 2006. Banks abroad, such as Denmark's largest banks, as well as two credit rating agencies, issued warnings about the situation. When, in 2007, the Icelandic banks established savings accounts, including the infamous Icesave accounts, to improve funding, their debt grew enormously. From 2006 until the crash of 2008, short-term debt alone grew from 400% of GDP to almost 900%.

The politics of protest, debt, and justice

Deep economic crises usually spread quickly to the political and social spheres, creating pressure for urgent action. In the immediate aftermath of the banking collapse, the question of who was to blame dominated public reaction and discourse as well as the more general demand for an explanation of what had happened. A general lack of trust in politicians prevented the Icelandic government from presenting a credible response to the crisis. The ensuing public protests reflected, in part, a search for interpretation. As a defensive mechanism, some government officials argued that the collapse of the banks was a consequence of the international financial crisis—that Iceland had become a victim of events that it could not control. But the privatization of the banks, the extravagant behavior of the Icelandic entrepreneurs with the full—and largely uncritical—support of all political parties, except for the Left-Greens, belied such a simple explanation. The mainstream media, such as the two largest television channels and the country's two biggest daily newspapers, played no major role in the interpretation of the crisis either. The media had taken part in the euphoria of the boom years and, with few exceptions, praised the achievements of bankers and Icelandic tycoons.

It was, therefore, to some extent the protest movement itself that offered the first interpretation of the crisis. Spontaneous action captured the spirit of the moment and challenged the legitimacy of the traditional political parties. The idea, borrowed from Argentina's street action in the 1990s, of overwhelming Parliament with noise by the banging of kitchen utensils created a name for it all: "The Pots and Pans Revolution." Public protest played a key role in bringing down the coalition government of the conservative Independence Party and the Social Democratic Alliance in early 2009. The enormous participation in the demonstrations—up to 25% of the Reykjavík population—put the Right on the defensive and paved the way for a sharp left-wing turn in Icelandic politics.

Jón Gunnar Bernburg and Anna Soffía Víkingsdóttir show how leftist protest leaders sought to neutralize right-wing attempts to portray the crisis as a global economic problem by blaming it, instead, on the privatization of the Icelandic banks and the neoliberal policies adopted during the mid-1990s and the early 2000s. The protest leaders were also concerned with framing their main demand in broad consensual terms; hence the emphasis on the resignation of the government rather than on more radical political and social goals. Thus, calls for a revolution or a "New Republic" did not become part of the collective vocabulary of the protesters, whose social make-up was diverse and whose political outlook was not uniform. The restricted political agenda also reflected the limits of mass mobilization in the absence of an enduring organizational base. As soon as the government resigned, the mass demonstrations ended, even if sporadic protests continued.

Whereas Bernburg and Víkingsdóttir explain how popular mobilization managed to discredit the "old regime" in 2008–2009, Helga Kristín Hallgrímsdóttir and Emmanuel Brunet-Jailly give some important clues as to how the Right managed to reinvent itself through collective action and stage a political comeback in 2013. In their treatment of the anti-Icesave movement, they show that it had the effect of increasing the political costs by political actors. The Icesave issue allowed new ideational connections and discursive alignments between elements from all sides of the political spectrum. Yet, as Hallgrímsdóttir and Brunet-Jailly suggest, the Independence Party and, especially, the Progressive Party were the main benefactors of the Icesave issue: after the two referenda and the EFTA court ruling, they succeeded in framing the issue in a populist and nationalistic way by portraying themselves as opposed to the interests of foreign banks and hostile governments and representing the interests of ordinary Icelandic citizens.

Thus, one can argue that similar tactics used against the Right after the financial collapse were adopted to discredit the Left in power. Indeed, the victory in the Icesave dispute and an electoral promise of a general debt relief program explain, to a large extent, the rehabilitation of the center-right parties in the 2013 elections. The same applies to the President of Iceland, Ólafur Ragnar Grímsson, whose reputation had been badly tarnished because of his enthusiastic support for the Icelandic banking expansion abroad in the period leading up to the crash; he regained his popularity after siding with the anti-Icesave movement and by refusing to sign the two Icesave bills, paving the way for his re-election to a fourth term in 2012.

As for political, economic, and social reactions to the crisis, the government was motivated by an acute need to explain to the public what had happened, to determine accountability, and to preserve a measure of social cohesion. Thus, in December 2008, the Icelandic Parliament appointed a Special Investigation Commission (SIC), which was given the task of examining the institutional mechanisms and practices that made Iceland so vulnerable in the financial crisis. Using the Report of the Special Investigation Commission and that of the Working Group on Ethics (WGE)—which became a separate part of the former when it was published in 2010—Vilhjálmur Árnason puts much blame for the crash on poor democratic practices and governance as well as on lax institutional morality. First, he argues that in a small society such as Iceland, the line between the professional and the personal—even the casual—is sometimes difficult to keep clear. Informal relationships may determine administrative practice, which greatly increases the likelihood of corruption. This led to reduced institutional capacity to recognize and react to the looming disaster. Second, he makes the point that an impoverished view of democracy damaged decision-making processes within the public administration, including the government itself and Parliament. In his view, an aggregative view of democracy, rather than a deliberative one, created a tendency to dismiss rational argument and deliberation from the political sphere, putting policy- and decision-making entirely in the context of opposed interests.

The informal interactions between regulatory institutions and businesses favored the former. The herd mentality—Árnason argues—shown by political, administrative, and media elites during the boom times played a role in providing ideological support for the Icelandic "business model." He further makes the case that oversight institutions, such as the Financial Supervisory Authority, failed to perform their duties due to an excessive legalistic reading of their mandate and their lack of assertiveness when dealing with the directors of financial companies. To him, the politicization of the Central Bank—the appointment of former prime minister, Davíð Oddsson, to its Board of Governors—also detrimentally affected the relationship between the bank and the government, because the ministers were former allies and opponents, creating mutual mistrust.

One has, of course, also to take into account the changed power relations between the government and the private sector resulting from the privatization drive. As Carl Schmitt stressed, when economic or other societal counter-forces are so strong that they are in a position to decide upon the "extreme possibility" from their point of view, they have become the new "political substance" of that entity.[6] What took place in Iceland arguably had much in common with the societal take-over practiced by the 19th-century American Robber Barons. Apart from controlling the banks, as well as the main insurance, shipping, retail, and aviation companies, they exerted political influence through ownership of major newspapers, private radio stations, and TV stations, and through their status as the largest party political donors. To accumulate social capital, they resorted—just like their 19th-century predecessors—to philanthropy, providing public and private institutions with financial support and sponsoring all kinds of cultural and sports events.

Valur Ingimundarson points to the many transitional justice elements that characterized the Icelandic response to the crash, including restorative justice features—such as the Special Investigation Commission Report—and retributive justice mechanisms through the criminal prosecutions of political, administrative, and financial actors. He also stresses the role of discredited elites in shaping and influencing societal transitions and their ability to re-emerge later on as political power brokers. Thus, the politics of transition is often not about defending or legitimizing a troubled past. The question is, rather—as Ruti Teitel has argued—to what degree the "old regime" can sustain itself by delegitimizing the "new" one and by infiltrating and influencing the transition. The dominant forces of the previous business and political elites, including former prime minister and Central Bank governor Davíð Oddsson, but also leading businessmen associated with the crash, not only survived, but shaped the "politics of reconstruction."

The SIC Report was unambiguous in its account of the actions and events leading to the financial crisis. But it did not create a consensus in its assessment of political—and in some cases possibly criminal—responsibility. Its authors suggested that a number of public officials, including former government ministers, could be criminally liable for their actions (or inaction) before October 2008. Two very different judicial approaches were made toward criminal accountability for acts contributing to the crisis. A Special Prosecutor was appointed in February 2009 to investigate alleged criminal action in connection with the collapse of Icelandic banks. The office has brought charges against many individuals for fraud, deception, and manipulation of financial markets.

Another mechanism for prosecuting public officials was initiated in 2010 with Parliament's decision to prosecute the former prime minister Geir Haarde. In accordance with the Law on Ministerial Responsibility, Haarde was tried by a Special Court, composed of 15 judges, which include lay members. Although the court found him not guilty on most of the charges, he was convicted for a violation of Article 17 of the Icelandic Constitution, which stipulates that the prime minister must convene special ministerial meetings to discuss matters of grave importance for the welfare of the state. On a superficial reading, this may be seen as a mere technical issue. But the Special Court used it to hold the former prime minister accountable for a failure to engage members of his own government in dealing with the country's desperate economic situation in the months before the banking collapse. Despite the guilty verdict, the court refrained from imposing a punishment, and the state was ordered to cover his legal expenses.

This contrast between the two approaches toward businessmen, on the one hand, and political leaders, on the other, is captured by Benjamin Constant's characterization of how political responsibility puts extraordinary restraints on political leaders:

> While we demand for ordinary citizens the safeguard of the most accurate precision and the guarantee of the letter of the law, ministers are exposed to a sort of arbitrariness exercised upon them both by their accusers and their judges. Yet, this arbitrariness is in the nature of the case itself; its defects must be softened by the solemnity of the procedures, the august character of the judges, and the moderation of the penalties.[7]

Constant argues that political leaders must submit to closer scrutiny and more severe and less predictable judgment of their actions than other citizens. Interestingly, however, this was not the most common reaction in Iceland. The fact that Prime Minister Haarde was singled out for prosecution, while other government ministers were spared, evoked sympathy for him among the public. An overwhelming majority had been in favor of prosecuting political leaders before Haarde's indictment by Parliament. When the Special Court convened, opinion polls showed that the majority had turned against the proceedings, judging them to be unfair.

In his analysis of the social response to the crisis, Stefán Ólafsson subscribes, in part, to the view that Iceland represented an alternative to the austerity policies in many other European countries, albeit with qualifications. He contends that even if the left-wing government was seriously restrained in adopting welfare policies due to high public debt, it was able to redistribute expenditures and tax burdens. It was a strategy of redistribution, which resulted in more equalization. Thus, cuts were directed more at education, health, and administration, while welfare transfers aimed at lower-income groups were increased. As a result, Iceland has regained its pre-crash status as the European country with the lowest combined risk of poverty and social exclusion. To Ólafsson, Iceland compares favorably with many crisis-hit European countries by achieving higher growth rates and by maintaining lower unemployment rates.

Constitutional reform as a societal transitional mechanism

The most idealistic response to the Icelandic crisis was undoubtedly the constitutional experiment. On the one hand, it reflected efforts to break away from the "politics of the past," which in the wake of the financial crisis had put a significant strain on the "social contract"; on the other, it was meant to symbolize a clean slate and to be a source of societal renewal. The decision to democratize and outsource the process of constitution-writing showed that political elites—devoid of trust and credibility after their failure—did not think they were capable of performing the task. The need to respond to the demand for a new democratic beginning outweighed any qualms about a direct parliamentary role in constitution-making, even if it was explicitly prescribed in the existing constitution.

As the novelty and luster of the exercise faded, the built-in tension between the competencies of the Constitutional Council and those of Parliament effectively destroyed the momentum for constitutional change during the tenure of the left-wing government from 2009 to 2013. There were other difficulties as well. Low voter participation in the elections for the Constitutional Assembly (37%) gave room to the criticism that Icelanders were not particularly interested in the enterprise at all. When the Supreme Court invalidated the elections on technical grounds, its legitimacy was also questioned. Parliament tried to sidestep this setback by reappointing the 25 elected Constitutional Assembly members (one of them declined reappointment) and change the Assembly's name to a Constitutional Council. But this act did not remove doubts about the Council's mandate. An apparent lack of interest by the parliamentary majority, which upon receiving the constitutional bill in 2011 seemed unsure of what to do with it, undermined the process.

To be sure, almost 50% of the electorate participated in a referendum on whether to base a new constitution on the bill prepared by the Constitutional Council in October 2012, with a large majority voting in favor. The result increased the legitimacy of the exercise, even if the referendum was non-binding. The voter turnout was, however, still lower than in most elections in Iceland. What was more, sharp and sustained criticism from a number of leading legal scholars and political scientists, who claimed that inconsistencies in the draft could lead to a constitutional crisis, did much to scuttle the project. Finally, the opposition to the draft by the center-right parties, which were on course to win the parliamentary elections in 2013, put the whole experiment on hold. Seeing that there was no chance that the constitutional bill would be passed by two successive parliaments, as the current constitution requires, the left-wing majority leaders agreed on a deal with the opposition, granting minor changes to the constitution, which supposedly will make further changes smoother, for example, by removing the requirement that Parliament must agree on them twice.

The attempt to reform the constitution reveals the same contrasts and paradoxes as many other policy initiatives of the crisis. Was it a fool's game, a

Table I.1 Overview of elections and referenda in Iceland 2009–2013

Dates	*Elections and referenda*	*Participation (%)*	*Outcome*
Spring 2009	Parliamentary elections	86	Majority government with the Social Democratic Alliance and the Left Green Movement
March 2010	First Icesave referendum	63	Rejection, 98%
November 2010	Elections to the Constitutional Assembly	37	25 members elected
April 2011	Second Icesave referendum	75	Rejection (59%)
October 2012	Referendum on the constitutional draft	49	Approval to "base a new constitution on the draft" (67%)
Spring 2013	Parliamentary elections	81	Majority government with the Progressive Party and the Independence Party.

remarkable innovation, and/or a lost opportunity? Should it be seen as a path-breaking experience, even contributing to future approaches in constitution-making? Was it doomed to fail because of political naivety and lack of support from the political elite? The exercise was rationalized by a need for extra-institutional intervention to ensure that the new constitution could be said to represent the will and feelings of the Icelandic people. Yet, in contrast to parliamentary elections, where voter turnout is traditionally high, there was not nearly as much interest in elections on the constitutional issue.

The parliamentary elections in 2009 and 2013 show over 80% participation; the Icesave referenda also generated a high voter turnout of 63% and 75%, respectively. On the other hand, the elections to the Constitutional Assembly and the referendum on the draft constitution in 2012 had much lower participation rates. Thus, there is no single narrative that clearly captures the constitutional reform process in Iceland. It was a contentious affair, ridden with difficulties at every instance, which revealed fundamental political rifts and polarization during the crisis. Nonetheless, whatever the final results, many participants and observers see the constitutional process as an important experiment in democratic innovation. This view is reflected in the contributions to this volume.

Jon Elster—together with Thorvaldur Gylfason and some other members of the Constitutional Council—argues that an ordinary legislature should, as a rule, not serve as a Constitutional Assembly or as a ratifying body. In either capacity, there is risk that it might act in a self-serving manner by adopting excessively legislative-centric constitutions or by rejecting proposals that reduce the power of the legislature or of the current legislators. In the Icelandic case, however, it was difficult to bypass Parliament, because any constitutional revisions had to be approved by two successive legislatures. In the absence of popular mobilization designed to pressure parliamentarians to ratify the draft proposed by the Council, Parliament eventually decided to step in and to exercise its power to take over the process. The government change in 2013, which involved political parties that were either hostile to—or critical of—the constitution-writing project, spelled its end as a crisis-response mechanism. The hope—expressed by some Council members—that the experiment can be revived in the future is dependent on different political constellations and conditions.

Most contributions on the constitutional project in this volume focus on the challenges it faced. Some writers laud the novelty of the experiment (Thorvaldur Gylfason, Jón Ólafsson, Björg Thorarensen, and Salvör Nordal), the link between democratic processes and constitutional reform (Ólafsson), and specific constitutional revisions, such as the strengthening of parliamentary competencies, the clarification of the role of the executive, and new measures designed to safeguard the independence of the courts (Thorarensen). Elster and Gylfason also believe that a *pouvoir constitué*, such as Parliament, ought not to have the power to block decisions of the *pouvoir constituant*, especially when the people, as in Iceland, had spoken twice, first in electing the members of the Constitutional Assembly (even if it was annulled on controversial grounds), and then in approving the constitutional draft.

Most of the contributors are, however, critical of the constitution-writing process itself. Elster is not convinced that the constitution had anything to do with the crisis. Public anger seems to have triggered a demand rather than a careful reflection about what might work. To him, specific weaknesses included the low turnout in the elections for the Constitutional Assembly, the skewed geographical distribution of the deputies, their lack of legal expertise, the cancellation of the election, and its replacement by a procedure with poorer democratic credentials.

The chair of the Council, Salvör Nordal, argues that an unclear mandate plagued the project from the start, especially the undefined and fuzzy relationship between the Assembly/Council and Parliament, and the confusion about whether a new constitution should be written or the existing one amended. Vilhjálmur Árnason believes that more participatory democracy, as proposed by the Council, was the wrong remedy for the weaknesses of democratic practices in Iceland (failure to adhere to proper rules and a lack of credible mechanisms of accountability and representation). And Jón Ólafsson questions the approach adopted by the Council to seek a consensus on the final document to avoid trade-offs, on the grounds that it created a tendency to leave the text open to different interpretations. In the aftermath of the Council's work it became clear, for example, that Council members who had unanimously agreed on the final text to be submitted to Parliament were far from unanimous on how to interpret their product.

Björg Thorarensen, Jón Ólafsson, and Pasquale Pasquino are especially critical of the Council for trying to sidestep Parliament. The implication is that the experiment was doomed to failure without the constitutionally prescribed input of legislators. To Ólafsson, the decision to write a new constitution instead of amending the old one also contributed decisively to the failure of the project. Gylfason, however, staunchly defends the Council's work and puts the blame on parliamentarians—acting out of self-interest—for ignoring the democratic will of the people as expressed in the referendum on the constitutional bill. This debate highlights a fundamental disagreement about the nature of popular participation in constitution-making. It is not only a question of whether "the people" should be involved in authoring and/or authorizing the constitution. It is also about the degree to which direct popular participation should be encouraged through referenda or other forms of democratic decision-making at the expense of representative democracy.

As the contributions to this volume demonstrate, the Icelandic crisis has to be approached from both domestic and international angles. While the liberalization and privatization agenda was promoted by Icelandic politicians, it echoed ideological trends in other countries. The Icelandic boom–bust experience also offers a test case for the macro-economic problems associated with the participation of small and vulnerable societies in integrated global financial markets. The political and social effects of the crisis are still being felt and contested in Iceland, and the legal aspects of the crash are being played out in domestic courts. The political question of Iceland's place in Europe has been sidelined after the current government shelved the EU membership application. The task of constitutional revisions was given to a commission controlled by political elites in 2013, even if some still hold out hope that the original experiment can be revived under different circumstances.

In short, the frantic drive for societal changes—unleashed by a collective shock in 2008—has, at least, temporarily given way to a less radical political agenda. Yet, while the transitional period has been without transformative elements, political battles are still being fought over issues related to the financial collapse. This means that political elites, who are still tainted by the collapse, are still grappling with the task of confronting a compromised past and of regaining public trust and legitimacy.

Notes

1 Anne Siebert, "Greek debt crisis: Lessons from Cyprus and Iceland," BBC website, accessed July 1, 2015, www.bbc.com/news/world-europe-33354036.

2 Other works on the Icelandic crises have tended to focus on specific aspects of the crisis, notably its economic causes, on Icelandic national discourses and identities, or on general narratives, predominantly journalistic ones in Icelandic, of the events in Iceland in 2008–2009. See, for example, Eiríkur Bergmann, *Iceland and the International Financial Crisis: Boom, Bust and Recovery* (New York: Palgrave Macmillan, 2014); Robert Z. Aliber and Gylfi Zoega eds., *Preludes to the Icelandic Financial Crisis* (New York: Palgrave Macmillan, 2011); Guðrún Johnsen, *Bringing Down the Banking System—Lessons from Iceland* (New York: Palgrave Macmillan, 2014); Ásgeir Jónsson, *Why Iceland? How One of the World's Smallest Countries Became the Meltdown's Biggest Casualty* (New York: McGraw-Hill, 2009); Gísli Pálsson and Paul Durrenberger eds., *Gambling Debt: Iceland's Struggle with the New World Order* (Boulder: University of Colorado Press, 2014); Guðni Th. Jóhannesson, *Hrunið* [The Crash] (Reykjavík: JPV,

2009); Roger Boyes, *Meltdown Iceland: How the Global Financial Crisis Bankrupted an Entire Country* (London: Bloomsbury, 2009); Stefán Gunnar Sveinsson, *Búsáhaldabyltingin* [The Pots and Pans Revolution] (Reykjavík: Almenna bókafélagið, 2013); Styrmir Gunnarsson, *Hrunadans og horfið fé. Skýrslan á 160 síðum* [Collapse and Vanished Money: The "Report" [of the Icelandic Investigative Commission] on 160 Pages] (Reykjavík, Veröld, 2010); Styrmir Gunnarsson, *Umsátrið* [The Siege] (Reykjavík: Veröld, 2009); Jóhann Hauksson, *Þræðir valdsins. Kunningjaveldi, aðstöðubrask og hrun Íslands* [Threads of Power: Nepotism, Favoritism and the Collapse of Iceland] (Reykjavík: Veröld, 2011); Ingi F. Vilhjálmsson, *Hamskiptin—Þegar allt varð falt á Íslandi* [Metamorphosis: When Anything Could Be Bought in Iceland] (Reykjavík: Bjartur, 2014); Ármann Thorvaldsson, *Frozen Assets: How I Lived Iceland's Boom and Bust* (Chichester: Wiley, 2009); Jón F. Thoroddsen, *Íslenska efnahagsundrið. Flugeldahagfræði fyrir byrjendur* [The Icelandic Economic Miracle: Rocket Economics for Beginners] (Reykjavík: Brúðuleikur, 2009); Ólafur Arnarson, *Sofandi að feigðarósi* [Courting Disaster] (Reykjavík: JPV, 2009); Einar Már Guðmundsson, *Hvíta bókin* [The White Book] (Reykjavík: Mál og menning, 2009).

3 "27 dæmdir í samtals 75 ára fangelsi," RÚV [Icelandic National Broadcasting Service], October 12, 2015, accessed December 12, 2015, www.ruv.is/frett/27-daemdir-i-samtals-75-ara-fangelsi.

4 See Már Guðmundsson, "Iceland's crisis and recovery: Are there lessons for the eurozone and its member countries?" Lecture, Athens, November 8, 2013, accessed March 19, 2015, www.sedlabanki.is/library/Skraarsafn/Raedur-erindi-og-greinar/MG%20Athens%20Nov%202013_final_07112013.pdf.

5 Tryggvi Thor Herbertsson and Gylfi Zoega, "A Microstate with Scale Economies: The Case of Iceland," Working Paper No. W0 2:10, Institute of Economic Studies, University of Iceland, December 2002.

6 Carl Schmitt, *The Concept of the Political*, Expanded Edition (Chicago and London: Chicago University Press, 2007), 39.

7 Benjamin Constant, *Political Writings*, ed. Biancamaria Fontana (Cambridge: Cambridge University Press, 1998), 230–231.

Bibliography

Aliber, Roger Z. and Gylfi Zoega eds. *Preludes to the Icelandic Financial Crisis*. New York: Palgrave Macmillan, 2011.

Arnarson, Ólafur. *Sofandi að feigðarósi* [Courting Disaster]. Reykjavík: JPV, 2009.

Bergmann, Eiríkur. *Iceland and the International Financial Crisis: Boom, Bust and Recovery*. New York: Palgrave Macmillan, 2014.

Boyes, Roger. *Meltdown Iceland: How the Global Financial Crisis Bankrupted an Entire Country*. London: Bloomsbury, 2009.

Constant, Benjamin. *Political Writings*, edited by Biancamaria Fontana. Cambridge: Cambridge University Press, 1998.

Guðmundsson, Einar Már. *Hvíta bókin* [The White Book]. Reykavik: Mál og menning, 2009.

Guðmundsson, Már. "Iceland's crisis and recovery: Are there lessons for the eurozone and its member countries?" Lecture, Athens, November 8, 2013. Accessed March 19, 2015. www.sedlabanki.is/library/Skr%C3%A1arsafn/R%C3%A6%C3%B0ur-erindi-og-greinar/MG%20Athens%20Nov%202013_final_07112013.pdf.

Gunnarsson, Styrmir. *Hrunadans og horfið fé. Skýrslan á 160 síðum* [Collapse and Vanished Money: The "Report" [of the Icelandic Investigative Commission] on 160 Pages]. Reykjavík, Veröld, 2010.

Gunnarsson, Styrmir. *Umsátrið* [The Siege]. Reykjavík: Veröld, 2009.
Hauksson, Jóhann. *Þræðir valdsins. Kunningjaveldi, aðstöðubrask og hrun Íslands* [Threads of Power: Nepotism, Favoritism and the Collapse of Iceland]. Reykjavík: Veröld, 2011.
Herbertsson, Tryggvi Thor and Gylfi Zoega. "A Microstate with Scale Economies: The Case of Iceland." Working Paper No. W0 2:10, Institute of Economic Studies, University of Iceland, December 2002.
Jóhannesson, Guðni Th. *Hrunið* [The Crash]. Reykjavík: JPV, 2009.
Johnsen, Guðrún. *Bringing Down the Banking System—Lessons from Iceland.* New York: Palgrave Macmillan, 2014.
Jónsson, Ásgeir. *Why Iceland? How One of the World's Smallest Countries Became the Meltdown's Biggest Casualty.* New York: McGraw-Hill, 2009.
Pálsson, Gísli and Paul Durrenberger eds. *Gambling Debt: Iceland's Struggle with the New World Order.* Boulder: University of Colorado Press, 2014.
Schmitt, Carl. *The Concept of the Political*, Expanded Edition. Chicago and London: Chicago University Press, 2007.
Siebert, Anne. "Greek debt crisis: Lessons from Cyprus and Iceland," BBC website. Accessed July 1, 2015. www.bbc.com/news/world-europe-33354036.
Sveinsson, Stefán Gunnar. *Búsáhaldabyltingin* [The Pots and Pans Revolution]. Reykjavík: Almenna bókafélagið, 2013.
Thoroddsen, Jón F. *Íslenska efnahagsundrið. Flugeldahagfræði fyrir byrjendur* [The Icelandic Economic Miracle: Rocket Economics for Beginners]. Reykjavík: Brúðuleikur, 2009.
Thorvaldsson, Ármann. *Frozen Assets: How I Lived Iceland's Boom and Bust.* Chichester: Wiley, 2009.
Vilhjálmsson, Ingi F. *Hamskiptin—Þegar allt varð falt á Íslandi* [Metamorphosis: When Anything Could Be Bought in Iceland]. Reykjavík: Bjartur, 2014.

Part I

The road to economic disaster

1 Iceland's financial crisis

An economic perspective

Gylfi Zoega

The idyllic sparsely populated Iceland became a symbol of the recent world recession when its banking system collapsed. The bankruptcies of the three largest banks were among the largest bankruptcies in world history.[1] If the banks in the United States had imposed comparable losses on a per capita basis on the outside world, these losses would have exceeded 60 trillion dollars. Remarkably, the extent of related-party lending in the Icelandic banking system was such that the default of only one of five owners of these three banks, who also happened to be among their biggest borrowers, would have brought the banking system down. The collapse was, thus, not only a part of the global crisis, affecting the world banking system, but also an inevitable consequence of market manipulation, related-party transactions, and excessive credit creation.

Iceland's financial crisis follows a growing number of similar crises. Charles P. Kindleberger and Robert Z. Aliber tell the story of financial turmoil going back to the Dutch tulip mania in the 17th century and the South Sea and Mississippi bubbles of the early 18th century. They list waves of four international crises that occurred in the past four decades. They all share common characteristics, in particular being caused by an inflow of capital into a country, an unsustainable rate of credit creation, and rising asset prices.

Following the oil price increases in the first half of the 1970s, Western banks channeled capital into South America, causing a boom in these countries that became a bust in the early 1980s, when the US Federal Reserve raised interest rates to high levels. The Latin financial crisis ensued, requiring a US-led bailout of Mexico. There was a subsequent flow of capital to Japan. When the Bank of Japan resisted the appreciation of the yen by buying foreign currency, the domestic money supply increased, as did real estate prices, until restrictions on lending to finance real estate investment caused the bubble to burst in the early 1990s. With a strong yen following the crisis, capital flowed to South East Asian countries: Thailand, Indonesia, Malaysia, and South Korea. Excessive lending by Thai banks gradually led to deterioration in the quality of their loan books, losses, and capital flight in 1997, which caused the Thai baht to depreciate, resulting in capital flight from Malaysia, Indonesia, and South Korea.

Thereafter, capital flowed to the United States, first causing a stock market boom at the end of the 1990s—the dot.com bubble—and then the real estate bubble in the 2000s. During the latter period, large current account surpluses developed in northern European countries, such as Germany, the Netherlands, Finland, and Sweden, and money was lent to Spain, Ireland, Portugal, Greece, and Iceland. A construction boom ensued in Spain and Ireland; the public sector had persistent deficits in Greece and Portugal; and a stock market boom, as well as a real estate boom, took place in Iceland, with consumption and investment rising and large current account deficits developing.

While China had current account surpluses, which it used to invest in US treasury bonds in the 2000s, Germany developed very large current account surpluses and lent huge sums to its trading partners. The German surpluses were not caused by demographic differences or by differences in the rate of growth of output.[2] Instead, the removal of capital controls in the European single market and the establishment of the euro—which removed exchange rate risk from investments within the currency area—appear to have created destabilizing capital flows, with savings surpluses from Germany and several other northern European countries being lent to Spain, Greece, Ireland, the Baltics, and Iceland.[3] These capital flows set the stage for both sovereign debt problems and bank insolvencies.

Every financial boom and bust has its share of law-breaking and the corruption of public officials. In many ways, history repeated itself in Iceland from 2003 to 2008; most of the characters had played the roles of bankers, politicians, and public officials in bygone periods. The abundance of data in Iceland, and the fact that this was a country with modern national accounts and small enough for the outsider to be able to understand the dynamics of the boom and bust, makes the crisis illuminating for anyone interested in financial turmoil. Iceland's experience is interesting in many respects. First, it shows the perils of capital flows for a country with flexible exchange rates. Second, it is a recent example of "irrational exuberance" and, in its size and impact on the economy, rivals earlier textbook examples of bubbles, such the Japanese real estate bubble of the 1980s. Third, it is hopefully unique in the extent to which a country's financial system was built on weak capital. It seems that many players in the financial sector were willing to cut corners and profit through questionable means during these years.

Macro-economic developments preceding the crisis

The macro-economic data were startling enough in Iceland: an inflow of capital elevated asset prices and the real exchange rate. Higher wealth and cheaper imports then propelled consumption and investment, which made output grow and unemployment fall. From 2003 to 2007, there was a credit-driven consumption and investment boom with a current account deficit that averaged 14% of gross domestic product (GDP). The M1 money supply increased by an average of 42% per year; real share prices increased by 35%, and real house prices by 12%.[4] The current account deficit rose from 5% of GDP in 2003 to 16% in 2007; unemployment fell to 2.3%, and gross foreign debt grew from a stable level of about 60% of GDP in the 1990s to nearly 700% before the collapse in mid-2008. Because the inflow of capital was unsustainable, it would only be a matter of time until the expansion ended in a sudden stop. The reversal of the capital flows in 2008 caused the exchange rate to collapse; consumption and gross domestic product to fall; investment to be reduced from 27% of GDP to 19% of a lower GDP; real imports to fall by 60% from 2006 to 2009; bank lending relative to GDP to contract by 54% from 2007 to 2012, and share prices to fall by 95%, and house prices by 13%, from peak to trough.[5]

These numbers tell only part of the story.[6] What sets Iceland apart from other capital recipient countries, such as Greece, Portugal, Spain, and the Baltic countries, was the rapid pace of growth of its banking sector prior to the collapse. The numbers speak for themselves. Total assets of the banking system amounted to one year's GDP in 2000 and one and a half years' GDP in 2003; they then rose to 238% of GDP in 2004, 376% in 2005, 534% in 2006, and 744% at the end of 2007.[7] This expansion was almost entirely driven by foreign borrowing. Foreign liabilities increased from 75% of GDP in 2003 to 476% of GDP at the end of 2007. At the same time, domestic liabilities rose from 60% to 268% of GDP. Local businessmen took the opportunity to borrow through Iceland's commercial banking system to finance the acquisition of businesses in other countries. This explained the unparalleled expansion of the country's banking system, whose assets grew from one year's GDP in 2000 to more than seven years' GDP at the end of 2007.[8] These businessmen also bought up businesses locally, where share prices rose by a factor of nine from their bottom value in 2001 to their peak value in 2007.

The boom was visible in the real economy in the form of imports of expensive cars and durable consumer goods, renovation of real estate, and foreign travel. However, it mostly took place in the electronic accounts of banks, limited-liability holding companies, and hedge funds. A stylized account would have commercial banks being owned by businessmen, who had the banks borrow from foreign banks, the latter being aware of the implicit government guarantee of all debt of the banks that made up Iceland's payment system. The banks then lent money to the owners' holding companies, charging foreign interest rates.

In this way, the borrowing from foreign banks, as well as the lending to local investment funds, is denominated in foreign currencies; the banks maintain an FX balance (assets and liabilities denominated in foreign currencies are equal), and the high domestic interest rates do not enter the transaction. But once the money is transferred to the owners' holding company, they can invest in domestic securities that pay much higher interest rates or rapidly rising stock prices. The investment funds reap accounting profits; their assets increase in value, and their costs are low due to low foreign interest rates. Profits can, then, be used to justify dividends or the paying of generous compensation schemes. There is an exchange rate risk, but this is not born by the actors; instead, the limited-liability companies will fail in the case of currency depreciation, transferring the losses to the banks and ultimately to the taxpayer and foreign creditors.

At the beginning of the Icelandic episode, one could find profitable investments in foreign businesses. These included foreign retail business, a large pharmaceutical company, and companies exporting fish products to the United Kingdom. The success of these investments increased confidence and convinced investors to make even more audacious decisions. The investment projects of local entrepreneurs gradually became less profitable and more risky, speculative, to use the Hyman Minsky classification of finance,[9] and, toward the end, Ponzi-like. The fortunes of the entrepreneurs were closely linked to those of the banks, since the banks had lent excessively to a handful of businessmen. When the banks could no longer borrow in foreign currencies to roll over their debt, they defaulted, because the amounts needed far exceeded the foreign exchange reserves of the Central Bank.

But what was the role of the general population if only a few businessmen had borrowed enough to be capable of causing a systemic collapse? Robert Aliber supplies a good account.[10] The story goes as follows. Current account surpluses in other countries—Germany and the Netherlands in Europe, Japan, China, and the Middle East—push up exchange rates and asset prices in other countries so as to induce these countries to spend their surplus savings.[11] The abundance of cheap capital in world financial markets from 2003 to 2008 had the effect of increasing the borrowing of Icelandic banks and investment funds and fueled a carry trade, which strengthened the exchange rate and made imported consumer goods cheaper. This increased consumption of goods and services and reduced exports; the population enjoyed a consumption boom, financed by bank credit, which helps explain the goodwill shown to the same businessmen before the collapse.

The Baltic countries, Greece, Ireland, Portugal, and Spain shared with Iceland a pattern of very high investment, rising asset price, low inflation, and high growth during this period, with a very large current account deficit in all countries except for Ireland.[12] In spite of the robust economic growth, inflation remained low in these countries. The economic growth was mainly driven by investment. House prices increased in all countries, propelled by the expansion of credit.[13] Stock prices rose at a rapid rate, but less than house prices, with one exception: the stock market boom in Iceland was much stronger than the house price boom.

Although all the crisis countries had large current account deficits prior to the crisis, their origins differed. In Iceland, there was an investment boom, but domestic saving remained more or less constant, masking falling private saving and increasing public saving. Government surpluses gradually reduced the level of sovereign debt. In Estonia, Latvia, and Lithuania, there was an investment boom, with the public sector in balance and steady or moderately increasing private saving. Ireland and Spain experienced an investment boom, accompanied by steady saving, public as well as private. Greece and Portugal had a persistent gap between saving and investment, mainly due to large government deficits. Thus, the public sector was more or less balanced or in surplus in Iceland, Ireland, and Spain, while it was in deficit in Greece and Portugal.

The inflow of capital in the period 2003–2008 distorted the allocation of production across sectors in Iceland as well as in the other countries.[14] Employment in the construction industry increased from 6.9% of total employment in 2003 to 9.8% in 2008; employment in financial services and insurance increased from about 4% of total employment to 5% in 2008.[15] The share of industries other than construction fell over time, as did the share of employment in agriculture and fisheries. The shifting allocation of employment was matched with a shift in the share of each industry in GDP. Construction and financial services took on increased significance in generating value added.[16]

What sets Iceland apart from the other crisis countries is the extent of speculation in comparison to the volume of enterprise—to paraphrase Keynes. Ireland and Spain also had rapid expansions of credit, but this was used to finance a construction boom. Irish banks financed the construction activities taking place in Ireland as well as overseas. The Spanish savings banks financed the buying of property in Spain, contributing to a bubble in house prices and a construction boom. But in Iceland, construction did not play the biggest role; instead, it was financial investments, speculation in the purest sense, taking the form of stock investments, foreign and domestic acquisitions, and currency speculation. While some of the foreign acquisitions turned out to be successful, others were much less so, and the domestic financial investments propelled a stock price bubble that, in the end, left most investors insolvent. Thus, Iceland's national accounts show only a small part of the financial imbalances that developed in the preceding years. The invisible economy, made up of the electronic entries of holding companies, investment banks, and commercial banks, was many times the size of the real national economy of Iceland.

Monetary policy was given the task of containing inflation in Iceland, while fiscal policy was used to promote long-term growth. Fiscal policy had the objective of lowering tax rates to spur investment and labor supply.[17] The rising tax revenues that were generated by the booming financial sector, rising wages, and import duties were used to increase government spending in addition to reducing government debt. Monetary policy bore the brunt of containing the domestic expansion. The Central Bank had been made independent by law in 2001 and guided by an inflation-targeting framework. It raised interest rates from 5.3% in 2003 to 15.5% in the months before the collapse in 2008. In so doing, it revealed many problems that plague independent monetary policy in a small country faced with perfect capital mobility. The Central Bank lost control of the money supply when commercial banks used external wholesale funding abroad to finance their credit expansion, charging the foreign rates of interest on loans to customers. The pace of credit expansion was breathtaking and unaffected by the high domestic currency interest rate.

The Central Bank tried to curb the expansion of credit by raising interest rates, but the prevalence of exchange-rate-linked loans bearing foreign interest rates meant that the transmission channel of monetary policy was very weak. In addition, a public mortgage system in which loans to households are indexed to the Consumer Price Index and carry a fixed rate of interest until maturity had the same effect. The weakness of the interest rate channel of monetary policy resulted in the Central Bank raising interest rates to 15.5% to curb domestic demand pressures. This fueled a carry trade, when foreign banks and investors took advantage of the interest differential by issuing bonds denominated in domestic currency.

During the expansionary phase, foreign currency loans became increasingly prevalent, especially in the business sector, and this also applied to businesses that had revenues in the domestic currency. Currency mismatch between debt repayments, revenues, and other costs were striking in the business sector, and a depreciation of the currency could, for this reason, very easily have triggered a financial crisis. For this reason, the Central Bank found it increasingly difficult to abandon its policy of high interest rates, realizing that lower interest rates would trigger a depreciation, which would damage balance sheets of businesses, and through the CPI indexation, household balance sheets. The reversal that occurred in 2008 made growth negative in all the countries, the most severe contractions taking place in some of the Eurozone countries and the fixed-exchange-rate countries such as Estonia, Latvia, and Lithuania. Stock prices fell, as did house prices.[18] The slump was characterized by a fall in the share of investment of GDP. Private debt accumulation was replaced by public sector deficits, which exceeded 10% of GDP in Greece, Iceland, and Ireland.[19]

Financial escapades become visible

Iceland would not have become a symbol of the global credit crunch if it had remained a passive recipient of the global saving glut. In spite of the country's ranking close to the top of the list of the least corrupt countries on the Transparency International list, the dissection of the remains of its financial system in the years since the collapse has revealed significant malfeasance; the expansion of the banking system appears to have been driven by market manipulation and related-party lending.

The privatization of the banks in a setting of capital mobility in a formerly repressed financial system with very limited experience of modern banking practices set the stage for subsequent events. The privatization process was mishandled; the banks were sold to individuals with political party connections and loyalties.[20] Gudrun Johnsen has described how the illusion of foreign bank participation was created in order to give offers by political cronies more credibility. Moreover, she also shows how the new owners of two of the biggest banks had no prior experience in banking, and how the selection process was distorted by the government and its agencies to ensure that the banks ended up in the "right" hands. In effect, individuals with connections to the two governing parties effectively took over one of the two largest banks.[21] As it turned out, the owners of the remaining large bank were just as risk-seeking as the politically connected owners of the first two.

Regulations were relaxed to facilitate the expansion of the banking system by making it easier for financial institutions to invest in non-financial businesses; to extend credit to directors; to invest in real estate companies; to lend money to buy own shares; to operate insurance companies; and to own other financial institutions.[22] These changes made it easier for the commercial banks to participate in leveraged buyouts, often in association with their owners or other clients.[23]

The owners of the banks set up a very complex system of ownership that hid related-party lending and made consolidated accounting difficult. They accumulated dividend payments through holding companies that also facilitated risky borrowing by limiting liability.[24] Instead, creditors and taxpayers bore the risk. The number of limited-liability companies in Iceland grew by 50% from 2003 to 2007, from 20,378 to 30,755.[25] Of these, about one in seven did not have a designated owner listed in the enterprise directory, or had unexplained ownership. As part of this cobweb of companies, one business group had borrowed in excess of 11% of all loans from the banking system and 90% of the capital of the one bank that it controlled.[26]

The expansion of credit required the capital of the banking system to grow rapidly. Due to low capital requirement, a 1-euro increase in capital enabled the banks to increase lending by 12 euros. Generating more equity was important to the bankers for the expansion of credit. Without the capital base increasing rapidly, the banks could not have grown as fast, and Iceland's problems would have been more manageable. One source of the rapid growth of capital in financial institutions was profits from investment in shares in other companies. But the main reason appears to have been the creation of capital through lending to buy own shares[27] as well as to employees, to clients, and to offshore subsidiaries.[28] From 2007 until the bank collapsed in 2008, 40–50% of total outstanding shares of Kaupthing Bank were pledged to the bank itself,[29] to give just one example. In this way, the financial statements were able to show more capital without the banks becoming more robust, since this weak capital did not provide any buffer against losses. But the stability of the banking system also depended directly on the level of stock prices. The banks financed equity for each other in a non-transparent way. It has been estimated that the banks carried the risk of about 25% of total capital on their own balance sheets,[30] which amounted to approximately 50% of core capital. Bank lending to finance the acquisition of shares in other banks also made the system vulnerable due to the interconnectedness of the banks and other financial institutions.[31]

From the outset, the market for shares in each of the banks was manipulated by the banks and their owners. According to Ulf V. Nielsson and Bjarni K. Torfason[32] and the Special Investigation Commission,[33] the banks' proprietary desks overall bought more of their own stocks than they sold. In 2008, the proprietary trading desks of the banks gradually accumulated their own shares, and then sometimes sold them to clients with borrowed money.

On the asset side of the banks' balance sheet, there were foreign-currency-denominated loans to limited-liability holding companies, which then invested in the stock market.[34] These companies were in many cases owned by the banks' owners. The accounting profits generated by the holding companies could then be used to justify dividend payment to the owners.[35] Also, the large volume of credit generated by the banks created accounting profits for the banks themselves, because allowances for losses were inadequate.[36] The under-reporting of risk allowed the owners of holding companies and the banks to extract wealth from these entities. In the months leading up to the collapse of the banks, some of the owners had managed to borrow vast sums from their bank at the last minute to meet margin calls at foreign banks or stow away in offshore banks. At the time of the collapse, lending to related parties came close to being equal to the banks' capital.[37] But the owners did not only borrow directly from the bank. Depositors were advised to withdraw deposits and put them into the bank's money market funds, where they collected much higher rates of interest from bonds issued by the bank's owners, who could not possibly have repaid the debt.[38] The Special Investigation Commission concludes that the operations of the Icelandic banks were intended to serve the interest of the larger shareholders.

The institutions that had the role of supervising and regulating the economy and the financial sector during this period were under-staffed when it came to dealing with an international banking system. While the banks had 8,400 employees at the end of 2007 and assets just below 7.5 times the country's annual GDP,[39] the Office of the Prime Minister had 26 employees at the time, the Ministry of Commerce 20, the Financial Supervisory Authority 47, and the Central Bank 115. Only two employees were responsible for financial markets when the banks were privatized in the early 2000s! In addition, the foreign currency reserves of the Central Bank were about 10% of the level of short-term foreign debt.[40] Attempts to establish swap lines with foreign central banks in the spring and summer of 2008 were largely unsuccessful due to the magnitude of the problem in comparison to the size of the Icelandic economy.[41]

Social pressures drown voices of protest

The lack of resistance to the bubble economy, among both the general public and politicians, may be partly explained by two factors. First, during the capital inflow, the standard of living was very high, while fiscal surpluses were created from increased tax revenues. As in many previous bubbles in other countries, the general population had a reason to justify the high value of the currency and asset prices. Carmen Rheinhart and Kenneth Rogoff title their book *This Time Is Different*—and this also applies to Iceland in the years prior to the collapse. The flow of capital into Iceland was justified by the low level of public debt, the sovereign's high credit ratings, and a culture of paying back debt. In addition, a myth was created about the superior abilities of Iceland's business community.[42]

To fully understand the period, one also has to take account of the failure of collective action to stop the bubble from growing before it was too late. As in Ireland during the same time period, political and economic power was concentrated within a golden circle, where people were of one view regarding the state of the economy. This made it difficult for anyone to point out the dangers, since anyone attempting to do so was either ignored or derided.[43] In essence, any one person has nothing to gain from pointing out the dangers of the speculative boom in a bubble economy, and is likely to be met by ridicule.

There was also a lack of verifiable information on the malfeasance that was occurring within the financial system. Only after the collapse did the extent of related-party lending and market manipulation become apparent. For all these reasons, there was a tendency to interpret the inflow of capital before the collapse as a sign of a dynamic, well-managed economy. This was also the case in most previous crises. The Japanese real estate bubble in the 1980s was justified by slogans such as "Japan number one."[44] The stock market bubble in the United States around 2000 was justified by the promise of the internet for future productivity. And the real estate boom that followed was accompanied by the observation that real estate prices in the United States could only continue to increase. In Europe, capital flowed into Ireland, labeled the "Celtic Tiger" and widely admired for its record of productivity growth in previous decades.

The problem of collective action also encouraged people to cut corners and violate ethical principles for financial gain. No one had any incentive—apart from appeasing his or her conscience—not to participate in profitable but dubious activities when rules and social norms were relaxed for private gain. Moreover, the increase in the aggregate volume of financial wealth helped make individuals more ready to put aside moral principles in return for a chance to get a larger slice of the pie. A prominent example is provided by accounting firms, some of which helped design questionable business practices that exaggerated the capital and profits of financial firms while not violating the letter of the law. Thus, risk was systematically under-reported and capital overestimated in financial statements.[45]

The downturn and its causes

An economy experiencing a capital inflow suffers a sudden stop when foreign investors lose confidence.[46] The sudden stop of the inflow of capital into Iceland in 2008 as financial markets abroad seized up due to the US subprime crisis reversed the macro-economic development of the previous years. A sudden depreciation of the currency occurred; the current account went into a surplus, output fell, and unemployment rose. This is what happened first in the spring of 2006, and then again, to a much greater extent, in 2008. The collapse was preceded by a mini-crisis in 2006, when, following the publication of negative reports by ratings agencies,[47] the banks' access to the European securities market became increasingly difficult. From then on, they managed to sell securities to American banks that packaged their debt securities into collateralized debt obligations (CDOs). The loss of access to remaining outside capital markets in 2008 caused the currency to tank; the loan book of the banks deteriorated, and in the end, the banks suffered bank runs that brought them down.

The total liabilities of the banking system as a ratio to the country's GDP were 744% at the end of 2007, and approached 1,000% in the weeks before the October 2008 collapse.[48] It was impossible for the sovereign to come to the help of the banking system with a capital injection, since the capital of the system was 77% of GDP at the end of 2008. But the greatest weakness lay in operating international banks in a very small currency area. The foreign liabilities of the banking system were close to five times GDP at the end of 2007, and seven times GDP at the time of the collapse. Deposits in foreign branches of the Icelandic banks alone were around seven billion pounds, or close to one year's GDP, and 5.3 times greater than the country's foreign reserves.[49] In only nine months, from late 2006 to the middle of 2007, one of the banks managed to collect deposits in its foreign branches equivalent to almost fivefold the foreign exchange reserves of the Central Bank.[50] The lack of a lender of last resort, and a vastly underfunded deposit guarantee scheme, could have been predicted to coordinate a modern bank run when foreign banks refused to roll over debt, making the banking system default on its external obligations.[51]

In addition to liquidity problems and a lack of a credible lender of last resort, the banking system was fragile because of its weak equity base and operational irregularities. The three Icelandic banks always satisfied minimum capital adequacy requirements, but a significant bulk of the equity could be termed weak, that is, not created through leverage.[52]

Conclusion

The dangers of destabilizing capital flows are well known from previous financial crises. What made the case of Iceland unique was the creation of a very large financial system in a short period of time without sufficient levels of (unleveraged) capital. Thus, large groups of interconnected entities were formed with little or no real capital. The buying and selling of businesses between related parties was used to prop up accounting goodwill, and value-to-market accounting was used to record unrealized profits from the stock market bubble. The cost of financing was under-reported because borrowing was in foreign currencies with no allowance made for the expected depreciation of the currency. Combined with the size of the banks in comparison to the GDP of Iceland and the lack of a credible lender of last resort, it was impossible to save the banking system.

One lesson from the episode is that the largest shareholders of limited-liability financial companies can have an incentive to profit as individuals while putting the businesses at risk through borrowing. While this has occurred elsewhere—the effect of the change of the US investment banks from partnerships to corporations is well documented—Iceland offers a very transparent case.[53] Second, the accounting profession acted not to guard other shareholders' and the public's interests but to help the corporate managers accomplish their objectives within the letter of the law. Third, the economics profession was misled by macroeconomic models that did not predict the turbulence.

The Central Bank's Dynamic Stochastic General Equilibrium (DSGE) model—similar to models used at central banks in other countries—would have predicted that the cessation of capital inflows would cause a sharp depreciation of the currency and inflation. Yet, the model does not have financial stocks and flows for sectors; nor does it include a banking system. The assumption of rational expectations would also not allow for the possibility of a speculative bubble of the magnitude seen in the stock market up to 2007. The macroeconomic models, moreover, did not capture the effect of higher interest rates, inducing investors to borrow in foreign currencies without taking into account the risk of depreciation.

Lastly, Iceland's experience shows the dangers of having an oversized banking system. It was the last factor that really set Iceland apart from the other crisis countries in the latest wave of financial crises. Having access to the European Central Bank saved the Irish banking system from collapse in the fall of 2008, while banks in the United States, the United Kingdom, and throughout the Eurozone were stabilized by a combination of central bank and government actions and guarantees. The Icelandic banks had no such support, because they were mostly operating in foreign currencies, which restricted the ability of the Icelandic Central Bank to intervene, and the Icelandic state was too small to be able to recapitalize the banks.

To sum up, the collapse of the banking system was preceded by distorted incentives in the financial system; excess savings in other countries searching for yield; an ethical lapse in corporate governance and accounting; the use of inappropriate economic models; an expansionary fiscal policy; and a monetary policy that did not take into account the institutional setup and incentives in financial markets. The financial system could not possibly survive all these failures.

Notes

1 Total assets of the banks were 182 billion dollars three months before the crash, which is about 1.8 times the assets of WorldCom before its failure in 2002 and almost three times the assets of Enron before its failure in 2001. Taken as one entity, the banks would come third in the history of bankruptcies in US history, with Lehman (691 billion dollars) and Washington Mutual (328 billion dollars) coming first and second. As separate entities, Kaupthing (83 billion dollars) would rank fifth, Landsbanki (50 billion dollars) ninth and Glitnir (49 billion dollars) 10th. The banking failures resulted in a loss of around 60 billion dollars to creditors. Source: Financial Services Authority of Iceland.

2 See Gudmundur S. Gudmundsson and Gylfi Zoega, "Age Structure and Current Account Imbalances," *Economic Letters* 123 (2014): 183–186.

3 See Olivier Blanchard and Francesco Giavazzi, "Current Account Deficits in the Euro Area: The End of the Feldstein-Horioka Puzzle?" Brookings Papers on Economic Activity 33, no. 2 (2002): 147–210; Margarita Katsimi and Gylfi Zoega, "European Integration and the Feldstein-Horioka Puzzle," Working Paper Series W143:01, Institute of Economic Studies, University of Iceland, 2014. These authors use the methodology of Feldstein and Horioka ("Domestic Saving and International Capital Flows," *The Economic Journal* 90 (358): 314–329) to test for a structural break in the relationship between investment and saving; the absence of a statistically significant relationship implies capital mobility.

4 The OMX15—which includes the 15 largest corporations—increased by a factor of six over the same period and by almost a factor of nine from its lowest point in 2001 to its peak value in 2007. See Ólafur G. Halldórsson and Gylfi Zoega, "Iceland's

Financial Crisis in an International Perspective," Working paper W10:02, Institute of Economic Studies, University of Iceland, 2010.

5 Numbers taken from *Statistics Iceland* (hagstofa.is) and the Central Bank of Iceland (sedlabanki.is), World Bank, *World Development Indicators*, and Trading Economics (tradingeconomics.com/iceland/stock-market).

6 Thorvaldur Gylfason et al., *Nordics in Global Crisis: Vulnerability and Resilience*, The Research Institute of the Finnish Economy (ETLA) (Taloustieto Oy, 2010). This work compares the economic conditions in the Nordic countries during these years.

7 Sigridur Benediktsdottir et al., "Lessons from a Collapse of a Financial System," *Economic Policy* 26, no. 66 (2011): 183–235. During 2008, the value of the Icelandic krona fell, and the total assets and liabilities of the banking system in relation to Iceland's GDP rose to 10 times GDP in September.

8 Halldorsson and Zoega, "Iceland's Financial Crisis in an International Perspective"; Benediktsdottir et al., "Lessons from a Collapse of a Financial System."

9 Hyman Minsky proposed a classification system of corporate debt in which a distinction is drawn between *hedge finance*, when a firm's operating profits are sufficient to offer the regular installments and interest on the debt; *speculative finance*, when they are only sufficient to pay the interest expenses; and *Ponzi finance*, when the firm needs to borrow to pay both installments and the interest on the debt. See Hyman Minsky, *Stabilizing an Unstable Economy* (New York: McGraw-Hill, 1986).

10 Robert Z. Aliber, "Introduction," in *Preludes to a Financial Crisis*, eds. Robert Aliber and Gylfi Zoega (London: Palgrave, 2011), 1–23.

11 This insight is related to that of Keynes, *The Economic Consequences of the Peace* (London: Macmillan, 1920), on the post-World War I transfer problem.

12 Estonia, Latvia, and Lithuania had an average rate of annual growth of GDP from 2003 to 2007 in excess of 7%; Ireland had annual growth of 5.3%, followed by Iceland at 4.5%, Greece at 4%, Spain at 3.5%, and Portugal at 1.40%. Portugal's boom actually occurred earlier, in the late 1990s, in the run-up to the adoption of the euro. Source: Organisation for Economic Co-operation and Development (OECD).

13 The average rate of change of house prices was 26.7% in Estonia, 30.1% in Lithuania, 13.0% in Spain, 16.6% in Iceland, and 7.6% in Greece. Source: national central banks. See Halldorsson and Zoega, "Iceland's Financial Crisis in an International Perspective."

14 Kjartan Hansson and Gylfi Zoega, "Capital Flows and Labour Market Distortion," Working Paper Series W13:05, Institute of Economic Studies, University of Iceland, 2013.

15 Numbers taken from *Statistics Iceland* (www.hagstofa.is).

16 Construction increased from 7.5% of GDP in 2003 to 11.7% of GDP in 2008, and financial services and insurance combined increased from 7.3% to 8.7%.

17 The government lowered corporate taxes from 30% to 18% at the end of 2001, and in February 2008, they were further lowered to 15%. The income tax rate was also lowered by 1% in each of the three years 2005, 2006, and 2007; property taxes were abolished; and the value added tax was lowered in 2007.

18 A record fall of 76% in stock prices occurred in Iceland, while house prices managed an annual fall of 25.8% in Estonia (Halldorsson and Zoega, "Iceland's Financial Crisis in an International Perspective").

19 Halldorsson and Zoega, "Iceland's Financial Crisis in an International Perspective."

20 This was later confirmed to be true by the parliamentary investigative committee into the causes of the financial collapse. See Rannsóknarnefnd Alþingis [Special Investigation Commission of the Icelandic Parliament], *Aðdragandi og orsakir falls íslensku bankanna 2008 og tengdir atburðir* [The causes and effects of the fall of the Icelandic banks and related events] (Reykjavík, Icelandic Parliament, 2010), chapter 6. Hereafter cited as "the SIC Report." See also Ulf V. Nielsson and Bjarni K. Torfason, "Iceland's Economic Eruption and Meltdown," *Scandinavian Economic History Review* 60, no. 1 (2012): 3–30.

21 The SIC Report, chapter 6.
22 Benediktsdottir et al., "Lessons from a Collapse of a Financial System."
23 The SIC Report, chapter 6.
24 See Gudrun Johnsen, *Bringing Down the Banking System: Lessons from Iceland* (New York: Palgrave Macmillan, 2014), 126.
25 Johnsen, *Bringing Down the Banking System*, 112.
26 See Johnsen, *Bringing Down the Banking System*, 120–121.
27 Offshore companies were the second largest shareholder in the Landsbanki (Johnsen, *Bringing Down the Banking System*).
28 The SIC Report. There is a resemblance to the case of Enron in the 1990s, which had employees invest in off-balance sheet-holding companies controlled by the Enron management that then bought shares in the company.
29 Johnsen, *Bringing Down the Banking System*, 138.
30 Aliber compares this situation to that of Japan in the 1980s; Japanese banks owned stocks directly, while the Icelandic banks financed stock through lending. See Robert Z. Aliber, "Monetary Turbulence and the Icelandic Economy," in *Preludes to the Icelandic Financial Crisis*, eds. Robert Aliber and Gylfi Zoega (London: Palgrave Macmillan, 2011), 302–326.
31 A report by Merrill Lynch in March 2006 described the dangers. It said:

> We cannot recall of a single other instance in Europe of where banks hold such substantial stakes in the local market (not to mention significant holding of their own shares, for whatever reason) or where they have to justify such an unusual state of affairs. Our point is merely that if the stock market were to decline rapidly, it would certainly impact the equities that the banks are apparently holding as hedges (such as they are), as well as the client portfolios, wherever they are.
> (Richard Thomas, "Icelandic Banks: Not What You Are Thinking," Merrill Lynch High Grade, March 7, 2006, accessed February 2, 2015, https://notendur.hi.is/ajonsson/kennsla2006/Merrill%20Lynch%20-%20Icelandic%20Banks.pdf.)

32 Nielsson and Torfason, "Iceland's Economic Eruption and Meltdown."
33 The SIC Report.
34 At the time of the collapse of the banks, 56% of Glitnir's loan portfolio was in foreign currency, as were 68% of Landsbanki's and 72% of Kaupthing's. Even 24.7% of loans to individuals were in foreign currencies. Johnsen, *Bringing Down the Banking System*.
35 According to the SIC Report, over 50% of loans were in the form of bullet loans, requiring the payment of neither interest nor principal.
36 Loan loss allowances were 0.77% of outstanding loans in 2007 in the Icelandic banks, while the comparable number was 0.86% in Deutsche Bank, 1.54% in Danske Bank, and 2.10% in HSBC (The SIC Report).
37 At the time of the collapse, one business group had borrowed what amounted to more than 50% of the three largest banks' total regulatory capital, making this one group a significant risk factor for the banking system as a whole. See Nielsson and Torfason, "Iceland's Economic Eruption and Meltdown."
38 In this way, the owners of Glitnir got around 300 million euros from depositors in the year 2008. Another money market fund, this one operated by the biggest of the three banks, Kaupthing, was used to invest in the parent company. During the latter half of 2006, this ratio was about 50% of the total assets of the fund, and even higher in 2008. See the SIC Report, chapter 6.
39 Benediktsdottir et al., "Lessons from a Collapse of a Financial System."
40 See Benediktsdottir et al., "Lessons from a Collapse of a Financial System."
41 The central bank got a swap line with the central banks of Denmark, Norway, and Sweden, amounting to 1.5 billion euros, after agreeing to specific terms involving responsible budget policy.

42 The President of Iceland made many speeches explaining the economic prosperity. The following quote is taken from a speech he gave at the Walbrook Club in London in 2005:

> Recently, I have often found myself cornered at various functions, especially here in London, and pressured to explain how and why daring Icelandic entrepreneurs are succeeding where others hesitate or fail, to reveal the secret behind the success they have achieved…
>
> How has it been possible to achieve such success in so many different fields and in such a short time, in areas where we definitely had no prior competitive advantage, areas such as pharmaceuticals and prosthetics, banking and finance, retail and fashion—to name only a few?
>
> Of course, many factors have contributed to the success of this voyage, but I am convinced that our business culture, our approach, our way of thinking and our behavior patterns, rooted in our traditions and national identity, have played a crucial role. All of these are elements that challenge the prevailing theories taught in respected business schools and observed in practice by many of the big American and British corporations. We are succeeding because we are different, and our track record should inspire the business establishment in other countries to re-examine their previous beliefs and the norms that they think will guarantee results. The range of Icelandic success cases provide a fertile ground for a productive dialogue on how the modern business world is indeed changing.

43 Paula Clancy et al., *Mapping the Golden Circle* (Dublin: TASC, 2010). It describes the overlap between the networks of bank and state boards in Ireland, while the Special Investigation Commission details the close relationship between politicians and bankers in Iceland during the same time period.

44 See, for example, Ezra F. Vogel, *Japan as Number One: Lessons for America* (Lincoln: Universe.com, 1980).

45 One example is the failure to account for expected losses in the banks' loan book due to lending in foreign currencies. Another is the creation of capital through accounting, such as the creation of goodwill through buying and selling companies within business groups controlled by one and the same party.

46 See Guillermo Calvo, "Capital Flows and Capital-Market Crises: The Simple Economics of Sudden Stops," *Journal of Applied Economics* 1, no. 1 (1998): 35–54.

47 A Fitch Ratings report published on February 22, 2006 stated that Fitch had revised the outlook on Iceland's long-term sovereign rating from stable to negative. Fitch described the macro-economic imbalances and raised concerns about how well the broader financial system would cope if the economy suffered a hard landing. Another report was written by economists at the Danske Bank. See Carsten Valgreen et al., "Iceland: Geyser Crisis," Danske Bank Research Paper, March 21, 2006, accessed February 2, 2015, www.mbl.is/media/98/398.pdf. It appeared in March 2006 titled "The Geyser Crisis." The authors are quite explicit in their warnings about the dangers facing the country.

48 Source: Central Bank of Iceland.

49 Using the median exchange rate of GBP on December 31, 2007; seven billion pounds multiplied by the exchange rate divided by the foreign exchange reserves of the Central Bank.

50 Johnsen, *Bringing Down the Banking System*, 87.

51 Willem Buiter and Anne Sibert, "The Icelandic Banking Crisis and What to Do about It: The Lender of Last Resort Theory of Optimal Currency Areas," in *Preludes to the Icelandic Financial Crisis*, eds. Robert Aliber and Gylfi Zoega (London: Palgrave Macmillan, 2011), 241–275.

52 Such weak equity was above 20% of the capital of Glitnir in mid-2008, and had increased significantly in the spring of 2008, when the bank lent funds to holding companies that then bought shares in the bank. The comparable figure was 60% for

Kaupthing, and also grew markedly in the spring of 2008. The share of weak capital was somewhat lower for Landsbanki. For all three banks put together, the share of weak capital was more than 25% of the capital base and more than 50% of core capital. See the SIC Report, chapter 9.

53 Other cases include the US savings and loans crisis in the 1980s, the Enron experience in the 1990s, and the issuing and reselling of mortgages in the United States in the first decade of this century. In all of these cases, the capital of financial institutions was exaggerated in financial statements by not taking credit risk adequately into account, and profits were also over-reported.

Bibliography

Aliber, Robert Z. "Monetary Turbulence and the Icelandic Economy." In *Preludes to the Icelandic Financial Crisis*, edited by Robert Aliber and Gylfi Zoega, 302–326. London: Palgrave Macmillan, 2011.

Benediktsdottir, Sigridur, Jon Danielsson, and Gylfi Zoega. "Lessons from a Collapse of a Financial System." *Economic Policy* 26, no. 66 (2011): 183–235.

Blanchard, Olivier and Francesco Giavazzi. "Current Account Deficits in the Euro Area: The End of the Feldstein-Horioka Puzzle?" Brookings Papers on Economic Activity 33, no. 2 (2002): 147–210.

Buiter, Willem and Anne Sibert. "The Icelandic Banking Crisis and What to Do about It: The Lender of Last Resort Theory of Optimal Currency Areas." In *Preludes to the Icelandic Financial Crisis*, edited by Robert Aliber and Gylfi Zoega, 241–275. London: Palgrave Macmillan, 2011.

Calvo, Guillermo. "Capital Flows and Capital-Market Crises: The Simple Economics of Sudden Stops." *Journal of Applied Economics* 1, no. 1 (1998): 35–54.

Clancy, Paula, Nat O'Connor, and Kevin Dillon. *Mapping the Golden Circle*. Dublin: TASC, 2010.

Feldstein, Martin and Charles Horioka. "Domestic Saving and International Capital Flows." *The Economic Journal* 90 (358): 314–329.

Gudmundsson, Gudmundur S. and Gylfi Zoega. "Age Structure and Current Account Imbalances." *Economic Letters* 123 (2014): 183–186.

Gylfason, Thorvaldur, Bengt Holmström, Sixten Korkman, Hans Tson Söderström, and Vesa Vihriala. *Nordics in Global Crisis: Vulnerability and Resilience*. The Research Institute of the Finnish Economy (ETLA). Taloustieto Oy, 2010.

Halldórsson, Ólafur G. and Gylfi Zoega. "Iceland's Financial Crisis in an International Perspective." Working Paper Series W10:02, Institute of Economic Studies, University of Iceland, 2010.

Hansson, Kjartan and Gylfi Zoega. "Capital Flows and Labour Market Distortion." Working Paper Series W13:05, Institute of Economic Studies, University of Iceland, 2013.

Johnsen, Gudrun. *Bringing Down the Banking System: Lessons from Iceland*. New York: Palgrave Macmillan, 2014.

Katsimi, Margarita and Gylfi Zoega. "European Integration and the Feldstein-Horioka Puzzle." Working Paper Series W143:01, Institute of Economic Studies, University of Iceland, 2014.

Keynes, John M. *The Economic Consequences of the Peace*. London: Macmillan, 1920.

Kindleberger, Charles P. and Robert Z. Aliber. *Manias, Panics, and Crashes: A History of Financial Crises*. London: Palgrave Macmillan, 2011.

Mackay, Charles. *Extraordinary Popular Delusions and the Madness of Crowds*. London: Richard Bentley, 1841.

Minsky, Hyman P. *Stabilizing an Unstable Economy*. New York: McGraw-Hill, 1986.

Nielsson, Ulf V. and Bjarni K. Torfason. "Iceland's Economic Eruption and Meltdown." *Scandinavian Economic History Review* 60, no. 1 (2012): 3–30.

Rannsóknarnefnd Alþingis [Special Investigation Commission of the Icelandic Parliament]. *Aðdragandi og orsakir falls íslensku bankanna 2008 og tengdir atburðir* [The Causes and Effects of the Fall of the Icelandic Banks and Related Events]. Reykjavik: Icelandic Parliament, 2010.

Reinhart, Carmen and Kenneth Rogoff. *This Time is Different: Eight Centuries of Financial Folly*. Princeton: Princeton University Press, 2009.

Sibert, Anne. "Overbanked and Undersized: Lessons from Iceland." In *Preludes to the Icelandic Financial Crisis*, edited by Robert Aliber and Gylfi Zoega, 329–340. London: Palgrave Macmillan, 2011.

Thomas, Richard. "Icelandic Banks: Not What You Are Thinking." Merrill Lynch High Grade, March 7, 2006. Accessed February 2, 2015. https://notendur.hi.is/ajonsson/kennsla2006/Merrill%20Lynch%20-%20Icelandic%20Banks.pdf.

Valgreen, Carsten, Lars Christensen, Peter Passing Andersen, and Rene Kallstrup. "Iceland: Geyser Crisis." Danske Bank Research Paper, March 21, 2006. Accessed February 2, 2015. www.mbl.is/media/98/398.pdf.

Vogel, Ezra F. *Japan as Number One: Lessons for America*. Lincoln: iUniverse.com, 1980.

2 The rise and fall of a financial empire

Looking at the banking collapse from the inside out

Gudrun Johnsen

The story of the rise and fall of the Icelandic banking system—from 2002 until its collapse in 2008—is instructive in many ways. It started out with the privatization process, where the first mistakes were made. Incentive schemes, then, had the effect of grossly misreporting bank equity levels, resulting in the rapid expansion of the balance sheets of the banks and in the buildup of poor quality loan portfolios. During the final phase, bank managers played tricks on central banks to avoid liquidity shortages, as they pledged bogus collateral in exchange for short-term lending facilities.

This chapter provides an overview of the events and business practices of bank managers, which led to the demise of the Icelandic banking system. One of the most surprising lessons is, perhaps, that even without all the data available today from the Special Investigation Commission (SIC), there were still enough public data available as early as 2005 to justify intervention by regulators to stop the unsustainable expansion of the Icelandic banks, that is, before 2006, the year the SIC called the point of no return.

The privatization process

When the Independence Party and the Progressive Party formed a coalition government in April 1995, they brought forward the vision of a stronger Icelandic economy, achieved by privatizing state enterprises that had been competing with private and public companies. These enterprises included the two largest banks at the time, Landsbanki and Búnaðarbanki. The government's ownership of banks and other financial companies had contributed to the lack of diversity in the market and had impeded the development of the Icelandic financial market, with negative consequences for the economy as a whole, as predicted by economic theories at the time.[1] The liberalization plan brought the promise of a modern financial system, devoid of politically motivated lending, and, even more importantly, a healthier economy with increased diversification.

Prime Minister Davíð Oddsson described the goal of liberalization during testimony to Parliament's Special Investigation Commission as follows:

> Financial services here were, of course, quite primitive, you see, very primitive, though many have forgotten; so people figured that with privatization, Iceland would have to attract the experience of market players who had been in this business in a free market elsewhere for 200 or 300 years; so many were very excited about that.[2]

The vision of those two parties was, therefore, quite clear. It reflected the idea that these banks would be bought by experienced market participants, most likely foreign banks, which had built up substantial expertise in financial services not to be found in Iceland at the time. For this reason, the sale of these two banks should bring accumulated knowledge and experience from abroad for the future development of the Icelandic financial market, which was essentially in its formative stage around that time. The vision was even larger. In an interview with the *Financial Times* in April 1998, Prime Minister Oddsson stated that the plan was to make Iceland an international financial center, but added that it would take a considerable amount of time.[3] The government, therefore, had a very ambitious plan for the Icelandic financial market.

Privatization, however, is not straightforward, and, to be successful, it requires good governance. The risk of moral hazard accompanies great financial interests. Privatization of banks is particularly precarious, given the delicate effect of the deposit money multiplier on financial stability and bankers' role in creating the money supply.[4] Banks may, then, end up in the hands of owners who have little or no experience of running them; hence, there is little or no insight into credit assessment and quality. Such ownership may lead to substandard lending or even reckless behavior, as Iceland so painfully experienced.

Privatization is more likely to yield positive results for society in the long run if the organizational setup is strong, with active oversight, and reputable independent experts chosen for the task. It is, however, not likely to succeed if a few "old friends" manage every step of the process and transparency is minimal. The privatization of the Icelandic banks in the early 2000s went awry from the very beginning, resulting in a complete failure on an unprecedented scale. Favored by the Independence Party, and with a little help from HSBC's representative advising on the execution of the private placement, a private holding company in the ownership of three investors, usually referred to as the Samson group, acquired a controlling stake in Landsbanki, with an exemption from the mandatory take-over rule, at 40% at the end of 2002.

The Samson Group claimed that it had not planned to buy a bank. Björgólfur Guðmundsson, a leading businessman of the group, testified that shortly after Samson sold the Bravo Beer Factory in St Petersburg, Russia, to Heineken, his son, Björgólfur Thor, and their business associate, Magnus Þorsteinsson, were at a cocktail party in London when they first met a man from HSBC, who mentioned that his bank had received a mandate from the Icelandic government to find buyers for Landsbanki. The individual also revealed that HSBC had talked to 17–20 potential buyers without success, and asked whether they were interested. This chance encounter evolved into a serious interest, leading to Samson taking part in the privatization process.[5]

Five groups of investors offered bids for the controlling stake in Landsbanki, all of them Icelandic. The Committee on Privatization (CoP) selected three of them for further discussions and met with each of them separately. During the bidding process, requirements toward bidders were profoundly changed, for example, from the prerequisite of having extensive experience and knowledge in running financial services to having *used* financial services.[6] The CoP's advisor, HSBC, compiled the answers from the investors and assigned a score for each factor. According to the SIC, there is no indication that HSBC used any information for these evaluations other than that which was provided by the bidders themselves. In other words, the SIC was not able to find any supporting materials from unbiased independent sources.[7]

During SIC testimony, a veteran of the CoP, Steingrímur Ari Arason, and the minister of commerce at the time, Valgerður Sverrisdóttir, described their disappointment on discovering that an employee of the CoP, a civil servant at the Ministry of Commerce, Skarphéðinn Berg Steinarsson, had met with the HSBC representative in London on his own to go over the evaluation model. The SIC discovered an e-mail from Edward Williams, the government's representative at HSBC, addressed to Steinarsson. The e-mail was dated August 29, 2002, shortly before Samson was declared the winning bidder by the CoP, and included the following explanation from Williams: "By defining the criteria and weighting carefully, it is possible to arrive at the 'right' result in selecting the preferred party, whilst having a semi-scientific justification for the decision that will withstand external critical scrutiny."[8]

Steingrímur Ari Arason, a representative of the minister of commerce since 1991, resigned from the CoP immediately after the sale of Landsbanki. Arason described the handling of the decision to select Samson as the main reason, claiming that he had never witnessed such unprofessionalism during his 11 years of service for the CoP.[9] Samson Group bought a 45.8% share in the bank, with a down payment of a third of the purchasing price and borrowing the remaining two-thirds from rival Búnaðarbanki.[10]

Having observed how businessmen close to the Independence Party were allowed to buy Landsbanki, the leaders of the other party in power, the Progressive Party, seem to have felt that it was their turn to cherry-pick the future owners of the other bank that was up for privatization. Búnaðarbanki was subsequently sold to a group of investors tightly linked to the Progressive Party, with the party's former minister of commerce, the CEO of an insurance company, and a shareholder in S-Group orchestrating the deal.[11]

HSBC completed the evaluation of the bids for Búnaðarbanki within two weeks and submitted the results at the beginning of November 2002 to the CoP. The CoP quickly selected the S-Group for further negotiations. One of the key factors in the decision was the involvement of a reputable international financial institution, Société Générale. The French bank was described as an advisor to the S-Group as well as a possible investor. HSBC's assessment of S-Group's knowledge and experience of financial markets depended on Societe General's participation in the investor group.[12]

The buyer agreement ("Head of Agreement") between the S-Group and the Icelandic government included Société Générale "and/or another international financial institution" as one of the investors. It required the S-Group to reveal by December 6 how large a share the French bank would invest in Búnaðarbanki; otherwise, the negotiations could be terminated.[13] On December 12, HSBC told the CoP that the participation of Société Générale would be confirmed the next day, but on December 13, the S-Group informed the CoP that information about an international investor in the group could not be revealed until the contract signing. The CoP responded by asking for more information. The HSBC advisor then notified them that "we do not have absolute comfort, but I think that it is reasonable to proceed on the back of what SocGen have told me."[14]

The process continued, and on January 6, 2003, the S-Group described the negotiations with an international financial institution as being well on their way. On January 9, the advisor from HSBC described that institution as a "good investor" for the Icelandic government, but did not reveal the name of the institution. The German bank Bayerische Landesbank was mentioned as an important financier at the CoP's meeting on January 10, but no international financial institution was mentioned at the CoP's last meeting, on January 14.[15]

The purchase agreement for Búnaðarbanki was signed on January 16, revealing for the first time the name of the international financial institution in the investor group, the German bank Hauck & Aufhäuser Privatbankiers KGaA. In a press release issued by the new owners of Búnaðarbanki, Hauck & Aufhäuser (H&A) was described as a privately owned bank with operations in Germany, Switzerland, and Luxembourg, specializing in "fund- and asset management for institutions and individuals, securities management for funds, and financial management for firms and individuals." The press release also stated that the German bank would provide valuable experience for growing Búnaðarbanki beyond the Icelandic market.[16]

The SIC found no evidence that Hauck & Aufhäuser ever provided valuable experience to Búnaðarbanki. In fact, its participation in the deal was questioned for several years following the sale. An Icelandic parliamentarian, who had submitted a formal inquiry to the minister of commerce, was informed that there was no reason to doubt that H&A had been a shareholder. However, during SIC testimony, Sigurjón Árnason, the vice president of operations at Búnaðarbanki at the time, explained: "[H&A] did not in fact have the means to participate [in the deal], despite the fact that Búnaðarbanki wasn't particularly big. That's why we always thought it was kind of strange when all this was happening."[17] After the sale, Búnaðarbanki management thought it would be appropriate to begin some form of cooperation with this new owner, which could, supposedly, be a great mentor. According to Árnason, Búnaðarbanki, therefore, sent one of its managers to Germany to meet with H&A to discuss the possibility of cooperation between the two banks. Much to their surprise, nobody at H&A knew anything about the deal. Furthermore, they had never heard of Búnaðarbanki in Iceland.[18]

Within five years of privatization, three of the largest banks had collapsed, two of which had been privatized. Together, these banks represented 97% of the Icelandic banking system in terms of bank assets. Their failure also had a severe impact on a number of smaller financial services companies and credit unions, such that, once the dust settled, 99% of the Icelandic banking system had collapsed.[19]

The unsustainable expansion of the banking system

Soon after the privatization of the Icelandic banks was completed, their funding efforts in the European bond market increased sharply. Landsbanki issued medium-term bonds in 2003 worth 850 million euros, which increased its balance sheet by 60%.[20] In only five years, the three Icelandic banks managed to borrow roughly 45 billion euros with bond issues abroad.[21] Even as the European Medium Term Note market (EMTN) was no longer an option in 2006, due to high rates as the credit default swap (CDS) premium grew fivefold in one year, the banks managed to issue bonds in the US market (USMTN). US investors saw an opportunity in bonds from the Icelandic banks, which had inherited the credit rating of the virtually debt-free Icelandic state, but were willing to pay rates more in line with financial institutions in developing countries, which carried a much lower credit rating. The Icelandic bonds, which carried high yields but seemingly little risk, were considered rare black swans and a welcome addition to US collateralized debt obligations (CDOs) in 2006.[22]

Yet, there were some early signs of trouble. Analysts from the rating agencies expressed a negative view toward the Icelandic banks when representatives from the Central Bank of Iceland (CBI) met with them in London in February 2006. They argued that that the growth of the Icelandic banks could not be maintained after they had tripled in size during the two years that had passed since privatization (see Table 2.1). A week later, Fitch Ratings issued its negative outlook regarding the Icelandic state and its access to financial markets. Iceland would have to reconsider its strategy and take action to reduce the risk in the Icelandic economy.[23] In March, both Merrill Lynch and Danske Bank issued detailed reports in which they highlighted what they considered an unsustainable case of rapid expansion and the looming refinancing challenge, and exposed their cross-ownership issues. Furthermore, they pointed out how unstable the Icelandic economy was at the time, with high inflation, negative current account, and low unemployment.[24] The Danske Bank report explained:

> On most measures, the small Icelandic economy is the most overheated in the OECD area. Unemployment stands at 1%, wage growth is above 7% and inflation is running above 4% despite a strong ISK. The current account deficit is closing in on 20% of GDP. The Icelandic central bank has been hiking rates substantially in order to cool the economy, and rates are now above 10%. Based on the macro data alone, we think the economy is heading for a recession in 2006–7. GDP could probably dip 5–10% in the

Table 2.1 Year end assets and liability values (million Icelandic krona), sum of the three banks

Year	*2003*	*2004*	*2005*	*2006*	*2007*	*2008*
Total assets (billion Icelandic krona)	1,451	2,946	5,419	8,475	11,354	14,437
Acquisitions (billion Icelandic krona)		797	726	0	58	0
Asset growth rate (%)		103	83.9	56.4	34.0	27.2
Organic growth (billion Icelandic krona)		713	1949	1988	3052	−219
Organic growth (%)		51.6	66.1	36.1	36.4	−1.9
Real organic growth (%)		43.5	59.5	27.2	28.8	−10.0

Source: Rannsóknarnefnd Alþingis [Special Investigation Commission of the Icelandic Parliament], in *Aðdragandi og orsakir falls íslensku bankanna 2008 og tengdir atburðir* [Causes and Effects of the Fall of the Icelandic Banks and Related Events], vol. 7 (Reykjavik: Icelandic Parliament, 2010), 91; Mark Flannery, "Iceland's Failed Banks: A Post-Mortem," in *Aðdragandi og orsakir falls íslensku bankanna 2008 og tengdir atburðir* [Causes and Effects of the Fall of the Icelandic Banks and Related Events], vol. 9 (Reykjavik: Icelandic Parliament, 2010), 89–107.

> next 2 years, and inflation is likely to spike above 10% as the ISK depreciates markedly. However, on top of the macro boom, there has been a stunning expansion of debt, leverage and risk-taking that is almost without precedents anywhere in the world. External debt is now nearly 300% of GDP, while short term external debt is just short of 55% of GDP. This is 133% of annual Icelandic export revenues.[25]

And their conclusion was very clear: "We look at early warning indicators for financial crises and conclude that Iceland looks worse on almost all measures than Thailand did before its crisis in 1997, and only moderately more healthy than Turkey before its 2001 crisis."[26] Rather than verifying the validity of the analysis and taking appropriate action, Icelandic politicians, businessmen, and financial supervisors reacted angrily to the criticisms and united in their own defense and their effort to convince the world that the Icelandic financial system was standing on firm ground.[27] The Icelandic Chamber of Commerce coordinated a counter-strategy with bankers and politicians. They went in search of well-known foreign economists who would be willing to provide the collusive mechanism needed and write reports that would counter the Danske Bank analysis. The purpose was to paint a positive picture of the Icelandic banking system, reassuring the world that Iceland's financial stability was intact. Two economists accepted this offer: Fredrick Mishkin in 2006 and Richard Portes in 2007.[28] The opportunity to take an honest look at what was happening in the light of serious and well-supported criticism was lost, and so was the opportunity to avoid the enormous losses that ensued when the system finally collapsed.

The campaign to save the reputation of the Icelandic banks and the banking system was quite successful, considering that the banks still managed to issue bonds worth another 11 billion euros in 2006, thanks in part to the efforts of Prime Minister Geir H. Haarde and others in government. However, as the market deemed the Icelandic banks unfit to take on more debt, the CDS premiums began climbing steadily in 2007. The rising cost of funding reflected the market's assessment of the banks and quickly became unsustainable for the three banks. Their rate climbed to 3% above interbank rates in London, compared with 0.3% above interbank rates three years earlier.[29] This constituted an institutional investor run on the banks, pricing the Icelandic banks out of the market, and was also marked by increased CDS activity, placing CDSs for the Icelandic banks among the 25 most actively traded in Europe in 2006.[30] Investors had, therefore, begun preparing for the default of the Icelandic banks, and even the Icelandic state, two years before the banks collapsed.

To keep the operations going, the Icelandic banks needed to search for alternative funding. In addition to issuing bonds in private placements, they turned their attention primarily to two sources of funding, the supremely informed central banks of Iceland and Europe, and the not-so-well informed depositors in London, Amsterdam, and elsewhere who had limited means of assessing the risk of making deposits in Landsbanki's Icesave accounts or Kaupthing's Edge accounts.[31]

The banks' skyrocketing growth of assets

The rapid growth of the Icelandic banks caught the attention of analysts and journalists abroad. When they inquired about the nature of the growth, Icelandic bankers and politicians alike had a simple explanation. They stated that the Icelandic banks had diversified internationally—they had bought assets abroad, including foreign financial institutions, to bring better service to their Icelandic customers who were expanding overseas. They insisted that the expansion of the banking system had little to do with Iceland, its economy, or its currency—the krona—and was a welcome diversification. The Icelandic economy, according to them, was, therefore, at no risk.

Government officials had no interest in carrying out an analysis that would test this explanation. Rather, they adopted it to shield themselves from criticism for failure to provide oversight. It was not until the SIC performed the analysis after the banks collapsed that the numbers revealed the truth.[32]

The SIC first calculated the internal growth of the banks, that is, growth excluding the impact of foreign acquisitions, concluding that it varied between 36% and 66% per year from 2003 to 2007 (see Table 2.1). The banks experienced a slight contraction from 2007 to 2008, or 1.9% when calculated in Icelandic krona, but their growth was eightfold from 2003 to 2007. Internal growth of this magnitude is without precedence. As a reference, the US Federal Deposit Insurance Corporation (FDIC) considers 5% total annual growth to be of concern if it lasts over four years.[33] The SIC then obtained data from authorities in Luxembourg and found that a considerable amount of the assets owned by the subsidiaries of the Icelandic banks was, in fact, tied to Icelandic risk in one way or another.[34] Claims by Icelandic bankers and politicians that the unprecedented growth was due to diversification and expansion in new markets, therefore, turned out to be incorrect.

The growth of the loan portfolios was so rapid that it is difficult for even experienced bankers and finance scholars to understand how it could have taken place. In 2001, bank credit to the private sector was equal to GDP, but then grew to five times GDP in 2008, even after Iceland's GDP had grown considerably.[35] When the banks collapsed, roughly 60% of their loan portfolios consisted of loans to holding companies or foreign companies. On further examination, many of the foreign companies turned out to be holding companies as well. The loan portfolios were, therefore, excessively exposed to one particular risk: holding company investments in listed and unlisted firms.[36] Although holding companies invest in various types of operations, they have certain characteristics that require them to be categorized as one particular sector. Holding companies do not produce anything themselves, and their owners have a tendency to put forth as little equity as possible. This, in turn, creates incentives that lead to increased risk-taking, in terms of both greater leverage and risk in investment choices, which can lead to either more profits, losses for creditors, or bankruptcy. Furthermore, in order to meet profitability requirements, the holding company is financially dependent on its subsidiary, and vice versa. If banks do not adequately determine related parties and the risk involved, they fail to charge the rate that should be required for that risk.

Up to 88% of Landsbanki's loans to holding companies consisted of bullet loans, requiring no payments during the life of the loan. Such loans are among the riskiest. Bullet loans also constituted around 43% of Landsbanki loans to Icelandic companies and around 10% of loans to individuals. Data from Kaupthing and Glitnir were not of the same quality, making it harder to determine the exact numbers, but indicated that their loan portfolios were not much different from that of Landsbanki.[37] Given that around 58% of the loan portfolios of the three banks provided no cash flow for the banks to meet their own obligations, they were excessively dependent on growth. The banks had, in a significant way, extended loans to borrowers that could make neither principal payments nor even interest payments during the loan periods. If those borrowers were, in fact, able to make interest payments on their loans, it must be considered very irresponsible to grant them loans without a cash flow at all. The Icelandic banks, therefore, operated more like a Ponzi scheme. To pay principal and interest on older loans, new loans had to be obtained. Once bond markets realized the nature of the excessive and unsustainable growth, they no longer wanted to be part of it.

Questionable banking practices: cross-ownership and market manipulation

The SIC conducted an extensive cross-ownership and financial dependency analysis of Icelandic firms to assess loan portfolio risk, in particular the exposure of borrowers to each other. Margrét Bjarnadóttir and Guðmundur Axel Hansen[38] carried out an analysis of all Icelandic firms from 2004 to 2008 and revealed a tight network of firms that either had owners in common, owned shares in each other, or represented controlling shares in each other. Simple and objective rules allowed Bjarnadóttir and Hansen to form groups of firms that could be considered related parties. The identification numbers of all the firms were then merged with identification numbers of bank customers to calculate lending to related parties. According to regulation 216/2007 of the Financial Supervisory Authority of Iceland (FME), a bank can lend no more than 25% of its equity base to financially related parties. The conclusion was that all three banks had exceeded the 25% when lending to the largest shareholders of the banks, allowing the shareholders to channel funds into their other firms. One of the groups, Baugur Group and others, consisted of 187 firms based on the widest definition of a financially related group, and managed to borrow as much as 85% of the equity base of Glitnir, but their related parties held around a 30% share in the bank.[39] Around 11% of the combined portfolio of the three banks consisted of loans extended to Baugur Group or related parties, or around six billion euros at its peak.[40]

A group of related firms, such as the ones associated with Baugur Group, Samson Group, or Milestone, is usually formed to obtain as much credit as possible with as little equity as possible. The business thereby manages to minimize its own risk and instead places it into someone else's hands. In the Icelandic case, the risk was mostly borne by banks and taxpayers. The loan portfolios of the banks rapidly deteriorated, as little equity was present to cushion any losses. Under those circumstances, investors are likely to gamble big in the hope of great returns, but with proportionally little impact on their other assets if an investment goes bad. Furthermore, they may already have paid themselves dividends to extract the little equity they had put into the deal to begin with.

A value of a loan is determined by the interest rates it carries, current interest rates in the market, and the probability of the loan being paid back. The loan value also reflects the expected value recovered in the case of a default, which, in turn, can be determined by the value of the collateral and how expensive it would be to claim cash from the pledged asset. When making an attempt to assess the quality of a loan book of the failed banks, the SIC quickly ran into difficulties due to the poor quality of systematic and electronic documentation of collaterals. Difficulties also rose from the one-to-many/many-to-one relationship between lending and collaterals.[41] The only data available on collaterals of the necessary quality were loans extended against collaterals in listed shares.

The analysis revealed a bleak picture, as it turned out that a large share of all outstanding shares in blue chip companies on the Icelandic stock exchange had been pledged as collateral into the banking system. Over 75% of all outstanding shares in closed end fund (and controlling shareholder of Glitnir Bank) FL-Group had been pledged as collateral. Between 40% and 50% of all outstanding shares in Exista (controlling shareholder in Kaupthing) had been pledged as collateral in the banking sector. Even 40% of Kaupthing had been pledged into Kaupthing.[42] This had an evident effect on the bankers' behavior in proprietary trading, especially in their own shares, as their own loan portfolio became increasingly dependent on stock market prices. Figures 2.1, 2.2, and 2.3 reveal striking asymmetric trading patterns of the banks on the Icelandic stock exchange, whereby shares in the banks are only bought (volume above 0), but hardly ever sold, on the exchange. The picture is reversed when after-hours trading is scrutinized, when all of the banks tend to sell over the counter, but buy on the stock exchange (see Figures 2.4, 2.5, and 2.6).

The pattern is further revealed by looking at how the banks behaved when trading the shares of the rival banks. There, proprietary trading looks much more like what can be expected of a normal profit-maximizing firm, buying and selling on the exchange, even-handedly, in a symmetric fashion (see Figures 2.7, 2.8, and 2.9). Several top-level managers of the three banks were, in early 2015, given stiff prison sentences for market manipulation on a massive scale.

The point of no return

The story of the Icelandic banks is, at times, both thrilling and exciting. Given the loan portfolios the banks accumulated from 2003 to 2008, as described above, they had no means to survive inevitable changes in world financial

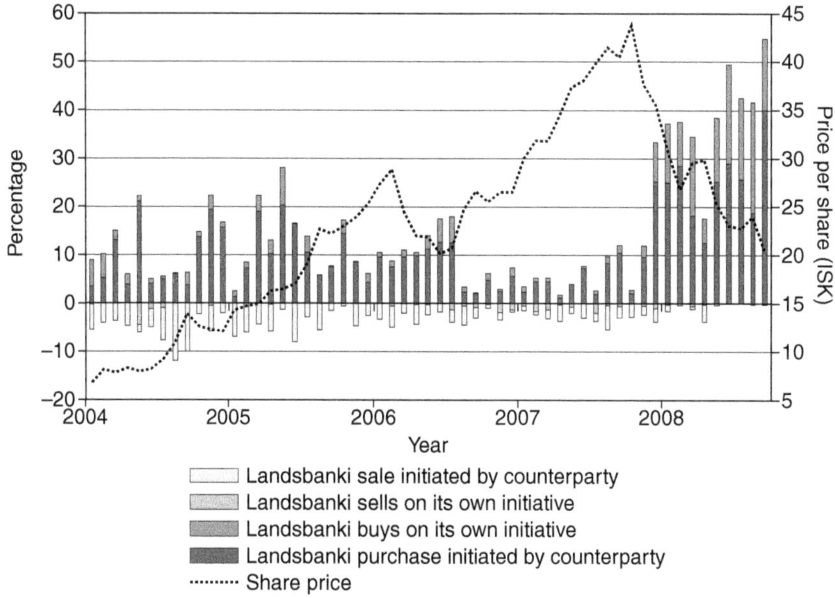

Figure 2.1 Landsbanki trading own shares. Percentage of all stock exchange turnover (source: Iceland Stock Exchange (ICEX) and Landsbanki Islands hf., SIC Report, Figure 30, Chapter 12, Volume 4, p. 48).

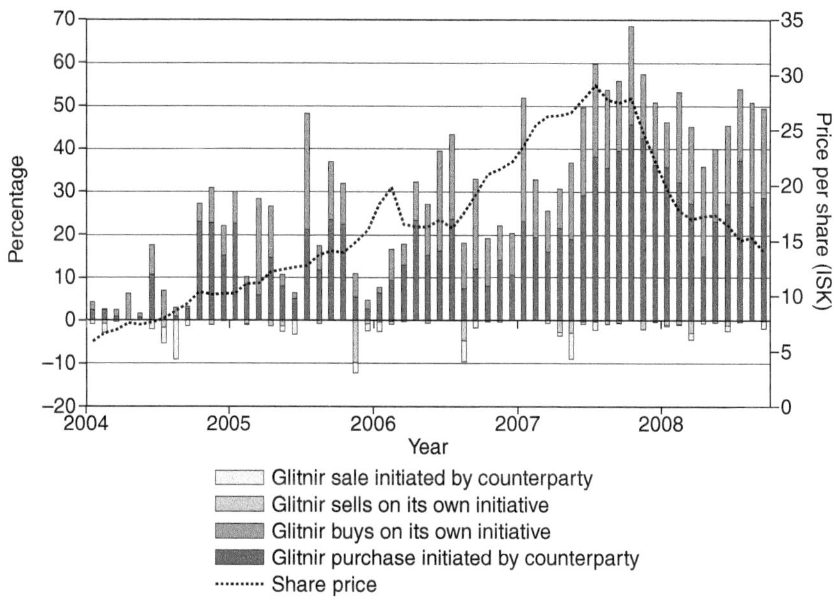

Figure 2.2 Glitnir trading own shares. Percentage of all stock exchange turnover (source: Iceland Stock Exchange (ICEX) and Glitnir bank hf., SIC Report, Figure 20, Chapter 12, Volume 4, p. 36).

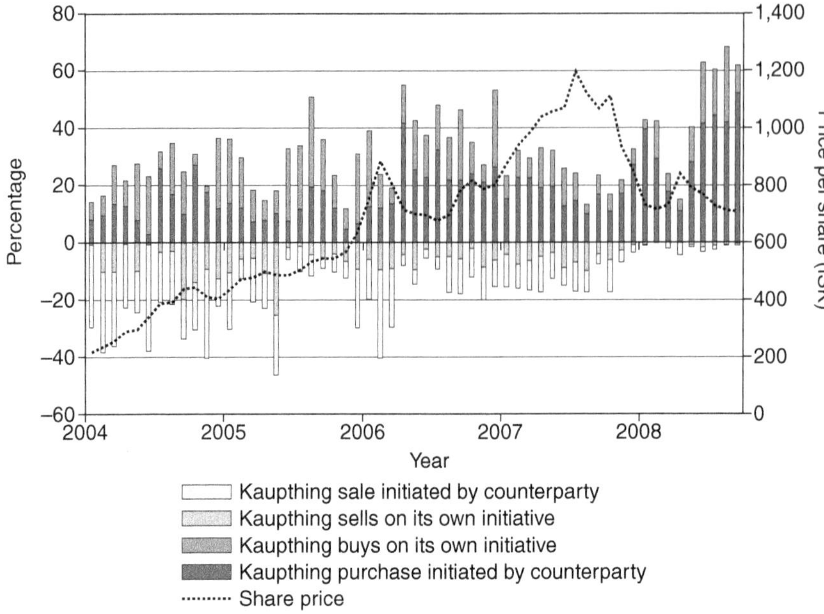

Figure 2.3 Kaupthing trading own shares. Percentage of all stock exchange turnover (source: Iceland Stock Exchange (ICEX), Kaupthing bank hf. and Iceland Securities Depository (ISD), SIC Report, Figure 8, Chapter 12, Volume 4, p. 24).

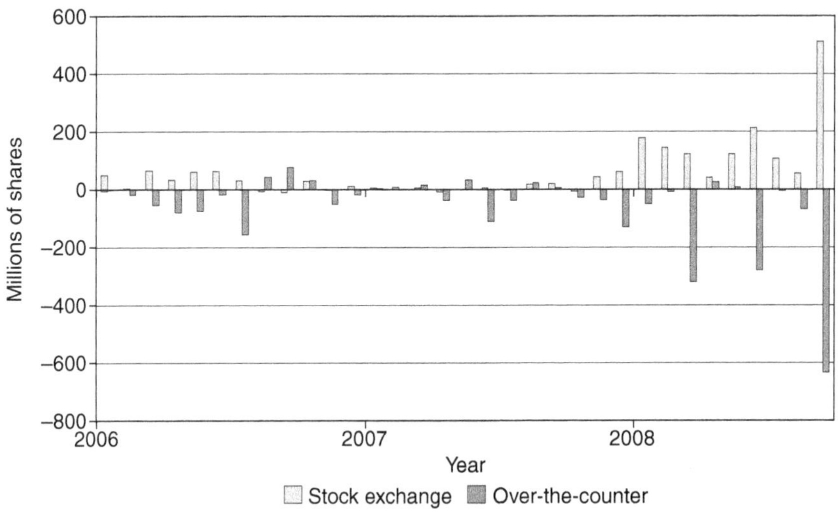

Figure 2.4 Buying and selling of own shares Landsbanki. Stock exchange transactions vs. over-the-counter (source: Landsbanki Islands hf., SIC Report, Figure 33, Chapter 12, Volume 4, p. 49).

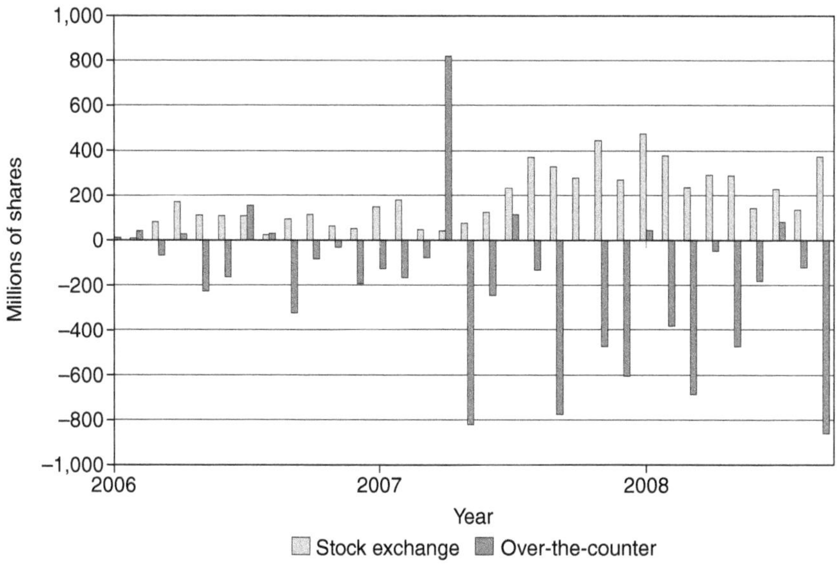

Figure 2.5 Buying and selling of own shares Glitnir. Stock exchange transactions vs. over-the-counter (source: Glitnir bank hf., SIC Report, Figure 23, Chapter 12, Volume 4, p. 37).

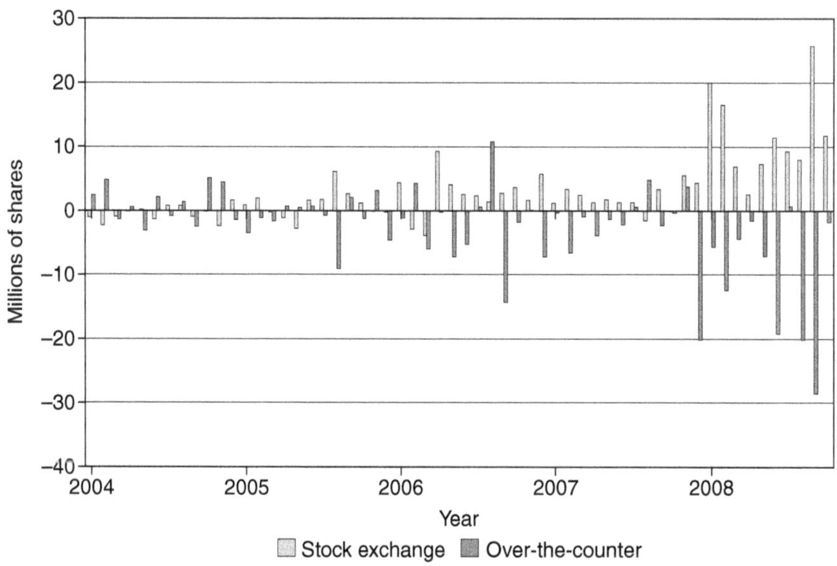

Figure 2.6 Buying and selling of own shares Kaupthing. Stock exchange transactions vs. over-the-counter (source: Iceland Stock Exchange (ICEX) and Kaupthing bank hf., SIC Report, Figure 13, Chapter 12, Volume 4, p. 26).

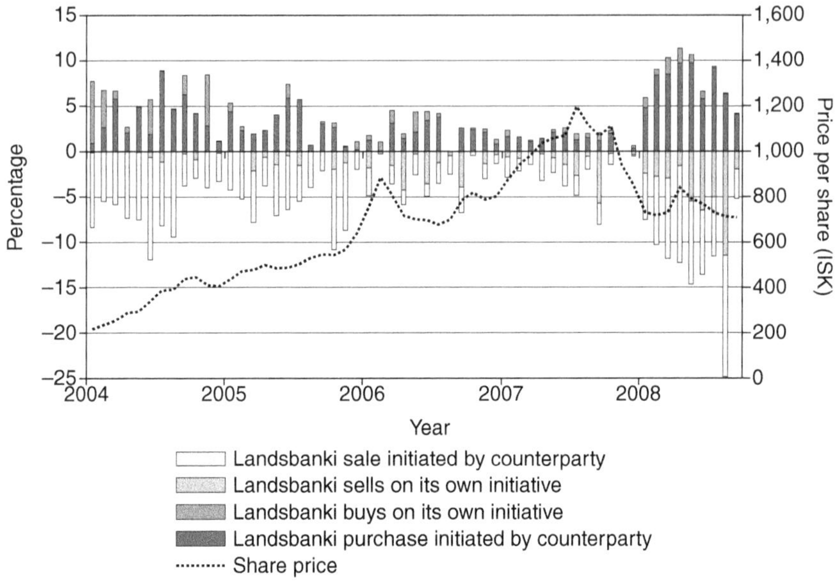

Figure 2.7 Landsbanki's trading in Kaupthing's shares. Percentage of all stock exchange turnover (source: Iceland Stock Exchange (ICEX) and Landsbanki Islands hf., SIC Report, Figure 14, Chapter 12, Volume 4, p. 33).

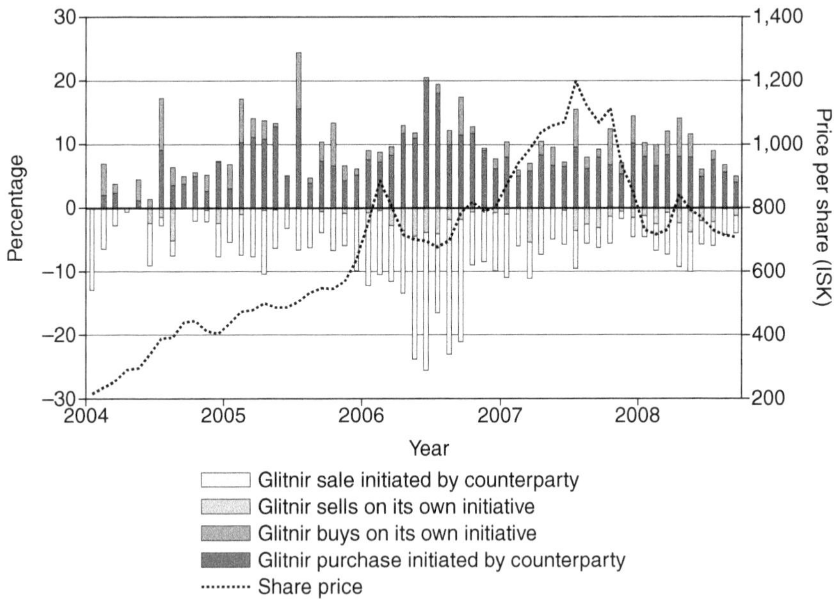

Figure 2.8 Glitnir's trading in Kaupthing's shares. Percentage of all stock exchange turnover (source: Iceland Stock Exchange (ICEX) and Glitnir bank hf., SIC Report, Figure 16, Chapter 12, Volume 4, p. 34).

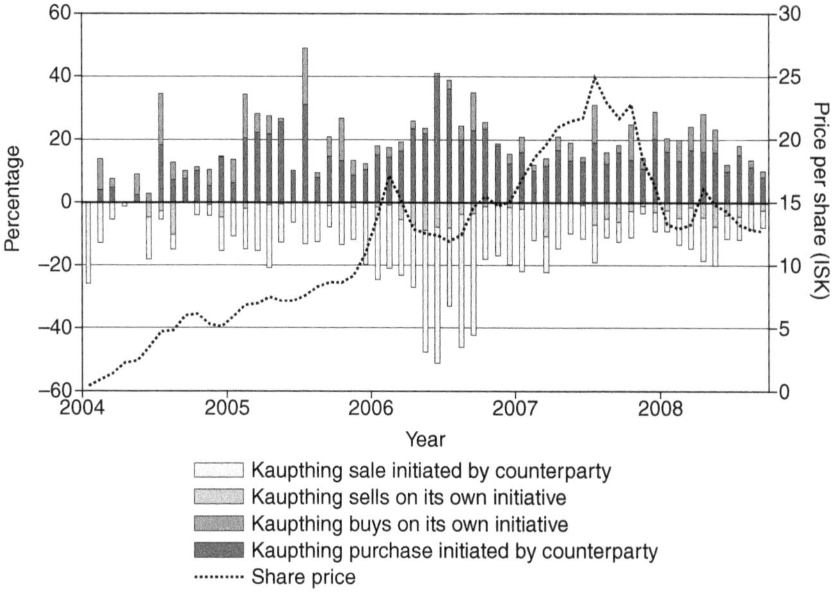

Figure 2.9 Kaupthing's trading in Glitnir's shares. Percentage of all stock exchange turnover (source: Iceland Stock Exchange (ICEX) and Kaupthing bank hf., SIC Report, Figure 24, Chapter 12, Volume 4, p. 46).

markets, even if those changes had not been as severe as they turned out to be in 2007 and 2008. In other words, it did not take an international financial crisis to bring down the Icelandic banks. Their portfolios were simply too weak, consisting of too many zero-coupon loans to borrowers who put down little equity and had, thus, little skin in the game. The equity of the three banks was also significantly overestimated and up to one-third falsified.[43]

The banks turned to two new funding sources to stay afloat after the wholesale run on them had started. In addition to raising funds with online savings accounts, they played a trick on the Central Bank of Iceland (CBI) by issuing bonds, which they swapped with each other and then brought to the CBI for collateralized lending.[44] The Icelandic bankers tried the same trick with the European Central Bank (ECB), but the ECB figured it out and stopped further collateralized lending to them. In the meantime, the CBI continued to provide funding until the end, adding a loan of last resort for Kaupthing immediately before it collapsed.[45]

Landsbanki suffered a run on the bank by deposit-holders in March 2008. Landsbanki's management told the prime minister as well as the foreign minister that the bank would have six days left if the run continued.[46] The foreign currency reserves of the CBI amounted to only about 20% of the deposits already in the Icesave accounts, yet the government took no action as a result. A run on a bank should prompt a central bank to provide a loan of last resort, according to the rules of Walter Bagehot from 1873, if and only if the bank needing the loan has adequate equity and good assets to use as collateral, and then only at a high rate.[47]

When Lehman Brothers fell in September 2008, customers with Icesave and Kaupthing Edge accounts lost faith in those banks and began withdrawing their funds again at an increasing rate. The withdrawals resulted in both Landsbanki and Kaupthing's subsidiary, KSF, being in breach of the British Financial Services Authority's (FSA) liquidity requirements. The CBI could not provide funds to Landsbanki, since it did not have the currency to do so.[48] Based on the reaction of the British authorities, as well as the testimony of the employees of the FSA in a case that the estate of Kaupthing filed against British authorities after the collapse, it was evident that they did not find it necessary to inject capital into a small bank like KSF to rescue it, since KSF's collapse would not have a systemic impact on the British financial system. It was, therefore, more economical, from a British standpoint, to use the authority of the FSA to move the deposits of Kaupthing Edge account holders in the United Kingdom to another financial institution instead of waiting to see whether KSF's assets would be enough to cover the assets of deposit-holders in the lengthy process that would follow.

The SIC found no evidence that KSF had ever formally asked for a loan of last resort, although Kaupthing discussed it informally with the FSA.[49] It is unlikely that such a request would have received much attention, given that KSF had been engaged in a 1.1 billion pound swap agreement with the parent company, Kaupthing, since the spring of 2008, in violation of its liquidity requirements. KSF, therefore, did not have the liquidity to meet withdrawals from Kaupthing Edge accounts, as it would have had if it had not violated the liquidity requirements placed on them by the FSA of holding 95% of all deposits on reserve in any given 24-hour cycle. When the violation was discovered, Kaupthing withdrew even more from the swap with KSF without providing the necessary collateral.[50] Kaupthing's final moment was, thus, determined by its senior management when they ignored the liquidity requirements set by British authorities. Kaupthing's loan of last resort from the CBI, equivalent to 400 million pounds, was not even enough for Kaupthing to provide the 300 million pounds to KSF that the management of KSF had promised, to keep it running, after the British authorities had moved the Kaupthing Edge accounts to ING Direct. Once KSF had fallen, the parent company Kaupthing went down as well, since loan covenants would kick in if any of Kaupthing's subsidiaries were to go under.

Conclusion

According to the SIC, the destiny of the Icelandic banks was determined as early as 2006. Although a counterfactual story is usually difficult to tell, it is evident from the available data that the loss would have been much reduced if action had been taken at that time.[51] Understandably, bankers and politicians have found it convenient to blame others for what happened to the Icelandic banks, such as foreign officials or unfavorable conditions abroad, akin to a natural disaster. These claims, however, have not been supported with data. On the contrary, the vulnerability that led to the banks' demise lay in the explosive growth of their loan portfolios. The portfolios were marked by ever-increasing risk due to high loan to value and poor collaterals, which, to a large degree, consisted of the banks' own listed shares as well as collaterals in the form of other listed and unlisted shares. A good banker would prefer to lend money to a borrower who is able to pay off his loan along with interest during the lifetime of the loan. A riskier loan would be extended to a borrower who would only be able to pay the interest on the loan during the lifetime of the loan, and the principal at the end of the lending period. The SIC's assessment, however, was that the majority of loans extended by the three banks were, indeed, to the riskiest type of customers one can find: to those who could neither pay interest nor make any payments off the loans during the lifetime of the loan. Hence, the most common form of loan in their portfolios was the bullet loan. At Landsbanki, up to 88% of the loans extended to holding companies were bullet loans.[52]

The lessons that can be drawn from the fall of the Icelandic banks are particularly important these days, as regulators around the world strive to reconstruct the institutional and regulatory framework responsible for controlling banks and other financial institutions. The cause of the collapse of the Icelandic banks lay primarily in the building blocks of the banks themselves: their incentive schemes, interconnectedness, cash flow, deprived loan portfolios, and vulnerable funding structure, including lack of equity funding.

Notes

1 See Rafael La Porta et al., "Government Ownership of Banks," *The Journal of Finance* 57, no. 1 (2002): 265–301.
2 Rannsóknarnefnd Alþingis [The Special Investigation Commission of the Icelandic Parliament], in *Aðdragandi og orsakir falls íslensku bankanna 2008 og tengdir atburðir* [The causes and effects of the fall of the Icelandic banks and related events], vol. 1 (Reykjavík: Icelandic Parliament, 2010), 23. Hereafter cited as "the SIC Report."
3 The SIC Report, vol. 1, 224.
4 James Tobin, "Commercial Banks as Creators of 'Money,'" Cowles Foundation Paper 205, reprinted in *Banking and Monetary Studies*, ed. Dean Carson (Homewood: Richard D. Irwin, 1963); N. G. Mankiw, *Macroeconomics* 4th ed. (New York City: Worth, 2000).
5 Gudrun Johnsen, *Bringing Down the Banking System: Lessons from Iceland* (New York: Palgrave Macmillan, 2014), 63.
6 The SIC Report, vol. 1, 246.
7 The SIC Report, vol. 1, 248.
8 The SIC Report, vol. 1, 263.
9 The SIC Report, vol. 1, 266; Johnsen, *Bringing Down the Banking System*, 67.
10 The SIC Report, vol. 1, 275–276; Johnsen, *Bringing Down the Banking System*.
11 Guðrún Johnsen, "Bankakerfið knésett," *Skírnir* 188 (2014): 9–36.
12 The SIC Report, vol. 1, 250–254; Johnsen, *Bringing Down the Banking System*, 88.
13 The SIC Report, vol. 1, 256.
14 The SIC Report, vol. 1, 256–257.

15 The SIC Report, vol. 1, 258; Johnsen, *Bringing Down the Banking System*, 69–71.
16 The SIC Report, vol. 1, 259; Johnsen, *Bringing Down the Banking System*, 69–71.
17 The SIC Report, vol. 1, 259; Johnsen, *Bringing Down the Banking System*, 70.
18 The SIC Report, vol. 1, 259; Johnsen, *Bringing Down the Banking System*, 71.
19 EFTA Court, *Judgment of the Court in Case E-16/11: Directive 94/19/EC on deposit-guarantee schemes — Obligation of result — Emanation of the State — Discrimination* (Strasbourg, January 28, 2013); Johnsen, *Bringing Down the Banking System*, 48.
20 Johnsen, *Bringing Down the Banking System*, 75.
21 The SIC Report, vol. 2, 20, figure 21.
22 Johnsen, *Bringing Down the Banking System*, 82.
23 Johnsen, *Bringing Down the Banking System*, 84.
24 Johnsen, *Bringing Down the Banking System*, 83.
25 Carsten Valgreen et al., "Iceland: Geyer Crisis," Danske Bank Research Paper, March 21, 2006, accessed December 1, 2015, www.mbl.is/media/98/398.pdf.
26 Carsten Valgreen et al., accessed May 2, 2015.
27 Johnsen, *Bringing Down the Banking System*, 86–87.
28 Johnsen, *Bringing Down the Banking System*, 86.
29 Johnsen, *Bringing Down the Banking System*, 87.
30 Johnsen, *Bringing Down the Banking System*, 85.
31 Johnsen, *Bringing Down the Banking System*, 85, 169.
32 Johnsen, *Bringing Down the Banking System*, 111.
33 "Federal Deposit Insurance Corporation," *Federal Register, Proposed Rules* 73, no. 201 (2008), accessed March 24, 2015, www.fdic.gov/regulations/laws/federal/2008/08propose1016.pdf; Mark Flannery, "Iceland's Failed Banks: A Post-Mortem," in *Causes and Effects of the Fall of the Icelandic Banks*, vol. 9, 93.
34 The SIC Report, vol. 2, 192–193, 196, figures 181 and 182.
35 Johnsen, *Bringing Down the Banking System*, 109.
36 Johnsen, *Bringing Down the Banking System*, 134–135; The SIC Report, vol. 2, 100–101, figures 29–30, 34.
37 Johnsen, *Bringing Down the Banking System*, 134–135; The SIC Report, vol. 2, 100–101, figures 29–30, 34.
38 Margrét V. Bjarnadóttir and Guðmundur Axel Hansen, "Rannsókn á krosseignartengslum og útlánum bankanna til tengdra aðila [Investigation into the cross ownership and bank credit to related parties]," in The SIC Report, vol. 9.
39 Bjarnadóttir and Hansen, "Investigation into the cross ownership and bank credit to related parties," 45, figure 23; The SIC Report, vol. 1, 293.
40 The SIC Report, vol. 2, 137.
41 Johnsen, *Bringing Down the Banking System*, 137.
42 Johnsen, *Bringing Down the Banking System*, 138–141.
43 Johnsen, *Bringing Down the Banking System*, 137–152; The SIC Report, vol. 3, chapter 9.
44 Johnsen, *Bringing Down the Banking System*, 93–96.
45 Johnsen, *Bringing Down the Banking System*, 101.
46 The SIC Report, vol. 6, 14.
47 Walter Bagehot, *Lombard Street: A Description of the Money Market* (New York: NuVision, 2008), 30.
48 The SIC Report, vol. 7, 157, 160–161.
49 The SIC Report, vol. 7, 165–166.
50 The SIC Report, vol. 7, 160–162.
51 Had the authorities stepped in and restructured the banking system in 2006, the online deposit accounts of Landsbanki, Icesave, would probably not have been set up, avoiding the long-standing dispute with the Dutch and the UK authorities over deposit insurance. Loans extended after 2006 were to a large degree granted to special

investment vehicles with next to no equity, to fund the purchase of shares in the banks themselves. Had the banks been restructured at that time, under strong leadership of their regulator, such loans would not have been extended and large losses would have been avoided by creditors and taxpayers who had to refinance the central bank, which became technically bankrupt as bank bonds backing loans of the central bank short-term lending facility proved worthless, to name one piece of supportive evidence of this.

52 Johnsen, *Bringing Down the Banking System*, 134.

Bibliography

Bagehot, Walter. *Lombard Street: A Description of the Money Market*. New York: NuVision, 2008.

Bjarnadóttir, Margrét V. and Guðmundur Axel Hansen. "Rannsókn á krosseignartengslum og útlánum bankanna til tengdra aðila [Investigation into the Cross Ownership and Bank Credit to Related Parties]." In *Aðdragandi og orsakir falls íslensku bankanna 2008 og tengdir atburðir* [Causes and Effects of the Fall of the Icelandic Banks and Related Events]. Vol. 9. Reykjavík: Icelandic Parliament, 2010.

Board of Governors of the Federal Reserve System. *Risks of Concentration of Credit and Nontraditional Activities*. Washington, DC: Board of Governors, March 26, 1993.

EFTA Court. *Judgment of the Court in Case E-16/11: Directive 94/19/EC on deposit-guarantee schemes — Obligation of result — Emanation of the State — Discrimination*. Strasbourg, January 28, 2013.

"Federal Deposit Insurance Corporation." Federal Register, Proposed Rules 73, no. 201 (2008), 61560–61597. Accessed March 24, 2015. www.fdic.gov/regulations/laws/federal/2008/08propose1016.pdf.

Flannery, Mark. "Iceland's Failed Banks: A Post-Mortem." In *Aðdragandi og orsakir falls íslensku bankanna 2008 og tengdir atburðir* [Causes and Effects of the Fall of the Icelandic Banks and Related Events]. Vol. 9, 89–107. Reykjavík: Icelandic Parliament, 2010.

Johnsen, Gudrun. *Bringing Down the Banking System: Lessons from Iceland*. New York: Palgrave Macmillan, 2014.

Johnsen, Guðrún. "Bankakerfið knésett," *Skírnir* 188 (spring 2014): 9–36.

Johnson, Simon, Rafael La Porta, Florencio Lopez-de-Silanes, and Andrei Shleifer. "Tunneling," *The American Economic Review* 90, no. 2 (2000): 22–27.

La Porta, Rafael, Florencio Lopez-De-Silanes, and Andrei Shleifer. "Government Ownership of Banks." *The Journal of Finance* 57, no. 1 (2002): 265–301.

Magnusson, Gylfi. "Lessons from a Small Country in a Financial Crisis or Dr. Minsky and Mr. Ponzi in Iceland." Working Paper Series W10:03, Institute of Economic Studies, University of Iceland, Reykjavík, 2010.

Mankiw, N. G. *Macroeconomics*. 4th ed. New York City: Worth, 2000.

Rannsóknarnefnd Alþingis [Special Investigation Commission of the Icelandic parliament]. The SIC Report. In *Aðdragandi og orsakir falls íslensku bankanna 2008 og tengdir atburðir* [Causes and Effects of the Fall of the Icelandic Banks and Related Events]. Reykjavík: Icelandic Parliament, 2010.

Thomas, Richard. "Icelandic Banks: Not What You Are Thinking." Merrill Lynch, High Grade, March 7, 2006. Accessed November 17, 2015. https://notendur.hi.is/ajonsson/kennsla2006/Merrill%20Lynch%20-%20Icelandic%20Banks.pdf.

Tobin, James. "Commercial Banks as Creators of 'Money.'" Cowles Foundation Paper 205. Reprinted from *Banking and Monetary Studies*, edited by Dean Carson. Homewood: Richard D. Irwin, 1963.

Valgreen, Carsten, Lars Christensen, Peter Passing Andersen, and Rene Kallstrup. "Iceland: Geyser Crisis." Danske Bank Research Paper, March 21, 2006. Accessed December 1, 2015. www.mbl.is/media/98/398.pdf.

3 The political economy of Iceland's boom and bust

Stefán Ólafsson

Introduction

The advent of Iceland's financial collapse was for the most part a typical financial bubble. It started as a mini bubble from 1998 to 2001, but then from 2003 onwards, it became one of the most extreme cases of a bubble economy ever seen, in relation to the size of the national economy.[1] When the bubble burst, it became one of the costliest financial crises of recent decades.[2] At the core was an excessive accumulation of external debt related to business speculation. Debt played a key role, both before and after the collapse. It fed the boom, and after the collapse, private debts were transferred to become public debts. At the same time, the household sector lost real earnings, which made it difficult to deal with fast-increasing pre-crisis debt levels. Corporate debt was, however, by far the largest part of the accumulated debt of the economy. While a housing bubble was a component of the economic developments, the extensive business speculation was the prime driver of the boom (the "Viking business raids")—and the bust.

The main theme of this chapter is the political economy of debt and speculation. It will be tied to issues of power and inequality by focusing on key actors and the gains they harvested. The study shows how classical theories of financial crises apply to the Icelandic saga, and how changing policy and institutional environments played a large role in the dramatic developments that engulfed Iceland. Key questions are: Why did it all happen? Why did it go so far? Who were the key players? And why did they do it?

Accounting for financial crises

Hyman Minsky's neo-Keynesian approach is the most prominent classical account of financial crises.[3] Minsky saw capitalism as a system prone to instability, and, thus, he rejected the neo-classical vision of capitalism as tending toward equilibrium. He located the source of instability in the key role played by the banking system in a capitalist economy. While Minsky followed Joseph Schumpeter in drawing attention to the centrality of the banking system in the capital accumulation process—due to its financing of entrepreneurial activity and trade—he had a different conception of capitalist fluctuations. Thus, he did not adhere to Schumpeter's idea of periodic cycles. Instead, he saw capitalism as characterized by cumulative destabilizing tendencies, such as those outlined by Thorstein Veblen, Gunnar Myrdal, John Maynard Keynes, and Nicholas Kaldor.[4]

These destabilizing tendencies come from the inherent entrepreneurial activity of economic development, that is, the financing of new developments, expansions, and innovations. The entrepreneurs (borrowers) are the optimists, pushing for more activities and debt financing, while the bankers (lenders) should be the conservative and critical party to the investment relationship. As the economy undergoes sustained expansion in a prosperous period, the tendency toward instability is brewing, since the good profits experienced on the upswing lead to laxer security and easier access to more investment capital. In other words, debt accumulates disproportionally. According to Minsky, financial fragility is an unavoidable part of the workings of the capitalist economy. The supply of credit is pro-cyclical; it increases during the boom and contracts after the bust.

The upswing is usually started by some innovations that inspire optimism, such as new technology (automobiles during the 1920s in the United States, new Integrated Circuit (IC) technology and dot.com firms in the late 1990s) or innovations in financial markets, such as liberalization (deregulation, shadow banking, eased surveillance, and fewer restraints) and new financial tools making debt accumulation easier (derivatives, structured investment vehicles, and general securitization). Financial liberalization featured largely as a source of instability in global financial markets from the 1980s onwards and in the present crisis.[5]

The new optimism of the upswing stimulates investment activities, and when asset prices start rising faster than before, it can feed increasing speculation, with spiraling effects. In a worst-case scenario, a manic condition can be created when the animal spirits of greed and strive take over, leading to over-investment, overheating, and bubble effects on asset prices (mainly stocks and real estates). During the buildup of the bubble, profits rise and investments appear to be very successful, inspiring further speculation with borrowed money. The provision of credit becomes more relaxed.

As Keynes remarked, the investor who is in the market during the boom considers himself a genius rather than just lucky due to operating in the middle of a bubble that provides gains to most investors. The rising profits also affect the bankers who provide credit more easily, not least when they themselves receive generous bonuses for higher rates of leverage and turnover. During the prosperous years on the upswing, the security of lending is typically reduced (from relatively secure *hedge financing* to the more risky *speculation financing*, and eventually to *Ponzi financing*, which is unsustainable). Hence, the tendency toward instability and higher risk levels is endemic to the workings of the capitalist system and not solely due to external shocks, even though they can play a role in fluctuations and periodic crises as well. External shocks are, however, important as sources of increased optimism at the beginning of an upswing.

When confidence erodes (for example, due to less profitable opportunities, higher interest rates, or reduced access to finance), panic may take over. Then, firms and investors in difficulties may need to liquidate assets to lower debts or service their interest cost. With panic sales of assets, the prices of assets fall, creating further spirals of contraction, bankruptcies, and eventually a banking crisis, if high debt levels are prevalent in the economy. Bankers typically contract the supply of credit as conditions deteriorate, exacerbating the problem. Hence, there is a need for Keynesian-style government stimulus measures in crisis conditions.

Regulation and empirical experience

Minsky also made much of the countervailing tendencies in the mixed economy, where big government provides regulatory restraints and the central bank acts as a lender of last resort. Thus, the institutional structure of regulation and restraint plays a large role in averting the excesses of the investment, accumulation, and speculation processes. The more effective and powerful these restraining forces are, the lower the risk of excess and crises.[6]

The Great Depression of the 1930s in the United States came in the wake of a boom period, which featured innovations and increasingly unrestrained capitalism, with predominantly laissez-faire government attitudes. That led to a bubble with accumulated debt levels and growing inequality, which eventually burst with the Wall Street Crash in the fall of 1929. The regulatory reforms of the Roosevelt Administration from 1933 onwards were a telling tale of successful applications of governmental power to restrain the tendencies of the financial market toward excesses, such as with the Glass–Steagall Act, stipulating a separation of risky investment banking from regular commercial banking. In addition, the government secured deposits and implemented significant surveillance and monitoring of banking operations to guard against excessive risk-taking. This system of financial regulation then prevailed in the post-war period until the 1970s.[7]

Carmen M. Reinhart and Kenneth S. Rogoff's[8] extensive statistical studies of financial crises further bear out the exceptional and, indeed, positive experience of the post-war system of financial regulation. Financial crises nearly disappeared from the developed capitalist world between 1945 and the early 1970s. Then, after regulations became more lax—and with growing liberalization of capital markets from the late 1970s, and more so from the 1980s onwards—the frequency of financial crises rapidly increased again, culminating in the Great Recession in 2008. In his book *Misunderstanding Financial Crises*, the financial economist Gary B. Gorton gives an enlightening and detailed historical account of the role of regulation in restraining and not restraining financial crises in the United States from the 19th century to the present, cementing the lessons from the Minskian approach.[9]

Yet, innovation in the financial markets from the late 1970s onwards eroded the effectiveness of the post-war system of regulation. Along with the adoption of neoliberal policies, this freed the capital markets from previous restraints, ending the quiet post-war period of no financial crises. Increased accumulation of debt, risks, and speculation prevailed once again, with the known consequences of growing frequency of financial crises and eventually the Great Recession, the second largest international financial crisis to emerge after the Great Depression.

Minsky was also concerned with the distributional aspects of accumulation and crisis tendencies. He saw inequality in the distribution of incomes as a major source of increased financial instability. Thus, consumption financed by debt rather than by wage increases (in step with productivity increases) was a clear risk factor, which, in fact, featured greatly in many nations in the advent of the present international financial crisis.[10] The same applies to excesses in debt-financed investments or speculation by the higher-income groups and entrepreneurs. A more secure buildup of investment capacity is preferable to searching for quick gains by means of debt-fed speculation. Once the bubble bursts, the Minskian approach would emphasize that governmental crisis-management strategies should primarily be directed toward relieving households facing reduced earnings and difficulties in meeting their mortgage commitments rather than toward saving banks.

The main lessons of the classical Minskian–Keynesian account of financial crises are the following:

- The tendency toward financial instability is inherent in capitalism. The supply of credit is pro-cyclical.
- Unless tempered by effective governmental regulation and effective central banking, the supply of credit slips loose, with growing risks of excesses and crises.
- Bubbles are fed by excessive debt accumulation.
- Growing risk-taking and excessive speculation bring down banks and start recessions.
- Entrepreneurs and financiers play a key role on the upswing, often gaining extensively.
- Governments and general taxpayers are typically landed with the consequences of the bust and recession.

In the next sections, these classical theories of financial crises will be applied to the Icelandic case, emphasizing the interplay between policy shifts, changing institutional environment, power distribution, and outcomes. It will be shown how Iceland changed from a highly statist policy environment to a growing neoliberal policy emphasis in a relatively short period of time. This was associated with growing power of finance and employers and rapidly growing inequality of income. An unfortunate combination of politics and business interests led to the largest bubble economy the world has seen to date, which then burst in 2008.

Accounting for the Icelandic boom and bust

Policy precondition: the shift toward neoliberalism

I have shown elsewhere that Icelandic society had strong statist characteristics in its political economy from the end of World War II.[11] These changed gradually from the 1960s onwards toward a more mixed economy, with growing marketization and less direct control of the economy by government, along with a growing welfare state. Still, the shift toward a more liberal political economy was later in the making than in most other Western countries. This meant that by the time neoliberal ideas started to make an inroad into Icelandic politics, they had a rather long road to travel, possibly making the transition faster and riskier.

While politicians on the Right were the main supporters of neoliberal ideas, many Social Democrats also viewed those ideas positively as a means of eroding the cronyist and protectionist remnants of the statist system, such as in agriculture and the fishing sector, as well as in regional policies in general. The main political platform for neoliberalism was the Independence Party (IP), which traditionally had been a rather modest right-of-center party by European standards, but still the party of employers and the upper middle class, even though it profiled itself as a "party for all classes" ("*stétt með stétt*"). What happened there was that from the late 1970s, a group of radical neoliberals had been formed, called the "The Locomotive Group" ("*Eimreiðarhópurinn*"), with the aim of promoting increased marketization, privatization, and smaller government. One of the famous slogans from that group was "Away with the Beast!" ("*Báknið burt!*"), referring to the size of government.[12]

In 1979, the group published an edited volume entitled *The Revolt of Neoliberalism* (*Uppreisn frjálshyggjunnar*). It contained essays from a group of individuals who all became highly influential in the IP in the coming decades, including Davíð Oddsson (prime minister from 1991 to 2004 and then governor of the Central Bank of Iceland from 2005 to 2009) and Hannes Hólmsteinn Gissurarson (the leading ideologist of Icelandic neoliberalism from that time to the present).[13] Others became influential politicians, lawyers, administrators, journalists, or businessmen. The publisher and editor of the book was Kjartan Gunnarsson, who became executive director of the IP in 1980 and held that position for 26 years. He was, thus, at the helm of the party until the end of 2006, when he devoted his energies fully to the governing of the recently privatized Landsbanki, having been the vice chair of its Board of Directors from 2003 (he had also served on the Board for a long time while the bank was fully in public ownership). Mr Gunnarsson was a prominent investor and perhaps the strongest personal symbol of the close interlinking of politics and business/finance that has prevailed for a long time in Iceland.

The aim of The Locomotive Group of neoliberals was to bend the policies of the IP toward the Right and to ride the rising wave of neoliberalism, which was already being felt in some Western countries.[14] Margaret Thatcher came to power in the United Kingdom in 1979, and shortly after Ronald Reagan took office as President of the United States. During the 1980s, the Icelandic neoliberals worked hard to increase the influence of neoliberal ideas, with the publications of articles, books, and journals and by importing most of the leading world authorities of neoliberalism to lecture, including Friedrich von Hayek, Milton Friedman, and James Buchanan, and ending with Arthur Laffer on the eve of the financial collapse of Iceland, that is, late in the autumn of 2007.[15] Given that

Icelandic politics had a rather long way to travel to gain a strong ground for such a policy shift, it is no surprise that it took most of the 1980s to shape political opinion both within and without the IP, but the group clearly gained a predominant position within the party, and in the society there was not much competition from the Left at the time. The collapse of Eastern European socialism in 1989 weakened the Left as a whole, if only symbolically, which facilitated the shifting of the whole political spectrum toward the Right. That made centrist political parties more open to neoliberal influences.

The policy shift gradually materialized, spreading a growing belief in the benevolence of unfettered markets and privatization, reservations about the role and size of government, deregulation, tax favors to firms and investors, and a laissez-faire attitude toward the role of government in finance and the economy in general. Even though this policy shift was quickly accepted within the IP, it took longer for the policies to gain ground for general implementation in the society at large. The IP did not enjoy majority support, so the full implementation of the ideology into government policy needed to pass through a governmental coalition and also to counter possible resistance from the union movement, which was, and is, strong, with about 85% of employees as members, and well organized in centralized federations.[16]

The IP came back to power in 1991, after a few years of a left-leaning government, with the old Social Democratic Party (SDP) as a coalition partner, and they reigned until 1995. At that time, the tide was generally turning in favor of more liberal market-oriented policies. The attitude toward privatization, for example, became more positive, and some initiatives in that direction were taken by that government. The shift was, however, modest and not particularly consequential.

Changed institutional environment

While the new ideology was gaining ground during the 1980s and early 1990s, the marketization of the fishing sector can be seen as an important landmark in paving the way for the further policy shift toward neoliberalism.[17] This was achieved by implementing a fishing quota system that involved a first step toward privatizing the rich fishing grounds in Icelandic waters, the fish in the sea, which had previously been treated as common ownership of the nation, open for all to utilize.

Owners of fishing boats were, in 1984, each allocated their share of total catches allowed. The allocation was based on the fishing experience of the three years prior to 1984. Hence, those who were already active in fishing were prioritized in this handout of massive monetary values. These fishing rights were then, in 1990, practically privatized and securitized by allowing a free transfer or trade of quotas, as well as by allowing their use as collateral for loans. The quotas could even be inherited from then on. Thus, the uncaught fish in the sea became de facto subjected to private property rights.

The transferable quota system was rationalized on the grounds of efficiency, that is, as a means of inhibiting overfishing and better tailoring the capacity of the fishing fleet to the size or possible harvest of the fishing stocks. That meant fewer and larger boats, increased concentration of ownership and larger size of fishing corporations, with considerable and varying regional influences. It also meant easier access to big capital, for example by selling or renting off quotas and by borrowing with the quotas as collateral. There soon emerged a new talk of "quota aristocracy." The prime beneficiaries of the increased efficiency in the fishing sector that this produced were the owners of the fishing fleet.

Another very important stepping stone in the policy environment that facilitated further influence of neoliberal policies was Iceland's entry into the European Economic Area (EEA) zone in 1994 (taking effect in 1995). This was particularly championed by the old SDP. The most consequential change associated with this was the free movement of capital across borders. The new institutional environment gave Icelandic financiers and business people full access to the global financial market for the first time since the inter-war period. Thus, capital controls and debt rationing became a thing of the past. Given the depth of that change, it is now possible, in hindsight, to say that the Icelandic authorities did not fully understand the implications that this could have for the finances and economy of the country. Perhaps the overextended belief in the self-regulating capacities of the unrestrained market also had something to do with it.

It might be thought that since Iceland was part of the EU financial regulatory environment, regulation should have been in order from 1995 onwards. Yet, just as in the United States, European financial markets had by that time outplayed governments and regulators, increasingly since the spreading of the liberalization tendencies of the 1980s, and with the emergence of various new instruments for financial manipulation. It was one of the main conclusions of the report of the Althingi's Special Investigating Committee into the fall of the banks (SIC) that regulators (the Central Bank of Iceland and the Financial Supervisory Authority) had grossly failed to carry out their duties. In fact, the governors of these institutions (including Davíð Oddsson, the most influential neoliberal politician) were found guilty of gross negligence by the Committee. The same applied to the government ministers who had duties in the relevant areas.[18]

From banking privatization to a bubbling economy

The government that came to power in 1995 was a coalition of the IP and the Progressive Party (PP), which used to be a farmers' party. The two parties presided over a society that had just entered a completely new global financial environment, where the language of privatization, competitiveness, free flows of capital, and market determination of economy and trade had become a mantra. The main political representatives of business interests in Icelandic politics had, thus, joined forces and seemed determined to make the most of the possibilities and economic benefits that the global market and domestic neoliberal politics were supposed to be able to deliver.

The road toward full neoliberalism and laissez-faire orientation was thus clear and well paved from 1995 onwards. Davíð Oddsson and Halldór

Ásgrímsson, the respective party leaders of the IP and PP, seemed to share the policy goals to a great extent. The cooperative movement heritage of the PP was a thing of the past after its business empire had collapsed during the 1980s. The PP's heritage of regional and welfare protectionism also receded into the background, because the party increasingly felt the need to court voters in the Reykjavík area. The population of the provincial areas was generally in decline. There was, thus, not much to keep the business interests that still remained within the PP from adopting neoliberal policies that clearly served their immediate interests.

The privatization of the main state banks, which began in 1998, proved to be the next major turning point in this new financial environment. The privatization itself was an odd affair, yet not unexpected. The government leaders had their hands on the process. Businessmen with close contacts to the IP leadership were allowed to buy the larger bank (Landsbanki). This happened even though the buyers in question had not delivered the best offer.[19] Businessmen close to the PP leadership got the other state bank (Búnaðarbankinn), which, in turn, was merged with Kaupthing security brokers to form Kaupthing Bank.

When the banks were fully privatized, at the beginning of 2003, the new owners, themselves prominent businessmen, immediately turned the banks into aggressive investment banks. They greatly increased their participation in leveraged mergers and acquisitions, first within Iceland but then, to a greater extent, in the neighboring countries. They also promoted an extensive use of offshore tax havens among Icelandic businessmen and financiers. All the main Icelandic banks opened subsidiaries in Luxembourg to serve wealthy Icelanders with private banking, making the most of the extra advantages that were on offer in tax havens in the Caribbean and elsewhere.[20] Iceland was by then set to become a leading platform for international casino capitalism.[21]

External debt escalated, and excessive risk behavior became predominant in the Icelandic financial and business environment, driven by the quest for accumulation of assets, profits, and bonuses.[22] It was as if the new owners of the banks had been issued licenses to print money—for their own pockets. With the easy flow of borrowed foreign capital at that time, at low interest rates, the economy had ample resources for rapid growth, which soon turned into an excessive but classic speculation bubble, as described by Minsky and Kindleberger.[23]

The main specialty of the Icelandic bubble economy was its extreme size, recklessness, and failings of the operators, both the private financial entrepreneurs and the governmental regulators and rulers. Thus, a shift of policy toward financial liberalization and laissez-faire attitude of government, along with changes in the institutional landscape, paved the way for pervasive financialization, privatization, and money culture, which fed excessive bubble economy developments.[24] Concentration of business ownership and financial power increased greatly, overshadowing democratically based political power.

Data on debt accumulation tell the fundamentals of the story in a clear way.

Debt accumulation—how much and who did it?

In Figure 3.1, the development of the total external debt level of the Icelandic economy from 1946 through 2008 is shown. Iceland started the post-war period as a debt-free country, indeed, with considerable assets abroad, primarily gained by exporting to the United Kingdom during World War II. As shown in the figure, the overall debt level of the economy rose very slowly through the decades, reflecting a considerable stability on that front. The early 1980s represented a slightly more decisive raising of the debt level, but a bigger turning point was during the late 1990s. In fact, there was a doubling of external debt from 1997 to 2001. In that period, the selling of part of the shares of the public banks had begun, and with that came an increased supply of credit to the Icelandic business community. The "Viking business raids" started at that time, albeit modestly compared with what was to come after the banks became fully owned by private individuals/corporations.

At the beginning of 2003, the former state banks were fully owned by private interests, handpicked from the ranks of favorites of the reigning political parties (the IP and the PP). That privatization process had all the hallmarks of a corrupt interlinking of politics and business.[25] The banks were, in fact, sold to business speculators rather than experienced bankers, and the new owners immediately turned their efforts toward acquisitions and take-overs, first within Iceland and then increasingly in the neighboring countries. Access to capital was easy in the international financial markets at that time, and the 117-year history of relatively

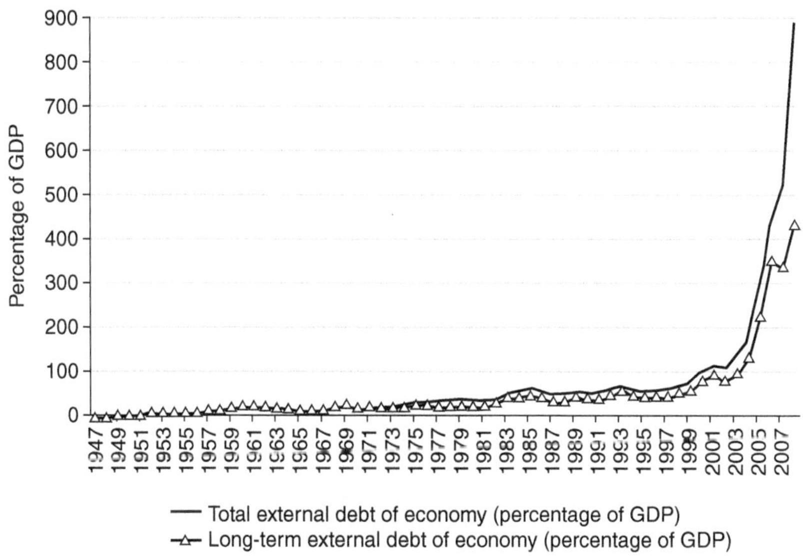

Figure 3.1 External debt of the Icelandic economy (% of GDP), 1946 to 2008. Total external debt and long-term debt (source: Central Bank of Iceland and National Economic Institute).

secure banking of the flagship of Icelandic banking, Landsbanki, helped to open the coffers of foreign lenders.

The predictable consequence can be seen in Figure 3.1. The external debt level started to increase significantly after 1998, and then at an unprecedented rate from 2003 onwards, in fact, as if there would be no tomorrow with repayment dates. Already by the end of 2004, Iceland had entered the rank of the world's most heavily indebted countries.[26] After that, the debt level multiplied in the advent of the collapse.

The graph in Figure 3.1 has two lines, the one with markers indicating long-term external debt of the economy and the unmarked line representing total external debt (in both cases as percentage of gross domestic product (GDP)). This includes all private and public debt; the increase was in private debt, since the government was paying down its debts in the advent of the crisis. The difference between the lines represents a change in the debt structures from 2006 onwards, with short-term loans (such as the Icesave savings accounts in the United Kingdom and Holland) becoming the main additions.

This came in the wake of serious warnings that were issued by the rating firms at the end of 2005 and by Danish bankers in early 2006.[27] The warnings featured risks associated with the very rapid growth of the banks and with cross-cutting ownerships. The Danish bankers indicated that it was only a question of time until there would be trouble. Even though the financial sector and government had some success in convincing the international financial market that all was well,[28] the supply of institutional credit to the Icelandic banks became more restrained and eventually stopped in 2007.[29]

Then two of the main banks turned toward accumulating deposit savings from the public in the United Kingdom with the "Icesave" and other savings accounts that were offered on the internet with some of the highest interest rates in the market. That worked. Landsbanki was the frontrunner in this, and offered the accounts through its UK subsidiary. Kaupthing Bank offered similar saving accounts later (Kaupthing Edge). Thus, the inflow into the Icesave accounts could be channeled directly to Iceland to relieve the tight liquidity position of the bank. The idea was to save the banks with this flow of money from individual savers in the United Kingdom, and later also in Holland.

This change of funding of the banks is reflected in Figure 3.1, indicating the growth of short-term financing from 2006, which is what the savings accounts provided, being a very volatile source that could easily evaporate in the face of loss of reputation or breach of confidence. Hence. the risk level was rapidly rising at that time.[30] After the warnings of late 2005 and early 2006 were issued, the overall debt level of the economy was to almost double, mainly as a result of short-term financing. The Central Bank facilitated this move, even as late as in the spring of 2008, by easing binding requirements. And then, in the last weeks of their lives, the banks got additional credit from the Central Bank of Iceland, with little or no security provided.[31]

So, the debt accumulation was extreme by all accounts. This was probably the most rapid expansion of a banking system in the history of mankind.

Reinhart and Rogoff said in a 2010 study that the growth of debt in Iceland was the most rapid they had ever seen in their survey of financial crises during the last eight centuries, including Ireland. Ireland's debt went up to similarly high levels, but started somewhat earlier. The speed was, thus, greater in the Icelandic bubble economy.[32]

What was the borrowed money for? Who were the main borrowers? Figure 3.2 gives the first direct answer to those questions. It shows how the debt of corporations or businesses increased in comparison to the debt of households. Government debt was being reduced in the advent of the crisis, as indicated above. By far the largest part of the increased accumulated debt consisted of corporate debt. This increased from 114% of GDP at the beginning of 2004 up to more than 380% at its peak in 2008. The expansion of household debt was modest by comparison, even though it was large. It increased from 85% of GDP in 2004 to 133% in early 2009, before coming down again. In addition, the banks held a part of the overall external debt, and there were also debts from within Iceland, particularly from the Occupational Pension Funds. Altogether, the size of the Icelandic banking sector was approaching 10 times the country's GDP when it collapsed in 2008.

So most of the accumulated debt was for business speculation, acquisitions, and leveraged take-overs, both in Iceland and abroad. In that sense, the Icelandic bubble was primarily a business speculation bubble. But there was also a housing bubble, even though that accounted for only a minor part of the whole affair.

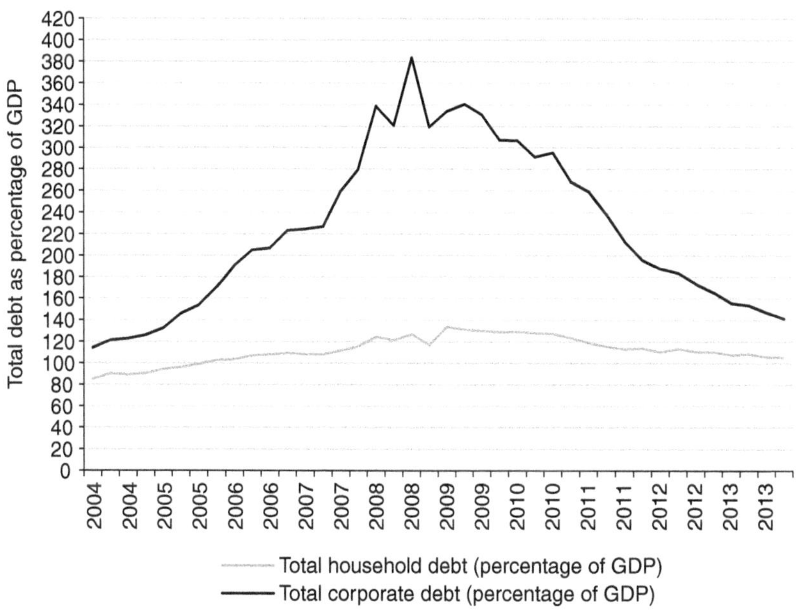

Figure 3.2 Total corporate and household debts 2004–2013 (source: Central Bank of Iceland, Financial Stability Report 2014, no. 1).

Why did they do it?

Speculation: "Wall Street on the Tundra"

Speculation for capital gains is a deviation from normal or rational behavior. "Mania," "irrational exuberance," and "bubbles" similarly refer to states out of the ordinary.[33] Hints of crowd or herd psychology are evoked. Keynes talked about "animal spirits." Still, Minsky argued that these are inherent aspects of the fluctuating capitalist economies. After all, the economy is a part of the human world, where rational and irrational aspects intermingle and coexist. The pure models of the "efficient market hypothesis" are removed from reality.[34]

During the 20th century, most of the manias and bubbles have involved real estate and business stocks, separately or jointly. In some cases, the bubbles are primarily housing bubbles (Japan in the late 1980s; Ireland, Spain, the United States, and the United Kingdom in the present crisis); in others, they have centered on speculation with shares in businesses or commodities (oil, gold, etc.). As noted above, the Icelandic bubble was primarily a business speculation bubble, with a minority role for a housing bubble as well. It was, indeed, an extreme affair by all standards.

In April 2009, soon after the financial meltdown in Iceland, the well-known financial journalist Michael Lewis wrote an article in *Vanity Fair* about the Icelandic case under the title "Wall Street on the Tundra." The point of this insightful article was the extreme extent of speculation in the Icelandic economy, even in comparison to the overblown importance of Wall Street in the United States. While the overall debt of the American economy went up to about 350% of GDP, the Icelandic one increased to about 850% in a shorter period of time. The financial economist Willem Buiter described the situation in pre-crisis Iceland as "collective insanity," while Robert Aliber talked about Iceland as "the perfect bubble" in its extremity.[35]

As noted, it was the financiers and businessmen who were the key players. The public Special Investigative Committee into the Fall of the Banks put the prime blame on the governors of the banks for making the excessive debt accumulation possible.[36] They fed the borrowed money onwards to businessmen and speculators as well. Asset prices rose steeply with the increasing inflow of capital into the emerging financial market, which had only recently come into contact with full freedom for movement of capital and also had a very immature and inexperienced stock market.[37] It turned out that it was easy to play this stock market.

The Icelandic stock market index rose by a factor of nine from 2003 to 2007. The American Dow Jones Index "only" doubled in about the same time period. The rise of share prices in the Icelandic bubble was also faster than in the United States of the Roaring Twenties, leading up to the collapse on Wall Street of 1929. Comparable cases are only to be found in South American countries (Argentina, Mexico, and Brazil) and the post-socialist economies of the Baltic states (Latvia, Lithuania, and Estonia), which also ventured deeply into market liberalization and laissez-faire policies after their independence was restored in 1991.[38]

By comparison, housing prices in Iceland increased by some 65% from 2003 to late 2007, a lower increase than in Ireland, the United States, Spain, and some other countries at the same time. The housing bubble was by no means the most consequential bubble effect in Iceland. It is also interesting to note that while corporate debt was reduced from 331% to 150% of GDP after the crisis hit, household debt was only reduced from the yearly average of 133% at its highest point to 105% at end of year 2013 (see Figure 3.2).

With such large increases in asset prices, particularly in stock prices, the greed and mania effects became quite pervasive in Iceland from 2003 to 2007. The money culture spread far beyond the business sector into the spheres of art, education, media, and science. Even some members of parliament took part in the speculation, and reliance on big donations for primaries and general elections grew exponentially, with the associated increase in the power of finance and business over politics.[39]

The similarity of the bubble years in the United States during the 1920s and the Icelandic bubble years of 2003 through 2008 has already been mentioned. Lastly, it is instructive to compare more directly the collapses in the respective stock market indices, the United States from 1929 to 1932 and Iceland from the summer of 2007 through 2010 (the initial values are set at 100 for both cases and the time scale synchronized in Figure 3.3).

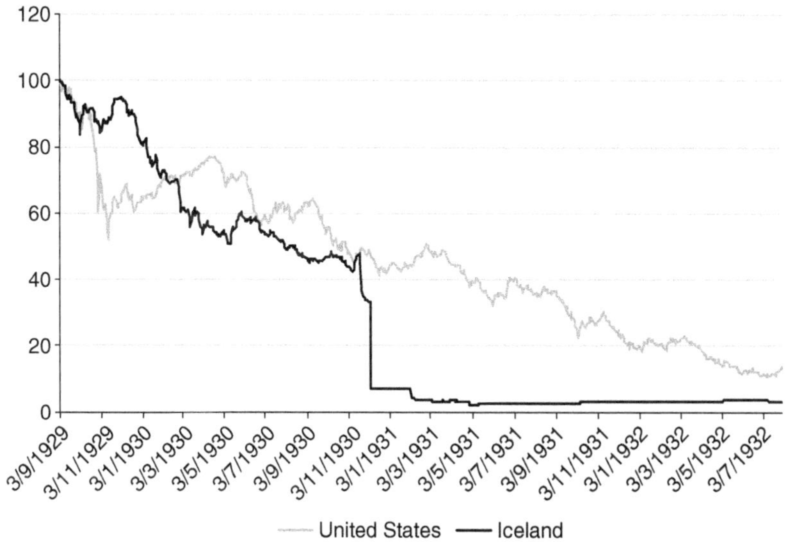

Figure 3.3 Two collapses: Wall Street 1929 and Iceland 2007–2008. Stock market share indexes, decline from highest value reached prior to collapse. The US peak was in August 1929; Iceland's peak was in July 2007 (both set at 100 in the figure) (source: Stefán Ólafsson, "Icelandic Capitalism," 2011).

On the whole, the Icelandic stock market collapse took a much shorter time to bottom out than the Wall Street Crash of 1929. It took about three years in the United States, but only about a year and a half in Iceland. And the Icelandic collapse was also deeper, as can be seen in the figure, especially with the big drop that came in October 2008 when the banks fell. That almost killed the stock market for the next two years. Thus, the indication regarding the speculation effect in the stock market is that the boom and the bust were more drastic in Iceland than in the United States, both in the Great Depression and in the contemporary Great Recession.

Increased inequality: big gains at the top

The lesson from the Minsky-Keynesian approach to financial bubbles and crashes is that the profit motive is the key driver of investment as well as speculation. The speculation effect reflects an excessive race for big gains, a situation of mania or euphoria, as Minsky characterized it. Lax regulation, oversight, and surveillance in a laissez-faire environment allow more room for maneuver. From that premise, it can be expected that the bubble economy and the financialization would have increased the earnings and wealth of the higher-income groups, since they are typically the ones involved in investments and speculation. And that is, indeed, what happened in Iceland. Inequality of incomes increased at an unprecedented rate from 1995 to 2007, with increased speed after 2003. The top incomes galloped way ahead of everyone else. This effect is shown in Figure 3.4, with Gini indices of inequality disaggregating the bubble effect on inequality.

In Figure 3.4, there are two measures of disposable income inequality: all taxable incomes including capital gains (the black columns) and all taxable incomes excluding the capital gains (the light gray columns). The difference between the two is then shown as the black line, giving the difference in the Gini coefficients for the two income concepts in the black and the gray columns. Capital gains reflect the income gained from sale of assets (stock, real estate, etc.). The main gains from the speculation activity on the stock market come up as capital gains in tax returns. The black line in Figure 3.4 shows the main bubble economy effect on income inequality, since the capital gains primarily flow to the highest-income groups.

Thus, income inequality started to increase from the Scandinavian low of about 0.19–0.21 Gini scores, gradually at first and then with increasing speed as the bubble economy gathered momentum from 2003 toward 2007. Capital gains were minor at the beginning of the period; hence, there was little difference at that time between the Ginis for the two income concepts. From 1995, the Ginis start to increase, and after 1999, the difference between the Ginis also increases, with growing financial earnings and their lower taxation.

The Gini for total earnings increased from 0.21 in 1995 to 0.43 at the top of the bubble in 2007. That is a gigantic increase by any standards. Excluding capital gains, the Gini increased from 0.20 in 1995 to 0.29 in 2007, which is an increase of 38%, way above the Organisation for Economic Co-operation and

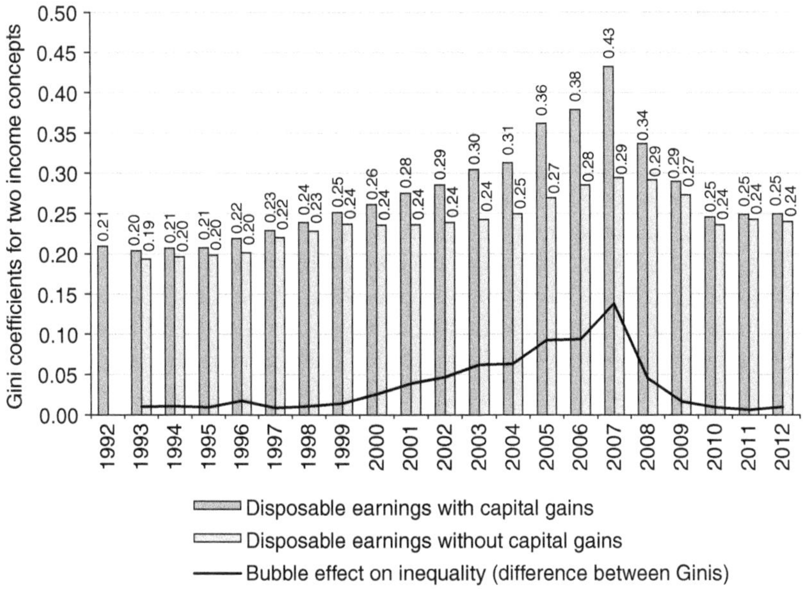

Figure 3.4 Development of income inequality in Iceland from 1993 to 2012. Two income concepts: disposable incomes including and excluding capital gains (source: Stefán Ólafsson and Arnaldur S. Kristjánsson (2012), with an update).

Development (OECD)'s benchmark for a "big change," that is, an increase of more than 14.5% in a period of 12 years.[40] The growth of income inequality during the height of the bubble economy was, therefore, extreme and unprecedented in Western societies of the post-war period. This extreme change resonates with other extremities of the bubble economy period.

The line showing the bubble economy effect in Figure 3.4 demonstrates clearly how the effect started to increase as early as 1999, soon after new legislation on lower taxation of financial earnings took effect (with a 10% tax rate, one of the very lowest in the OECD), along with growth of the previously immature stock market. It is also interesting to see how rapidly the level of inequality came down again after the bubble burst in 2008. This was also an unprecedented decline in inequality. The effect of capital gains largely disappeared during the crisis. Significant interest earnings remained, however, since many owners of stock managed to transfer their assets to savings accounts before the collapse of the banks.[41]

Ólafsson's and Kristjánsson's assessment of what explains the respective developments of income inequality before and after the collapse indicates that the overall growth of inequality from 1995 to 2007 was explained mainly by the bubble effect on financial earnings and governments' tax and benefit policies. About two-thirds of the increased inequality was accounted for by growing financial earnings (which were also taxed at lower rates than employment earnings from 1999 onwards), and the remaining third was due to government tax and benefits policy.

One may ask why the key players in the bubble economy developments did what they did, with such devastating consequences for the national economy and taxpayers. The theoretical account of Minsky and the empirical evidence presented here provides the clearest answer. They were going for massive private gains, which truly materialized during the bubble period.

The top 1% income share increased from about 4% in 1994 to nearly 20% of total pre-tax incomes in 2007, when the comparable group in the United States was receiving 23.5% of the total pre-tax household incomes of the country. This was an unprecedented and exceptional increase in Iceland. At the height of the bubble economy, between 2005 and 2007, financial earnings amounted to 82–85% of the total earnings of the top 1% in Iceland. More than half of the financial earnings of those years consisted of capital gains, emanating from speculation.[42] The Icelandic business and financial elite was, indeed, flying high.

Debates within Iceland about the causes of the collapse have sometimes pointed to a small number of individual businessmen and bankers, who are singled out as totally and solely responsible. Supporters of neoliberal policies and leaders of the neoliberal experiment have gone furthest in such arguments, even blaming the whole crash on only one prominent businessman. A related claim is that individuals failed, but the policy was not to blame. Alternatively, it has been argued that foreigners are to blame: the governments and governors of central banks in the United States and neighboring countries, for refusing to lend Iceland sufficient sums to bail out the banks before their collapse. The same spokesmen have also blamed the UK government for freezing Icelandic banking assets in the United Kingdom by means of clauses in anti-terrorist laws after the banking collapse had already started.[43]

These are, however, weak arguments. It was, indeed, a blessing that central bankers and governments of neighboring countries turned down requests to provide Iceland with the loans needed to save the banks from collapse. The sums required were of such an order that the Icelandic economy would never have been able to pay them back. All were unanimous in directing the Icelandic authorities toward the International Monetary Fund (IMF) for the ultimate crash program for a failed state.

As regards the number of gainers who were on board the bubble train, it is obvious that the banking collapse was not solely the work of one, or even a few, individuals.[44] It was a systemic failure, related to policy, institutions, power, and interests. There were many more who gained than the most prominent Viking business raiders or the individual bankers, even though they played a particularly important role.

Our analysis of income distribution data shows that those who gained greatly were well spread over the top 10% of income receivers, and even toward the top 12–15%.[45] But still, the biggest gainers were the top 1%. In fact, the higher up the income scale one goes, the greater the financial earnings, and particularly the capital gains. Hence, we can argue that despite a prominent role for the top elite of business and finance leaders, the big gainers and supporters were a significantly larger group.

Conclusions

The argument has been made here that the Icelandic financial crisis was the result of a typical but excessive financial bubble, which emerged in the decade before the banking collapse. The Icelandic bubble economy was the largest bubble ever seen, that is, in relation to the size of the national economy. The ensuing bust was also gigantic, and one of the costliest financial crises in history.

Minsky's classical neo-Keynesian account of such events applies well to the Icelandic case. What was special in Iceland was the enormity of the bubble and some special local effects connected to extensive interlinking of politics and business, as well as to weak moral standards in a country with insufficient respect for rules. A laissez-faire policy attitude, mixed with goals of liberalization of finance and business, poses extra risks in such an environment. It has been shown how the Minskian approach gives a strong explanatory account by outlining the roles of policy shifts, liberalization, institutional changes, and emergence of new leaders of the financial system of the country, following the privatization of the state banks. The imbalances of the global financial market, giving easy access to credit, also played a role in making the extremity of the whole affair possible. Debt accumulation and speculation reached previously unseen heights, and the top income groups reaped tremendous gains. These were the prime drivers of the unfortunate adventure.

Notes

1 Robert Z. Aliber and Gylfi Zoega eds., *Preludes to the Icelandic Financial Crisis* (New York: Palgrave Macmillan, 2011); also Carmen M. Reinhart and Kenneth S. Rogoff, *This Time Is Different: Eight Centuries of Financial Folly* (Princeton: Princeton University Press, 2009); Charles P. Kindleberger and Robert Z. Aliber, *Manias, Panics, and Crashes. A History of Financial Crises* (New York: John Wiley and Sons, 2005); Hyman P. Minsky, *Stabilizing an Unstable Economy* (New York: McGraw-Hill, 2008/1986).

2 Luc Laeven and Fabián Valencia, "Systemic Banking Crisis Database: An Update," IMF, Working Paper no. 12/163, accessed January 10, 2014, www.imf.org/external/pubs/ft/wp/2010/wp10146.pdf.

3 Hyman Minsky, *Stabilizing an Unstable Economy*; also Gerald A. Epstein and Martin H. Wolfson eds., *The Handbook of Political Economy of Financial Crises* (Oxford: Oxford University Press, 2013).

4 Jan Kregel, "Political Economy Approaches to Financial Crisis: Hyman Minsky's Financial Fragility Hypothesis," in *The Handbook of Political Economy of Financial Crises*, 2013.

5 Reinhart and Rogoff, *This Time Is Different*; also Jennifer S. Taub, "What We Don't Talk About When We Talk About Banking," in *The Handbook of Political Economy of Financial Crises*, 2013 and Kindleberger and Aliber, *Manias, Panics, and Crashes.*

6 Martin H. Wolfson, "An Institutional Theory of Financial Crises," in *The Handbook of Political Economy of Financial Crises*, 2013; also Damon Silvers, "Deregulation and the New Financial Architecture," in *The Handbook of Political Economy of Financial Crises*, 2013.
7 David M. Kotz, "Changes in the Postwar Global Economy and the Roots of the Financial Crisis," in *The Handbook of Political Economy of Financial Crises*, 2013; Wolfson, "An Institutional Theory of Financial Crises"; also Hyman Minsky, "The Financial Instability Hypothesis," Working Paper no. 78, Levy Economics Institute of Bard College, accessed February 15, 2014, www.levyinstitute.org/pubs/-wp74.pdf.
8 Reinhart and Rogoff, *This Time Is Different*; see also their *A Decade of Debt*, Policy Analyses in International Economics 95 (New York: Peterson Institute of International Economics, 2010).
9 Gary B. Gorton, *Misunderstanding Financial Crises: Why We Don't See Them Coming* (New York: Oxford University Press, 2012).
10 cf. Kregel, "Political Economy Approaches to Financial Crisis."
11 Stefán Ólafsson, "Icelandic Capitalism: From Statism to Neoliberalism and Financial Collapse," in *Nordic Varieties of Capitalism*, special edition of *Comparative Social Research*, vol. 28, ed. Lars Mjöset (Amsterdam: Emerald, 2011).
12 Eiríkur Bergmann, *Iceland and the International Financial Crisis: Boom, Bust and Recovery* (New York: Palgrave Macmillan, 2014).
13 A 2001 book by Gissurarson, "*Hvernig getur Ísland orðið ríkasta land í heimi?*" [How Can Iceland Become the Richest Country in the World?], was a very clear manifesto for the plan of making Iceland an international tax haven and financial center. That book was very influential on the right wing of Icelandic politics, and a vice president of the Central Bank wrote a rather positive review of it in the bank's journal (Bjarni Bragi Jónsson, "Hannes Hólmsteinn Gissurarson: Hvernig Ísland getur orðið ríkasta land í heimi?" *Fjármálatíðindi* [Bulletin of Monetary Affairs] 39, no. 1 (2002)). Even though the book was very superficial and Lafferian in its arguments, it was probably more influential than many have thought. After all, it was where the idea of Iceland as an international financial center was clearly formulated.
14 Peter Evans and William H. Sewell Jr, "The Neoliberal Era: Ideology, Policy, and Social Effects", in *Social Resilience in the Neoliberal Era*, eds. Peter A. Hall and Michèle Lamont (Cambridge: Cambridge University Press, 2013); David Harvey, *A Brief History of Neoliberalism* (Oxford: Oxford University Press, 2007); and Mark Blyth, *Great Transformations: Economic Ideas and Institutional Change in the Twentieth Century* (Cambridge: Cambridge University Press, 2002).
15 Laffer came to Iceland to lecture (at the request of local neoliberals) at a time when the international credit crunch had put the financial markets practically on hold and the risk of financial setback was a real threat in many countries, not least in Iceland. Laffer was put in front of the largest part of the Icelandic financial and business elite and the right-wing politicians, to tell them that Iceland was such an outstanding model for freedom that many wanted to bring their money onto Icelandic shores. Even though Iceland had been running at a double-digit trade deficit persistently from 2004 and debts had risen astronomically, he claimed that "there is no such thing as an overheated economy" in an interview in *Morgunblaðið*. He was treated as royalty in the main private press as well as on state TV, so the message was well rubbed in. This is, no doubt, a rare case of successful preaching of black supposedly being white!
16 Katrín Ólafsdóttir and Stefán Ólafsson, *Economics, Politics and Welfare in Iceland: Booms, Busts and Challenges* (Oslo: Fafo Institute, 2014), accessed January 11, 2015, www.fafoarkiv.no/pub/rapp/20360/20360.pdf; see also OECD, *Employment Outlook 2009* (Paris: OECD, 2009).
17 Eiríkur Bergmann, *Iceland and the International Financial Crisis.*
18 Rannsóknarnefnd Alþingis [Special Investigation Commission of the Icelandic Parliament—SIC]. *Aðdragandi og orsakir falls íslensku bankanna 2008 og tengdir*

atburðir [The Causes and Effects of the Fall of the Icelandic Banks and Related Events] (Reykjavík: Rannsóknarnefnd Alþingis, 2010); see also Guðrún Johnsen, *Bringing Down the Banking System: Lessons from Iceland* (New York: Palgrave Macmillan, 2014).

19 A controversial publication of private e-mails of a prominent IP member, Mr Styrmir Gunnarsson, an influential editor of *Morgunblaðið* at the time, has him on record talking about the need to get the Landsbanki into the hands of individuals "on good speaking terms with the IP." cf. Special Investigation Commission, *Causes and Effects of the Fall of the Icelandic Banks*. See also the interesting Ingi Freyr Vilhjálmsson, *Hamskiptin. Þegar allt varð falt á Íslandi* [Metamorphosis: When Anything Could Be Bought in Iceland] (Reykjavík: Bjartur, 2014).

20 Magnús Sveinn Helgason, "Íslenskt viðskiptalíf—breytingar og samspil við fjármálakerfið," Appendix 5 to the Report of the Special Investigation Committee (Reykjavík: Rannsóknarnefnd Alþingis, 2010), accessed February 16, 2015, www.rna.is/media/skjol/RNAvefVidauki5.pdf; also Eríkur Bergmann, *Iceland and the International Financial Crisis*.

21 Susan Strange, *Casino Capitalism* (Oxford: Basil Blackwell, 1986); see also Ármann Thorvaldsson, *Ævintýraeyjan—uppgangur og endalok fjármálaveldis* (Reykjavík: Bókafélagið, 2009), and Ásgeir Jónsson, *Why Iceland? How One of the World's Smallest Countries Became the Meltdown's Biggest Casualty* (New York: McGraw-Hill, 2009), for two insiders' accounts of the buildup and operations of Kaupthing Bank, the largest of the Icelandic banks.

22 cf. Special Investigation Commission, *Causes and Effects of the Fall of the Icelandic Banks* and Guðrún Johnsen, *Bringing Down the Banking System*.

23 Kindleberger and Aliber, *Manias, Panics, and Crashes*; and Minsky, *Stabilizing an Unstable Economy*.

24 cf. Vilhjálmsson, *Hamskiptin*, on the pervasiveness of the money culture; see also Jóhann Hauksson, *Þræðir valdsins—kunningjaveldi, aðstöðubrask og hrun Íslands* (Reykjavík: Veröld, 2011). The latter book analyzes power relations and business–politics networking in the context of Iceland's financial collapse.

25 cf. Johnsen, *Bringing Down the Banking System*; Vilhjálmsson, *Hamskiptin*; and Hauksson, *Þræðir valdsins*.

26 cf. Central Bank of Iceland, *Fjármálastöðugleiki 2007* [Financial Stability Report 2007], no. 1 (Reykjavík: Seðlabanki Íslands, 2007).

27 Carsten Valgreen et al., "Iceland: Geyser Crisis," Danske Bank Research paper, March 21, 2006, accessed February 5, 2014, https://notendur.hi.is/ajonsson/kennsla2006/Danske%20Bank%20-%20Geyser%20Crises%20%28Mars%202006%29.pdf.

28 Frederic Miskin and Tryggvi Þór Herbertsson, "Financial Stability in Iceland," Iceland Chamber of Commerce, May 2006, accessed February 16, 2015, www.vi.is/files/555877819financial+stability+in+iceland+screen+version.pdf.

29 Guðrún Johnsen, *Bringing Down the Banking System*.

30 Special Investigation Commission (SIC), *Causes and Effects of the Fall of the Icelandic Banks*.

31 Johnsen, *Bringing Down the Banking System* and Special Investigation Commission, *Causes and Effects of the Fall of the Icelandic Banks*.

32 Carmen M. Reinhart and Kenneth Rogoff, "A Decade of Debt". NBER Working Paper No. 16827, February 2011, accessed March 16, 2015, www.nber.org/papers/w16827.

33 Kindleberger and Aliber, *Manias, Panics, and Crashes*.

34 James Crotty, "The Realism of Assumptions Does Matter: Why Keynes-Minsky Theory Must Replace Efficient Market Theory as the Guide to Financial Regulatory Policy," in *The Handbook of Political Economy of Financial Crises*, 2013.

35 Information provided at the 2011 Reykjavík conference of the IMF and the Central Bank of Iceland, under the title "Iceland's Recovery—Lessons and Challenges" (see www.imf.org/external/np/seminars/eng/2011/isl/, accessed January 2015).

36 Special Investigation Commission, *Causes and Effects of the Fall of the Icelandic Banks*, 2010.
37 Johnsen, *Bringing Down the Banking System*.
38 Ólafsson, "Icelandic Capitalism."
39 Vilhjálmsson, *Hamskiptin*; and Special Investigation Commission, *Causes and Effects of the Fall of the Icelandic Banks*.
40 Stefán Ólafsson and Arnaldur Sölvi Kristjánsson, "Þróun tekjuskiptingarinnar 1993 til 2010" [Development of the Income Distribution from 1993 to 2010], *Icelandic Review of Politics and Administration* 8, no 1 (2012). Also OECD, *Growing Unequal?* (Paris: OECD, 2008).
41 Ólafsson and Kristjánsson, "Þróun tekjuskiptingarinnar 1993 til 2010."
42 Stefán Ólafsson and Arnaldur Sölvi Kristjánsson, "Income Inequality in Boom and Bust: A Tale from Iceland's Bubble Economy," in *Income Inequality: Economic Disparities and the Middle Class in Affluent Countries*, eds. Janet Gornick and Markus Jäntti (Palo Alto: Stanford University Press, 2013).
43 Styrmir Gunnarsson, *Umsátrið—fall Íslands og endurreisn* (Reykjavík: Veröld, 2009); see also Bergmann, *Iceland and the International Financial Crisis*.
44 Johnsen, *Bringing Down the Banking System*; also Special Investigation Commission, *Causes and Effects of the Fall of the Icelandic Banks*.
45 See the data analysis in Ólafsson and Kristjánsson, "Income Inequality in Boom and Bust"; and also, by the same authors, "Þróun tekjuskiptingarinnar 1993 til 2010."

Bibliography

Aliber, Robert Z. and Gylfi Zoega eds. *Preludes to the Icelandic Financial Crisis*. New York: Palgrave Macmillan, 2011.

Atkinson, Anthony B. and Thomas Piketty. *Top Incomes: A Global Perspective*. Oxford: Oxford University Press, 2010.

Atkinson, Anthony B., Thomas Piketty, and Emmanuel Saez. "Top Incomes in the Long Run of History." *Journal of Economic Literature* 49, no. 1 (2011): 3–71.

Bagus, Philipp and David Howden. *Deep Freeze—Iceland's Economic Collapse*. Auburn Alabama: Ludvig von Mises Organization, 2011.

Bergmann, Eiríkur. *Iceland and the International Financial Crisis: Boom, Bust and Recovery*. New York: Palgrave Macmillan, 2014.

Blyth, Mark. *Great Transformations: Economic Ideas and Institutional Change in the Twentieth Century*. Cambridge: Cambridge University Press, 2002.

Central Bank of Iceland. *Fjármálastöðugleiki 2014* [Financial Stability Report 2014], no. 1. Reykjavík: Seðlabanki Íslands, 2014.

Central Bank of Iceland. *Fjármálastöðugleiki 2007* [Financial Stability Report 2007], no. 1. Reykjavík: Seðlabanki Íslands, 2007.

Crotty, James. "The Realism of Assumptions Does Matter: Why Keynes–Minsky Theory Must Replace Efficient Market Theory as the Guide to Financial Regulatory Policy." In *The Handbook of Political Economy of Financial Crises*, edited by Gerald A. Epstein and Martin H. Wolfson, 133–158. Oxford: Oxford University Press, 2013.

Epstein, Gerald A. and Martin H. Wolfson eds. *The Handbook of Political Economy of Financial Crises*. Oxford: Oxford University Press, 2013.

Evans, Peter and William H. Sewell. "The Neoliberal Era: Ideology, Policy, and Social Effects." In *Social Resilience in the Neoliberal Era*, edited by Peter. A. Hall and Michèle Lamont, 35–68. Cambridge: Cambridge University Press, 2013.

Gissurarson, Hannes Hólmsteinn. *Hvernig getur Ísland orðið ríkasta land í heimi?* Reykjavík: Nýja bókafélagið, 2001.

Gorton, Gary B. *Misunderstanding Financial Crises: Why We Don't See Them Coming.* New York: Oxford University Press, 2012.

Gunnarsson, Kjartan ed. *Uppreisn frjálshyggjunnar*. Reykjavík: Kjartan Gunnarson, 1979.

Gunnarsson, Styrmir. *Umsátrið—fall Íslands og endurreisn*. Reykjavík: Veröld, 2009.

Harvey, David. *A Brief History of Neoliberalism*. Oxford: Oxford University Press, 2007.

Hauksson, Jóhann. *Þræðir valdsins. Kunningjaveldi, aðstöðubrask og hrun Íslands* [Threads of Power: Nepotism, Favoritism and the Collapse of Iceland]. Reykjavík: Veröld, 2011.

Helgason, Magnús S. "Íslenskt viðskiptalíf—breytingar og samspil við fjármálakerfið." Appendix 5 to the Report of the Special Investigation Committee. Reykjavík: Rannsóknarnefnd Alþingis, 2010. Accessed February 16, 2015, www.rna.is/media/skjol/RNAvefVidauki5.pdf.

Johnsen, Guðrún. *Bringing Down the Banking System—Lessons from Iceland*. New York: Palgrave Macmillan, 2014.

Jónsson, Ásgeir. *Why Iceland? How One of the World's Smallest Countries Became the Meltdown's Biggest Casualty*. New York: McGraw-Hill, 2009.

Jónsson, Bjarni Bragi. "Hannes Hólmsteinn Gissurarson: Hvernig Ísland getur orðið ríkasta land í heimi?" *Fjármálatíðindi* [Bulletin of Monetary Affairs] 39, no 1 (2002): 61–67.

Kindleberger, Charles P. and Robert Z. Aliber. *Manias, Panics, and Crashes: A History of Financial Crises*. New York: John Wiley and Sons, 2005.

Kotz, David M. "Changes in the Postwar Global Economy and the Roots of the Financial Crisis." In *The Handbook of Political Economy of Financial Crises*, edited by Gerald A. Epstein and Martin H. Wolfson, 395–410. Oxford: Oxford University Press, 2013.

Kregel, Jan. "Political Economy Approaches to Financial Crisis: Hyman Minsky's Financial Fragility Hypothesis." In *The Handbook of Political Economy of Financial Crises*, edited by Gerald A. Epstein and Martin H. Wolfson, 159–171. Oxford: Oxford University Press, 2013.

Laeven, Luc and Fabián Valencia. "Systemic Banking Crisis Database: An Update". IMF, Working Paper no. 12/163. Accessed January 10, 2014. www.imf.org/external/pubs/ft/wp/2010/wp10146.pdf.

Lewis, Michael. "Wall Street on the Tundra." *Vanity Fair*, April 2009. Available at www.vanityfair.com/culture/2009/04/iceland200904.

Minsky, Hyman Philip. *Stabilizing an Unstable Economy*. New York: McGraw-Hill, 2008/1986.

Minsky, Hyman Philip. "The Financial Instability Hypothesis," Working Paper no. 78, Levy Economics Institute of Bard College, accessed February 15, 2014, www.levyinstitute.org/pubs/-wp74.pdf.

Miskin, Frederic and Tryggvi Þór Herbertsson. "Financial Stability in Iceland." Iceland Chamber of Commerce, May 2006. Accessed February 16, 2015. www.vi.is/files/555877819financial+stability+in+iceland+screen+version.pdf.

OECD. *Growing Unequal?* Paris: OECD, 2008.

OECD. *Employment Outlook*. Paris: OECD, 2009.

OECD. *Divided We Stand. Why Inequality Keeps Rising*. Paris: OECD, 2011.

Ólafsdóttir, Katrín and Stefán Ólafsson. *Economy, Politics and Welfare in Iceland: Booms, Busts and Challenges*. Oslo: Fafo Research Monograph, 2014. Accessed January 11, 2015. www.fafoarkiv.no/pub/rapp/20360/20360.pdf.

Ólafsson, Stefán. "Icelandic Capitalism: From Statism to Neoliberalism and Financial Collapse." In *Nordic Varieties of Capitalism*. Special edition of *Comparative Social Research*, vol. 28, edited by Lars Mjöset, 1–52. Amsterdam: Emerald, 2011.

Ólafsson, Stefán and Arnaldur Sölvi Kristjánsson. "Þróun tekjuskiptingarinnar 1993 til 2010" [Development of the Income Distribution from 1993 to 2010]. *Icelandic Review of Politics and Administration* 8, no. 1 (2012): 39–72.

Ólafsson, Stefán and Arnaldur Sölvi Kristjánsson. "Income Inequality in Boom and Bust: A Tale from Iceland's Bubble Economy." In *Income Inequality: Economic Disparities and the Middle Class in Affluent Countries*, edited by Janet Gornick and Markus Jäntti, 416–439. Palo Alto: Stanford University Press, 2013.

Rannsóknarnefnd Alþingis [Special Investigation Commission of the Icelandic Parliament]. *Aðdragandi og orsakir falls íslensku bankanna 2008 og tengdir atburðir* [The Causes and Effects of the Fall of the Icelandic Banks and Related Events]. Reykjavík, Rannsóknanefnd Alþingis, 2010.

Reinhart, Carmen M. and Kenneth Rogoff. *This Time Is Different: Eight Centuries of Financial Folly*. Princeton: Princeton University Press, 2009.

Reinhart, Carmen M. and Kenneth Rogoff. "A Decade of Debt." New York: Peterson Institute of International Economics, 2010. Accessed March 16, 2015. www.piie.com/publications/chapters_preview/6222/01iie6222.pdf.

Saez, Emmanuel. "Update on Statistics on Income Inequality." Accessed February 12, 2014. http://eml.berkeley.edu/~saez/#income.

Silvers, Damon. "Deregulation and the New Financial Architecture." In *The Handbook of Political Economy of Financial Crises*, edited by Gerald A. Epstein and Martin H. Wolfson, 430–446. Oxford: Oxford University Press, 2013.

Taub, Jennifer S. "What We Don't Talk About When We Talk About Banking." In *The Handbook of Political Economy of Financial Crises*, edited by Gerald A. Epstein and Martin H. Wolfson, 447–466. Oxford: Oxford University Press, 2013.

Valgreen, Carsten *et al.*, "Iceland: Geyser Crisis," Danske Bank Research paper, March 21, 2006, accessed February 5, 2014, www.mbl.is/media/98/398.pdf.

Vilhjálmsson, Ingi F. *Hamskiptin—Þegar allt varð falt á Íslandi* [Metamorphosis: When Anything Could Be Bought in Iceland]. Reykjavík: Bjartur, 2014.

Wolfson, Martin H. "An Institutional Theory of Financial Crises." In *The Handbook of Political Economy of Financial Crises*, edited by Gerald A. Epstein and Martin H. Wolfson, 172–190. Oxford: Oxford University Press, 2013.

Þorvaldsson, Ármann. *Ævintýraeyjan- uppgangur og endalok fjármálaveldis*. Reykjavík: Bókafélagið, 2009.

Part II

The political and societal responses to the crisis

4 Political opportunity, framing, and mobilization in Iceland's post-crash protests

Jón Gunnar Bernburg and Anna Soffía Víkingsdóttir

The financial crisis triggered much contentious collective action in Iceland. Within days of the collapse of the banking system in October 2008, social activists and other concerned citizens began to organize public meetings in midtown Reykjavík. The public meetings became regular events and spread to towns around the country, with thousands of individuals attending them. Focused on attributing blame for the crisis and its anticipated effects on the public, the meetings became a forum for intellectuals, activists, and other critics to challenge, among other things, the attempts of government leaders to define it as a global problem. Instead, the protesters framed the crash as a local disaster, blaming it on the authorities.[1] The message was echoed in the news and social media—and, in an emotionally charged situation, it reflected a collective effort to make sense of the evolving crisis.

The key demand of protesters was that the government, along with the governor of the Board of Directors of the Central Bank and the director of the Financial Supervisory Authority, should take responsibility for the crisis by stepping down with a promise of new elections. When government leaders refused to resign, protest leaders threatened stronger protest actions. Eventually, large-scale demonstrations broke out on January 20, 2009. Modeling themselves on South American *cacerolazo* demonstrations, protesters gathered in front of Parliament, banging kitchen utensils (pots, pans, and spoons), some engaging in vandalism and conflict with police. The scale and intensity of the protests, which went on for several days, created an enormous pressure on the coalition government—composed of the center-right Independence Party and the Social Democratic Alliance—to resign, which it did on January 26. After a transitional minority left-wing coalition government was formed, it was decided to call a general election in the spring of 2009. Once the protests had "successfully" brought down the government, large-scale mobilization vanished, and institutional politics ruled again in Iceland.

The Icelandic protests provide an interesting case for studying how crises prompt large-scale collective action.[2] The global financial crisis has led to protests in many (but not all) countries hit hard by the crisis, such as Greece, Spain, and Lithuania.[3] But, being the first victim of the crisis,[4] Iceland was the first country to respond to it with popular protest. The Icelandic protests, thus, did not follow an international protest wave. Public participation in the Icelandic protests was enormous, as was the level of support. Surveys conducted after the protests have confirmed this point. Based on a random sample of 609 adults from the Reykjavík area, one study has estimated that about 25% of the population were involved in the "pots and pans" protests in January 2009 at least once, and that 16% participated repeatedly.[5] The survey also found a high level of support for the protests; 57% of the survey respondents indicated having been in favor of the actions of protesters at the time of the demonstrations. Asking about general support for the protests, other surveys have found a public support rate of up to 70%.[6] These findings indicate that the Icelandic protests were one of the largest of the recent post-crash protests in Europe.[7]

This chapter explores how the crisis triggered these large-scale protests. Our analysis is guided by the notion that disruptive changes, such as crises, lead to collective action by evoking purposive, "agency-driven" action.[8] As Doug McAdam, James D. McCarthy, and Meyer N. Zald[9] argue, disruptive changes can lead to revolutions and large political protest by creating *political opportunities*, that is, by rendering the authorities vulnerable to challenge. However, as these authors emphasize, political opportunities do not automatically cause collective action. Changes entailing political opportunities lead to collective action only when individuals define the change in the historical context as an opportunity to mobilize others in a challenge and "take advantage" of the perceived opportunity by engaging in strategic mobilizing efforts, including framing (giving speeches, writing articles, performing contention, etc.[10]), and organizational work (for example, organizing meetings, rallies, and other acts of contention). In what follows, we discuss how the bank crisis changed the political and social context in Iceland, and then use grounded work to explore the resulting mobilization efforts and the interpretations of actors involved in such work, as well as of common protesters.

Grounded work

Our grounded research work consists of a discourse analysis and semi-structured interviews with 24 individuals. The discourse analysis studied framing work performed by critics and activists in the period from early October 2008 to January 20, 2009 (20 public meeting speeches and 50 media articles/interviews appearing in major media news outlets), and by government leaders (20 media interviews, announcements, and speeches). We coded all the texts for thematic content, using the method of grounded theory.[11]

We define three of our interviewees as "mobilization entrepreneurs" (all of them agreed to be named in this work). Most importantly, we interviewed artist and activist Hörður Torfason, the leading organizer of the Saturday protest meetings. We also interviewed well-known novelist and social critic Einar Már Guðmundsson, who was a prominent "message maker" both at the public meetings and in the media in this period. Finally, we interviewed poet Steinar Bragi, who was a prominent protest advocate in the pots and pans protests. We asked about the reasons that these individuals had for engaging in mobilization work, about their strategies, and about their perceptions of the post-crash situation.

We define 21 of the interviewees as common protesters, that is, individuals who attended the pots and pans protests in January 2009 (nine of these individuals were women). We selected them by using a blend of snowball and purposive sampling. Although social activists are over-represented (eight interviewees defined themselves as having been "activists" at the time of the protests), the group is heterogeneous in other respects. Age ranged from 19 to 67 years, and employment ranged from unemployed to students to working professionals. We asked open-ended questions about reasons and events leading these individuals to participate in the protests (for example, "Lead me through how it was that you first went to the pots and pans protests") as well as about their experiences of the financial crisis (for example, "Did the crisis damage your financial situation?"). The interviews were conducted from May through December 2012. Although more than three years had passed, interviewees expressed little difficulty in recalling their experiences. As Karl-Dieter Opp and Christiane Gern[12] have argued, people can usually recall historically unique and emotion-provoking protests even months or years later (of course, through their own subjective lenses). We coded all the interviews for thematic content using the method of grounded theory.[13]

The emergence of political opportunity

In the 1990s and 2000s, Iceland was, like many other countries, affected by the global shift toward increased dominance of market logics in politics, economy, and culture.[14] In the political realm, the changes were led by the center-right Independence Party, a party whose traditional conservatism was replaced in the 1990s by an outspoken "neoliberal" agenda of economic deregulation and privatization. With the continuous support of more than one-third of Icelandic voters, this party had, for the most part, led successive governments from 1993 up to the January 2009 protests. It had implemented, among other things, the privatization of Iceland's three state banks in the early 2000s, creating the conditions for their enormous expansion abroad, and for the subsequent economic boom.[15] In this period, the political leadership could argue that their neoliberal agenda had created economic prosperity[16]—and would continue to do so.

But this development created discontent on the Left, especially from "new left" groups, such as environmentalists, human rights activists, and feminists, who criticized growing inequality and privatization of public services, the invasion of culture by market forces and materialism, and the environmental damage caused by the construction of hydroelectric plants and aluminum smelters. In the political realm, the Left-Green Movement represented these oppositional views, and small activist groups emerged, sometimes organizing isolated small-scale protests.[17] But, such counter-voices had limited ground in public opinion; the majority of the public supported the government while living standards kept rising in a booming economy.

If prospects for mobilizing the public in opposition against the government were slim prior to the crisis, the collapse of the banking system changed the situation, temporarily creating an opportunity for opponents of the country's right-wing political leadership to mobilize the public in a challenge against it. Specifically, a widespread perception of opportunity emerged when the crisis simultaneously created a credibility crisis for the government and disrupted the taken-for-granted reality of the public.

Credibility crisis

If state fiscal crises are known to make ruling authorities vulnerable to challenge,[18] the Icelandic banking collapse created such a crisis. It instantly became associated with scandals and blunders, creating a credibility crisis for the country's political leadership and undermining its ability to provide the public with a credible explanation of the disaster. The outspoken endorsement by government leaders of the expansion of the banks and companies prior to the crash became a political liability in its aftermath, especially for the Independence Party and its neoliberal agenda. The authorities had not only celebrated and promoted growth in the financial sphere,[19] but had dismissed all warnings of its unsustainability. Reports about the irresponsible risk behavior of the banks had started to emerge two years prior to the crisis,[20] but, even in the months leading up to the crash, government leaders insisted that such warnings were unwarranted.[21] As Prime Minister Geir Haarde put it in a speech at Iceland's Chamber of Commerce in February 2008,

> [W]e still see negative coverage by individual analysts and media agencies, [characterized by] factual errors and descriptions about the Icelandic economic system that are grossly exaggerated. [We are concerned] that these parties do not pay attention to … the information available to everyone that shows the strong position of the banks and the Treasury. *There seem to be other forces at work here than the search for the truth* (italics added).[22]

In a context of apparent blunder, critics could argue that government leaders had failed to look out for the public's interest due to the government's neoliberal agenda or incompetence, or both. When the crisis struck, the public learned that the banks had accumulated an unsustainable foreign debt burden,[23] thus creating a huge systemic risk before the downfall of the banks. Neither the government nor its supervisory agencies (the Central Bank and the Financial Supervisory Authority) seemed to have acted in any significant way to prevent this risky development. That the global crisis had not created a comparable systemic breakdown in other countries, at this point in time, made it even more difficult for the authorities to blame global forces for the situation.

Perhaps it was inevitable, given the extreme uncertainty about Iceland's fate in the aftermath of the bank crash, that the actions of the government designed to contain the evolving crisis undermined its legitimacy even more. First, due to the risk of losing the entire foreign exchange reserves, the authorities applied for assistance to the International Monetary Fund (IMF), the first Western state to do so in 30 years.[24] Thus, aside from hurt national pride,[25] austerity measures controlled by external actors were anticipated. Such measures, especially if pushed through by foreign agents such as the IMF, are known to undermine government legitimacy and trigger protest.[26]

Second, to rescue the domestic banking system, including the public's savings in the fallen banks, the government enacted an emergency legislation enabling it to refinance new banks and take over the domestic affairs of the fallen banks (allowing the much larger foreign part of the banks' operations to go bankrupt). Aside from enormous cost to the state, the laws protected only Icelanders and, thus, resulted in liability claims from powerful foreign entities. In particular, due to pressure from the "international community," the authorities were forced to negotiate with the governments of Britain and the Netherlands about liability for the "Icesave" accounts: lost savings accounts of over 400,000 individuals and entities in these countries.[27] The Icesave affair damaged the authorities' legitimacy. Not only did it threaten Iceland's economy, creating widespread anxiety among the public, but it seemed to demonstrate how the banks had been allowed to take enormous risks on behalf of the Icelandic public. Moreover, the Icesave affair undermined the legitimacy of the authorities by making them vulnerable to criticism about serving foreign capitalist interests.[28]

Disruption of the taken-for-granted

Social movement theorists have argued that disasters and crises can trigger collective action because such events can disrupt the taken-for-granted reality of many individuals at the same time. David A. Snow and others[29] have argued that the stable routines of everyday life render most people unreflective in their perceptions of reality, which are, thus, based largely on taken-for-granted assumptions (for example, "banks are trustworthy"; "government acts in the public's interest"). But, events that disrupt or threaten routine life, "the taken-for-granted substrate of everyday life,"[30] can undermine the habitual acceptance by individuals of their situations. When such disruption is experienced collectively, as can occur in a crisis, an opening emerges for re-interpretation of shared meanings, beliefs, and identities, thus facilitating the emergence of radical or activist frames. Elizabeth Borland and Barbara Sutton's study of the Argentinean crisis in the early 1990s has illustrated this point.[31] Through interviews with women, these researchers have shown how disruption of everyday lives can create room for activist frames and identities.

The financial crisis created a collectively experienced disruption in taken-for-granted reality. The scale of the crisis was unexpected and sudden, and it undermined the public's fundamental assumptions about their social reality. Used to the idea of living in a highly affluent and secure society, the Icelandic public was suddenly cast into a state of uncertainty about fundamental aspects of its current and future way of life. Not only did the crisis disrupt most people's positive expectations about their economic well-being, but it also disrupted their trust in major social institutions, including the country's political system. Opinion polls from this period show a dramatic fall among the public in both economic expectations and trust in major institutions.[32]

Our interviews with protest participants reveal how the disruption in the taken-for-granted reality created a need for many individuals to make sense of the crisis, for example, by going to public meetings. Thus, some interviewees recalled feeling an urge to understand the situation. Typically, a 50-year-old male professional who had never engaged in activism before experienced the crisis as "a surreal situation, total chaos."[33] Another protester, a female, 22-year-old music teacher, described her experience:

> [T]he confusion, it was just such a shock … we did not know anything, everyone just clueless with their lives on the line … I went to the meetings to get information, you know, just to meet other people and talk together, to find out what was going on.[34]

In this vein, several interviewees described the post-crash confusion, anxiety, and frustration by mentioning a protest sign reading "damn fucking fuck" (*Helvítis fokking fokk*), displayed by a young man at an early public meeting. The media highlighted the sign as symbolizing the public's confusion and frustration; the sign has since then represented part of the imagery of the post-collapse frustrating confusion.[35]

In short, the financial crisis disrupted the public's taken-for-granted reality, creating a shared need among the public (and the media) to make sense of it (to establish a frame). Since the crisis undermined the credibility of the authorities, it gave extraordinary publicity and attention to radical voices coming out to frame it at public meetings and elsewhere.

Perception of opportunity

Social movement scholars have argued that for emerging political opportunities to lead to collective action, individuals need to define them as such.[36] Our grounded work illustrates how both "protest entrepreneurs" and protest participants defined the crisis as an opportunity for mobilizing others in a challenge against Iceland's long-standing political leadership. Protest leader Torfason put it this way:

> Prior to the crisis people lived on some cloud … if you tried to talk to them about the structure of society they had no interest, but rather asked where you bought this sweater; did you get a new car? They talked in money and about having things…[37]

Activists and protest entrepreneurs experienced a turnaround in prospects for mobilizing a popular challenge. In the words of protest advocate Steinar Bragi,

> I perceived the post-crash situation as an opportunity for all to bring up their opinions ... a dominating ideological system had fallen and everyone was open to something new to commit to ... I felt very strongly that society could change.[38]

Moreover, demonstrating this point further, known novelist and social critic Einar Már recalls extraordinary reactions to his critical writings about societal affairs after the bank crash: "All of a sudden what I had been saying fitted in ... I've never felt such enormous instantaneous reaction to anything I've written."[39]

Not only mobilization entrepreneurs defined the post-crash situation as an opportunity for challenge. The perception was shared by many supporters of left-wing politics who prior to the crisis had resented the long-standing reign of the Right. For them, the crisis had "exposed" the flaws of the government's unfettered neoliberalism and corruption, for all to see. As Sigurður, a 29-year-old writer and protester, puts it:

> I was very skeptical about 'the expansion' [the business expansion abroad referred to in Iceland as the *útrásin*] ... and then all this happened and then it was like an 'I told-you-so moment' for me and others who had been on the leftwing.[40]

If such "told-you-so" sentiments were common among those aligned with the Left, the actions of critics, activists, and other mobilization agents amplified such sentiments and associated them with a moral call for protest. They did so by framing the crisis not as an economic crisis but as a moral-democratic crisis.

Framing the crisis

A politically motivated conflict over how to define the crisis emerged at the moment it struck Iceland. Government leaders immediately came out framing it as an "international financial storm," insisting that global forces external to government were to blame.[41] According to them, the Icelandic government had abided by international regulations and market principles, but these unfortunately had created unexpected problems for Iceland. Their actions (or inactions) prior to the crisis could be defined as unwise only in hindsight. Prime Minister Haarde characterized it as follows in a newspaper interview right after the bank crash:

> We thought we had the best laws in that area, founded on the EEA (European Economic Area) Agreement. The most tragic hole in those regulations ... is that banks were able to promise state responsibility ... for savings accounts created in other countries [...] ... the Icelandic government [did not create this problem...], although it has to deal with it now.[42]

Yet, the crisis continued to undermine the credibility of government leaders, weakening their ability to influence public opinion. Perceiving the situation as a window of opportunity, activists began to create a platform for countering the authorities' framing of the crisis. Within days of the crash, artist and activist Hörður Torfason organized an outdoor public meeting on a Saturday, locating it on *Austurvöllur*, a national symbolic square facing Iceland's Parliament, calling on the public to come and discuss the crisis. Several hundred individuals attended the first meeting. Speeches were held, with speakers selected by Torfason himself. He recalls: "I decided to call a meeting … to gather intellectuals and artists who had knowledge and insights into the issue, to give speeches and try to explain it to us."[43]

In the subsequent weeks, the "Saturday meetings" became weekly events, sometimes attended by several thousand individuals. The meetings, in turn, inspired a series of "citizens' meetings"—mass indoor meetings with speakers focused on specific topics related to the crash—and cabinet ministers were asked to come and sit on the stage and answer the questions of citizens (one of the largest of these meetings was broadcast live on national television). The discourse emerging at all of these public meetings echoed in the mass and social media—and intellectuals and critics brought the message home by giving interviews and writing articles in national newspapers and web-based news media.

The public meetings became a novel forum for intellectuals and critics to challenge the government's "global-problem" framing of the crisis. According to them, the Icelandic public had not been a mere victim of global forces but of a misguided and corrupt leadership. Not only did the economic situation need a remedy; also required was a change in Iceland's politics, representing a challenge to the ruling political parties, especially the Independence Party. Two major "diagnostic" themes emerged. First, critics appealed to pre-existing left-wing discontent in Iceland by emphasizing that the government's neoliberal agenda had promoted greed and policies favoring the rich and that its belief in market principles had led them to allow the financial elite, now exposed as corrupt and incompetent, to profit (and crash) at the public's expense. One speaker at a Saturday meeting held in November 2008 captured this sentiment in the following way:

> [This] economic and political bankruptcy … is neither a natural catastrophe nor an accident … [but] the effect of a man-made global financial system that Icelandic politicians [allowed to take control of] Iceland's economy. There were men who made those decisions, in the name of ideology created by men. It is that ideology, and those men, who are responsible for [the current situation].[44]

Second, critics appealed to a pre-existing discourse in Iceland about the failure of Icelandic politics to break away from nepotism and cronyism, a discourse that had been associated with the longevity of the political elite, especially the Independence Party.[45] In this vein, political corruption was said to have caused incompetence and rule of "special interests" in political decisions prior to the crisis, undermining the public good. An intellectual and government critic put it this way at a large citizens' meeting broadcast live on national television at the end of November 2008:

> Icelandic business life was for a long time infiltrated by politics. The privatization of banks ... was meant to change that structure ... [But] The government failed.... It gave the state banks to men with party connections but no experience directing banks. In their hands the banks grew immensely and secretly cast a heavy responsibility on the nation. The Central Bank, the Government and the Financial Affairs did nothing, until the dam broke.[46]

Emergence of a collective action frame

Framing theory argues that the emergence of a "diagnostic" frame that identifies a public problem and blames it on illegitimate processes can potentially mobilize many in collective action.[47] It is, however, unlikely to do so without the co-emergence of action-oriented, "prognostic," and "motivational" definitions. Prognostic definitions refer to definitions that specify the type of collective action needed to remedy the problem (for example, a call for protest), while motivational definitions provide "call-to-arms" motivations for individuals to participate in collective action (by equating participation with honor or by emphasizing the urgency and efficiency of protesting).[48]

As weeks went by, a collective action frame did indeed emerge. Protest organizers and meeting speakers began to call for intensifying protest activity in conjunction with specific demands that rhymed with their diagnostic framing of the crisis. Thus, they began to threaten more disruptive protest unless the government resigned and called a general election. Demanding the resignation of the government became the manifest aim of the protests. A known novelist wrote in a national newspaper:

> A government that cannot fire those who need to be fired will itself be fired.... If not next Saturday, then the following Saturday... A promise of a new election soon is the only promise that the nation can accept from this government.[49]

Importantly, the demand for the resignation of the government followed by a new election was strategically derived by means of consensus framing on the part of protest entrepreneurs. Our interview with protest leader Torfason underscores this point:

> I talked to people and asked what they wanted ... there were all kinds of squirts, but [everyone] wanted the government out.... I listened and I summarized ... that is how I came up with these demands. I laid out these demands at each and every meeting and asked the people: 'IS THIS WHAT YOU WANT?' ... and everyone shouted 'YES!'[50]

This manifest aim had a strong mobilizing potential. It resonated well with the widespread popular sense of justice and democratic procedure. But at the same time, it fell short of radical ideas about "revolution" and a "new republic."

To many activists, these demands were "minimum demands." As one speaker put it at the final Saturday meeting, which was held at the end of January 2009, a few days after the government resigned, "By getting [...these demands] through a new mass movement was showing its claws, to practice for the real battle."[51] However, the moment of mass mobilization ended when the government resigned; once that key demand was met, the protests stopped attracting large numbers to Austurvöllur Square.

Finally, motivational "call-to-arms" framing emerged.[52] Speakers at the protest meetings emphasized the seriousness of the current moral-democratic crisis, for example, by telling stories of how banks, with the help of the government, had victimized individuals (by tricking them into investing their savings in unsecure ways and into borrowing too much prior to the crisis). Also, speakers emphasized the moral propriety of collective action, arguing that "as long as no one has resigned, we are all guilty accepting the crime."[53] Moreover, speakers defined collective action as urgent, emphasizing that the system had failed and that it was, therefore, the right time for taking action to change it.

Importantly, although organized for speech-making, the public meetings became a forum for left-wing activists, such as "anarchists," to perform contentious acts. For example, at a large Saturday meeting, a young activist used a ladder to climb on top of the Parliament building and pulled up the flag of an Icelandic food-chain store ("Bónus") associated with one of the financial moguls and owner of one of the fallen banks. Symbolizing civil disobedience, the message was clear: the state is controlled by the rich and their interests. Such ongoing contentious acts were covered by the news media, and worked to associate the public meetings with anticipation of public disorder and civil disobedience.

Also, protest organizers were instrumental in creating anticipation. In January 2009, protest organizer Torfason[54] claimed in a media interview that the protests (referring to the public meetings) were "just beginning", that they were about to "start for real," and that "protesters have just been practicing" for what was coming. In Torfason's words, the tactic was to "imply things vaguely to create tension and anticipation."[55]

In short, inspired by a perception of political opportunity (and, of course, their pre-existing ideologies and commitments), left-wing critics and social activists created a public platform in the aftermath of the bank crash; that is, they organized public meetings, to counter the attempts of government leaders to frame the crisis as a global economic problem. Such agents appealed to and invigorated pre-existing left-wing discontent in Iceland with the long-standing right-wing political leadership, by framing the crisis as a moral-democratic crisis, calling for reform by means of protest.

Exploring voices on the ground

We have yet to study the forces underlying participation of individual citizens in the protests. Providing a starting point for addressing the issue,[56] Bernburg has examined participation in the January 2009 protest by surveying a sample representing the population of the Reykjavík area. Conducted several months after the protests, the survey measured protest participation along with social and economic characteristics and political attitudes. The study found two major results. First, in spite of the economic severity of the crisis, personal economic strain appeared to have played only a minor role in motivating individual citizens to protest. Thus, protest participation was not, as a rule, tied to socio-economic factors (income, education, wealth, financial hardship),[57] and it was only modestly associated with experiencing economic loss in the crisis.[58] Instead, the study indicated that political attitudes played a pivotal role in mobilizing individuals to participate in the protests, showing that protesters were many times more likely than non-protesters to support left-wing politics and to believe in the reality of political corruption.

Thus, the framing of the crisis as manifesting unfettered neoliberalism and corruption apparently mobilized many individuals whose attitudes were congruent with this frame. Underscoring this point, our interviews with protesters illustrate considerable alignment of protesters with the collective action frame that emerged at the public meetings and elsewhere (while none of our interviewees mentioned personal financial problems as a reason for protesting). Many of our interviewees said that they protested because the crisis had "exposed" the corruption and incompetence of politicians, especially of the ruling political leadership and leading officials (particularly the director of the Central Bank, former prime minister and strongman leader of the Independence Party in the 1990s and early 2000s). In the words of Hanna, a 29-year-old female college student, the crisis destroyed the idea "...that we [Icelanders] were somehow better than others ... [As in other countries] there is corruption and power play."[59] Likewise, Víkingur, a working-class male in his sixties, said:

> It was endless corruption to give certain men state property [referring to the sale of the state banks in the early 2000s] and let them do what they wanted ... [for example,] serving themselves tens of millions in monthly salaries.... [Moreover, consider the] election funds of politicians ... if I give you twenty millions I expect something back ... that is just how it works...[60]

Moreover, several interviewees expressed an alignment with the view that the political leadership's neoliberal agenda had caused the crisis: due to a strong faith in private enterprise and rule of market forces, government leaders had ignored all warnings and allowed the rich to victimize the public, then refused to accept responsibility for their mistakes. Typically, in the words of Hanna, "It is so much injustice to have represented some [neoliberal] ideals, and when the ideals do not work they just keep on ruling and refuse to admit it."[61] And Gunnhildur, a 51-year-old real estate agent: "The authorities just brought all normal defenses, almost paralyzed the Financial Supervisory Agency and never listen to any."[62]

The interviews illustrate how individuals who had been discontented with the authorities prior to the crisis were receptive to this view, and they also illustrate how activists already committed to opposition saw the crisis and the protests as an opportunity for challenging the establishment. Representing such accounts, Eydís, a 26-year-old student, said:

> [I]t doesn't take much to get me to protest against the Independence Party ... [But the protests were] also a forum for different fighting issues ... people brought flags "Iceland out of NATO" and there was "Iceland–Palestine" ... it wasn't just one issue.[63]

Motivational framing appears to have played a role, as many interviewees expressed sentiments about the moral propriety and efficiency of the protests. Thus, some interviewees recalled experiencing a "duty" to protest. For example, Jón said: "I just thought it was my social duty to express my discontent ... I felt a little bit like a soldier in a movement."[64] Furthermore, many interviewees described a perception of efficacy stemming from their expectation about a huge protest as well as the enormous number of people showing up at the protests. Some interviewees recall "moments" when they realized how many people were showing up at the protests. Guðmann, an unemployed 19-year-old, characterized this feeling:

> I was sure that it would have an effect ... standing there in a crowd ... with I don't know how many and yelling INCOMPETENT GOVERNMENT ... there was so much solidarity and there were so many, that they just couldn't ignore this, that was the mood, you could just feel that people were not going to let this go on anymore.[65]

Our interviews illustrate how the manifest aim of the protests, to demand the resignation of the government, created strong consensus among protesters. All interviewees agreed that the government had to resign and that a new election had been necessary to "clean out the bad elements" and to "get rid of those who slept on the job."[66] In the words of Sigurður, a 29-year-old writer, "[The aim was to] get rid of the government ... that may have been the only thing that tied us together, very loosely but enough to form this unity."[67]

But, not all interviewees agreed on the methods of protest. Activists kept busy during the protest performing symbolic acts such as burning benches, and some of them wore masks to conceal their identities. While some interviewees agreed with such methods, some (including the protest leaders) thought that they were harming the protest because it was giving the authorities and others a chance to label the protesters "a mob." One interviewee, commenting on the Saturday meetings, said:

> I thought they were good for the most part but it bothered me that there were some stupid people trying to light them up ... it meant that for the rest of us people could call us a mob but we weren't, we were just ordinary people protesting...[68]

While agreement with the collective action framing appears to have played a key role in protest mobilization, other mobilization forces were important as well. Thus, in line with previous protest research,[69] our interviews indicate that social incentives were an important force underlying protest mobilization. Thus, some interviewees describe the protests as an exciting site of social gathering, of meeting friends, and for experiencing rare feelings of solidarity and belonging. These features of the protests were probably an important part of the attraction for some to participate in the protests. Ingibjörg, a 23-year-old student, described her feelings at the protests:

> [T]here were so many people and then people were really united and I just felt an atmosphere where everyone were beating the same rhythm and someone was dancing over there and I just, woah! I never thought that this could happen in Iceland … I never expected that Icelanders could be so united.[70]

Conclusion

Despite Iceland's weak tradition of mass protest, public participation in the January 2009 protests was enormous (about 25%), as was the level of public support. Exploring how the financial crisis spurred this high degree of protest mobilization, we have assumed that disruptive changes such as crises, and the political opportunities that crises can entail, lead to collective action only through "agency-driven" mobilizing work.[71] Accordingly, we have tried to identify how the crisis created political opportunity, and then explored the interpretations and actions of actors engaged in mobilization work as well as of protesters.

We argue that the financial crisis in Iceland created an opportunity for activists and left-wing critics to mobilize the public in a collective challenge. Two major changes were crucial in creating this opportunity. First, the financial crisis was associated with scandals and blunders that undermined the credibility of government leaders, thus undercutting their ability to avert blame for the crisis. Second, at the same time, the crisis disrupted the public's taken-for-granted reality, undermining common assumptions. As theorists have argued,[72] when such disruption is experienced collectively, as can occur in an economic crisis,[73] an opening emerges for radical frames and identities.

The bank crash created a shared and emotionally charged need among the Icelandic public to define the crisis, creating a rare opportunity for radical framing and protest mobilization. Our grounded work illustrates how mobilization actors perceived the crisis as an opportunity to mobilize a challenge against Iceland's long-standing, right-wing political leadership. The situation inspired activists to organize public meetings and create a public forum for critics to challenge the authorities. Thus, as government leaders tried to neutralize the situation by framing the crisis as an "international financial storm," critics appealed to and amplified pre-existing left-wing discontent with the ruling right-wing authorities by framing the crisis as a problem of corruption and unfettered neoliberalism. Both these issues had been associated with the political leadership prior to the crisis,[74] but the crisis made them more credible and salient for the public than they had been prior to the crisis.

Furthermore, based on this diagnostic framing, a collective action frame emerged as critics called for protest to enforce democratic reform. Strategically derived by protest entrepreneurs, the manifested "common denominator" aim of the protests, namely, the resignation of the government followed by an election, resonated with the public's sense of democratic procedure. Moreover, framing the crisis as a "moral shock"[75] made it possible to appeal to values of justice, and associate protest participation with moral duty.[76] Finally, the ongoing, often strategic, collective action activity in the fall of 2008 and early January 2009 was crucial in building enough anticipation that a large-scale protest would occur.

Our interviews with protesters illustrate how alignment with this collective action frame, and the political-ideological interests motivating its emergence, mobilized individuals to participate in the January 2009 protests. Issues of political corruption, unfettered neoliberalism, and lack of responsibility and accountability on the part of government leaders were often mentioned as the main reasons for protesting. Some protesters expressed a strong sense of moral duty to participate in the protests. Underscoring the role of political attitudes in the protests are findings from a participation survey, showing that left-wing political attitudes and attitudes toward extended corruption strongly predict protest participation, while economic strain played only a modest role in participation.[77]

Our interviews with mobilization entrepreneurs illustrate their common perception of political opportunity, but more interviews are needed to accomplish a thick description of the experiences of this group. Also, the data that we have analyzed in this chapter, focused on framing work, has provided limited insight into the organizational work underlying the public meetings and the protests, such as methods of recruitment and information flow. We should point out, though, that while some politicians, particularly members of the Left-Green Movement, were outspoken about their support for the protest movement,[78] we find no evidence of organizational cooperation between protesters and established political parties.[79] In this sense, the protests reflected a spontaneous, "grassroots" movement that did not have a lasting organizational base, which, in turn, explains why protest mobilization continued only insofar as the manifest goal of the protests resonated strongly with public opinion. That the mass mobilization vanished as soon as the government resigned on January 26, 2009 bears witness to this fact. Certainly, the simple demand for government resignation and new elections was a key in uniting protesters, contributing to the enormous public mobilization in the protests. But, at the same time, this demand fell short of more radical reformist ideas emerging at the public meetings and elsewhere, ultimately leaving many activists disappointed with the success of the Icelandic *cacerolazo* protests.

Notes

1 See Jón Gunnar Bernburg, "Overthrowing the Government: A Case Study in Protest," in *Gambling Debt: Iceland's Struggle with the New World Order*, ed. Gísli Pálsson and Paul Durrenberger (Boulder: University of Colorado Press, 2014), 63–78; Jón Gunnar Bernburg, *Economic Crisis and Mass Protest: The Pots and Pans Revolution in Iceland* (Ashgate, In Press); Guðni Th. Jóhannesson, *Hrunið* [The Crash] (Reykjavík: JPV, 2009).

2 See Elizabeth Borland and Barbara Sutton, "Quotidian Disruption and Women's Activism in Times of Crisis, Argentina 2002–2003," *Gender & Society* 21, no. 5 (2007): 700–722; Kurtulus Gemici, "Moral Economy Redux: Social Protests in Turkey after the 2001 Economic Crisis," *Mobilization* 18, no. 2 (2013): 143–160.

3 See Donatella della Porta and Alice Mattoni eds., *Spreading Protest: Social Movements in Times of Crisis* (Colchester, UK: ECPR Press, 2013); Kerman Calvo, "Fighting for a Voice: the Spanish 15-M/Indignados Movement," in *Understanding European Social Movements*, eds. Cristina Flesher Fominaya and Laurence Cox (New York: Routledge, 2013), 236–253; Cristina Flesher Fominaya and Laurence Cox, "Conclusion: Anti-Austerity Protests in European and Global Context—Future Agendas for Research," in *Understanding European Social Movements*, eds. Cristina Flesher Fominaya and Laurence Cox (New York Routledge, 2013), 236–253; Hank Johnston and Seraphim Seferiades, "The Greek December, 2008," in *Violent Protests, Contentious Politics, and the Neoliberal State*, eds. Seraphim Seferiades and Hank Johnston (Burlington: Ashgate, 2012), 149–156; Hanspeter Kriesi, "The Political Consequences of the Financial and Economic Crisis in Europe: Electoral Punishment and Popular Protest," *Swiss Political Science Review* 18 (2013): 518–522; Spyros Sakellaropoulos, "On the Causes and Significance of the December 2008 Social Explosion in Greece," *Science & Society* 76, no. 3 (2012): 340–364; Woolfson, " 'Hard times' in Lithuania: Crisis and 'Discourses of Discontent' in Post-Communist Society," *Ethnography* 11, no. 4 (2010): 487–514.

4 See Sigriður Benediktsdottir et al., "Lessons from a Collapse of a Financial System," *Economic Policy* 26, no. 66 (2011): 183–235; Ásgeir Jónsson, *Why Iceland? How One of the World's Smallest Countries Became the Meltdown's Biggest Casualty* (New York: McGraw-Hill, 2009); Thorolfur Matthiasson, "Spinning Out of Control: Iceland in Crisis," *Nordic Journal of Political Economy* 34, 3 (2008): 1–19.

5 Jón Gunnar Bernburg, "Economic Crisis and Popular Protest in Iceland, January 2009: The Role of Perceived Economic Loss and Political Attitudes in Protest Participation and Support," *Mobilization* 20, no. 2 (2015): 231–252.

6 Eva Önnudóttir, "Búsáhaldabyltingin: pólitískt jafnræði og þátttaka almennings í mótmælum," in *Rannsóknir í félagsvísindum*, ed. Silja Bára Ómarsdóttir (Reykjavík: Félagsvísindastofnun Háskóla Íslands, 2011), 36–44.

7 Compare Wolfgang Rudig and Georgios Karyotis, "Beyond the Usual Suspects? New Participants in Anti-Austerity Protests in Greece," *Mobilization* 18, no. 3 (2013): 313–330.

8 James M. Jasper, "Introduction: From Political Opportunity Structures to Strategic Interaction," in *Contention in Context: Political Opportunities and the Emergence of Protest*, eds. Jeff Goodwin and James M. Jasper (Stanford: Stanford University Press, 2012), 1–36.

9 Doug McAdam et al., "Introduction: Opportunities, Mobilizing Structures, and Framing Processes—Toward a Synthetic, Comparative Perspective on Social Movements," in *Comparative Perspectives on Social Movements: Political Opportunities, Mobilizing Structures, and Cultural Framings*, eds. Doug McAdam, John D. McCarthy, and Mayer N. Zald (Cambridge: Cambridge University Press, 1996).

10 See Robert D. Benford and David A. Snow, "Framing Processes and Social Movements: An Overview and Assessment," *Annual Review of Sociology* 26 (2000):

611–639; David A. Snow et al., "Frame Alignment Processes: Micromobilization, and Movement Participation," *American Sociological Review* 51 (1986): 464–481; David A. Snow and Robert D. Benford, "Ideology, Frame Resonance, and Participant Mobilization," *International Social Movement Research* 1 (1988): 197–217; for application, see McAdam, "The Framing Function," 338–355; Anthony Oberschall, "Opportunities and Framing in the Eastern European Revolts of 1989," 93.

11 Barney Glaser and Anselm Strauss, *The Discovery of Grounded Theory* (Chicago: Aldine, 1967).

12 Karl-Dieter Opp and Christiane Gern, "Dissident Groups, Personal Networks, and Spontaneous Cooperation: The East German Revolution of 1989," *American Sociological Review* 58 (1993): 659–680.

13 Glaser and Strauss, *The Discovery of Grounded Theory.*

14 See Durrenberger and Pálsson, *Gambling Debt*; Kristín Loftsdóttir, "Vikings of the Past and Present: Icelandic National Identities in a Neoliberal World," in *Gambling Debt*, 3–14; Arnaldur Sölvi Kristjánsson and Stefán Ólafsson, "Heimur hátekjuhópanna: Um þróun tekjuskiptingar á Íslandi 1993–2007," *Stjórnmál og stjórnsýsla* 5, no. 1 (2009): 93–212; Stefán Ólafsson, "Íslenska efnahagsundrið: Frá hagsæld til frjálshyggju og efnahagshruns," *Stjórnmál og stjórnsýsla* 4, no. 2 (2008): 231–256; Thröstur Olaf Sigurjónsson, "Privatization and Deregulation: A Chronology of Events," in *Preludes to the Icelandic Financial Crisis*, eds. R. Z. Aliber and Gylfi Zoega (London: Palgrave Macmillan, 2010), 26–50; for theory, see Jón Gunnar Bernburg, "Anomie, Social Change and Crime: A Theoretical Examination of Institutional-Anomie Theory," *British Journal of Criminology* 42 (2002): 729–742.

15 Richard Portes and Friðrik Már Baldursson, *The Internationalization of Iceland's Financial Sector* (Reykjavík: Viðskiptaráð Íslands, 2007).

16 See Forsætisráðuneytið, "Ræða forsætisráðherra, Geirs H. Haarde, á Viðskiptaþingi 13. febrúar 2008" [Prime Minister's Address at Iceland's Congress of Commerce February 13, 2008], accessed March 19, 2015, www.forsaetisraduneyti.is/radherra/raedurGHH/nr/2865.

17 "Mótmæli erlendra gegn Kárahnjúkavirkjun: Níu samtök og 680 einstaklingar," *Fréttablaðið*, February 24, 2003, 10.

18 See Paul D. Almeida, "Opportunity Organizations and Threat Induced Contention: Protest Waves in Authoritarian Settings," *American Journal of Sociology* 109 (2003): 345–400; David G. Ortiz and Sergio Béjar, "Participation in IMF-Sponsored Economic Programs and Contentious Collective Action in Latin America, 1980–2007," *Conflict Management and Peace Science* 30, no. 5 (2013): 492–515; John Walton and Charles Ragin, "Global and National Sources of Political Protest: Third World Responses to the Debt Crisis," *American Sociological Review* 55 (1990): 876–890.

19 Forsætisráðuneytið, *Alþjóðleg fjármálastarfsemi á Íslandi* [International Finance in Iceland] (Reykjavík: Committee of Prime Minister on International Finance, 2006).

20 "Iceland: Geyser crisis," Danske Bank March 21, 2006, accessed December 1, 2015, https://notendur.hi.is/ajonsson/kennsla2006/Danske%20Bank%20-%20Geyser%20Crises%20(Mars%202006).pdf.

21 Thröstur Olaf Sigurjónsson et al., "Viðbrögð tengslanets við gagnrýni á fjármálastöðugleika Íslands," *Stjórnmál & stjórnsýsla* 7, no. 1 (2011): 161–184; Rannsóknarnefnd Alþingis [The Special Investigation Commission of the Icelandic parliament], *Aðdragandi og orsakir falls íslensku bankanna 2008 og tengdir atburðir* [The Causes and Effects of the Fall of the Icelandic Banks and Related Events] (Reykjavík: Icelandic Parliament, 2010).

22 Forsætisráðuneytið, February 13, 2008.

23 Matthíasson, "Spinning Out of Control," 1–19.

24 Matthíasson, "Spinning Out of Control."

25 See Eiríkur Bergmann, *Iceland and the International Financial Crisis: Boom, Bust, and Recovery* (New York: Palgrave Macmillan, 2014); Loftsdóttir, "Vikings of the Past."

26 See Gemici, "Moral Economy Redux," 143–160; Ortiz and Béjar, "IMF-Sponsored Economic Programs," 492–515; Walton and Ragin, "Political Protest," 879–890.
27 For an overview, see Benediktsdóttir et al., "Lessons from a Collapse," 183–235; Matthíasson, "Spinning Out of Control," 1–19; Jónsson, *Why Iceland?*
28 See Ortiz and Béjar, "IMF-Sponsored Economic Programs," 492–515; Walton and Ragin, "Political Protest," 879–890.
29 David A. Snow et al., "Disrupting the "Quotidian": Reconceptualizing the Relationship Between Breakdown and the Emergence of Collective Action," *Mobilization* 3, no. 1 (1998), 1–22.
30 Snow et al., "Disrupting the 'Quotidian'," 4.
31 Borland and Sutton, "Times of Crisis," 700–722.
32 Berglind Hólm Ragnarsdóttir et al., "The Global Financial Crisis and Individual Distress: The Role of Subjective Comparisons after the Collapse of the Icelandic Economy," *Sociology* 47, no. 4 (2013): 755–775; Bernburg, *Economic Crisis and Mass Protest.*
33 Protester, interviewed by Linda Björk Guðmundsdóttir, May 30, 2012, interview recorded and transcribed.
34 Protester, interviewed by Linda Björk Guðmundsdóttir, May 7, 2012, interview recorded and transcribed.
35 Jóhannesson, *Hrunið.*
36 McAdam et al., "Introduction;" Jasper, "Introduction."
37 Hörður Torfason, interviewed by Jón Gunnar Bernburg, October 18, 2012, recorded and transcribed.
38 Steinar Bragi, interviewed by Anna Soffía Víkingsdóttir, November 21, 2012, recorded and transcribed.
39 Einar Már Guðmundsson, interviewed by Jón Gunnar Bernburg, October 23, 2012, recorded and transcribed.
40 Protester, interviewed by Linda Björk Guðmundsdóttir, July 23, 2012, recorded and transcribed.
41 Haarde, "Special Circumstances"; see Jóhannesson, *Hrunið.*
42 Interview with Geir H. Haarde, *Morgunblaðið*, October 12, 2008.
43 Hörður Torfason, interviewed by Jón Gunnar Bernburg, October 18, 2012, recorded and transcribed.
44 Viðar Þorsteinsson, speech at Austurvöllur, November 8, 2008.
45 Svanur Kristjánsson, "Brothætt lýðræði: Valdsmenn í sókn," *Skírnir* 186 (2012): 303–337.
46 Thorvaldur Gylfason, speech at a citizens' meeting in Háskólabíó, November 24, 2008.
47 Benford and Snow, "Framing Processes," 611–639.
48 Robert D. Benford, "'You Could Be the Hundredth Monkey': Collective Action Frames and Vocabularies of Motive within the Nuclear Disarmament Movement," *The Sociological Quarterly* 34, no. 2 (1993): 195–216; Rachel L. Einwohner, "Opportunity, Honor, and Action in the Warsaw Ghetto Uprising of 1943," *American Journal of Sociology* 109 (2003): 650–676.
49 Hallgrímur Helgason, "Ábyrgð Samfylkingarinnar," *Fréttablaðið*, November 20, 2008, 24.
50 Hörður Torfason, interviewed by Jón Gunnar Bernburg, October 18, 2012, recorded and transcribed.
51 Protester, interviewed by Linda Björk Guðmundsdóttir, July 15, 2012, recorded and transcribed.
52 Benford, "Hundredth Monkey," 195–216.
53 Andri Snær Magnason, speech at Austurvöllur Square, November 15, 2008.
54 "Hörður: Mótmælin rétt að byrja," *Morgunblaðið*, January 11, 2009, accessed March 19, 2015, www.mbl.is/frettir/innlent/2009/01/11/hordur_motmaelin_rett_ad_byrja.

55 Hörður Torfason, interviewed by Jón Gunnar Bernburg, October 18, 2012, recorded and transcribed.
56 Bernburg, "Economic Crisis and Popular Protest," 231–252.
57 While unrelated to socio-economic status, protest participation had a nonlinear relationship with age: it increased slightly up to about age 40 and then decreased sharply with age. The fact that the crisis had a severe impact on many individuals who were paying off mortgages and consumption loans (for example, car loans), many of whom were between 30 and 50 years of age, may have rendered this age group particularly susceptible to experiencing injustice and frustration. Also, the study found that residential proximity to the protest site (that is, living near to downtown Reykjavík) significantly predicted protest participation (but not protest support).
58 The association between experiencing economic loss and protest participation was actually quite pronounced among individuals who thought that the crisis had harmed them more than most others. However, only 18% of the study's sample reported this experience, weakening the overall association.
59 Protester, interviewed by Linda Björk Guðmundsdóttir, May 23, 2012, recorded and transcribed.
60 Protester, interviewed by Anna Soffía Víkingsdóttir, November 20, 2012, recorded and transcribed.
61 Protester, interviewed by Linda Björk Guðmundsdóttir, May 23, 2012, recorded and transcribed.
62 Protester, interviewed by Anna Soffía Víkingsdóttir, October 11, 2012, recorded and transcribed.
63 Protester, interviewed by Linda Björk Guðmundsdóttir, August 1, 2012, recorded and transcribed.
64 Protester, interviewed by Linda Björk Guðmundsdóttir, May 5, 2012, recorded and transcribed.
65 Protester, interviewed by Linda Björk Guðmundsdóttir, July 27, 2012, recorded and transcribed.
66 Protester, interviewed by Anna Soffía Víkingsdóttir, November 20, 2012, recorded and transcribed.
67 Protester, interviewed by Linda Björk Guðmundsdóttir, July 23, 2012, recorded and transcribed.
68 Protester, interviewed by Anna Soffía Víkingsdóttir, September 23, 2012, recorded and transcribed.
69 Opp and Gern, "Dissident Groups," 659–680.
70 Protester, interviewed by Anna Soffía Víkingsdóttir, December 12, 2012, recorded and transcribed.
71 See Jasper, "Introduction," 1–36; Oberschall, "Opportunities and Framing," 93.
72 Snow et al., "Disrupting the 'Quotidian'," 1–22.
73 Borland and Sutton, "Times of Crisis," 700–722.
74 Kristjánsson, "Brothætt lýðræði," 303–337.
75 James M. Jasper, "Introduction," 1–36.
76 See Einwhoner, "Warsaw Ghetto Uprising," 650–676.
77 Bernburg, *Economic Crisis and Popular Protest*, 231–252.
78 Stefán Gunnar Sveinsson, *Búsáhaldabyltingin* [The Pots and Pans Revolution] (Reykjavík: Almenna bókafélagið, 2013).
79 Several of our interviewees talked about feeling angry when claims were made (by partisan agents) in the Icelandic media that the protests were organized by politicians or political parties. Protest organizer Torfason claimed in our interview with him to have been careful in keeping established politics out of the protests.

Bibliography

Almeida, Paul D. "Opportunity Organizations and Threat Induced Contention: Protest Waves in Authoritarian Settings." *American Journal of Sociology* 109 (2003): 345–400.

Benediktsdottir, Sigridur, Jon Danielsson, and Gylfi Zoega. "Lessons from a Collapse of a Financial System." *Economic Policy* 26, no. 66 (2011): 183–235.

Benford, Robert D. " 'You Could Be the Hundredth Monkey': Collective Action Frames and Vocabularies of Motive within the Nuclear Disarmament Movement." *The Sociological Quarterly* 34, no. 2 (1993): 195–216.

Benford, Robert D. and David A. Snow. "Framing Processes and Social Movements: An Overview and Assessment." *Annual Review of Sociology* 26 (2000): 611–639.

Bergmann, Eiríkur. *Iceland and the International Financial Crisis: Boom, Bust, and Recovery.* New York: Palgrave Macmillan, 2014.

Bernburg, Jón Gunnar. "Anomie, Social Change and Crime: A Theoretical Examination of Institutional-Anomie Theory." *British Journal of Criminology* 42 (2002): 729–742.

Bernburg, Jón Gunnar. "Overthrowing the Government: A Case Study in Protest." In *Gambling Debt: Iceland's Struggle with the New World Order*, edited by Gísli Pálsson and Paul Durrenberger, 63–78. Boulder: University of Colorado Press, 2014.

Bernburg, Jón Gunnar. "Economic Crisis and Popular Protest in Iceland, January 2009: The Role of Perceived Economic Loss and Political Attitudes in Protest Participation and Support." *Mobilization* 20 (2015): 231–252.

Bernburg, Jón Gunnar. *Economic Crisis and Mass Protest. The Pots and Pans Revolution in Iceland.* London and New York: Routledge, 2016.

Borland, Elizabeth, and Barbara Sutton. "Quotidian Disruption and Women's Activism in Times of Crisis, Argentina 2002–2003." *Gender & Society* 21, no. 5 (2007): 700–722.

Calvo, Kerman. "Fighting for a Voice: the Spanish 15-M/Indignados Movement." In *Understanding European Social Movements*, edited by Cristina Flesher Fominaya and Laurence Cox, 236–253. New York: Routledge, 2013.

Della Porta, Donatella and Alice Mattoni eds., *Spreading Protest: Social Movements in Times of Crisis* (Colchester, UK: ECPR Press, 2013).

Einwohner, Rachel L. "Opportunity, Honor, and Action in the Warsaw Ghetto Uprising of 1943." *American Journal of Sociology* 109 (2003): 650–676.

Fominaya, Cristina Flesher and Laurence Cox. "Conclusion: Anti-Austerity Protests in European and Global Context—Future Agendas for Research." In *Understanding European Social Movements*, edited by Cristina Flesher Fominaya and Laurence Cox, 254–258. New York: Routledge, 2013.

Forsætisráðuneytið. *Alþjóðleg fjármálastarfsemi á Íslandi* [International Finance in Iceland]. Reykjavík: Committee of Prime Minister on International Finance, 2006.

Forsætisráðuneytið. "Ræða forsætisráðherra, Geirs H. Haarde, á Viðskiptaþingi 13. febrúar 2008" [Prime Minister's Address at Iceland's Congress of Commerce February 13, 2008]. Accessed March 19, 2015. www.forsaetisraduneyti.is/radherra/raedurGHH/nr/2865.

Forsætisráðuneytið, "Ávarp forsætisráðherra vegna sérstakra aðstæðna á fjármálamarkaði" [Prime Minister's Address due to Special Circumstances in the Financial Market]. Accessed March 19, 2015. www.forsaetisraduneyti.is/radherra/raedurGHH/nr/3034.

Gemici, Kurtulus. "Moral Economy Redux: Social Protests in Turkey after the 2001 Economic Crisis." *Mobilization* 18, no. 2 (2013): 143–160.

Glaser, Barney, and Anselm Strauss. *The Discovery of Grounded Theory.* Chicago: Aldine, 1967.

Helgason, Hallgrímur. "Ábyrgð Samfylkingarinnar [The Responsibility of the Social Democratic Alliance]." *Fréttablaðið*, November 20, 2008.

Torfason, Hörður: "Mótmælin rétt að byrja"[The Protests Are Just Beginning]. *Morgunblaðið*, January 11, 2009. www.mbl.is/frettir/innlent/2009/01/11/hordur_motmaelin_rett_ad_byrja/.
"Iceland: Geyser crisis." Danske Bank March 21, 2006. Accessed December 1, 2015. https://notendur.hi.is/ajonsson/kennsla2006/Danske%20Bank%20-%20Geyser%20Crises%20(Mars%202006).pdf.
Jasper, James M. "Introduction: From Political Opportunity Structures to Strategic Interaction." In *Contention in Context: Political Opportunities and the Emergence of Protest*, edited by Jeff Goodwin and James M. Jasper, 1–36. Stanford: Stanford University Press, 2012.
Jasper, James M. and Jane D. Poulsen. "Recruiting Strangers and Friends: Moral Shocks and Social Networks in Animal Rights and Anti-Nuclear Protests." *Social Problems* 42, no. 4 (1995): 493–512.
Johannesson, Guðni Th. *Hrunið* [The Crash]. Reykjavík: JPV, 2009.
Johnston, Hank, and Seraphim Seferiades. "The Greek December, 2008." In *Violent Protests, Contentious Politics, and the Neoliberal State*, edited by Seraphim Seferiades and Hank Johnston, 149–156. Burlington: Ashgate, 2012.
Jónsson, Ásgeir. *Why Iceland? How One of the World's Smallest Countries Became the Meltdown's Biggest Casualty*. New York: McGraw-Hill, 2009.
Kriesi, Hanspeter. "The Political Consequences of the Financial and Economic Crisis in Europe: Electoral Punishment and Popular Protest." *Swiss Political Science Review* 18 (2013): 518–522.
Kristjánsson, Arnaldur Sölvi and Stefán Ólafsson. "Heimur hátekjuhópanna: Um þróun tekjuskiptingar á Íslandi 1993–2007 [The World of Higher Income Earners: The Development of Income Distribution in Iceland 1993–2007]." *Stjórnmál og stjórnsýsla* 5, no. 1 (2009): 93–212.
Kristjánsson, Svanur. "Brothætt lýðræði: Valdsmenn í sókn [Fragile Democracy: Power Politicians on the Offensive]." *Skírnir* 186 (2012): 303–337.
Loftsdóttir, Kristín. "Vikings of the Past and Present: Icelandic National Identities in a Neoliberal World." In *Gambling Debt: Iceland's Struggle with the New World Order*, edited by Gísli Pálsson and Paul Durrenberger, 3–14. Colorado: University of Colorado Press, 2014.
McAdam, Doug. 1996. "The Framing Function of Movement Tactics: Strategic Dramaturgy in the American Civil Rights Movement." In *Comparative Perspectives on Social Movements: Political Opportunities, Mobilizing Structures, and Cultural Framings*, edited by Doug McAdam, John D. McCarthy, and Mayer N. Zald, 338–355. Cambridge: Cambridge University Press, 1996.
McAdam, Doug, James D. McCarthy, and Meyer N. Zald. "Introduction: Opportunities, Mobilizing Structures, and Framing Processes—Toward a Synthetic, Comparative Perspective on Social Movements." In *Comparative Perspectives on Social Movements: Political Opportunities, Mobilizing Structures, and Cultural Framings*, edited by Doug McAdam, John D. McCarthy, and Mayer N. Zald, 1–22. Cambridge: Cambridge University Press, 1996.
McCarthy, James D. and Ronnelle Paulsen. "Specifying the Relationship between Social Ties and Activism." *American Journal of Sociology* 99 (1993): 640–667.
Matthiasson, Thorolfur. "Spinning Out of Control: Iceland in Crisis." *Nordic Journal of Political Economy* 34 (2008): 1–19.
"Mótmæli erlendra gegn Kárahnjúkavirkjun: Níu samtök og 680 einstaklingar [Foreign Protests against the Kárahnjúka Hydroelectric Plant: Nine Organizations and 680 Individuals]." *Fréttablaðið*, February 24, 2003.

Oberschall, Anthony. "Opportunities and Framing in the Easter European Revolts of 1989." In *Comparative Perspectives on Social Movements: Political Opportunities, Mobilizing Structures, and Cultural Framings*, edited by Doug McAdam, John D. McCarthy, and Mayer N. Zald, 93–121. Cambridge UK: Cambridge University Press, 1996.

Oberschall, Anthony. "Opportunities and Framing in the Transition to Democracy: The Case of Russia." In *Comparative Perspectives on Social Movements: Political Opportunities, Mobilizing Structures, and Cultural Framings*, edited by Doug McAdam, John D. McCarthy and Mayer N. Zald, 122–140. Cambridge: Cambridge University Press, 1996.

Ólafsson, Stefán. "Íslenska efnahagsundrið: Frá hagsæld til frjálshyggju og efnahagshruns [The Icelandic Economic Miracle: From Prosperity to Liberalism and Economic Collapse]." *Stjórnmál og stjórnsýsla* 4, no. 2 (2008): 231–256.

Önnudóttir, Eva. "Búsáhaldabyltingin: pólitískt jafnræði og þátttaka almennings í mótmælum [The Pots and Pans Revolution: Political Equality and Public Participation in Protests]." In *Rannsóknir í félagsvísindum*, edited by Silja Bára Ómarsdóttir, 36–44. Reykjavík: Félagsvísindastofnun Háskóla Íslands, 2011.

Opp, Karl-Dieter and Christiane Gern. "Dissident Groups, Personal Networks, and Spontaneous Cooperation: The East German Revolution of 1989." *American Sociological Review* 58 (1993): 659–680.

Ortiz, David G. and Sergio Béjar. "Participation in IMF-Sponsored Economic Programs and Contentious Collective Action in Latin America, 1980–2007." *Conflict Management and Peace Science* 30, no. 5 (2013): 492–515.

Pálsson, Gísli and Paul Durrenberger eds. *Gambling Debt: Iceland's Struggle with the New World Order*. Boulder: University of Colorado Press, 2014.

Petrie, Michelle. "A Research Note on the Determinants of Protest Participation: Examining Socialization and Biographical Availability." *Sociological Spectrum* 24 (2004): 553–574.

Portes, Richard and Friðrik Már Baldursson. *The Internationalization of Iceland's Financial Sector*. Reykjavík: Viðskiptaráð Íslands, 2007.

Ragnarsdóttir, Berglind Hólm, Jón Gunnar Bernburg, and Sigrún Ólafsdóttir. "The Global Financial Crisis and Individual Distress: The Role of Subjective Comparisons after the Collapse of the Icelandic Economy." *Sociology* 47, no. 4 (2013), 755–775.

Rudig, Wolfgang and Georgios Karyotis. "Beyond the Usual Suspects? New Participants in Anti-Austerity Protests in Greece." *Mobilization* 18, no. 3 (2013): 313–330.

Sakellaropoulos, Spyros. "On the Causes and Significance of the December 2008 Social Explosion in Greece." *Science & Society* 76, no. 3 (2012): 340–364.

Sigurjónsson, Thröstur Olaf. "Privatization and Deregulation: A Chronology of Events." In *Preludes to the Icelandic Financial Crisis*, edited by R. Z. Aliber and Gylfi Zoega, 26–50. London: Palgrave Macmillan, 2010.

Sigurjónsson, Thröstur Olaf, David Schwartzkopf, and Auður Arna Arnardóttir. "Viðbrögð tengslanets við gagnrýni á fjármálastöðugleika Íslands [Network Response to Criticisms of Iceland's Financial Stability]." *Stjórnmál & stjórnsýsla* 7, no. 1 (2011): 161–184.

Skocpol, Theda. *States and Social Revolutions: A Comparative Analysis of France, Russia and China.* Cambridge: Cambridge University Press, 1979.

Snow, D. and S. C. Byrd. "Ideology, Framing Processes, and Islamic Terrorist Movements." *Mobilization* 12 (2007): 119–36.

Snow, David A. and Robert D. Benford. "Ideology, Frame Resonance, and Participant Mobilization." *International Social Movement Research* 1 (1988): 197–217.

Snow, David A., E. Burke Rochford, Jr, Steven K. Worden, and Robert D. Benford. "Frame Alignment Processes: Micromobilization, and Movement Participation." *American Sociological Review* 51 (1986): 464–481.

Snow, David A., Daniel M. Cress, Liam Downey, and Andrew W. Jones. "Disrupting the "Quotidian:" Reconceptualizing the Relationship between Breakdown and the Emergence of Collective Action." *Mobilization* 3, no. 1 (1998): 1–22.

Sveinsson, Stefán Gunnar. *Búsáhaldabyltingin* [The Pots and Pans Revolution]. Reykjavík: Almenna bókafélagið, 2013.

Walton, John and Charles Ragin. "Global and National Sources of Political Protest: Third World Responses to the Debt Crisis." *American Sociological Review* 55 (1990): 876–890.

Woolfson, Charles. "'Hard times' in Lithuania: Crisis and 'Discourses of Discontent' in Post-Communist Society." *Ethnography* 11, no. 4 (2010): 487–514.

5 Contentious politics, political expediency, and the real costs of the Icesave debt

Helga Kristín Hallgrímsdóttir and Emmanuel Brunet-Jailly

The controversy over the repayment of the debt incurred as a result of the so-called "Icesave" accounts—the high-interest accounts offered by subsidiaries of Landsbanki in the United Kingdom and the Netherlands—emerged first in late 2008 and continued to play a prominent role in Icelandic politics until 2013.[1] The 2008 crash of Landsbanki led to a run on both Icelandic and foreign deposit accounts; despite the UK government's decision to freeze UK-held assets (through invoking the 2001 Anti-Terrorism, Crime, and Security Act), British and Dutch account holders lost access to their deposits. The British and Dutch governments compensated their own citizens for their losses. The Icesave depositors in the United Kingdom received full repayments, and those in the Netherlands a compensation of up to 100,000 euros. The two governments then demanded remuneration with interest and costs from the Icelandic government, on the grounds that Iceland should be held liable for guaranteeing savings up to about €20,887 per depositor, in accordance with European banking rules.

The dispute over whether the Icelandic government was responsible for repayment of the Icesave debts, and for how much, dominated the political debate in Iceland for several years.[2] The No side, by far the more vocal, included not only interested citizens, such as bloggers and community activists, but also grassroots groups and political parties from all sides of the political spectrum, and members of parliament. The No side eventually prevailed: the Icesave repayment deal was defeated in two separate referenda. The Icelandic government did not honor any of the repayment deals that were brokered; and Iceland's victory in 2013 at the court of the European Free Trade Association (EFTA) has effectively put the issue to rest.[3]

The Icelandic crash was only one of several calamitous fiscal events, which shook Europe and North America in the wake of the 2008 economic meltdown. Common responses to the crisis included public bailouts of private corporations and the adoption of fiscal austerity measures.[4] The success of the anti-Icesave movement, therefore, has implications significantly beyond local Icelandic politics. Social movement success—in particular, when a protest movement is able not only to mobilize support but also to enforce a policy response—is a rare enough phenomenon on its own to warrant investigation. However, set in the context of the much more nebulous effects of the wave of anti-austerity protests that swept Europe in 2010–2011,[5] the outcomes of the Icesave protest are even more interesting. The success of the anti-Icesave movement can be put within a complex and multi-level governance framework that included not only domestic political players but also international and supranational monetary and political institutions, especially the International Monetary Fund (IMF).

The focus of this chapter is on this intersection of protest politics and governance structures, and how it created the circumstances for the triumph of the anti-Icesave movement. The central question that frames our research is whether, and how, contentious politics around Icesave may have altered the political and economic costs associated with the Icesave debt for state actors in Iceland. Two disparate theoretical lenses underpin our approach to this question: political process theory and theories of participatory governance. We argue that merging these perspectives provides a fuller explanation of the efficacy of protest in the complex governance structures that characterize the current socio-historical context.

Our data are drawn from qualitative interviews with a range of actors involved in the Icesave dispute, including activists, political actors, and academics. They were conducted at three different points in time: August 2012, December 2012, and July 2013. We asked respondents to speak both specifically about the Icesave dispute as well as more generally about their sense of the political context in Iceland during and in the aftermath of the 2008 crisis. Our findings suggest that protest around the Icesave dispute did, indeed, alter governance structures, even if temporarily, by *increasing* the political costs of repayment for Icelandic political actors. We conclude by suggesting that further work exploring conceptual and empirical intersections between the literature on governance and the social movement scholarship may prove fruitful for understanding social movement mobilization and political change in the current fiscal and political climate.

The context: a brief history of the Icesave dispute

As discussed elsewhere in this volume, a confluence of economic errors and faults, including the lack of oversight of the Icelandic banking sector, the significant undercapitalization of Icelandic banks, especially in their overseas ventures, and the global fallout of the subprime mortgage crisis in the United States, led to the collapse of Iceland's three major banks, literally overnight.[6] The effects included erosion of Iceland's currency (the krona) and a substantial decline in gross domestic product (GDP) (which fell by 25%).[7] In addition, given certain peculiarities of the Icelandic banking system, in which a significant portion of mortgages and personal loans were either low-interest loans denominated in foreign currencies or high-interest loans indexed to inflation, the economic crash resulted in a rapid spike in household debt levels and a concomitant decline in the standard of living for Icelanders.

The crash was met with significant social protest and a rise in grassroots political activity, which included the formation of new political parties.[8] Prior to the crash, Icelandic society had been characterized by high levels of social trust and consensus, in addition to shared national pride in the exploits of the "útrásarvíkingar" (roughly translated as "corporate raider-vikings"), who were largely considered responsible for the extraordinary economic growth experienced between 2005 and 2007.[9] The time period after the crash, however, was characterized not only by the "pots and pans revolution" but also by intense debate over the nature of democracy, citizenship obligations and rights, and political transparency, all of which culminated in the formation of a body to review and rewrite the Icelandic constitution, and the decision to open up negotiations for accession to the European Union in July 2009.[10] It was against this backdrop that the government (first, the center-right/center-left government in power at the time of the crisis, and then the left-wing government that was formed in 2009) entered into negotiations for financial aid from international creditors and neighboring nations.[11]

The negotiations for financial assistance have to be viewed within the context of international censure regarding the loss of foreign deposits in the Icesave accounts. In effect, resolving the Icesave debt was both explicitly and implicitly a condition of receiving financial aid.[12] Ultimately, loans from the IMF were secured, estimated to cover up to about 42% of the financial gap faced by the state, but on the condition that Iceland negotiate agreements with all international creditors regarding lost deposits of Icelandic banks in foreign countries.[13] In early 2009, the Icelandic government sent an envoy to broker a settlement with the United Kingdom and Holland regarding the repayment of the losses suffered by Dutch and British citizens due to the collapse of the Icelandic banks. The result was an agreement to reimburse the Dutch and British governments what they had paid out in deposit guarantees to their own citizens, up to a maximum of 20,887 euros per account holder.[14]

The first repayment agreement (often referred to as "Icesave I") was tabled and passed by the Icelandic Parliament in September 2009. This agreement named a total sum of 3.8 billion euros, to be repaid with interest, a sum that represented about 44% of Iceland's GDP at the time. During the debate over the bill, the Icelandic Parliament imposed a 14-year time limit to the debt repayment; this condition, however, was not acceptable to the Dutch and UK governments. A subsequent revised agreement ("Icesave II") maintained the same terms, but with no expiry date to the debt. "Icesave II" was hotly debated in Parliament, and was only narrowly passed in December 2009.[15]

A number of activist groups from all sides of the political spectrum emerged to protest this second Icesave agreement.[16] Critical here were the activities of a small and organized group called *InDefence.* This group was established in October 2008 in response to the decision of the British government to invoke anti-terrorism legislation in its efforts to prevent the run on British-held Icesave accounts following the collapse of Landsbanki. InDefence was also instrumental in mobilizing protest against "Icesave II"—following the passage of the bill in December 2009—through mounting an online petition against the repayment deal. Over a period of less than two weeks, the petition gathered over 56,000 signatures, which were delivered to the President of Iceland, Ólafur Ragnar Grímsson, in early January 2010.[17] A few days later, in an apparent response to mounting public pressure, the President exercised his right to refuse to sign the bill into law and thereby triggered a referendum.[18] The vote was held in March 2010; an overwhelming majority, 98.1%, voted against the agreement. A subsequent revision ("Icesave III") was again defeated in a referendum held in April of 2011 (59.77% voted against).[19] After this second defeat, no additional efforts were made to broker a new deal.[20]

Since that time, there have been two additional developments of importance: first, almost all the Icesave debt has been paid out from the liquidated assets of Landsbanki.[21] Second, in January 2013, the EFTA Court ruled in favor of Iceland in a case brought against it by the European Free Trade Surveillance Association. The Dutch and British governments subsequently brought a case against the Icelandic Depositors' and Investors' Fund (DIGF) before the EFTA Court for several billion Euros (representing a combination of arrears and interest payments).[22] But in September 2015, the DIGF reached an agreement with the Dutch Central Bank and the British Financial Services Compensation Scheme (FSCS), which represented a full and final settlement of the claims resulting from Icesave between the three countries. The agreement was consistent with the 2013 EFTA ruling, which did not make the Icelandic state liable for ensuring payments of minimum guarantees to depositors. Yet, as noted, the Landsbanki estate had already repaid most of the original claims.

Political process theory and theories of participatory governance

While there has been a great deal of scholarship on the economic aspects of the financial crisis, less attention has been given to its political effects. This is an important problem. In Europe, for instance, there is some evidence of a link between the crisis, the subsequent implementation of austerity programs, and a rise in nationalism, Euro-skepticism, and xenophobic politics.[23] In Iceland, the crisis gave rise to new local and national political parties, grassroots organizations, and both renewed interest in European accession and Euro-skepticism. In fact, there have been few periods in Iceland that have seen such an intense pace of change in political discourse as the years between 2008 and 2014.

Contentious politics[24] refers to the broad range of "politics in which people make concerted claims bearing on each other's interests."[25] In Iceland, several new protest movements, as well as new political parties, were formed in the wake of the economic crisis. Some of these movements were aimed at the Icesave agreements, while others were more broadly concerned with correcting governance deficits that were understood to have been behind the crisis itself as well as the initial political response to it. Protest over the Icesave repayment deals was voiced in newspapers, through op-eds and letters to the editors, on individual blogs (from a range of voices, including politicians, students, journalists, and members of the public) and through social media; in addition, positions around Icesave were incorporated into political campaigns of both mainstream and alternative political parties.[26] In other words, contentious politics around the Icesave dispute occupied political space that included grassroots activism as well as "politics as usual."

As noted, one of the most interesting aspects of the Icesave dispute is its outcome. Not only did mobilization against the Icesave repayment deals raise awareness of the issue and stimulate political debate, but it arguably led to a concrete policy result: the refusal to honor a negotiated settlement with the United Kingdom and the Netherlands after a government bill had been defeated in a referendum. The conditions and circumstances that led to these events are of considerable interest, given the general consensus in the literature that outcomes of protest are exceedingly difficult to assess.[27]

Political process theories seek to identify what aspects of the political context lower or raise the cost of protest, and, by extension, constrain or enable movement success.[28] The key concept in this literature is political opportunity structure (POS). POS is constituted of the static (or more structural) features of government (including such elements as the governance architecture and how sensitive it is to the demands and programmatic claims of groups outside the political establishment) as well as the dynamic events that reshape them.[29] It is a loose conceptual framework that encompasses a range of political phenomena (electoral politics, institutional configurations, and historical precedents of political protest); its central premise, though, is that the outcomes of contentious politics are largely dependent on "institutional structure and the ideological disposition of those in power."[30]

Political process theories, however, are somewhat hobbled by an assumption that protest politics occur within finite or enclosed governance structures, in which policy-makers and state actors have both the capacity and the resources to act (or not to act) on claims that are made by contentious political actors. The Icesave dispute illustrates the limits of this theoretical and empirical rendering: while contentious political claims around Icesave were directed toward elected officials in Iceland, these same individuals were embroiled in difficult and tense relationships around this issue with officials from the IMF, the EFTA, and the United Kingdom and Holland.[31] In other words, "those in power" were in positions of political dependence inside a supranational governance structure, within which actions in response to claims from grassroots activists as well as supranational agencies entailed potentially high political costs. The challenges associated with protest and politics in this context of complex and opaque supranational governance are amply illustrated by the relatively modest impact of the wave of anti-austerity protests that swept Europe in 2010.[32]

The concept of political opportunity, therefore, must account for not only opportunities for claims-makers and activists but also how social movement activity itself creates political opportunities for state actors and policy-makers. Political process theory highlights how characteristics of the state make activism more or less costly and its outcomes more or less successful. However, contentious politics also transforms the state in ways that change the costs and benefits for future activists; by extension, in the current context of supranational governance, contentious politics can either raise or lower the costs for elected officials of complying with or resisting extra-national governance.

The concept of governance refers to the dynamic way in which politics is practiced on the ground by governmental and non-governmental organizations, civil society organizations, and civic actors.[33] It has taken on renewed significance in examining the relationships between local, state, and global governments in the context of supranational economic and political agreements, such as the European Union and the North American Free Trade Agreement (NAFTA).[34] One focus here, particularly in the EU context, has been on understanding *participatory* governance, and whether it enhances democratic decision-making and political clout of local decision-makers.[35] The specific events in Iceland after 2008—the protest movement that emerged, and the shift of governance realities in Iceland—suggest the need for a look at the interplay of governance and contentious politics.

The Icesave dispute: the role of governance and democratic engagement

We present here findings from just over 30 interviews with actors involved in the Icesave debates. Respondents were identified through a variant of snowball sampling. We began by contacting individuals with prominent web-presences in the dispute. At the close of the interview, each respondent was asked to identify four to five additional contacts from other organizations, both with similar political views and with contrary political views. Our goal was to build a sample representative of the range of views and interests.[36] The resultant sample included about equal numbers of elected politicians and social activists. This latter category included individuals who were active members of partisan and non-partisan organizations that took a position on the Icesave issue, and it also included people who were active in the dispute as individuals (for example, through blogging or academic and non-academic writing).

Interviews were conducted at three different times, but were transcribed immediately and analyzed using Dedoose, a qualitative software analytical package. During the interviews, we asked our respondents to talk generally about Icelandic politics as well as specifically about the impact and consequence of the Icesave dispute in terms of governance, citizenship participation, and democratic engagement.[37] Respondents are identified by randomly generated initials and by their location inside the political field: politician, political official, activist, or academic. The interviews were transcribed verbatim; language or grammatical errors in the respondent quotes were not corrected.

Icesave and the Icesave referenda as democratic achievement

As stated above, many respondents, from across the political spectrum, discussed Icesave in terms of its implications and effects on the exercise of democracy. For one respondent, the referendum exemplified democracy in action:

> One of the most significant first acts was the gathering of signatures for the President … and in general, the fact that we had our first national

> referendum like this was an extremely significant transformation and change. Because we managed, by figuring out weaknesses ... in our system ... we found a way for people to have their say about it.[38]

A similar sentiment was expressed by another respondent, who, in addition to highlighting the democratic intent of the anti-Icesave movement, juxtaposed these intentions with what were characterized as the non-democratic impulses of the government of the time: "We were running against the government [sic], as the government was trying its utmost to pass the legislation as quickly as possible to get it signed before we could have enough names on the petition."[39]

Respondents also discussed the referendum in terms designed to juxtapose it with the "politics of the past," which were, in contrast, characterized by cronyism, backroom deals, and lack of accountability. As one respondent recollected from the initial Icesave deal,

> [T]he first person I see is [an official from the negotiating committee].... I asked him: So, why are we in such a hurry? [in reaching an agreement to repay] ... he said, Well, I got so bored with it. I wanted to go on a summer holiday ... this is what [this official] on the single largest commitment of the state of Iceland, financially said to us in the middle of the crisis...[40]

In stark contrast to this picture of political cynicism, another respondent, also a member of parliament, characterized the Icesave movement and the call for a referendum as being dually motivated by moral and ethical commitment to democratic decision-making:

> Well I think people just realized that it was unfair and immoral to let the general public pay the debt that was brought on by bankers that were criminals. I mean it was ... people just took a moral stance and said, we're not going to pay this. This is not our debt and we're not going to pay it.[41]

Similar arguments around democratic accountability were used to explain why the President conceded to the anti-Icesave petition. For instance, one respondent, a political activist, suggested that the President's refusal to sign the Icesave bill into law came about because he recognized that there had appeared a significant gap between the parliamentary politics and the will and desires of the Icelandic population:

> I think people were really, really angry. He got emails. There was writing in the newspaper. A big percentage signed. They wanted him to do something, to say No, that we wanted to vote on this. It's because of this realization that you're living in a society where if you have no say in anything, then we have a tool in the constitution that gives people voice.... He decided to use that. This power that people have. To give it to the people.... If it was a power play on his part, it doesn't really matter. It doesn't concern me. It was the pressure of people who wanted to have a say.[42]

From this perspective, contentious politics around Icesave had the effect of awakening from a long slumber the dormant legislative powers of the President. This perspective underlines a view among many of our respondents that the dispute was about something much more fundamental than simply the legal and economic implications of the Icesave legislation. Rather, Icesave was a symbol of how deficits in democracy had brought Iceland to a place of crisis, and how the route out of crisis required thinking about how to revive principles of democratic decision-making and accountable governance.

Icesave and the Icesave referenda as political expediency

At the same time, and in stark contrast, some of our respondents suggested that positions around whether or not to repay the Icesave debt were motivated by concerns around political careerism and expediency rather than around democracy and political accountability. In this telling of the Icesave events, anti-Icesave positions were not only politically expedient, but they also allowed right-of-center parties an avenue into populist claims around nationalism and sovereignty. In turn, by infusing the Icesave debate with these claims, anti-Icesave political positions gave renewed credibility to demands to halt accession talks to the European Union:

> The political opposition [the Independence Party] got large guns to shoot because they could destroy the EU application as a part of the program. Even though the federation of employers and labor unions were in favor of negotiating with the EU … [anti-Icesave claims became] a policy with the only goal of trying to kill the government. They were not thinking about whether it was good or not to join the EU or get a contract on the table from which we could form an attitude towards. It was just a destructive measure. And they went on and on. It was an issue in which it was so easy to mislead the public [by saying] always, we will not pay the debts of corrupt bankers.[43]

In fact, according to one respondent, the political opposition purposefully and even cynically used the controversy over the Icesave bills in order to set the government up for failure: "the political opposition decided to make an issue [with Icesave]. They wanted to incite splits within the party."[44] From this perspective, the referendum gave the President a political reason to refuse to sign the Icesave bill into law: "and I know now that the president was glad to have gotten this as an excuse. Then he could do it [not sign] without being blamed by the politicians."[45]

Not surprisingly, respondents who emphasized these more cynical and political opportunistic aspects of the Icesave dispute also downplayed the democratic intents and purposes of the referendum. For example, as recounted by HG, an activist in a left-of-center social movement, the process was not only cynical but also corrupt:

> That [first] referendum was a phony referendum, in the sense that most who voted against the contract [Icesave deal] thought they were voting for not paying anything. That's the way it was talked about. Either Iceland pays or not, but not paying was never an option ... so what the President did was produce a national referendum on a phony basis, actually. Even if you tried to say that to people, there was no chance you could get them to listen to that. It was also framed in that the IMF and EU is forcing us to pay it ... now, we little people, we're not going to pay.... This was really a corrupt process. Corrupt on part of the political opposition in particular. Corrupt on the part of the President, because he did this in bad faith, and did nothing to explain the issues in a realistic way.[46]

In essence, from this perspective, both politicians as well as some activists cynically manipulated the debate. Specifically, rather than highlighting possible solutions, to "solve this gracefully," the Icesave debates obscured the real facts about the case, including that the final repayment deal could involve much smaller amounts of money than had been named in the initial bill, and, that there were likely going to be real political costs associated with not paying:

> It was a dirty process. The last contract we had that was made, as it was already clear by then, the assets of the fallen banks would cover 90% and now it seems like they will cover more than 100%. Iceland might land with interest costs, which is only a gentleman's way of solving it. We'd pay maybe half a % in GDP but it would be worth it as a PR issue to the world. We solved this gracefully. That's the way I wanted it to be done. Of course you can, with 20 or 30 billion krona, you can build another Harpa[47] but not much more than that.[48]

Similarly, the President's decision to exercise a veto was also framed by some respondents as having to do with political careerism, rather than a moral or ethical attachment to principles of democratic decision-making and accountability:

> Here's why I think our president said No the two times. My speculation is that it is first and foremost politics. Then it was pressure from the public. He didn't agree with the government and the contract they brought. The first deal was horrible. He didn't agree. Then there was this petition. 60,000 people signed and that's a lot for a nation of 300,000. We only have 200,000 voters. If 60,000 of those 200 sign a petition, then he had a moral obligation not to sign it. So there were two things: politics and public pressure.[49]

The complexity of this was well summed up by one of our respondents, a member of parliament who discussed the two sides of the Icesave issue as follows:

> In many ways you have to think of Icesave as a politicized issue. The way it's built up by the IP [the center-right Independence Party] the ideologues,

> as a nationalistic issue. Is this a grassroots movement or a propaganda ploy to make the government that took over after the crash look that bad ... for me this is the question. Where between these extremes lies the truth? [I think that] it is a grassroots movement with a lot of sincere people. They petitioned the President. Getting signatures. I do not doubt the sincerity of these people. Where are Icelanders now when it turns out that Icesave is being paid out by the funds of the collapsed banks? Probably the government doesn't have to pay a krona. The taxpayer doesn't have to pay anything. Maybe we were stuck in a future discussion for a very long time. It made the government look horrible and it hasn't recovered from the two referendums it lost. And of course it became the ticket to get the president re-elected. He was scorned, despised before the veto. These were his meal tickets into the next elections.[50]

In sum, from this perspective, Icesave was simultaneously the site of real and sincere politics around reforming democracy in Iceland as well as the vehicle for the cynical manipulation of public opinion in order to help bring about the collapse of the center-left coalition government that had been elected after the crash. Both of these interpretations of the Icesave dispute are relevant in order to understand the outcome of the Icesave protests and implications for governance structures.

Conclusion

The Icesave disputes showcase citizen political engagement in an era in which participation in general has been declining.[51] In this chapter, our focus has been on examining the relationship between protest politics—or contentious politics—and the governance structure, with an eye to understanding the outcomes of the anti-Icesave movement. We conclude by arguing that contentious politics around Icesave had political governance implications in, at least, two ways. First, there is the role of the Icesave referendum in delegitimizing the left-wing government coalition between 2009 and 2013. Our findings suggest that the Icesave dispute created a tipping point, at which the left-wing parties lost discursive control of their traditional ideological territory: the protection of public interest. Arguably, this loss of control was ceded in the immediate aftermath of the 2009 election, first to social movements and new political parties. But, as we have seen also in the 2013 election results, it was ultimately relinquished to the right-wing parties.

Indeed, during the 2013 election campaign, the traditional right-wing parties—the Independence Party and the Progressive Party—were able to use their opposition to Icesave to couch themselves as against a "corrupt" banking system and for the ordinary Icelandic citizen. This is clearly something of a paradox, although the extent to which this loss of discursive control was responsible for the election results in 2013 (which saw the return of a center-right government) is a matter for a separate research study. Nonetheless, it is clear that from 2009 onward, the Icesave dispute muddied traditional ideological and normative distinctions between the Left and the Right in Iceland. These blurred boundaries have been exploited to some effect by some of the newer political parties (such as the Best Party, which won the Reykjavík municipal elections in 2010) and the Pirate Party.

Second, the actions of the President, whether motivated by political expediency or concerns around government accountability, have also done much to alter governance and the political opportunity structure in Iceland. Indeed, respondents who emphasized the Icesave referendum as an issue of democratic accountability also pointed out that, by exercising his presidential veto twice in a row, Grímsson had changed perceptions of governance and the role of citizen participation in political decision-making.

At the same time, the results of the most recent election can be understood as an indication that there has been a rebalancing of some structural elements in Icelandic politics; the new constitution was shelved, and most of the small, political parties that were formed as alternatives to the dominant four have either dissolved or appear to be in abeyance, with the notable exception of the Pirate Party, which outperformed all the other parties in popular opinion polls for most of 2015.

One of the central lessons of our research is that social movement activism and governance contexts, whether local, national, or global, should be studied together. We return here to the question implied by the title of the chapter: in the end, what was the real cost of the Icesave debt? While many of our respondents did speak about and have a sense of the fiscal realities associated with paying the debt, it is also clear that they understood that Icesave was a political issue, with political costs. These costs could be borne in the global, supranational context, or they could be costs with local, national implications. Raising the value of resistance in local governance contexts, the anti-Icesave movement appeared to lower the political costs of not paying in the supranational governance context, for state and political actors.

We conclude by suggesting the need for future research, especially comparative, that explores the intersection between protest, national politics, and supranational governance in other contexts. In addition, there is a need for more empirical work examining the intersections between the Icesave dispute and the public debates around the Icelandic Constitutional Council.

Notes

1 André Broome, "Negotiating Crisis: The IMF and Disaster Capitalism in Small States," *The Round Table* 100, no. 413 (2011): 155–167; Jon Danielsson, "The First Casualty of the Crisis: Iceland," *VoxEU*, November 12, 2008; Már Guðmundsson, "The Icelandic Economy Two Years after the Crash," Speech by the Governor of the National Bank of Iceland at a meeting of the Icelandic-American Chamber of Commerce, New York, October 19, 2010; Thorvaldur Gylfason, "Iceland: How Could This Happen?" CESifo Working Paper, January, 2014; David O'Brien, "The Icelandic Banking Crisis: Causes, Effects & Implications," *Social & Political Review* (2010): 125; Robert H. Wade and Silla Sigurgeirsdottir, "Iceland's Rise, Fall, Stabilisation and Beyond," *Cambridge Journal of Economics* 36, no. 1 (2012), 127–144.

2 K. Amber Curtis et al., "I Save for Icesave: Self-Interest and Sovereign Debt Resettlement," Working Paper, Institute of Behavioral Science, University of Colorado at Boulder, May, 2012; Baldur Þórhallsson and Christian Rebhan, "Iceland's Economic Crash and Integration Takeoff: An End to European Union Scepticism?" *Scandinavian Political Studies* 34, no. 1 (2011): 53–73.

3 More recently, however, both the United Kingdom and the Netherlands have launched new cases against Iceland's depositor guarantor fund directly to recoup some of their losses. These new suits, which were filed in February 2014, amount to a total of 8.6 billion dollars, or about two-thirds of Iceland's GDP. At the time of the writing of this chapter, neither lawsuit had been heard by a court. Richard Milne, "Icesave Dispute Resurrected in Court," *Financial Times*, February 10, 2014, accessed March 19, 2015, www.ft.com/intl/cms/s/0/6e350fe6–927b-11e3–8018–00144feab7de.html?siteedition=uk#axzz3IhmQDBdC.

4 Joseph Stiglitz, "The Global Crisis, Social Protection and Jobs," *International Labour Review* 152, no. 1 (2013): 93–106; Joseph E. Stiglitz, *Freefall: America, Free Markets, and the Sinking of the World Economy* (New York: WW Norton & Company, 2010).

5 Tova Benski et al., "From the Streets and Squares to Social Movement Studies: What Have We Learned?" *Current Sociology* 61, no. 4 (2013): 541–561.

6 Curtis et al., "I Save for Icesave: Self-Interest and Sovereign Debt Resettlement"; Valur Ingimundarson, " 'A Crisis of Affluence': The Politics of an Economic Breakdown in Iceland," *Irish Studies in International Affairs* 21, no. 1 (2010): 57–69.

7 Þórhallsson and Rebhan, "Iceland's Economic Crash and Integration Takeoff: An End to European Union Scepticism?"

8 Kristín Loftsdóttir, "The Loss of Innocence: The Icelandic Financial Crisis and Colonial Past," *Anthropology Today* 26, no. 6 (2010): 9–13; Kristín Loftsdóttir, "Colonialism at the Margins: Politics of Difference in Europe as Seen through Two Icelandic Crises," *Identities* 19, no. 5 (2012): 597–615; Baldur Þorhallsson, "The Corporatist Model and its Value in Understanding Small European States in the Neo-Liberal World of the Twenty-First Century: The Case of Iceland," *European Consortium for Political Research* 9 (2010): 375–386; Þorhallsson and Rebhan, "Iceland's Economic Crash and Integration Takeoff."

9 Þorgerður Einarsdóttir and Gyða Margrét Pétursdóttir, "Greining á skýrslu rannsóknarnefndar Alþingis frá kynjafræðilegu sjónarhorni" [Analyses of the Special Investigation Commission Report from a Gendered Perspective], in Skýrsla þingmannanefndar til að fjalla um skýrslu rannsóknarnefndar Alþingis [Report of Parliament on the Report of the Special Investigation Commission] (Reykjavik: Icelandic Parliament, 2010), 209–67; Kristín Loftsdóttir, "Colonialism at the Margins;" Ann-Sofie Nielsen Gramaud, "The Vikings Are Coming! A Modern Icelandic Self-Image in the Light of the Economic Crisis," Nordeuropa Forum 1 (2010): 87–106.

10 Össur Skarphéðinsson, "Accession Is a Logical Next Step," *European Voice* July 22, 2009, accessed March 19, 2015, www.europeanvoice.com/article/accession-is-a-logical-next-step.

11 Broome, "Negotiating Crisis;" Arthur L. Centonze, "Iceland's Financial Meltdown," *Journal of Financial Education* 37, no 1/2 (2011): 131–166.

12 Centonze, "Iceland's Financial Meltdown."

13 Centonze, "Iceland's Financial Meltdown."

14 Curtis et al., "I Save for Icesave."

15 Hardarson and Kristinsson, "Iceland."

16 Loftsdóttir, "Colonialism at the Margins."

17 "The Icesave Dispute—In Defence of Iceland." Icenews, October 19 2009, www.icenews.is/2009/10/19/the-icesave-dispute-%E2%80%93-in-defence-of-iceland/#axzz42HNXuwS8, accessed March 7, 2016; Gylfason, Thorvaldur. *From Collapse to Constitution: The Case of Iceland.* Milan: Springer, 2013.

18 Finnur Magnusson, "Opening Pandora's Box: The Refusal of a President to Sign a Bill from Parliament," *Zeitschrift für öffentliches Recht* 65, no. 2 (2010): 203–224; Steven D. Roper, "Are All Semipresidential Regimes the Same? A Comparison of Premier-Presidential Regimes," *Comparative Politics* (2002): 253–272.
19 Landskjörstjórn, "Niðurstaða talningar við þjóðaratkvæðagreiðsluna 9. apríl 2011," accessed March 15, 2015, www.landskjor.is/landkjorstjorn/frettir-tilkynningar/nr/101.
20 Maria Elvira Mendez-Pinedo, "The Icesave Dispute in the Aftermath of the Icelandic Financial Crisis: Revisiting the Principles of State Liability, Prohibition of State Aid and Non-Discrimination in European Law," *European Journal of Risk Regulation* 3 (2011): 335.
21 Loftsdóttir, "Colonialism at the Margins"; Thorsteinn Thorgeirsson and Paul van den Noord, "The Icelandic Banking Collapse: Was the Optimal Policy Path Chosen?" (Central Bank of Iceland Working Paper No. 62. Central Bank of Iceland, Reykjavík, 2013).
22 Mendez-Pinedo, "State Liability, Prohibition of State Aid and Non-Discrimination in European Law," 335.
23 Mabel Berezin, "The Normalization of the Right in Post-Security Europe," in *Politics in the Age of Austerity*, eds. Armin Schäfer and Wolfgang Streeck (Cambridge, UK: Polity, 2013); Douglas R. Imig and Sidney G. Tarrow, *Contentious Europeans: Protest and Politics in an Emerging Polity* (Lanham: Rowman & Littlefield, 2001); Mario Pianta, "Democracy Lost: The Financial Crisis in Europe and the Role of Civil Society," *Journal of Civil Society* 9, no. 2 (2013): 148–161; Simon Usherwood and Nick Startin, "Euroscepticism as a Persistent Phenomenon," *JCMS: Journal of Common Market Studies* 51, no. 1 (2013): 1–16.
24 Charles Tilly, *Contention and Democracy in Europe, 1650–2000* (Cambridge: Cambridge University Press, 2004), 6.
25 Helga Leitner et al., "The Spatialities of Contentious Politics," *Transactions of the Institute of British Geographers* 33, no. 2 (2008): 157–172; Sidney Tarrow, "Social Movements in Contentious Politics: A Review Article," *The American Political Science Review* 90, no. 4 (1996): 874–883; Sidney Tarrow, *Power in Movement. Social Movement and Contemporary Politics* (Cambridge: Cambridge University Press, 2011); Sidney Tarrow, "Silence and Voice in the Study of Contentious Politics: Introduction," in *Silence and Voice in the Study of Contentious Politics*, eds. Ronald Aminzade et al. (Cambridge: Cambridge University Press, 2001): 1–13.
26 The current Prime Minister of Iceland, Sigmundur Davíð Gunnlaugsson, in fact, initially gained prominence through his participation in InDefense.
27 Edwin Amenta and Michael P Young, "Making an Impact: Conceptual and Methodological Implications of the Collective Goods Criterion," in *How Social Movements Matter*, eds. Doug McAdam, Marco Guigni, and Charles Tilly (Minneapolis: University of Minnesota Press, 1999), 22–41; Mary Bernstein, "Nothing Ventured, Nothing Gained? Conceptualizing Social Movement "Success" in the Lesbian and Gay Movement," *Sociological Perspectives* 46, no. 3 (2003): 353–379; Marco Giugni, "How Social Movements Matter: Past Research, Present Problems, Future Developments," in *How Social Movements Matter*, eds. Doug McAdam, Marco Guigni, and Charles Tilly (Minneapolis: University of Minnesota Press, 1999), 13–33; Suzanne Staggenborg, "Can Feminist Organizations Be Effective?" in *Feminist Organizations: Harvest of the New Women's Movement*, eds. Martin Ferree and Patricia Yancey Myra (Philadelphia: Temple University Press, 1995), 339–355.
28 Charles Tilly, *From Mobilization to Revolution* (New York: McGraw-Hill, 1978).
29 Herbert Kitschelt, "Political Opportunity Structures and Political Protest: Anti-Nuclear Movements in Four Democracies," *British Journal of Political Science* 16, no. 1 (1986): 57–85; Jung-eun Lee, "Insularity or Solidarity? The Impacts of Political Opportunity Structure and Social Movement Sector on Alliance Formation," *Mobilization: An International Quarterly* 16, no. 3 (2011): 303–324; Doug McAdam,

"Conceptual Origins, Current Problems, Future Directions," in *Comparative Perspectives on Social Movements: Political Opportunities, Mobilizing Structures, and Cultural Framings*, eds. Doug McAdam, John D. McCarthy, and Mayer N. Zald (Cambridge: Cambridge University Press, 1996), 23–40; *Political Process and the Development of Black Insurgency, 1930–1970* (Chicago: University of Chicago Press, 2010); David S. Meyer and Suzanne Staggenborg, "Movements, Countermovements, and the Structure of Political Opportunity," *American Journal of Sociology* 101, no. 6 (1996): 1628–1660.

30 McAdam, "Conceptual Origins, Current Problems, Future Directions," 25.

31 Broome, "Negotiating Crisis: The IMF and Disaster Capitalism in Small States"; Danielsson, "The First Casualty of the Crisis: Iceland."

32 Benski et al., "From the Streets and Squares to Social Movement Studies: What Have We Learned?"

33 Crispian Fuller and Mike Geddes, "Urban Governance under Neoliberalism: New Labour and the Restructuring of State-Space," *Antipode* 40, no. 2 (2008): 252–282; Mike Geddes, "Partnership and the Limits to Local Governance in England: Institutionalist Analysis and Neoliberalism," *International Journal of Urban and Regional Research* 30, no. 1 (2006): 76–97; Valeria Guarneros-Meza and Mike Geddes, "Local Governance and Participation under Neoliberalism: Comparative Perspectives," *International Journal of Urban and Regional Research* 34, no. 1 (2010): 115–129.

34 Emmanuel Brunet-Jailly, "NAFTA, Economic Integration, and the Canadian-American Security Regime in the Post-September 11, 2001 Era: Multi-Level Governance and Transparent Border?" *Journal of Borderlands Studies* 19, no. 1 (2004): 123–142; Bas Denters and Lawrence E. Rose, *Comparing Local Governance: Trends and Developments* (New York: Palgrave Macmillan, 2005).

35 Chris Aulich, "From Citizen Participation to Participatory Governance," *Commonwealth Journal of Local Governance* 2 (2009): 44–66; Michael Cuthill and John Fien, "Capacity Building: Facilitating Citizen Participation in Local Governance," *Australian Journal of Public Administration* 64, no. 4 (2005): 63–80; Brigitte Geissel, "Participatory Governance: Hope or Danger for Democracy? A Case Study of Local Agenda 21," *Local Government Studies* 35, no. 4 (2009): 401–414; Antonio Postigo, "Accounting for Outcomes in Participatory Urban Governance through State–Civil-Society Synergies," *Urban Studies* 48, no. 9 (2011): 1945–1967; Michael R. Woodford and Susan Preston, "Strengthening Citizen Participation in Public Policy-Making: A Canadian Perspective," *Parliamentary Affairs* 66, no. 2 (2013): 345–363.

36 Janice M. Morse, "The Significance of Saturation," *Qualitative Health Research* 5, no. 2 (1995): 147–149.

37 We note here that because Iceland is a small country, and many of our respondents are known to one another, anonymity and confidentiality are hard to achieve. We maximized the anonymity of our data by conducting the interviews in English, so that idiosyncratic phrasings and other characteristic types of speaking would not be apparent in the interviews.

38 Interview with [MP] conducted by Helga Kristin Hallgrimsdottir and Emmanuel Brunet-Jailly, recorded and transcribed December, 2012.

39 Interview with [NH] conducted by Helga Kristin Hallgrimsdottir and Emmanuel Brunet-Jailly, recorded and transcribed August, 2012.

40 Interview with [MP] conducted by Helga Kristin Hallgrimsdottir and Emmanuel Brunet-Jailly, recorded and transcribed December, 2012.

41 Interview with [RT] conducted by Helga Kristin Hallgrimsdottir and Emmanuel Brunet-Jailly, recorded and transcribed July, 2013.

42 Interview with [SA] conducted by Helga Kristin Hallgrimsdottir and Emmanuel Brunet-Jailly, recorded and transcribed December, 2012.

43 Interview with [RW] conducted by Helga Hallgrimsdottir, recorded and transcribed July, 2013.

44 Interview with [LT] conducted by Helga Kristin Hallgrimsdottir and Emmanuel Brunet-Jailly, recorded and transcribed July, 2013.
45 Interview with [KM] conducted by Helga Kristin Hallgrimsdottir, recorded and transcribed August, 2012.
46 Interview with [HG] conducted by Emmanuel Brunet-Jailly, recorded and transcribed July, 2013.
47 Harpa is a performance and conference center in downtown Reykjavík. Construction on Harpa commenced in January 2007 but was halted in the immediate aftermath of the financial crisis. Construction resumed once the government decided to fully fund the building (for a total cost of 164 million euros, according to publicly available estimates).
48 Interview with [HG] conducted by Emmanuel Brunet-Jailly, recorded and transcribed July, 2013.
49 Interview with [PL] conducted by Emmanuel Brunet-Jailly and Helga Hallgrimsdottir, recorded and transcribed August, 2012.
50 Interview with [FR] conducted by Helga Hallgrimsdottir and Emmanuel Brunet-Jailly in Reykjavík, August, 2012.
51 Guarneros-Meza and Geddes, "Local Governance and Participation under Neoliberalism"; Peter Somerville, "Democracy and Participation," *Policy & Politics* 39, no. 3 (2011); Andrea Cornwall et al., "States of Citizenship: Contexts and Cultures of Public Engagement and Citizen Action," IDS Working Papers No. 363 (2011); Ruth Lister, "Inclusive Citizenship: Realizing the Potential 1," *Citizenship Studies* 11, no. 1 (2007): 49–61.

Bibliography

Amenta, Edwin and Michael P. Young. "Making an Impact: Conceptual and Methodological Implications of the Collective Goods Criterion." In *How Social Movements Matter*, edited by Doug McAdam, Marco Guigni, and Charles Tilly, 22–41. Minneapolis: University of Minnesota Press, 1999.

Arter, David. " 'Big Bang' elections and Party System Change in Scandinavia: Farewell to the 'Enduring Party System'?" *Parliamentary Affairs* 65, no. 4 (2012): 822–844.

Aulich, Chris. "From Citizen Participation to Participatory Governance." *Commonwealth Journal of Local Governance* 2 (2009): 44–66.

Benski, Tova, Lauren Langman, Ignacia Perugorrí, and Benjamín Tejerina. "From the Streets and Squares to Social Movement Studies: What Have We Learned?" *Current Sociology* 61, no. 4 (2013): 541–561.

Berezin, Mabel. "The Normalization of the Right in Post-Security Europe." In *Politics in the Age of Austerity*, edited by Wolfgang Streeck and Armin Schäfer, 239–261. Cambridge: Polity, 2013.

Bernstein, Mary. "Nothing Ventured, Nothing Gained? Conceptualizing Social Movement "Success" in the Lesbian and Gay Movement." *Sociological Perspectives* 46, no. 3 (2003): 353–379.

Broome, André. "Negotiating Crisis: The IMF and Disaster Capitalism in Small States." *The Round Table* 100, no. 413 (2011): 155–167.

Brunet-Jailly, Emmanuel. "NAFTA, Economic Integration, and the Canadian-American Security Regime in the Post-September 11, 2001 Era: Multi-Level Governance and Transparent Border?" *Journal of Borderlands Studies* 19, no. 1 (2004): 123–142.

Centonze, Arthur L. "Iceland's Financial Meltdown." *Journal of Financial Education* 37, no. 1/2 (2011): 131–166.

Cornwall, Andrea, Steven Robins, and Bettina Von Lieres. "States of Citizenship: Contexts and Cultures of Public Engagement and Citizen Action." IDS Working Papers, no. 363 (2011): 1–32.
Curtis, K. Amber, Joseph Jupille, and David A Leblang. "I Save for Icesave: Self-Interest and Sovereign Debt Resettlement." Working Paper, Institute of Behavioral Science, University of Colorado at Boulder, May, 2012.
Cuthill, Michael and John Fien. "Capacity Building: Facilitating Citizen Participation in Local Governance." *Australian Journal of Public Administration* 64, no. 4 (2005): 63–80.
Danielsson, Jon. "The First Casualty of the Crisis: Iceland." *VoxEU*, November 12, 2008.
Denters, Bas and Lawrence E. Rose. *Comparing Local Governance: Trends and Developments*. New York: Palgrave Macmillan, 2005.
Einarsdóttir, Þorgerður and Gyða Margrét Pétursdóttir. "Greining á skýrslu rannsóknarnefndar Alþingis frá kynjafræðilegu sjónarhorni" [Analyses of the Special Investigation Commission Report from a Gendered Perspective]. In *Skýrsla þingmannanefndar til að fjalla um skýrslu rannsóknarnefndar Alþingis*, 209–267. Reykjavík: Icelandic Parliament, 2010.
Fuller, Crispian and Mike Geddes. "Urban Governance under Neoliberalism: New Labour and the Restructuring of State-Space." *Antipode* 40, no. 2 (2008): 252–282.
Geddes, Mike. "Partnership and the Limits to Local Governance in England: Institutionalist Analysis and Neoliberalism." *International Journal of Urban and Regional Research* 30, no. 1 (2006): 76–97.
Geissel, Brigitte. "Participatory Governance: Hope or Danger for Democracy? A Case Study of Local Agenda 21." *Local Government Studies* 35, no. 4 (2009): 401–414.
Giugni, Marco. "How Social Movements Matter: Past Research, Present Problems, Future Developments." In *How Social Movements Matter*, edited by Doug McAdam, Marco Guigni, and Charles Tilly, 13–33. Minneapolis: University of Minnesota Press, 1999.
Guarneros-Meza, Valeria and Mike Geddes. "Local Governance and Participation under Neoliberalism: Comparative Perspectives." *International Journal of Urban and Regional Research* 34, no. 1 (2010): 115–129.
Guðmundsson, Már. "The Icelandic Economy Two Years after the Crash." Speech by the Governor of the National Bank of Iceland at a meeting of the Icelandic-American Chamber of Commerce, New York, October 19, 2010.
Gylfason, Thorvaldur. "Iceland: How Could This Happen?" CESifo Working Paper, January, 2014.
Hardarson, Ólafur Th. and Gunnar Helgi Kristinsson. "Iceland." *European Journal of Political Research* 49, no. 7–8 (2010): 1009–1016.
"The Icesave Dispute—In Defence of Iceland." Icenews, October 19, 2009, www.icenews.is/2009/10/19/the-icesave-dispute-%E2%80%93-in-defence-of-iceland/#axzz42HNXuwS8, accessed March 7, 2016.
Imig, Douglas R. and Sidney G. Tarrow. *Contentious Europeans: Protest and Politics in an Emerging Polity*. Lanham: Rowman & Littlefield, 2001.
Ingimundarson, Valur. "'A Crisis of Affluence': The Politics of an Economic Breakdown in Iceland." *Irish Studies in International Affairs* 21, no. 1 (2010): 57–69.
Johnson, Simon and Robert Robertson, "UK, Dutch File $4.8 Billion Icesave Debt Claim against Iceland Fund." *Reuters*, February 10, 2014.
Kitschelt, Herbert. "Political Opportunity Structures and Political Protest: Anti-Nuclear Movements in Four Democracies." *British Journal of Political Science* 16, no. 1 (1986): 57–85.

Landskjörstjórn. "Niðurstaða talningar við þjóðaratkvæðagreiðsluna 9. apríl 2011." Accessed March 15, 2015. www.landskjor.is/landkjorstjorn/frettir-tilkynningar/nr/101.

Lee, Jung-eun. "Insularity or Solidarity? The Impacts of Political Opportunity Structure and Social Movement Sector on Alliance Formation." *Mobilization: An International Quarterly* 16, no. 3 (2011): 303–324.

Leitner, Helga, Eric Sheppard and Kristin M. Sziarto. "The Spatialities of Contentious Politics." *Transactions of the Institute of British Geographers* 33, no. 2 (2008): 157–172.

Lister, Ruth. "Inclusive Citizenship: Realizing the Potential." *Citizenship Studies* 11, no. 1 (2007): 49–61.

Loftsdóttir, Kristín. "Colonialism at the Margins: Politics of Difference in Europe as Seen through Two Icelandic Crises." *Identities* 19, no. 5 (2012): 597–615.

Loftsdóttir, Kristín. "The Loss of Innocence: The Icelandic Financial Crisis and Colonial Past." *Anthropology Today* 26, no. 6 (2010): 9–13.

McAdam, Doug. "Conceptual Origins, Current Problems, Future Directions." In *Comparative Perspectives on Social Movements: Political Opportunities, Mobilizing Structures, and Cultural Framings*, edited by Doug McAdam, John D. McCarthy, and Mayer N. Zald, 23–40. Cambridge: Cambridge University Press, 1996.

McAdam, Doug. *Political Process and the Development of Black Insurgency, 1930–1970.* University of Chicago Press, 2010.

Magnusson, Finnur. "Opening Pandora's Box: The Refusal of a President to Sign a Bill from Parliament." *Zeitschrift für öffentliches Recht* 65, no. 2 (2010): 203–224.

Mendez-Pinedo, Maria Elvira. "The Icesave Dispute in the Aftermath of the Icelandic Financial Crisis: Revisiting the Principles of State Liability, Prohibition of State Aid and Non-Discrimination in European Law." *European Journal of Risk Regulation* 3 (2011): 330–356.

Meyer, David S. and Suzanne Staggenborg. "Movements, Countermovements, and the Structure of Political Opportunity." *American Journal of Sociology* 101, no. 6 (1996): 1628–1660.

Morse, Janice M. "The Significance of Saturation." *Qualitative Health Research* 5, no. 2 (1995): 147–149.

Nielsen Gramaud, Ann-Sofie. "The Vikings Are Coming! A Modern Icelandic Self-Image in the Light of the Economic Crisis." *Nordeuropa Forum* 1 (2010): 87–106.

O'Brien, David. "The Icelandic Banking Crisis: Causes, Effects & Implications." *Social & Political Review* (2010): 100–125.

Pianta, Mario. "Democracy Lost: The Financial Crisis in Europe and the Role of Civil Society." *Journal of Civil Society* 9, no. 2 (2013): 148–161.

Postigo, Antonio. "Accounting for Outcomes in Participatory Urban Governance through State–Civil-Society Synergies." *Urban Studies* 48, no. 9 (2011): 1945–1967.

Roper, Steven D. "Are All Semipresidential Regimes the Same? A Comparison of Premier-Presidential Regimes." *Comparative Politics* 34, no. 3 (2002): 253–272.

Schonlau, Matthias and Elisabeth Liebau. "Respondent-Driven Sampling." *Stata Journal* 12, no. 1 (2012): 72–93.

Skarphéðinsson, Össur. "Accession Is a Logical Next Step." *European Voice*, July 22, 2009. Accessed March 15, 2015. www.europeanvoice.com/article/accession-is-a-logical-next-step.

Somerville, Peter. "Democracy and Participation." *Policy & Politics* 39, no. 3 (2011): 417–437.

Staggenborg, Suzanne. "Can Feminist Organizations Be Effective?" In *Feminist Organizations: Harvest of the New Women's Movement*, edited by Martin Ferree and Patricia Yancey Myra, 339–355. Philadelphia: Temple University Press, 1995.

Stiglitz, Joseph. "The Global Crisis, Social Protection and Jobs." *International Labour Review* 152, no. 1 (2013): 93–106.

Stiglitz, Joseph E. *Freefall: America, Free Markets, and the Sinking of the World Economy*. New York: WW Norton & Company, 2010.

Tarrow, Sidney. "Social Movements in Contentious Politics: A Review Article." *The American Political Science Review* 90, no. 4 (1996): 874–883.

Tarrow, Sidney. "Silence and Voice in the Study of Contentious Politics: Introduction." In *Silence and Voice in the Study of Contentious Politics*, edited by Ronald Aminzade et al., 1–13. Cambridge: Cambridge University Press, 2001.

Tarrow, Sidney. *Power in Movement. Social Movement and Contemporary Politics*. Cambridge: Cambridge University Press, 2011.

Thorgeirsson, Thorsteinn and Paul van den Noord. "The Icelandic Banking Collapse: Was the Optimal Policy Path Chosen?" Central Bank of Iceland Working Paper No. 62. Reykjavík: Central Bank of Iceland, 2013.

Tilly, Charles. *From Mobilization to Revolution*. New York: McGraw-Hill, 1978.

Tilly, Charles. *Contention and Democracy in Europe, 1650–2000*. Cambridge: Cambridge University Press, 2004.

Usherwood, Simon and Nick Startin. "Euroscepticism as a Persistent Phenomenon." *JCMS: Journal of Common Market Studies* 51, no. 1 (2013): 1–16.

Wade, Robert H. and Silla Sigurgeirsdottir. "Iceland's Rise, Fall, Stabilisation and Beyond." *Cambridge Journal of Economics* 36, no. 1 (2012): 127–144.

Woodford, Michael R. and Susan Preston. "Strengthening Citizen Participation in Public Policy-Making: A Canadian Perspective." *Parliamentary Affairs* 66, no. 2 (2013): 345–363.

Þórhallsson, Baldur. "The Corporatist Model and Its Value in Understanding Small European States in the Neo-Liberal Century. The Case of Iceland." *European Consortium for Political Research* 9 (2010): 375–386.

Þórhallsson, Baldur and Christian Rebhan. "Iceland's Economic Crash and Integration Takeoff: An End to European Union Scepticism?" *Scandinavian Political Studies* 34, no. 1 (2011): 53–73.

6 Democratic practices, governance, and the financial crash

Vilhjálmur Árnason

In this chapter, I discuss democratic practices in the period of transition in Iceland during the years before and after the financial collapse. I draw on the analyses of the Special Investigation Commission of the Icelandic Parliament (SIC) and the Working Group on Ethics (WGE), which were charged with the task of explaining the causes of the crash. In the first sections, I focus on the explanations in the reports that concern democratic practices in a broad sense—in politics, administration, and the media—and how they failed to resist, and may even have facilitated, the course of events. Subsequently, I describe and reflect, critically, on democratic experiments in Iceland after the collapse, and argue that they have not contributed to the kind of improvements envisioned by the SIC and the WGE. I argue that the flaws of democratic practices both before and after the crisis are rooted in a narrow understanding of democracy, as vote-centric aggregation of preferences, regardless of whether they have been fleshed out in the spirit of liberal or republican politics.

Investigations of the financial collapse

The Icelandic financial crisis has been thoroughly investigated. In the wake of the collapse of the three leading Icelandic banks in October 2008, the Icelandic Parliament passed a law regarding a Special Investigation Commission, which was given the task of finding out the truth about the events that led to the financial collapse and explaining its causes. The SIC consisted of three members. One was a legal scholar who was a member of the Supreme Court and former Professor of Law at the University of Iceland, and the second was another lawyer who had served as the Ombudsman of *Althingi*, the Icelandic Parliament. The third member was an economist who had been an assistant professor at Yale University. SIC delivered an extensive report in nine volumes to parliament on April 12, 2010, explaining the main causes of the collapse.[1]

The law on the SIC contains an article on the WGE, which states that in "relation to the work of the special investigation commission, there shall be an inquiry of whether the collapse of the banks and related financial setbacks can to some extent be explained by morality and work practices."[2] It is, furthermore, stipulated that the members should be educated in philosophy, history, sociology, political science, media studies, or other comparable disciplines. The members of the WGE were appointed by the governing committee of Parliament, and it consisted of two philosophers and a historian.[3] The WGE delivered its report to Parliament in April 2010, as Volume 8 of the final report of the SIC.[4] In the letter of ordinance from the Speaker of Parliament to the members of the WGE in January 2009, it was stated that the inquiry was not to be limited to morality and work practices in the financial sector; other sectors of society could come under scrutiny as well. In light of this, the WGE decided to assess morality and work practices in three main sectors or social spheres: the business and financial sector, the administrative and political sector, and the social and cultural sector. Although the main focus of the SIC's report was on the financial sphere, the events were inevitably related to policies and decisions made within the political and administrative arenas. The WGE set the explanations of the SIC in an even wider context by relating these events and decisions to political ideology, prevailing social values, and a lack of resistance in the public sphere to the developments that led to the collapse.[5]

The main conclusions of both the SIC and the WGE emphasized the intricate relations between the collapse of the banks and political practices in Iceland. The SIC puts this in a nutshell in the following passage:

> [W]hen the size of the financial system of a country is, for instance, threefold its gross domestic product, the competent authorities of the country have, in general, the potential to set rules for the financial system to comply with and to ensure compliance with such rules. However, when the size of the financial system of a country is nine times its gross domestic product the roles are reversed. This was the case in Iceland. It appears that both the parliament and the government lacked both the power and the courage to set reasonable limits to the financial system. All the energy seems to have been directed at keeping the financial system going.[6]

This implies two key aspects that relate to the role of politics in the course of events. On the one hand, it refers to the question of how the financial system came to be so large in the first place and, on the other hand, why the banks were not downsized when signals of danger started to show. Discussion of these two aspects leads to the core of Icelandic political practices and shows clearly that such complicated events as the financial collapse cannot be explained without tracing various interrelated threads. Methodological and moral individualism, which is prevalent in the mundane and often political discourse about the causes of the financial collapse, is an inadequate and distorting way to deal with complex social phenomena.[7] This was explicitly recognized by the WGE, which summarized its main conclusion in this way: "Although several individuals, in the financial, administrative, political and the public sphere, showed negligence and sometimes reprehensible action, the most important lessons to draw from these events are about weak social structures, political culture and public institutions."[8]

In what follows, I will show how this claim is substantiated by an analysis of events, decisions, and policies in the administrative and political sector, as well as of working practices in the media. These are chosen because they exemplify democratic practices, governance, and institutional morality in Iceland in the advent of the financial collapse.

Policies of regulation

Regulatory or supervising agencies, needless to say, play an important role in a democratic society by ensuring that financial institutions work within the boundaries of the law and do not pose a threat to economic stability. They are to serve as watchdogs of the public interest by setting firm and fair limits to the activities of private financial companies and informing the authorities of the state of affairs. A precondition for being able to fulfill these functions is that these institutions have professional competence, integrity, and independence. The two main regulatory agencies of the financial sector in Iceland, the Financial Supervisory Authority (FME) and the Central Bank of Iceland (CBI), received rather harsh criticism in the SIC and WGE reports for failing to carry out their supervisory duties properly. The FME was mainly criticized for a lack of both professional and technical expertise, as well as for wrong prioritization in its work. As a consequence, the agency was unable to have the necessary overview of the standing, activities, and complex ownership of the financial institutions. The FME was also criticized for a lack of firmness and assertiveness in its interaction with financial companies.[9] "The Authority did not sufficiently ensure that formal procedures were followed in cases where it had been discovered that regulated entities did not comply with the laws and regulations applicable to their operations."[10]

In the WGE report, it is shown how the policy of trusting the directors of financial companies, regarding them as co-operators in the task of maintaining good working practices in the financial sector, characterized the way in which FME carried out its supervising duties. This is striking, not least in light of the fact that the financial investment culture in Iceland had not developed internal structures and practices that could have provided reasons for this trusting approach. On the contrary, there were several indicators that the new culture within the banks emphasized image-making and entertainment at the cost of reliable banking policies and compliance. At one time in Glitnir Bank, for example, there was one compliance officer, while 13 were employed in the events and entertainment department.[11] Compliance officers who were interviewed by WGE complained that it had been made most difficult for them to fulfill their function; they were bombarded with minor errands that made them unable to grasp the whole picture. "This was like rowing a small boat against an oil tanker," one said, claiming a total lack of respect for good business practices within the bank.[12] The compliance officers were critical of both the directors of the banks and the FME for not supporting them in their attempt to combat poor banking practices.

One explanation for the FME's trusting approach—and its lack of assertiveness toward financial companies—is the informal style of interaction that is practiced in a small society where people tend to know each other and to be on speaking terms. This acquaintance and informality factor played a major role in the interaction between the chairman of the CBI Board of Governors and the political authorities. The chairman, Davíð Oddsson, was Prime Minister of Iceland for 13 years, from 1991 to 2004, the years of the financial liberalization of the Icelandic economy and privatization of the banks. As was customary at the time, he was guaranteed a good position in the public sector once he decided to leave formal politics. During his time as chairman of the Board of Governors of the CBI, 2005–2009, the government ministers were former political allies and opponents, which radically affected the interaction between the CBI and the government. This both created mutual mistrust and affected the way in which information from CBI was understood. The governors of the CBI heeded serious warning signals from their European colleagues,[13] but did not manage to convey them clearly to Icelandic politicians. Instead of official documents being provided, informal meetings were held, where sometimes alarming information was passed on, without leading to any firm response. Furthermore, the ministers did not keep any minutes from these informal meetings. These working practices prevented transparency and accountability and were incompatible with democratic governance.[14]

The Icelandic supervisory agencies can also be criticized for the narrow legalistic thinking in their approach.[15] There are several striking examples of this in the SIC Report. One is when Icelandic bankers and supervisors met with the European Central Bank governor, Jean-Claude Trichet, who had voiced serious concerns about the number of loans going to the Icelandic banks, which, in turn, pledged "abnormal, artificial" bonds as collateral: "FME director Jónsson commented that although he didn't know the rules of the ECB, he would assume that the banks were operating 'within the formal rules of the ECB.'"[16] Another example is when British and Dutch authorities resisted the plans of the Icelandic bank, Landsbanki, to set up Icesave accounts in the United Kingdom and the Netherlands. They were worried that a small country like Iceland would have weak securities, but the spokesmen of FME argued that it was illegal to restrict the operation of the banks within the European Economic Area. In a report to the SIC, the director said that the Dutch had been voicing "macro-economic concerns," while the FME had made sure that the bank was not breaking any laws.[17]

The restrictive formal legalism demonstrated by these examples is relevant because it is one way in which supervisory agencies tend to serve, inadvertently perhaps, the special interests of financial companies at the cost of the public interest. This is especially true in a culture like the one that developed within the Icelandic banks, where legal expertise was used primarily to find loopholes in the law and to go as far as possible regardless of the moral objectives that were the rationale for the legal framework in the first place. When lawyers and other experts work uncritically in the service of the aims of directors of the banks, the consequence is a moral void, lacking professional resistance to reckless behavior.

This reduction of professionalism to technical skill facilitated a narrow legalistic approach and fed into a mentality of like-mindedness that was preached by the young bankers. This mentality was behind the policy of weeding out experienced bankers, bred in a more traditional institutional atmosphere of precaution, and replacing them with younger people who would adapt to the new business model of risk and continuous growth. As one of the directors of Kaupthing said, "It is very hard to change a culture without changing employees."[18]

Even though all these factors relating the institutional mentality and lack of professional morality within the financial companies are significant, they must not be overrated. A major reason why the supervisory practices were not stronger is that political authorities did not emphasize this aspect sufficiently to enable the agencies to keep up with the growth of the banks. This was no coincidence, for it reflected a deliberate policy to enable the financial companies to grow. At the same time, the message to the supervisory agencies was that regulation should be efficient, yet not burdensome. The ideology behind this policy was worded quite explicitly by the Icelandic Chamber of Commerce, which served like a think tank for the government during this period.[19]

This message shows the heart of the political ideology of liberalization, which was behind the growth of the banks. Effectiveness was the euphemistic term for a laissez-faire policy agenda, aiming at deregulation of the economic sector generally, to increase its competiveness and give the financial entrepreneurs more leeway for their actions. Liberty in this context is understood primarily in a negative sense of having space where one is free from interference or external control.[20] However, ideas about how the actors were to gain moral autonomy within that space, by cultivating a responsible culture of self-regulation, are strikingly absent, even though they form the background for sensible ideas of self-regulation in the first place.

Political practices

The period that is sometimes referred to as the "Icelandic financial adventure" started in the 1990s with the financial liberalization of the public sector. Part of this was the privatization of the Icelandic banks, which was completed in 2003. This process started out with the goals of having both well-distributed ownership and a controlling shareholder, preferably a foreign one with extensive knowledge and experience of operating financial services.[21] The outcome, however, was quite different, "laden with political favoritism and back-room deals,"[22] and the banks were sold to Icelandic financial investors with little experience of operating financial services. The three banks grew rapidly during their first three years due to easy access to loans on the international markets. They received good ratings by international companies, and benefited both from the good standing of the Icelandic treasury and from the favorable reputation of Nordic banks. The young bankers seemed to be doing exceedingly well, and they soon enjoyed the status of national heroes in Iceland. Financial groups formed around the three banks owned various kinds of services, such as in the field of transportation and media. Under the banner of corporate social responsibility,[23] they contributed, generously, to culture, charity, and sports, making the directors of the financial companies appear as major public benefactors.

This strong social and economic standing of the banks forms an important background for explanations of the reactions of Icelandic authorities when difficulties arose in 2006. When Fitch Ratings, Merrill Lynch, and Danske Bank all issued negative outlooks for the Icelandic banks in February and March 2006, leading Icelandic politicians and even regulators reacted angrily, defending the banks against unfair foreign criticism. Major themes in the defense were that the criticism was rooted primarily in envy, because of the success of the Icelandic bankers, and in ignorance of why they were so clever. In Iceland, the matter was analyzed primarily as a problem of perception or image. Instead of looking into the standing of the banks, representatives of the government sided with the bankers in an effort to convince the world that there was no need to worry. Moreover, the government officially endorsed a report about financial stability in Iceland, which was commissioned by the Icelandic Chamber of Commerce as a response to the Geyser report of Danske Bank.[24]

The Prime Minister, Geir Haarde, attended a meeting in May 2006 in New York with the main author of the report, Frederick S. Mishkin, Professor of Economics at the Columbia University Business School, to reassure the financial world about the solid standing of the Icelandic banks. A similar message was given at a press conference in Copenhagen in March 2008,[25] where the Icelandic Prime Minister, the Minister for Foreign Affairs, Ingibjörg Sólrún Gísladóttir, and the chairman of Kaupthing Bank, Sigurður Einarsson, were joined by Richard Portes, Professor of Economics at London Business School, who co-authored another commissioned report about the Icelandic banks.[26]

These reactions demonstrate the solidarity among Icelandic authorities with the banks. Politicians, academics, and businessmen joined hands in defending the image of the banks to the bitter end. The chief financial analyst at Danske Bank, Lars Christensen, one of the authors of the Geyser report, described it as follows:

> [T]he main problem in Iceland was the pervasive collusion: politicians, public officials and regulators were all in the same team. Those who were supposed to protect the economy and the public interests were the cheerleaders of the expansionists in the banks. [...] There was no independent voice. In response to criticism like the Geyser report, everyone united as "we" against "them," as if there was a conspiracy to damage the Icelandic banks.[27]

A serious consequence of this active involvement of government officials in the affairs of the private banks was that it intertwined the credibility of the Icelandic banks with that of the state and, thus, implicated the Icelandic public even more.

A persistent criticism of Icelandic governance in the SIC Report concerns the lack of professional practices in relation to policy and decision-making. At no stage in the period of the expansion and eventual downfall of the banks was there a systematic collection and analysis of information about the financial system. Key information such as ownership of the banks, their debtors and cross-lending relations between the banks, or the size of the possible financial commitments that might fall on the state if things went bad, was not even available to a special consultation group of high-ranking government officials that was set up with the aim of taking precautionary measures in the event of a possible financial crisis.[28] The crucial decision of the state to take over Glitnir Bank at the end of September 2008 was made without a careful assessment of the effects it might have on the other banks and the Icelandic financial system.[29]

These are only two of several examples in the SIC Report of poor documentation and lack of professional working practices to underpin planning and decision-making. Here, again, we encounter a characteristic of the acquaintance and informality factor pervasive in a small society where the soil was fertile for naïve trust and solidarity. This apparent state of innocence, however, was also motivated by financial interests and close bonds between the political and financial sectors. The WGE mapped the monetary contributions received by individual politicians and political parties from the main financial companies in Iceland in the years 2006 and 2007. It turned out that all political organizations in Iceland, with the exception of the Left-Green Party, had received substantial amounts from the financial companies, mostly in order to finance primaries of individual politicians. It has been calculated that while the US financial industry donated 180 million dollars to political campaigns in 2010, or 60 cents per person, the roughly comparable Icelandic figure was eight dollars per person in 2006, or 14 times as much.[30] Moreover, 10 members of parliament were in considerable debt to the banks, to an average of $12 million.

For decades, until 2007, Icelandic politicians, especially members of the largest party, the center-right Independence Party, which has had close relations to business and industry, have resisted regulation of financial donations to politicians. In spite of this, Iceland has always scored very high on international monitoring of corruption, mainly because the key measure is bribery of public officials. Such corruption hardly exists in Iceland, but the relationship between the financial and political sectors has always been close and has affected political practices. It has been argued that the symbiosis of politics and business was the main cause for the weak business culture that brought down the Icelandic economy.[31] This systemic type of corruption is not measured by the main monitoring agencies. One of the major aims of the privatization of the banks was to reduce political interference in the financial sector, but as a consequence, it became dominant in all sectors of society. There were, therefore, strong reasons for undertaking a study of the relationship between power and democracy in Iceland, as had been done in the other Nordic countries.[32] But a proposal in Parliament in 2004 to launch such a study, focusing on how power was being transferred from politics to private financial blocks in Iceland, did not get sufficient political support.

The media and the public sphere

A most interesting aspect of the relationship between power and politics in Iceland is the way in which the workings of power have changed from the vertical interference of politicians toward a more subtle horizontal influence of financial forces.[33] Clear examples of this surfaced in the WGE investigation of the media in the advent of the financial crisis. Apart from the Icelandic National Broadcasting Service, RÚV television and radio, all the major media services in Iceland were owned and operated by the financial groups that owned the three large banks. However, the social changes also affected the practices of RÚV, regardless of state ownership. The director of RÚV testified in the WGE hearings that the reporters there had become quite skillful in dealing with the declining power of politicians, but that they did not know how to deal with the new, more friendly and inviting type of power that came with the financial regime:

> [T]his big change in society regarding increased power of the business sector may have escaped us and we had no proper experts in analyzing the business life. And those who became close to being knowledgeable were simply bought out by the banks.[34]

Once they started working for the banks, professional reporters were transformed into cunning information technicians whose means uncritically served the ends of the employers—often at the cost of serving the public interests in a democratic society.[35]

A pervasive theme relating to manifestations of horizontal power in the stories of media directors for the WGE was the one of self-censorship. According to them, owners of the media rarely threatened reporters or directly interfered with their ways of working. But the fact of being in a small country, where there are few media, owned by even fewer corporations, had the effect that people were afraid of being stigmatized as difficult or even critical. They did not want to resist the tide of events in society because then they might lose their jobs. An editor of one of the two leading newspapers put this succinctly:

> A few corporations dominated everything and if people […] came into opposition with one or two men even, they would literally not have any job opportunities. I think that this is at least part of the explanation, that people were afraid of losing their very subsistence.[36]

This mentality may also have had an effect on the willingness of citizens to voice their criticism in the public sphere. Media reporters were critical of how unwilling specialists at the universities had been to comment on the financial practices during this time. The media in a small society are unusually dependent on the contribution of specialists for interpretation of complex matters and battling misleading image-making and spin produced by powerful players in society. The Icelandic media proved unable to provide this resistance in the years preceding the financial crisis.

A special report, commissioned by WGE, on the media coverage of the banks and financial companies from 2006 to 2008 concluded that this reporting had generally framed issues in a favorable way for the companies.[37] Independent analysis was lacking, and reporting was largely based on material prepared by the banks' PR staff. The argument that it was the role of professional media in a democratic society to resist the forces, in both the private and the public sphere, that distort information and misuse power to undermine open discussion has been challenged by a few spokesmen of the Icelandic media. They argued that if the media did anything other than mirror what was happening in society each time, media reporters would be participating in politics.[38] The media should, therefore, not be criticized for reflecting the dominant mentality and atmosphere during these years. The aforementioned acquaintance and informality factor prevailing in Icelandic society also colored the interaction between financial reporters and the bankers. Some media directors claimed in the WGE hearings that they had been worried about the friendliness that had characterized this relationship. The blurring of the demarcations between news and entertainment in the media also contributed to this factor.

This was part of the "overall national pride in the success of the banks," as the former director general of the Finnish Financial Supervision Authority wrote in a report for the Prime Minister's Office after the financial collapse. He correctly pointed out that the "nation, up to its highest echelons, supported and admired the banks."[39] The media contributed to—and nourished—this mentality, and interviews with the bankers and stories about their luxurious lifestyle were popular in the media. The WGE commissioned a report from a social psychologist about how both general group dynamics and characteristics of a small nation contributed to the course of events that led to the financial collapse.[40] The report shows how the public had strong incentives to believe the economy was going well and the financial sector was successful and thriving. As consumers, they gained from this state of affairs, and as citizens of a small nation, they took pride in it. Almost everything in their surroundings reinforced their belief, and they were likely to reject or deem invalid information that contradicted it. The members of the *demos* were happy consumers, enjoying the fruits of the apparent economic prosperity, and had no incentives to act as vigilant citizens.

Weaknesses in Icelandic democratic culture

The political and institutional practices discussed above reflect a certain understanding of democracy, which is quite compatible with what Jürgen Habermas has characterized as the "liberal model"[41] and Will Kymlicka calls the "aggregative model" or "vote-centric democracy."[42] Kymlicka argues that this practice of democracy does not provide any mechanism for shaping an informed public opinion or for developing a fair consensus in society. The main emphasis is on the legitimacy of exercising political power through popular elections whereby the citizens express their preferences. These preferences are regarded as fundamentally private and existing independently of the political process. This squares well with the liberal emphasis on political liberty, where citizens can enjoy freedom from politics and concentrate on their pursuits as consumers or workers in the private or occupational spheres. They only exercise their political liberty at the moment of voting, when the deeds and policies of politicians are put to the democratic test. In-between elections, political representatives exercise political power within the boundaries of the law and constitution.

As in many other countries, Icelandic political culture is characterized by dominant party leaders who are key ministers in the government. Ministers are responsible for their set of issues and can make major decisions without consulting Parliament or other members of government. Neglect and even distrust of professional advice is partly rooted in the vote-centric, aggregative understanding of democracy according to which politicians are elected to govern, and specialists outside the formal political sphere should not limit their power. Though not confined to Iceland, it played a significant role in the course of events that led to the financial collapse.[43] A clear example of this style of governance is that the National Economic Institute in Iceland, which was the main source of professional advice for the government in economic affairs, was abolished in 2002. This has been explained as an "act of revenge" on behalf of the then Prime Minister, Davíð Oddsson, who was unhappy with the critical reports of the institute.[44] The official political reasons for the decision were that such an institution was obsolete, since the government had many other sources of information and advice about the economy, such as the financial analysis departments of the banks. This trust placed in the private banks, coupled with distrust of independent professional advice, reduced the resistance to, and facilitated, the course of events.

Another example of the relevant weakness of Icelandic political culture is the prevailing attitude toward democratic accountability, which is often understood in terms of criminal liability. In Marion Young's words, criminal liability means that "one assigns responsibility to a particular agent (or agents) whose actions can be shown to be causally connected to the circumstances for which responsibility is sought."[45] This type of responsibility, however, is not well suited to accountability in politics and administration, which refers to a sphere of tasks and concerns that a person can be rightly expected to take care of. The agent need not be strictly liable for a past wrong, but has failed to see to it that certain practices have functioned properly or had appropriate outcomes. These are role-specific obligations that people have "by virtue of their social roles or positions."[46] Some Icelandic ministers and administrators, for example, can rightly be held accountable because something went terribly wrong "on their watch", without being liable for causing the financial collapse. One of the conclusions of the SIC Report was that three ministers, the three governors of the CBI, and the director of the FME had shown negligence "by omitting to respond in an appropriate fashion to the impending danger for the Icelandic economy that was caused by the deteriorating situation of the banks."[47]

This conclusion of the report was not published until April 2010, or 18 months after the collapse of the banks, and the handling of these negligence charges will not be discussed here. What interests me is that no Icelandic politician or public administrator resigned in the wake of the financial collapse in October 2008. It was not until late January 2009 that the Minister of Business Affairs in the Icelandic government resigned and relieved the director of FME of his duties. This was just a day before the entire government resigned due to riots and general public pressure, which were largely fueled by the fact that politicians and major public administrators of financial affairs had not assumed responsibility. The financial collapse and the political response to it created serious mistrust in the political system among the Icelandic public. The liberal, aggregative model of representative democracy that had been practiced in Iceland suffered a serious blow, and the prevalent political practices received thorough criticism in the SIC Report. Yet, this criticism, which was mainly aimed at poor working practices and lack of professionalism, has not effectively fed into the process of democratization that has characterized Icelandic society since the financial collapse.

Post-crash democratic experiments

As David Held put it, "democracy has been championed as a mechanism that bestows legitimacy on political decisions when they adhere to proper principles, rules and mechanisms of participation, representation and accountability."[48] The criticism in the reports of the SIC and the WGE can be summarized by saying that Icelandic democracy has suffered from not adhering to proper principles, rules, and mechanisms of representation and accountability. Both Parliament and the Prime Minister's Office responded to this criticism with reports aimed at improving policies, governance, and professionalism in working practices, within both the legislative and executive spheres.[49] It is indicative of the prevailing understanding of democracy that these policy documents were not associated with strengthening democracy. The ideas in these three reports, however, were aimed at strengthening democratic practices and institutions, as they had been understood in the SIC and WGE reports.

The discourse about democracy in Iceland during the years after the financial collapse has centered on increasing participation of the public in political decision-making. This is understandable in a society where trust in formal politics and institutions has plummeted and where there is a political crisis of legitimacy.[50] This engenders democratic emphasis, which leads to "a polemical understanding of politics as directed against the state apparatus," as Habermas has aptly described the republican model of democracy.[51] Democratic participation can take on many different forms, and in Iceland, the channels chosen for it have been, in the spirit of accumulative, vote-centric democracy, increased participation of the public in national referenda and other elections. This has been done without developing, in Held's words, the "proper principles, rules and mechanisms of participation." The value and success of direct democracy is contextual, in the sense that it is dependent on the background conditions of the political culture and institutions in the society at issue. If these conditions are poor, citizens can be easily exploited by populist appeals to direct democracy and the will of the nation.[52] Unfortunately, this has happened in Iceland, as I will indicate through a brief discussion of democratic exercises in the wake of the financial collapse. These experiments have received international attention and, misleadingly, have been seen as signs of strong Icelandic democracy. To the contrary, I have argued that the type of democratization they represent has exploited the weaknesses of Icelandic society.[53]

The two National Forums that were held in Iceland in 2009 and 2010 have been seen as an exercise in participatory democracy.[54] In both cases, hundreds of people gathered in Reykjavík's largest sports arena for a full day of discussion.[55] In the former case, the subject matter was said to be "re-evaluation of the basic values upon which society is founded and a clearer vision for the future," required by the circumstances in the wake of the financial collapse.[56] Due to the methodology used in the meeting and the ideology behind it, the results of the gathering were statements about basic moral values and virtues—such as honesty, integrity, and justice—that were too general to have any bearing on policy or political practices. The purpose was to collect a large number of ideas and to hold elections among the participants about their importance without any prior critical analysis or discussion. This approach is rooted in the ideology of the "Anthill," referring to the fact that a collection of ants demonstrates a certain instinctive intelligence that is not shown by individual ants. It was projected into the human political context in a national forum where the collective insight and consciousness of the public, which is hidden from each and every individual, is to be harnessed. One of the major spokesmen of "The Anthill" described its mission as pursuing a "unique flavor of crowd-sourced democracy," while aptly comparing it to making a business plan for a large company that has a similar number of employees as the population of Iceland.[57]

From the viewpoint of democracy, this was a futile exercise. In fact, there are reasons for stating that the citizens' genuine interest and motivation for contributing to the "re-evaluation of the basic values upon which society is founded and a clearer vision for the future" were exploited by the way in which the whole affair was conducted. Moreover, an ambitious plan promised to follow up on the ideas discussed at the meeting by working with Parliament, government, special interest groups, and grassroots movements did not materialize. This is not surprising, since it is hard to see how such general results could have served as guiding ideas for any substantial changes in social or institutional policy.

Despite the flaws that characterized the National Forum in 2009, the government decided to embark on another national forum a year later, introduced in an act of Parliament with the specific purpose of providing guidance for a National Assembly on a new constitution for Iceland. In this case, the task was aimed at giving the participants a direct input into the process of revising the Icelandic constitution: "The National Assembly is to be held in order to call for the public's viewpoints and points of emphasis regarding the organization of the country's government and constitution and its changes."[58] From a democratic point of view, it is certainly commendable to engage the public in the process of revising the constitution. Their views were not only sought at the end of the process in a referendum about a completed document, but at the beginning, to set the stage for the revision and to feed into the public discussion. However, there are numerous critical remarks to be made about this way of engaging the public in a democratic process and how it was subsequently used in the debate about the bill for the constitution. Even though the anthill ideology was not as conspicuous this time around, the methodology was basically the same as in the former national forum. This precluded any deliberation or critical reasoning about ideas, and the emphasis was on articulation of basic general values, accumulation, and calculation of preferences.

The main difference between the two forums lies in the output, which in 2010 fed directly into the work of the Constitutional Committee (consisting of experts who oversaw the constitutional process) and the Constitutional Council. In fact, some of the major changes to the current constitution in the bill of the Constitutional Council mirrored ideas from the National Forum, such as equal voting rights for all, public ownership of the country's natural resources, sharper division of powers, increased participatory democracy, and more personalized choice of members of parliament for voters. However, a major weakness in the constitutional process was the way in which some of the main spokesmen of the Constitutional Council used the ideas collected in the National Forum. Instead of seeing them as food for democratic debate and discussion, they were referred to as "conclusions of the people," which should not be changed either by the Council or by Parliament. In this way, the National Forum was turned into an authoritative voice to settle and silence public debate rather than to ignite and feed into it. This is especially strange in light of the methodology of the forum, which did not provide the opportunity for thoughtful deliberation and critical debate.

It is important to bear in mind that the constitutional process was initiated in response to the financial collapse in an atmosphere of serious mistrust of political authorities. This mistrust, however, was partly explained by the fact that the SIC Report on Icelandic governance had revealed a serious lack of professional practices in relation to policy- and decision-making. Sadly, the democratically important attempt to revise the constitution was radically affected by many of the flawed working practices in politics and administration that were pointed out in the SIC and WGE reports. For example, expert criticism of the bill from the Constitutional Council was met with scorn and suspicion.[59] These reactions were reminiscent of the times leading up to the crisis, when critics of the apparent financial success of the Icelandic banks were met with accusations of ill will, envy, and ignorance. One aspect of the constitutional bill that several scholars pointed out as questionable was that the new constitution would introduce more radical participatory democracy and personalized voting in Iceland than in any other European country. This, like other changes to the constitution, had been made without any research on the possible effects that it would have for Icelandic politics, or on the experience of other nations with comparable policies.[60] As is common in Icelandic politics, the main principles of rational policy-making—such as careful agenda-setting and analysis—were violated in the process, which largely explains its flaws and eventual failure.[61]

Conclusion

In this chapter, on the basis of the reports of a Special Investigation Commission of the Icelandic Parliament and a Working Group on Ethics, I have tried to demonstrate how flawed practices in politics, administration, and the media failed to provide resistance to—and partly facilitated—the events that led up to the Icelandic financial collapse. Both these reports focused on institutional failures, weak governance, and lack of professionalism, and argued for improvement in political and administrative practices as key factors in the task of strengthening Icelandic democracy. I briefly analyzed democratic experiments in the wake of the collapse that have emphasized direct participatory democracy. While this emphasis is understandable in a society that is suffering from a loss of trust in major institutions and is ridden by a political crisis of legitimacy, it is argued that direct participatory democracy does not provide remedies to the weaknesses of Icelandic democratic practices revealed in the SIC and WGE reports.

In a context of weak democratic practices, institutions, and media, which form background conditions for successful participatory democracy, they lend themselves to manipulation and do not produce any significant political results. On the contrary, the kind of democratization the post-crash exercises represent has exploited the weaknesses of Icelandic society demonstrated by the parliamentary reports. This is largely due to a narrow understanding of democracy as vote-centric, regardless of whether or not it implies other direct public participation. In light of this understanding, the recommendations of the SIC and WGE reports about strengthening practices in politics and administration with the objective of improving decision-making, accountability, and responsible governance are not even associated with democracy. Instead of using the analysis of these reports as an occasion for reflecting on the conditions for collective will formation through the channels of deliberation and decision-making in both formal politics and the informal public sphere, the emphasis has been on spontaneous action and expression of preferences as the heart of democratic thinking. The failures of this approach will hopefully feed into a valuable learning process of a nation in the ongoing search for a stronger democracy.

Notes

1 Rannsóknarnefnd Alþingis [The Special Investigation Commission of the Icelandic parliament], *Aðdragandi og orsakir falls íslensku bankanna 2008 og tengdir atburðir* [The Causes and Effects of the Fall of the Icelandic Banks and Related Events], 9 vols, eds. Páll Hreinsson, Sigrídur Benediktsdóttir, and Tryggvi Gunnarsson. (Reykjavík: Icelandic Parliament, 2010). Hereafter quoted as the SIC Report. In English, see Chapter 2, "Summary of the Report's Main Conclusions" and Chapter 21, "Causes of the Collapse of the Icelandic Banks—Responsibility, Mistakes and Negligence," accessed December 1, 2015, www.rna.is/eldri-nefndir/addragandi-og-orsakir-falls-islensku-bankanna-2008/skyrsla-nefndarinnar/english/.

2 *Lög um rannsókn á aðdraganda og orsökum falls íslensku bankanna 2008 og tengdra atburða* nr. 142/2008 [Law no. 142/2008], art. 1.

3 The members are: Vilhjálmur Árnason (the author of this chapter), Professor of Practical Philosophy at the University of Iceland (Chair); Salvör Nordal, a philosopher and director of the Centre for Ethics at the University of Iceland; and historian Kristín Ástgeirsdóttir, former parliamentarian for the Women's Movement and current director of the Equal Status Council in Iceland.
4 See Vilhjálmur Árnason, "Moral Analysis of an Economic Collapse—an Exercise in Practical Ethics," *Etikk i praksis* 4 (2010): 101–123.
5 There have also been two other investigative commissions related to the financial collapse that are not discussed in this chapter: one on the Housing Finance Fund and the other on the savings and loans institutions in Iceland. Moreover, a Special Prosecutor has been working since February 1, 2009, investigating the suspicions of criminal actions in the preceding period, in connection with or in the wake of the collapse of the Icelandic banks.
6 "Summary of the Report's Main Conclusions," the SIC Report, 17.
7 Vilhjálmur Árnason, "Something Rotten in the State of Iceland. 'The Production of Truth' about the Icelandic Banks," in *Gambling Debt: Iceland's Rise in the Global Economy*, eds. Gísli Pálsson and Paul Durrenberger (Boulder: University Press of Colorado, 2014), 47–59.
8 "The Main Conclusion of the Working Group on Ethics," the SIC Report, accessed December 1, 2015, www.rna.is/media/skjol/WorkingGroupOnEthics_Summary.pdf.
9 "Summary of the Report's Main Conclusions," 16–17.
10 "Summary of the Report's Main Conclusions," 17.
11 Vilhjálmur Árnason et al., "Siðferði og starfshættir í tengslum við fall íslensku bankanna 2008" [Morality and Working Practices in Relation to the Collapse of the Icelandic Banks 2008], in the SIC Report, vol. 8, 55.
12 "Morality and Working Practices in Relation to the Collapse of the Icelandic Banks 2008," 51–52.
13 cf. Gudrun Johnsen, *Bringing Down the Banking System. Lessons from Iceland* (New York: Palgrave Macmillan, 2014), 77–78, 101–102.
14 The SIC Report, vol. 8, 146.
15 Thorarinn G. Pétursson reporting to the SIC, August 4, 2009, the SIC Report, vol. 8, 124.
16 Johnsen, *Bringing Down the Banking System*, 102. The quote is from the SIC Report, vol. 2, chapter 7, 47.
17 The SIC Report, vol. 8, 123–124.
18 "Eftir höfðinu dansa limirnir" [The Limbs Dance after the Head], interview with Ármann Þorvaldsson in the newspaper *Fréttablaðið*, October 25, 2006; the SIC Report, vol. 8, 191.
19 "90 tillögur að bættri samkeppnishæfni Íslands" [90 Suggestions for Improved Competitiveness of Iceland] (Reykjavík: Icelandic Chamber of Commerce, 2007),19.
20 cf. Isiah Berlin, *Four Essays on Liberty* (Oxford and London: Oxford University Press, 1969), esp. 121–124.
21 Johnsen, *Bringing Down the Banking System*, chapter 5.
22 Johnsen, *Bringing Down the Banking System*, 59.
23 David Sigurthorsson, "The Icelandic Banking Crisis: A Reason to Rethink CSR?" *Journal of Business Ethics* 111 (2012): 147–156.
24 "Iceland: Geyser Crisis," Danske Bank, March 21, 2006, accessed December 1, 2015, https://notendur.hi.is/ajonsson/kennsla2006/Danske%20Bank%20-%20Geyser%20Crises%20(Mars%202006).pdf; Frederic S. Mishkin and Tryggvi Th. Herbertsson, "Financial Stability in Iceland," Icelandic Chamber of Commerce, May, 2008, accessed December 1, 2015, http://rafhladan.is/bitstream/handle/10802/3564/555877819Financial%20Stability%20in%20Iceland%20Screen%20Version.pdf?sequence=1.
25 These examples are described and analyzed in Árnason, "Something Rotten in the State of Iceland."

26 Richard Portes and Friðrik Már Baldursson, *The Internationalisation of Iceland's Financial Sector* (Reykjavík: Iceland Chamber of Commerce, 2007).
27 Interview with author, Copenhagen, April 30, 2009; the SIC Report vol. 8, 158.
28 I describe this example in Árnason, "Moral Analysis of an Economic Collapse."
29 "Causes of the Collapse of the Icelandic Banks—Responsibility, Mistakes and Negligence," 157.
30 Thorvaldur Gylfason, "From Collapse to Constitution: The Case of Iceland," CESifo Working Paper No. 3770, Center for Economic Studies & Ifo Institute, Ludwig-Maximilians University, Munich, 2012.
31 Vlad Vaiman et al., "Weak Business Culture as Antecedents of Economic Crisis: The Case of Iceland," *Journal of Business Ethics* 98 (2011): 259–272.
32 cf. Norbert Götz, "Introspective Performance: The Scandinavian Power Investigation as a Politico-Cultural Practice," *Journal of Contemporary European Studies* 21 (2013): 341–356.
33 cf. Michel Foucault, "Two Lectures," in *Power/Knowledge*, ed. Colin Gordon (Brighton: Harvester Press, 1980), 78–108.
34 The SIC Report, vol. 8, 199.
35 Cf. Kay Weaver et al., "From Propaganda to Discourse (and Back Again): Truth, Power, the Public Interest and Public Relation," in *Public Relations. Critical Debates and Contemporary Practice*, eds. Jacquie L'Etang and Magda Pieczka (Mahwah, NJ: Lawrence Erlbaum Associates, 2006), 17.
36 The SIC Report, vol. 8, 206.
37 Friðrik Þór Guðmundsson et al., "Media Coverage in Iceland about Banks and Financial Companies 2006–2008," in the SIC Report, vol. 8, 247–269.
38 Magnús Björn Ólafsson, "Spegill, spegill" [Mirror, Mirror], *Krítík*, November 4, 2010, accessed December 1, 2015, http://wayback.vefsafn.is/wayback/20111126000000/http://kritik.is/greinar/20/spegill-spegill-herm-thu-mer-hvad-i-frettum-fegurst-er/.
39 Kaarlo Jännäri, "Report on Banking Regulation and Supervision in Iceland: past, present and future," March 30, 2009, 37, 22.
40 Hulda Þórisdóttir, "Afsprengi aðstæðna og fjötruð skynsemi: Aðdragandi og orsakir efnahagshrunsins á Íslandi frá sjónarhóli kenninga og rannsókna í félagslegri sálfræði" [Situational Determinants and Bounded Rationality: Causes and Consequences of the Icelandic Economic Collapse from the Viewpoint of Social Psychology], in the SIC Report, vol. 8, 275–297.
41 Jürgen Habermas, "Three Normative Models of Democracy," in *The Inclusion of the Other*, eds. Ciaran Cronin and Pable de Greiff (Cambridge: Polity Press, 1998), 239–252.
42 Will Kymlicka, *Contemporary Political Philosophy: An Introduction* (Oxford: Oxford University Press, 2002), 290–291.
43 cf. the SIC Report, vol. 8, 184.
44 The SIC Report, vol. 8, 157.
45 Iris Marion Young, "Responsibility and Global Justice: A Social Connection Model," *Social Philosophy and Policy* 23 (2006): 116.
46 Young, "Responsibility and Global Justice," 119.
47 "Summary of the Report's Main Conclusions," 18.
48 David Held, *Models of Democracy* (Cambridge: Polity Press, 2006), 261.
49 The three reports are: (1) *Eftirlit Alþingis með framkvæmdarvaldinu* [Parliamentary Supervision of the Executive Branch], delivered to the Icelandic Parliament October 1, 2009, accessed December 1, 2015, www.althingi.is/pdf/eftirlit_althingis_med_framkvaemdavaldinu_skyrsla.pdf; (2) *Skýrsla starfshóps forsætisráðherra um viðbrögð stjórnsýslunnar við skýrslu rannsóknarnefndar Alþingis* [Report of a Working Group of the Prime Minister about Reactions to the SIC Report], delivered to the Prime Minister May 7, 2010, accessed December 1, 2015, www.forsaetisraduneyti.is/frettir/nr/4266; (3) *Skýrsla þingmannanefndar til að fjalla um skýrslu rannsóknarnefndar*

Alþingis [Parliamentary Report about the SIC Report], delivered to the Icelandic Parliament September 11, 2010, accessed December 1, 2015, www.althingi.is/altext/138/s/1501.html.

50 Gylfason, "From Collapse to Constitution: The Case of Iceland."

51 Habermas, "Three Normative Models of Democracy," 247.

52 cf. Virginia Beramendi et al., eds., *Direct Democracy: The International IDEA Handbook* (Stockholm: IDEA, 2008).

53 Vilhjálmur Árnason, "Financial Collapse and Democratic Reconstruction in Iceland," in *Retrenchment or Renewal? Welfare States in Times of Economic Crisis*, eds. Guðmundur Jónsson and Kolbeinn Stefánsson (Helsinki: NordWel, 2013).

54 I have discussed these in Vilhjálmur Árnason, "'To Model a New Way of Democracy' The Case of National Forums in Iceland," in *Developing Democracies: Democracy, Democratization and Development*, eds. Michael Böss, Jørgen Møller, and Svend-Erik Skaaning (Aarhus: Aarhus University Press, 2013).

55 In the 2009 meeting, 1231 attended; in the 2010 meeting, about 950 people participated.

56 "Þjóðfundur um nýjan sáttmála" [National Forum on a New Social Contract], accessed December 1, 2015, www.thjodfundur2009.is/thjodfundur/um_thjodfundinn/.

57 Althea Legaspi, "The Many Ants of Iceland" [Interview with Guðjón Már Guðjónsson], *Foreign Policy*, January 11, 2010, accessed December 1, 2015, www.foreignpolicy.com/articles/2010/01/11/the_many_ants_of_iceland.

58 *Lög um stjórnlagaþing* nr. 90/2010 [Act on a Constitutional Assembly no. 90/2010], English translation available from http://thjodfundur2010.is/other_files/2010/doc/Act-on-a-Constitutional-Assembly.pdf.

59 Valgerður Bjarnadóttir [chair of the Constitutional Committee in the Icelandic Parliament], "Stjórnarskrá fólksins skotin í kaf" [Constitution of the People Shot Down], accessed December 1, 2015, http://blog.pressan.is/valgerdur/2012/11/09/strjornarskra-folksins-skotin-i-kaf/.

60 Gunnar Helgi Kristinsson, "Stjórnlagaráð var algjörlega umboðslaus samkunda fræga fólksins" [The Constitutional Council was the Gathering of the Famous without a Mandate], *Eyjan.pressan.is*, December 13, 2012, accessed December 1, 2015, http://eyjan.pressan.is/frettir/2012/12/13/stjornlagarad-var-algjorlega-umbodslaus-samkunda-fraega-folksins/.

61 Gunnar Helgi Kristinsson, "Raunhæf skynsemi eða stefnufálm" [Bounded Rationality or Policy Fumble], *Stjórnmál og stjórnsýsla* 9 (2013): 257–277.

Bibliography

"90 tillögur að bættri samkeppnishæfni Íslands" [90 Suggestions for Improved Competitiveness of Iceland]. Reykjavík: Icelandic Chamber of Commerce, 2007.

Árnason, Vilhjálmur. "Moral Analysis of an Economic Collapse—an Exercise in Practical Ethics." *Etikk i praksis* 4 (2010): 101–123.

Árnason, Vilhjálmur. "Something Rotten in the State of Iceland. 'The Production of Truth' about the Icelandic Banks." In *Gambling Debt: Iceland's Rise in the Global Economy*, edited by Gísli Pálsson and Paul Durrenberger, 47–59. Boulder: University Press of Colorado, 2014.

Árnason, Vilhjálmur. "'To Model a New Way of Democracy' The Case of National Forums in Iceland." In *Developing Democracies: Democracy, Democratization and Development*, edited by Michael Böss, Jørgen Møller, and Svend Erik Skaaning, 203–216. Aarhus: Aarhus University Press, 2013.

Árnason, Vilhjálmur. "Financial Collapse and Democratic Reconstruction in Iceland." In *Retrenchment or Renewal? Welfare States in Times of Economic Crisis*, edited by Guðmundur Jónsson and Kolbeinn Stefánsson, 329–347. Helsinki: NordWel, 2013.

Árnason, Vilhjálmur, Salvör Nordal, and Kristín Ástgeirsdóttir. "Siðferði og starfshættir í tengslum við fall íslensku bankanna 2008" [Morality and Working Practices in Relation to the Collapse of the Icelandic Banks 2008]. In *Aðdragandi og orsakir falls íslensku bankanna 2008 og tengdir atburðir* [The Causes and Effects of the Fall of the Icelandic Banks and Related Events]. Vol. 8. Reykjavík: Icelandic Parliament, 2010.

Beramendi, Virginia, Andrew Ellis, Bruno Kaufman, Miriam Kornblith, Larry LeDuc, Paddy McGuire, Theo Schiller, and Palle Svensson, eds. *Direct Democracy: The International IDEA Handbook*. Stockholm: IDEA, 2008.

Berlin, Isaiah. *Four Essays on Liberty*. Oxford: Oxford University Press, 1969.

Bjarnadóttir, Valgerður. "Stjórnarskrá fólksins skotin í kaf" [Constitution of the people Shot Down]. Accessed December 1, 2015. http://blog.pressan.is/valgerdur/2012/11/09/strjornarskra-folksins-skotin-i-kaf/.

Eftirlit Alþingis með framkvæmdarvaldinu [Parliamentary Supervision of the Executive Branch]. Delivered to the Icelandic Parliament October 1, 2009. Accessed December 1, 2015. www.althingi.is/pdf/eftirlit_althingis_med_framkvaemdavaldinu_skyrsla.pdf.

Foucault, Michel. "Two Lectures." In *Power/Knowledge*, edited by Colin Gordon, 78–108. Brighton: Harvester Press, 1980.

Götz, Norbert. "Introspective Performance: The Scandinavian Power Investigation as a Politico-Cultural Practice." *Journal of Contemporary European Studies* 21 (2013): 341–356.

Guðmundsson, Friðrik Þór, Kjartan Ólafsson, Valgerður Jóhannsdóttir, and Þorbjörn Broddason. "Media Coverage in Iceland about Banks and Financial Companies 2006–2008." In *Aðdragandi og orsakir falls íslensku bankanna 2008 og tengdir atburðir* [The Causes and Effects of the Fall of the Icelandic Banks and Related Events]. Vol. 8, 247–269. Reykjavík: Icelandic Parliament, 2010.

Gylfason, Thorvaldur. "From Collapse to Constitution: The Case of Iceland." CESifo Working Paper No. 3770, Center for Economic Studies & Ifo Institute, Ludwig-Maximillian University, Munich, 2012.

Habermas, Jürgen. "Three Normative Models of Democracy." In *The Inclusion of the Other*, edited by Ciaran Cronin and Pable de Greiff, 239–252. Cambridge: Polity Press, 1998.

Held, David. *Models of Democracy*. Cambridge: Polity Press, 2006.

"Iceland: Geyser Crisis." Danske Bank March 21, 2006. Accessed December 1, 2015. https://notendur.hi.is/ajonsson/kennsla2006/Danske%20Bank%20-%20Geyser%20Crises%20(Mars%202006).pdf.

Jännäri, Kaarlo. "Report on Banking Regulation and Supervision in Iceland: Past, Present and Future." March 30, 2009. Accessed March 21, 2016. https://eng.forsaetisraduneyti.is/media/frettir/KaarloJannari__2009.pdf.

Johnsen, Gudrun. *Bringing Down the Banking System. Lessons from Iceland*. New York: Palgrave Macmillan, 2014.

Kristinsson, Gunnar Helgi. "Stjórnlagaráð var algjörlega umboðslaus samkunda fræga fólksins" [The Constitutional Council was the Gathering of the Famous without a Mandate]. *Eyjan.pressan.is*, December 13, 2012. Accessed December 1, 2015. http://eyjan.pressan.is/frettir/2012/12/13/stjornlagarad-var-algjorlega-umbodslaus-samkunda-fraega-folksins/.

Kristinsson, Gunnar Helgi. "Raunhæf skynsemi eða stefnufálm" [Bounded Rationality or Policy Fumble], *Stjórnmál og stjórnsýsla* 9 (2013): 257–277.

Kymlicka, Will. *Contemporary Political Philosophy: An Introduction*. Oxford: Oxford University Press, 2002.

Legaspi, Althea. "The Many Ants of Iceland" [Interview with Guðjón Már Guðjónsson]. *Foreign Policy*, January 11, 2010. Accessed December 1, 2015. www.foreignpolicy.com/articles/2010/01/11/the_many_ants_of_iceland.

Mishkin, Frederic S. and Tryggvi Th. Herbertsson. "Financial Stability in Iceland," Icelandic Chamber of Commerce, May, 2008.

Ólafsson, Magnús Björn. "Spegill, spegill" [Mirror, Mirror]. *Krítík*, November 4, 2010. Accessed December 1, 2015. http://wayback.vefsafn.is/wayback/20111126000000/http://kritik.is/greinar/20/spegill-spegill-herm-thu-mer-hvad-i-frettum-fegurst-er/.

Portes, Richard and Friðrik Már Baldursson. *The Internationalisation of Iceland's Financial Sector*. Reykjavík: Iceland Chamber of Commerce, 2007.

Rannsóknarnefnd Alþingis [The Special Investigation Commission of the Icelandic Parliament]. *Aðdragandi og orsakir falls íslensku bankanna 2008 og tengdir atburðir* [The Causes and Effects of the Fall of the Icelandic Banks and Related Events]. 9 vols, edited by Páll Hreinsson, Sigrídur Benediktsdóttir, and Tryggvi Gunnarsson. Reykjavík: Icelandic Parliament, 2010.

Sigurthorsson, David. "The Icelandic Banking Crisis: A Reason to Rethink CSR?" *Journal of Business Ethics* 111 (2012): 147–156.

Skýrsla starfshóps forsætisráðherra um viðbrögð stjórnsýslunnar við skýrslu rannsóknarnefndar Alþingis [Report of a Working Group of the Prime Minister about Reactions to the Report of the Special Investigation Commission]. Delivered to the Prime Minister May 7, 2010. Accessed December 1, 2015. www.forsaetisraduneyti.is/frettir/nr/4266.

Skýrsla þingmannanefndar til að fjalla um skýrslu rannsóknarnefndar Alþingis [Parliamentary Report about the Report of the Special Investigation Commission]. Delivered to the Icelandic Parliament on September 11, 2010. Accessed December 1, 2015. www.althingi.is/altext/138/s/1501.html.

Vaiman, Vlad, Throstur Olaf Sigurjonsson, and Páll Ásgeir Davídsson. "Weak Business Culture as Antecedents of Economic Crisis: The Case of Iceland." *Journal of Business Ethics* 98 (2011): 259–272.

Weaver, Kay, Judy Motion, and Juliet Roper. "From Propaganda to Discourse (and Back Again): Truth, Power, the Public Interest and Public Relation." In *Public Relations. Critical Debates and Contemporary Practice*, edited by Jacquie L'Etang and Magda Pieczka, 7–22. Mahwah, NJ: Lawrence Erlbaum Associates, 2006.

Young, Iris Marion. "Responsibility and Global Justice: A Social Connection Model." *Social Philosophy and Policy* 23 (2006): 98–116.

"Þjóðfundur um nýjan sáttmála" [National Forum about New Social Contract]. Accessed December 1, 2015. www.thjodfundur2009.is/thjodfundur/um_thjodfundinn/.

Þórisdóttir, Hulda. "Afsprengi aðstæðna og fjötruð skynsemi: Aðdragandi og orsakir efnahagshrunsins á Íslandi frá sjónarhóli kenninga og rannsókna í félagslegri sálfræði" [Situational Determinants and Bounded Rationality: Causes and Consequences of the Icelandic Economic Collapse from the Viewpoint of Social Psychology]. In *Aðdragandi og orsakir falls íslensku bankanna 2008 og tengdir atburðir* [The Causes and Effects of the Fall of the Icelandic Banks and Related Events]. Vol. 8, 275–297. Reykjavík: Icelandic Parliament, 2010.

7 The politics of transition, memory, and justice

Assigning blame for the crisis

Valur Ingimundarson

Introduction

The generic term "transitional justice"—whether involving trials, truth commissions/reports, lustration, or apologies—has been used to describe efforts to confront a society's "tainted" past, condemnation, and reconciliation between conflicting parties.[1] Iceland's response to the economic disaster had many such features, even if it was not about a civil conflict or a transition from an authoritarian to a democratic regime. In this chapter, I explore the Icelandic crash by focusing on the use of transitional justice mechanisms and on the politics of memory to "come to terms" with a collective shock.

In Iceland, special measures were adopted in the immediate aftermath of the banking collapse to react to a state of exception, containing both backward-looking and forward-looking narratives. To assign responsibility and culpability, the government—composed of the Independence Party and the Social Democratic Alliance—and Parliament used an uneven mixture of retributive and restorative justice instruments as part of its crisis management response. To begin with, the Special Investigation Commission (SIC) was appointed, charged with producing a "truth report" on the fall of the banks, and, subsequently, the Special Prosecutor's Office was established to prosecute potential financial crimes. When the government fell in January 2009, its successor, the Social Democratic–Left-Green government, added an act of lustration by seeking the removal of the three governors of the Icelandic Central Bank. As a political move, it was particularly aimed at the former head of the Independence Party, Davíð Oddsson—the long-serving former Prime Minister—who after leaving the government in 2005 had been appointed to the top post at the Central Bank.[2]

Parliament later filed impeachment charges against former Prime Minister Geir Haarde, who resigned as head of the Independence Party after the fall of his government, for dereliction of duties after it had been suggested in the SIC Report that he and two other ministers might have broken the Law on Ministerial Responsibility. The Special Prosecutor, moreover, indicted leading bankers and businessmen for criminal wrongdoing in connection with the banking collapse. Political elites refrained, however, from creating a Truth and Reconciliation Commission, even if such bodies are meant to achieve political stability in the collective national interest after societal disasters. Such a move was considered politically unviable in Iceland. It could not only have complicated criminal prosecutions but possibly also have required amnesties, which would have triggered—without doubt—strong popular opposition. Thus, the punitive aspects clearly trumped the restorative ones in the official response to the crisis.

To address popular demands for some sort of democratic renewal and a break with the past, Parliament also approved the creation of the Constitutional Assembly—later changed into a Constitutional Council—entrusted with the task of reviewing the constitution. Historically, such constitutional rewriting has often been associated with political and economic upheaval.[3] In the Icelandic case, it reflected efforts to address the demands of the "pots and pans revolution" after the financial collapse. Finally, Iceland's 2009 application for EU membership can be interpreted as a future-oriented move—in a time of national crisis—to attract political and financial aid abroad and societal stability at home. Yet, despite much popular and elite support for efforts to deal with a collective misfortune, the transitional process in Iceland exposed deep political divisions—a fact that explains, in part, its failures and shortcomings. The abandonment of the constitutional experiment and the EU accession process—and the controversial punitive proceedings against the former Prime Minister, which resulted in a verdict on a minor charge—are cases in point. As Ruti Teitel has argued, the key question in political transitions is whether or not the ideological undoing of the "old regime," which is critical to political change, will succeed.[4]

To simplify, one can describe the Icelandic experience as a struggle—within the context of the politics of memory—between two metanarratives. On the one hand, the Left—which was brought to power by the banking collapse—blamed the crash on the Right, arguing that its neoliberal policies and ideology had, over a period of 18 years, transformed Icelandic society, with catastrophic results. On the other, the Right pointed to the global financial crisis as a key factor in instigating the crash, together with Icelandic bankers who had acted with supreme recklessness. Both sides—and the population in general—agreed on interpreting the economic collapse as a national disaster, affecting Icelandic society as a whole. However, the political question of how to account and assign blame was contested from the start.

Defining the nature of a societal shock

On the eve of the banking collapse—when Iceland was faced with a bank run at home and abroad—an Emergency Law was passed by the Icelandic Parliament to ensure that deposit holders were given priority over bond holders and to pave the way for all domestic assets to be transferred to new banks. What this meant was that the banking system shrank from being nine times the size of Iceland's gross domestic product (GDP) when the banks fell, to twice its size. Hence, Iceland did not socialize the bulk of the losses of the banks—an impossible task anyway, given the gargantuan banking system. But to avert a sovereign debt default, it was forced to get an International Monetary Fund (IMF) bailout and emergency loans from the Nordic countries and Poland after desperate overtures to Western countries and, later, to Russia for financial assistance came to nothing.

The view has been put forward that the Icelandic crisis was less severe than originally portrayed.[5] It has been contended that despite serious social disturbances, there was never a revolutionary situation. While the crash was considered a national disaster, it was not the result of a civil war or of violence perpetrated by a dictatorial regime. There was never enough public support in Iceland for using extra-parliamentary means to challenge the political system itself. While the political volatility, unpredictability, and contingency that characterized the post-crash situation could have created such scenarios, they did not materialize. And it is certainly overblown to put the Icelandic situation on a par with the systemic injustice of repressive rule in Eastern Europe or Central America. The transition process was never about abandoning dictatorship in favor of democracy. Finally, political stabilization in Iceland has, as noted, not been preconditioned on a quasi-religious societal healing associated with truth-telling—and implied apology and forgiveness—followed by an amnesty for the perpetrators. There have been no public testimonies or hearings, apart from the criminal case against former Prime Minister Haarde, even if a strong case can be made for them, since political and economic elites have refused to shoulder any responsibility for the crash.

This raises the question of whether the situation in Iceland should be compared to the banking crises in Scandinavia in the 1990s rather than to countries undergoing transitions after major societal ruptures. While such a view may have considerable merit on the surface, a simple comparison between the Scandinavian economic crises in the 1990s and the Icelandic one will not do, because such an interpretation fails to account for fundamental differences. It is true that the severe Finnish economic contraction was, as was the case in Iceland, caused by a massive credit expansion based largely on foreign debt following a deregulation drive. It led to high-risk company take-overs and failed foreign investments. Governmental intervention included bank take-overs, direct financial assistance, and blanket guarantees to banks. What compounded the crisis was the break-up of the Soviet Union, which wiped out 20% of Finnish exports in one fell swoop.[6] But even if the Finnish banking crisis resulted in a deep recession and very high unemployment, it did not produce a political crisis or lead to criminal trials. Similarly, despite a considerable drop in Sweden's GDP and a steep increase in the unemployment rate, there was no financial collapse or political turmoil.[7] Sweden did not need an IMF rescue program or experience severe political volatility, criminal prosecutions, or a government downfall. The Icelandic case was far more serious than those of the Scandinavian countries: it was a crisis of economic sustainability as well as of political legitimacy.

Thus, there is no need to downplay the seriousness of the Icelandic experience. It was a collective shock—the most profound political and economic crisis since the founding of the Icelandic Republic. The riots that followed the banking collapse in Iceland had not been witnessed in Iceland since it joined NATO in 1949,[8] with the parliamentary building being stoned and government ministers and parliamentarians physically threatened. The many demonstrations—and civic forum meetings—directed against the government in 2008–2009 played a decisive role in bringing it down. It was an act of intensive extra-parliamentary pressure from below, which made it politically impossible for the Social Democratic Alliance to stay in a coalition government with the Independence Party. What is more, the political system was put under enormous strain, with the political elite thoroughly discredited. Indeed, the purges of the heads of the Central Bank and Financial Supervisory Authority, the Special Investigation "Truth Report," the appointment of a Special Prosecutor, the indictment of the former Prime Minister, and the decision to embark on constitutional rewriting—have many of the characteristics of societies in transition.

This does not mean that transitions need to be transformative, or that pre-crisis elites have lost their influence. What is more, a strong argument can be made for abandoning the practice of restricting transitional justice mechanisms to the process of moving from authoritarianism to democracy. Civil conflicts or economic disasters can take place in democratic states, with far-reaching consequences. The "troubles" in Northern Ireland come to mind, which produced two official "truth-seeking" inquiries within the time span of 38 years—to account for Bloody Sunday in 1972—with two radically different conclusions: the first exonerating the British army (1972) and the second making it responsible for the killings (2010). The politics of justice and regret after societal shocks can emerge without "regime change" or democratic consolidation. And, needless to say, crimes do not have to be committed—or covered up—by an authoritarian regime.[9] Democratic governments are perfectly capable of doing so. For this reason, a transitional justice framework—with obvious qualifications regarding the non-violent nature of the previous regime and the crimes involved—is theoretically useful to explain the Icelandic experience. It was about a societal reckoning, and the moralistic terms associated with the politics of justice and memory—responsibility, culpability, and victimhood—were central in the Icelandic discourse.

Juggling restorative and retributive justice

The specific formal political and judicial mechanisms that were adopted to deal with the Icelandic crash served both retributive and restorative aims. The Office of the Special Prosecutor—charged with the task of investigating what illegal activities were involved in bringing about the financial collapse—focused on investigating three of Iceland's major banks for fraud, market manipulation, and money laundering. The Norwegian-French investigator and former French presidential candidate Eva Joly was hired, for a while, as a special consultant. The Special Prosecutor began issuing criminal charges against the heads of the banks in 2011. The former heads of the major banks—together with many other influential bank employees—have received stiff prison sentences for financial crimes, including fraud and market manipulation.[10] In addition, the former highest-ranking official of the Finance Ministry was sentenced to a two-year prison term for insider trading, and the heads of one of the smaller banks in Iceland received prison terms for financial crimes. The punitive aspect of the Icelandic response to the financial crisis differs markedly from that of other countries experiencing major economic turmoil—such as Greece or Portugal—where criminal prosecutions of politicians, bankers, and businessmen were not part of a "reckoning with the past" or a future-oriented "reconstruction" agenda.

The 2,000-page Report of the Special Investigation Commission was highly critical of the owners of the Icelandic banks, government ministers, leading private businessmen, and government regulators. It concluded that the collapse of the banking system was, in fact, inevitable by the end of 2006—an argument admittedly open to contestation on the grounds of being too teleological and deterministic—and contending that the banks had committed fraud by artificially inflating the value of their stocks. Three former ministers—Prime Minister Haarde, Minister of Finance Árni Mathiesen, and Minister of Commerce Björgvin G. Sigurðsson—were singled out for having possibly violated Iceland's 1963 Law on Ministerial Responsibility. Five other former officials were accused of acting with negligence in failing to prevent Iceland's banking collapse in 2008: the three governors of the Central Bank, including former Prime Minister Oddsson, and the former director of the Financial Supervisory Authority. In addition, former Foreign Minister, Ingibjörg Sólrún Gísladóttir, was assigned responsibility as the leader of the Social Democratic Alliance, even if the 1963 law was not seen as being applicable in her case or those of the Central Bank officials.[11]

The report was not limited to an analysis of the collapse of the banking system. The criticism of the political elite in the report of the Working Group on Ethics (WGE) specifically mentioned the role of the President of Iceland, Ólafur Ragnar Grímsson, in promoting—uncritically—the unsustainable Icelandic business expansion abroad. It also took the media and the academic community to task for complicity or silence. Indeed, as the report details, clichés about modern-day Viking territorial conquerors became household metaphors for the foreign investment drive preceding the collapse. Such metaphors were promoted by Iceland's leading businessmen and seconded by large segments of the political elite and the media to trump up a new and unique Icelandic business model based on essentialist national characteristics, such as high-stakes risk-taking, decisive and quick decision-making, and anti-bureaucratic flexibility.[12]

Given its sweeping scope, the Report of the Special Investigation Commission served a broad truth-seeking function. Its mandate was, after all, to "seek the truth relating to the events leading to, and the causes of, the downfall of the Icelandic banks, and related events."[13] The commission did not, however, operate through an open process or organize any public staging of truth-telling. The publication of the report, which took two years to complete, was delayed twice, which proved frustrating for a public in desperate need of explanation for what had happened. But when the report was finally made public, it briefly served a cathartic purpose. It managed to do what Brandon Hamber and Richard A. Wilson term the main rationale for truth commissions: to give a collective identity to a divided nation.[14] It was met with overwhelming approval across the political spectrum, and, instantly, became a foundational document: an accepted version of a national narrative on the crash.

Despite the positive reaction, truth reports[15] are usually based on the premise that a pursuit of unity is a coherent practice and that individual and national processes are largely equivalent.[16] Predictably, different groups—in a deeply polarized Icelandic society—interpreted the report differently. It satisfied the expectations of the Left by singling out culprits and by detailing the devastating consequences of a tainted privatization and deregulation drive; to the Right, its account of the insider trading practices of a leading group of the banking and business elite was particularly welcomed. Thus, the report was not about societal reconciliation, which involves long-term processes beyond the capacity of any short-term commission.[17] But it clearly achieved its object of unmasking as a lie the official truth of the preceding period.[18] It contributed to the creation of social knowledge indispensable to the politics of transition[19] by offering answers that were seen as being morally and politically viable.

Given the report's reified status, it did not come as a surprise that a cross-party parliamentary committee—appointed to consider and act on the findings of the Special Investigation Commission—only parroted the latter's findings. In its own report, the committee decided, if not unanimously, that legal action should be taken against the three ministers as well as the former Minister of Foreign Affairs, Ingibjörg Sólrún Gísladóttir, because of her status as the head of the Social Democratic Alliance, which made her the party's most influential member of the coalition government with the Independence Party.[20] Echoing the conclusion of the Special Investigation Commission, the heads of the Central Bank and the Financial Supervisory Authority were spared on the grounds that the law did not apply to them. And the ministers who had privatized the banks were also excluded, since they could not be prosecuted three years after the alleged violations.

When the issue came to a vote in Parliament in 2010, the majority of MPs decided only to refer the case of Haarde to a Special Court, *Landsdómur*, with 33 voting in favor and 30 against; proposals to indict the other three were defeated. The vote was deeply controversial because some Social Democratic members of parliament decided to vote for Haarde's impeachment, but to shield their own ministers, notably Ingibjörg Sólrún Gísladótttir, from indictment. A case put forward to provide justice and closure after a collective trauma sparked, instead, a debate over whether one politician should bear sole responsibility for the collapse. There was little support for such a reductionist interpretation even among those strongly favoring criminal prosecution. The indictment against Haarde claimed that he displayed "serious malfeasance of his duties as prime minister in the face of major danger looming over Icelandic financial institutions and the state treasury, a danger that he knew of or should have known of."[21] It was the first time a Western leader had been charged with crimes associated with the global financial crisis. Haarde was indicted on several counts, such as seriously neglecting his ministerial duties; failing to assess the financial risks facing Iceland; refraining from initiating measures to reduce the size of the Icelandic banking system; and not ensuring that the Icelandic banks offering saving accounts in the United Kingdom and Netherlands were split off into subsidiary companies in those countries before the collapse of the banking system.[22]

The law underpinning the Special Court is a curious phenomenon, not only because the indictments emanate from Parliament instead of the Public Prosecutor, but also because of the composition of the court itself.[23] It is made up of 15 members: five Supreme Court justices, a district court president, a constitutional law professor, and eight people chosen by Parliament every six years. Thus, as a hybrid court composed of professional judges and legal specialists together with political appointees, the separation of legislative and judicial powers does not apply to its proceedings. In 2011, the Special Court dropped the two first charges against Haarde, concerning gross negligence and failure to have the financial risks assessed, but continued with the case based on the four remaining charges.

After some delay, the trial took place from March 5–16, 2012. In a strange case of Icelandic pragmatism, which triggered no public debate, the criminal proceedings were held at the Center for Cultural Heritage—the National Culture House—in the heart of Reykjavík. A celebratory, if elitist, "site of memory," serving the purpose of national and collective belonging, was, thus, turned into a venue for deeply divisive proceedings—into a provisional criminal court house in a trial over a former Prime Minister. The spectators could, if they wanted to whet their cultural appetite during a trial recess, observe the old manuscripts of the Icelandic Sagas or visit an exhibition of Iceland's National Hero, Jón Sigurðsson, in the same building.

Over 40 persons offered testimonies, including the ministers who escaped impeachment by Parliament, the former heads of the Central Bank, and the former directors of the failed Icelandic banks, several of whom were charged with criminal conduct by the Special Prosecutor. As a media event, the trial was something of a spectacle—with considerable foreign[24] and all-consuming domestic interest. This was the first time that all the major players in the banking collapse had testified one after another in a court of law. Camaraderie was very much on display—with witnesses affectionately greeting the accused—reminiscent of a reunion of old friends.

As a contribution to retributive justice, however, the testimonies proved noticeably meager. No real new information was brought to light at the trial. Haarde acknowledged that he had had limited faith in the idea—being pushed by politicians and bankers during the period leading up to the crash—of making Iceland an international financial center. But he blamed the banks—which had engaged in irresponsible, high-risk, and unlawful conduct—and the international financial crisis for the disaster. Neither he nor the government, he argued, were in a position to do anything such as reducing the size of the banks or pressuring them to relocate abroad.[25] In other words, "action" was not an option, because the crisis was beyond the control of the government. It was a narrative fitting a Shakespearean tragedy—with the main protagonists unaware of an impending, if unavoidable, disaster—in which the fate of the banking system was already predestined and there was no room or scope to act. To do anything would only have hastened the downfall of the banks by undermining their credibility in global markets. Hence, misleading public statements or silence on the part of high government officials, such as the Prime Minister and Foreign Minister,[26] over the real state of the banks were justified as an attempt to prevent something worse. While the economic situation was precarious, there was no way of knowing—Haarde claimed—that the entire banking system was being threatened.[27]

To be sure, some foreign economists and journalists had warned of an impending disaster in the years and months prior to the crash.[28] But such views were, as a rule, not taken at face value but rejected as biased in Iceland. Echoing this interpretation, the former ministers who testified at the trial claimed that the banking collapse could only have been averted if something had been done several years before it took place. To respond to accusations that they reacted irresponsibly by not having formal government meetings on the rapidly deteriorating economic situation from February until October 2008, they stated that banking and financial matters were discussed in general terms. In addition, they admitted that the possibility of reducing the size of the banks had been broached, even if nothing came out of it. It would have been impossible, they argued, to do so in 2008 because there were no willing buyers at that time.[29] To paraphrase the testimony—with some exaggeration—inaction was the prudent and judicious move in a situation beyond human control; action would only have initiated a self-fulfilling prophesy of doom.

The central bankers blamed the banks for recklessness and indefensible risk-taking.[30] Former Central Bank governor, Davíð Oddsson, made the point that he had warned the government, in the strongest possible terms, that the Icelandic banks were facing serious difficulties recapitalizing themselves, as the European banks no longer believed in their stability.[31] The heads of the failed banks blamed the international financial crisis as well as the government and the Central Bank for the fall of the banks.[32] It was a rehash of arguments repeated endlessly since the crash. Those who expected the first public staging of truth-telling to be a cathartic moment must have been disappointed. There were no public confessions, apologies, or admission of responsibility or mistakes. The testimonies amounted to a collective self-defense of the actions taken by the political and economic elites before the crisis.

The Special Court, it turned out, convicted Haarde of only one criminal charge, without punishment—of failing to hold government meetings over the precarious state of the banking system ahead of its collapse—and cleared him on three others: of not doing anything to reduce the size of the banking system, of not making sure that the Icesave internet accounts of the Landsbanki in Britain and the Netherlands were transferred to a subsidiary, and of failing to produce better results from the government's 2006 report on financial stability. Haarde himself castigated the court for meting out political justice, calling the verdict "ludicrously laughable."[33] Earlier, he had termed the affair a political trial and farce, bordering on persecution. He added that he had "a clean slate"—using a language characteristic of transitional justice proceedings.[34] His own actions had actually helped save Iceland from economic ruin and national bankruptcy by rushing through the Emergency Law. What was more, he appealed his conviction to the European Court of Human Rights, which has agreed to review his case. The counter-argument, based on the finding of the Special Investigation Commission, was that Haarde should be held accountable for doing nothing to avert an unmitigated economic disaster.

After the trial, the Icelandic public were divided on the question of whether the proceedings should have been held, with roughly half supporting the indictment and the other half against.[35] The pressure to hold Haarde responsible proved far weaker than it had been in the beginning, because many saw it as being grossly unfair to charge him alone. It also confirms a tendency—experienced in other countries undergoing transitions—that the call for retribution is stronger in the immediate aftermath of a major societal rupture and that sentences tend to get far more lenient as time elapses. In the case of Iceland, however, this has to be qualified, since bankers continued to receive severe prison sentences seven years after the financial collapse.

The case against Haarde is an instance of political justice, to be sure. The majority of political representatives in Parliament issued the charges. The Public Prosecutor claimed that she was bound by law to prosecute the case on the premises spelled out by Parliament.[36] And echoing the political nature of the process, eight out of 15 members of the Special Court were, as noted, political appointees, who did not require any legal background (even if some of them had legal training). Nonetheless, the nature of the trial should not come as a surprise. It underscores the point that direct and indirect transitional justice mechanisms after societal shocks—for both restorative and retributive justice—are always part of a highly politicized and contested process.

As is usually the case in societies grappling with a tainted past, the "old regime"—in business or politics—not only has to be reckoned with but can also stage a comeback. While historical events cannot be reversed, it does not follow, as Nenad Dimitrijević has pointed out, that the dividing line between the past and the present is clear-cut. What happened under the "old regime" has, rather, undergone a transformation: having lost the capacity to act as an officially sanctioned and hegemonic social and political narrative, the old patterns still survive.[37] Such political displacement can best be captured in the words of the Prince in Giuseppe Tomasi de Lampedusa's novel *The Leopard*: "If we want things to stay as they are, things will have to change."[38]

Thus, the question is not about defending or legitimizing a compromised past. It is rather, to what degree the "old regime" can sustain itself by delegitimizing the "new" one and by infiltrating and influencing the transition. Thus, after being forced out of the Central Bank, Oddsson was hired as the editor-in-chief of the second largest newspaper in Iceland, the conservative *Morgunblaðið*, which he used to propagate his own interpretation of the economic collapse as part of an intervention in the politics of memory. In addition, he played an important role in fighting the left-wing government policies on the EU application and the constitutional project. What was more, the media empire, which includes the largest newspaper, *Fréttablaðið*, and a private TV station, Channel 2, is still controlled by the wife of Jón Ásgeir Jóhannesson, one of the leading businessmen in Iceland in the 2000s. As the former CEO of Baugur Group, he had extensive dealings with all the major Icelandic banks and a controlling stake in Glitnir Bank before the banking collapse. After the privatization of the Icelandic banks, he and the new owners of the banks had been locked in a power struggle with Oddsson and his political allies, which lasted until the crash. It was, to some degree, re-enacted within a different political context and on another public stage during the reconstruction period. Thus, dominant elements of the previous business and political elite not only survived, but also shaped the politics of transition in Iceland.

Conclusion

In the aftermath of the crash, Icelanders had to deal not only with the consequences of an economic and political crisis but also with its causes and the events leading up to it. I have argued here that transitional justice mechanisms have influenced Iceland's effort to confront the past. Consistently with other national cases of societal traumas, there has been a tendency to single out a few culprits in an effort to evade questions of wider societal responsibility.[39] One can question the decision to limit accountability to negligent politicians, incompetent regulators, or unscrupulous bankers and businessmen. The media, especially the most influential privately owned media, were arguably co-opted by the Icelandic moguls who owned them as well as by the banks. Academia also took part in legitimizing the business practices of economic elites. And, while this was almost a taboo in the public debate, a sizable number of Icelanders took huge financial risks and participated willingly in get-rich-quick schemes.

The transitional rituals and processes also included the division of political time into "before" and "after."[40] The case against Geir Haarde can be seen as having been backward-looking and based on a law dating back all the way to the year 1905 after Iceland was granted home rule from Denmark. It was archaic because the law had never been used. But it was rooted in a common past—the constitution of 1944 and the 1963 Law on Ministerial Responsibility—which is required to ensure historical continuity. At the same time, the idea of rewriting the constitution—to take an example—was projected as a forward-looking and liberalizing project designed to break away from the past, a precondition for a new beginning. Thus, the political measures adopted by the left-wing government were, in part, directed at the right-wing policies and ideology of the "old regime." But as part of a political agenda to adopt a future-oriented societal transformative agenda, they did not succeed. The government's initial popularity quickly evaporated in the face of the magnitude of the crisis.

The notion of collective victimhood raises the question of societal reconciliation after the crash; as I noted, the pressure for accountability has not been followed by South African-style calls for reconciliation as a form of public staging of truth-telling followed by an amnesty, except in the general form of debt relief. Ironically, if not surprisingly, two of the most visible players in the crash—rival businessmen and former stakeholders in the Icelandic banks, Björgólfur Thor Björgólfsson and Jón Ásgeir Jóhannesson—called for a Truth and Reconciliation Commission.[41] The problem with such a course of action is obvious: it can be seen as a self-serving vehicle for restorative truth-telling without legal accounting or retributive justice. Thus, the idea to opt exclusively for restorative justice mechanisms in the name of societal reconciliation would not only shield potential perpetrators from retributive justice; it would also provide the heavily compromised state with implicit power to "wipe the slate clean." For this reason, it is not surprising that this idea did not receive any public support.

No uncontested narratives about the causes and nature of the crash or about the assignment of responsibility have emerged. Despite strong backing for the Special Investigation Report, its long-term impact has been limited. Its findings have not served as a blueprint for "societal reconstruction," even if they have been used as a reference point. Indeed, the whole politically enacted process of assigning blame and responsibility has been characterized by conflict, ambiguity, and contingency. To be sure, there has been much support for bringing bankers and businessmen to justice. But when it comes to the political elite, things have been much murkier. As it happened, all the parties, except for the Left Greens and the small Civic Movement—which won seats in the 2009 elections but was dissolved before the 2013 elections—were, in one way or another, implicated in the crash. Having stayed out of government from 1995 until 2007, the Social Democratic Alliance had no influence over the economic policies adopted by the center-right government during this period. But it could not evade all responsibility, because it had supported the frenzied Icelandic business and banking expansion as part of the coalition government with the Independence Party from 2007 to 2009.

Even if the Independence Party reclaimed its status as the largest party in Iceland in the 2013 elections, it has been damaged by the crash and failed to restore its electoral base after its historical loss in 2009. After entering a coalition government with the Progressive Party, it was unable to stop the criminal proceedings against Haarde. Yet, it has been successful in dismantling core aspects of the agenda of the left-wing government, such as the EU application and the constitutional experiment. In addition, in a symbolic act designed to rehabilitate Haarde, he was appointed Ambassador to the United States. Yet, all these issues had already divided the former left-wing government during its tenure. The Independence Party has not been able to absolve itself of responsibility for the societal disaster or to replace one interpretive account—or truth regime—with another, while preserving, in a historical sense, a common national narrative.[42] The outcome of the politics of memory in Iceland will, in the end, be determined—at least partly—by the relative strengths of the forces vying for control. As things now stand, no universal version of the "truth" about the

Icelandic crisis has developed. But the struggle discussed here is what the politics of transition and justice in Iceland is about. And instead of closure, it is still an open-ended process, with no fixed outcome. What is clear, however, is that the crash did not lead to any permanent realignment of power relations in Icelandic politics.

Notes

1 See Neil J. Kritz ed., *Transitional Justice: How Emerging Democracies Reckon with Former Regimes.* 3 vols. (Washington, DC: United States Institute of Peace Press, 1995); Naomi Roht-Arriaza ed., *Impunity and Human Rights in International Law and Practice* (New York: Oxford University Press, 1995); A. James McAdams ed., *Transitional Justice and the Rule of Law in New Democracies* (Notre Dame: University of Notre Dame Press, 1997); Ruti Teitel, *Transitional Justice* (Oxford: Oxford University Press, 2000); Jon Elster, *Closing the Books: Transitional Justice in Historical Perspective* (Cambridge: Cambridge University Press, 2004); Jon Elster ed., *Retribution and Reparations in the Transition to Democracy* (Cambridge: Cambridge University Press, 2006); Carmen González Enríquez et al. eds., *The Politics of Memory: Transitional Justice in Democratizing Societies* (Oxford: Oxford University Press, 2001).

2 Davíð Oddsson refused to give up his position until he was forced to do so in 2009, when a government-sponsored bill on the reorganization of the Central Bank was passed by parliament. See "Lög um breytingar á lögum nr. 36/2001 um Seðlabanka Íslands" [Law on the Changes of the Law Number 36/2001 on Icelandic Central Bank], accessed December 4, 2015, www.althingi.is/altext/stjt/2009.005.html.

3 Jon Elster, "Forces and Mechanisms in the Constitution-Making Process," *Duke Law Journal* 45, no. 2 (1995): 364–396.

4 Teitel, *Transitional Justice*, 116.

5 See, for example, Jón Ólafsson, "An Experiment in Iceland: Crowdsourcing a Constitution" (unpublished manuscript).

6 Seppo Honkapohja, "The 1990s financial crisis in Nordic Countries (Bank of Finland Research Discussion Papers, 5 2009), accessed March 7, 2016, www.riksbank.se/Upload/Dokument_riksbank/Kat_foa/2009/6_8nov/Honkapohja.pdf.

7 On the Swedish crisis, see P. Englund, "The Swedish Banking Crisis: Roots and Consequences," *Oxford Review of Economic Policy* 15, no. 3 (1999): 80–97.

8 See Valur Ingimundarson, *The Rebellious Ally: Iceland, the United States and the Politics of Empire, 1945–2006* (St Louis and Dordrecht: Republic of Letters Publishing, 2011), 29–33.

9 See Mano Toth, "The Myth of the Politics of Regret," *Millennium: Journal of International Studies* 42, no. 2 (2015): 551–566.

10 See *Eyjan*, webzine, December 18, 2011; *Morgunblaðið*, February 22, 2012; *Viðskiptablaðið*, December 12, 2013; *Kjarninn*, webzine, February 12, 2015.

11 Rannsóknarnefnd Alþingis [The Special Investigation Commission of the Icelandic parliament], *Aðdragandi og orsakir falls íslensku bankanna 2008 og tengdir atburðir* [The Causes and Effects of the Fall of the Icelandic Banks and Related Events] (Reykjavík: Icelandic Parliament, 2010); see also, "Report of the Special Investigation Commission (SIC)"). Summaries in English, http://sic.althingi.is/.

12 See, for example, Ólafur Ragnar Grímsson, "How to succeed in modern business: lessons from the Icelandic voyage" (speech by the President of Iceland at the Walbrook Club, London), May 3, 2005, accessed December 4, 2015, http://forseti.is/media/files/05.05.03.Walbrook.Club.pdf.

13 See the mandate of the Special Investigation Commission, available at www.rannsoknarnefnd.is/.

14 Brandon Hamber and Richard A. Wilson, "Symbolic Closure through Memory, Reparation and Revenge in Post-Conflict Societies," in *The Role of Memory in Ethnic Conflict*, eds. Ed Cairns and Mícheál D. Roe (Houndmills, Basingstoke and New York: Palgrave Macmillan, 2003), 144.

15 On truth commissions, see Priscilla Hayner, *Unspeakable Truths: Confronting State Terror and Atrocity* (New York: Routledge, 2001); Beth Rushton, "Truth and Reconciliation? The Experience of Truth Commissions," *Australian Journal of International Affairs* 60, no 1 (2006): 125–141; Charles Maier, "Doing History, Doing Justice: The Narrative of the Historian and of the Truth Commission," in *Truth vs. Justice: The Moral Efficacy of Truth Commissions: South Africa and Beyond*, eds. Robert Rotgber and Dennis Thompson (Princeton: Princeton University Press, 2000), 261–278; David Crocker, "Truth Commissions, Transitional Justice, and Civil Society," in ibid., 99–121; Nenad Dimitrijevic, "Justice beyond Blame: Moral Justification of (the Idea) of a Truth Commission," *Journal of Conflict Resolution* 50, no. 3 (2006): 368–382.

16 Hamber and Wilson, "Symbolic Closure through Memory, Reparation and Revenge in Post-Conflict Societies," 144.

17 See Rushton, "Truth and Reconciliation? The Experience of Truth Commissions," 131.

18 Teitel, *Transitional Justice*, 91.

19 Dimitrijević, "Justice beyond Blame: Moral Justification of (the Idea) of a Truth Commission," 376–377.

20 "Skýrsla þingnefndar til að fjalla um skýrslu rannsóknarnefndar Alþingis" [Parliamentary Report on the Report by the Icelandic Investigative Commission] (September 2010), accessed December 4, 2015, www.althingi.is/altext/138/s/1501.html.

21 "Tillaga til þingsályktunar um málshöfðun gegn ráðherrum" [Parliamentary Proposal on an Indictment against Ministers], September 11, 2010, accessed December 4, 2015, www.althingi.is/altext/138/s/1502.html.

22 "Tillaga til þingsályktunar um málshöfðun gegn ráðherrum."

23 On the Special Court, see, for example, Sigurður Líndal, "Um ráðherraábyrgð og landsdóm" [On Ministerial Responsibility and the Special Court], *Skírnir* 184, no. 2 (2010): 522–532; Svala Ísfeld Ólafsdóttir, "Rökstólar: Landsdómur og ráðherraábyrgð" [Debate: The Special Court and Ministerial Responsibility], *Úlfljótur* 64, no. 2 (2011): 290–294; Helgi Jóhanesson, "Rökstólar: Landsdómur og ráðherraábyrgð," *Úlfljótur* 64, no. 2 (2011): 282–283; Hróbjartur Jónatansson, "Rökstólar: Landsdómur og ráðherraábyrgð," *Úlfljótur* 64, no. 2 (2011): 285–289; Andri Árnason, "Ráðherraábyrgð" [On Ministerial Responsibility], *Tímarit lögfræðinga* 3 (2009): 239–261.

24 See, for example, *New York Times*, *Guardian*, *Der Spiegel*, and *CNN*, March 5, 2012; *Le Monde*, March 7, 2012.

25 The testimony of Geir Haarde before the Icelandic Special Court (*Landsdómur*), March 5, 2012, accessed March 19, 2015, www.landsdómur.is/adalmedferd/nr/9.

26 *Financial Times*, March 27, 2008; *Iceland Review*, March 12, 2008, accessed March 19, 2015, www.icelandreview.com/icelandreview/Daily_News/?ew_0_a_id=302521.

27 The testimony of Geir Haarde before the Icelandic Special Court, March 5, 2012.

28 See Carsten Valgreen et al., "Iceland: Geyser Crisis," March 21, 2006, accessed December 4, 2015, www.mbl.is/media/98/398.pdf; Robert Aliber, "Monetary turbulence and the Icelandic economy" (lecture, University of Iceland, May 5, 2008); Anne C. Sibert and Willem Buiter, "The Icelandic Banking Crisis and What to Do about It: The Lender of Last Resort Theory of Optimal Currency Areas," *CEPR Policy Insight*, no. 26 (October 2008), accessed March 19, 2015, http://willembuiter.com/iceland.pdf; see also Robert Wade, "Iceland Pays Price for Financial Excess," *Financial Times*, July 1, 2008.

29 The testimony of Ingibjörg Sólrún Gísladóttir, former Foreign Minister, March 12, 2012, accessed March 19, 2015, www.landsdómur.is/adalmedferd/nr/41; the testimony of Árni Mathiesen, former Minister of Finance, March 13, 2012, accessed March 19, 2015,

www.landsdómur.is/adalmedferd/nr/29; the testimony of Björgvin G. Sigurðsson, former Minister of Commerce, March 6, 2012, accessed March 19, 2015, www.landsdómur.is/adalmedferd/nr/34.

30 The testimony of Davíð Oddsson, former Central Bank governor, March 6, 2012, accessed March 19, 2015, www.landsdómur.is/adalmedferd/nr/36; the testimony of Ingimundur Friðriksson, former Central Bank governor, March 7, 2012, accessed March 19, 2015, www.landsdómur.is/adalmedferd/nr/42.

31 The testimony of Davíð Oddsson, March 6, 2012.

32 See the testimony of Hreiðar Már Sigurðsson, former CEO of Kaupthing Bank, March 8, 2012, accessed March 19, 2015, www.landsdómur.is/adalmedferd/nr/40; Sigurður Einarsson, former chair of the Board of Kaupthing Bank, March 19, 2012, accessed March 19, 2015, www.landsdómur.is/adalmedferd/nr/57; Sigurjón Þ. Árnason, former director of Landsbanki, March 12, 2012, accessed March 19, 2015, www.landsdómur.is/adalmedferd/nr/59; Lárus Welding, former director of Glitnir Bank, March 12, 2012, accessed March 19, 2015, www.landsdómur.is/adalmedferd/nr/55.

33 *Eyjan*, April 24, 2012.

34 See "Former Iceland Prime Minister on Trial," *RTE News*, September 5, 2011, accessed March 19, 2015, www.rte.ie/news/2011/0905/iceland.html; see also *Vísir*, September 28, 2010, accessed March 19, 2015, www.visir.is/geir-segir-akaeruna-jadra-vid-politiskar-ofsoknir/article/201013381550.

35 *Eyjan*, February 13, 2012, accessed December 1, 2015, http://eyjan.is/2012/02/13/thjodin-klofin-vegna-akaeru-a-hendur-geir-haarde-svipadur-fjoldi-vill-haetta-vid-og-malid-afram/.

36 See *Morgunblaðið*, January 27, 2012.

37 Dimitrijević, "Justice beyond Blame: Moral Justification of (the Idea) of a Truth Commission," 371.

38 Giuseppe Tomasi de Lampedusa, *The Leopard*, trans. Archibald Colquhoun (London: Fontana, 1963), 29.

39 See, for example, Martha Minow, *Between Vengeance and Forgiveness: Facing History after Genocide and Mass Violence* (Boston: Beacon Press, 1998), 40–47.

40 See Ruti Teitel, *Transitional Justice*, 116.

41 See *Eyjan*, March 23, 2012; *DV*, March 28, 2012.

42 See Teitel, *Transitional Justice*, 115.

Bibliography

Árnason, Andri. "Ráðherraábyrgð" [On Ministerial Responsibility]. *Tímarit lögfræðinga* 3 (2009): 239–261.

Árnason, Árni Páll. "Iceland's Recovery." Address at the Conference, "Iceland's Recovery—Lessons and Challenges," October 27, 2011, Reykjavík.

Cairns, Ed, and Mícheál D. Roe eds. *The Role of Memory in Ethnic Conflict*. Houndmills, Basingstoke and New York: Palgrave, 2003.

Crocker, David. "Truth Commissions, Transitional Justice, and Civil Society." In *Truth vs. Justice: The Moral Efficacy of Truth Commissions: South Africa and Beyond*, edited by Robert Rotgber and Dennis Thompson, 99–121. Princeton: Princeton University Press, 2000.

Dimitrijević, Nenad. "Justice beyond Blame: Moral Justification of (the Idea) of a Truth Commission." *Journal of Conflict Resolution* 50, no. 3 (2006): 368–382.

Elster, Jon. *Closing the Books: Transitional Justice in Historical Perspective*. Cambridge: Cambridge University Press, 2004.

Elster, Jon ed. *Retribution and Reparations in the Transition to Democracy*. Cambridge: Cambridge University Press, 2006.

Englund, P. "The Swedish Banking Crisis: Roots and Consequences." *Oxford Review of Economic Policy* 15, no. 3 (1999): 80–97.
Enríquez, Carmen González, Alexandra Barahona de Brito, and Paloma Aquilar eds. *The Politics of Memory: Transitional Justice in Democratizing Societies.* Oxford: Oxford University Press, 2001.
Grímsson, Ólafur Ragnar. "How to succeed in modern business: lessons from the Icelandic voyage." Speech at the Walbrook Club, London, May 3, 2005. Accessed December 4, 2015. http://forseti.is/media/files/05.05.03.Walbrook.Club.pdf.
Hamber, Brandon, and Richard A. Wilson. "Symbolic Closure through Memory, Reparation and Revenge in Post-Conflict Societies." In *The Role of Memory in Ethnic Conflict*, edited by Ed Cairns and Mícheál D. Roe, 144–168. Houndmills, Basingstoke and New York: Palgrave Macmillan, 2003.
Hayner, Priscilla. *Unspeakable Truths: Confronting State Terror and Atrocity.* New York: Routledge, 2001.
Honkapohja, Seppo. "The 1990s financial crisis in Nordic Countries (Bank of Finland Research Discussion Papers, 5 2009), accessed March 7, 2016, www.riksbank.se/Upload/Dokument_riksbank/Kat_foa/2009/6_8nov/Honkapohja.pdf.
Ingimundarson, Valur. "A 'Crisis of Affluence': The Politics of an Economic Breakdown in Iceland." *Irish Studies in International Affairs* 21 (2010): 57–63.
Ingimundarson, Valur. *The Rebellious Ally: Iceland, the United States and the Politics of Empire, 1945–2006.* St Louis and Dordrecht: Republic of Letters Publishing, 2011.
Jóhanesson, Helgi. "Rökstólar: Landsdómur og ráðherraábyrgð [Debate: The Special Court and Ministerial Responsibility]." *Úlfljótur* 64, no. 2 (2011): 282–283.
Jónatansson, Hróbjartur. "Rökstólar: Landsdómur og ráðherraábyrgð [Debate: The Special Court and Ministerial Responsibility]." *Úlfljótur* 64, no. 2 (2011): 285–289.
Kritz, Neil J. ed. *Transitional Justice: How Emerging Democracies Reckon with Former Regimes.* 3 vols. Washington, DC: United States Institute of Peace Press, 1995.
Lampedusa, Giuseppe Tomasi de. *The Leopard.* Translated by Archibald Colquhoun. London: Fontana, 1963.
Líndal, Sigurður. "Um ráðherraábyrgð og landsdóm" [On Ministerial Responsibility and the Special Court]. *Skírnir* 184, no. 2 (fall 2010): 522–532.
"Lög um breytingar á lögum nr. 36/2001 um Seðlabanka Íslands" [Law on the Changes of the Law Number 36/2001 on Icelandic Central Bank]. Accessed December 4, 2015. www.althingi.is/altext/stjt/2009.005.html.
McAdams, A. James ed. *Transitional Justice and the Rule of Law in New Democracies.* Notre Dame: University of Notre Dame Press, 1997.
Maier, Charles. "Doing History, Doing Justice: The Narrative of the Historian and of the Truth Commission." In *Truth vs. Justice: The Moral Efficacy of Truth Commissions: South Africa and Beyond*, edited by Robert Rotgber and Dennis Thompson, 261–278. Princeton: Princeton University Press, 2000.
Minow, Martha. *Between Vengeance and Forgiveness: Facing History after Genocide and Mass Violence.* Boston: Beacon Press, 1998.
Ólafsdóttir, Svala Ísfeld. "Rökstólar: Landsdómur og ráðherraábyrgð" [A Debate: The Special Court and Ministerial Responsibility]. *Úlfljótur* 64, no. 2 (2011): 290–294.
Ólafsson, Þorvarður Tjörvi and Karen A. Vignisdóttir. "Staða íslenskra heimila í aðdraganda og kjölfar hrunsins. Lokaniðurstöður á greiningu á stöðu íslenskra heimila" [The state of Icelandic households preceding and following the crash. Final results of an analysis of the state of Icelandic households]. Public lecture at the Central Bank of Iceland, April 3, 2012. Accessed December 4, 2015. www.sedlabanki.is/lisalib/getfile.aspx?itemid=9536.

Ólafsson, Jón. "An Experiment in Iceland: Crowdsourcing a Constitution" (unpublished manuscript).

Rannsóknarnefnd Alþingis [The Special Investigation Commission of the Icelandic Parliament]. *Aðdragandi og orsakir falls íslensku bankanna 2008 og tengdir atburðir* [The Causes and Effects of the Fall of the Icelandic Banks and Related Events]. Reykjavík: Icelandic Parliament, 2010.

Roht-Arriaza, Naomi ed. *Impunity and Human Rights in International Law and Practice*. New York, Oxford University Press, 1995.

Rotgber, Robert, and Dennis Thompson eds. *Truth vs. Justice: The Moral Efficacy of Truth Commissions: South Africa and Beyond*. Princeton: Princeton University Press, 2000.

Rushton, Beth. "Truth and Reconciliation? The Experience of Truth Commissions." *Australian Journal of International Affairs* 60, no 1, 2006: 125–141.

Samtök fjármálafyrirtækja [Icelandic Financial Services Association]. "Niðurfærsla lána heimila 196,4 milljarðar króna um áramót" [Debt Relief in the Amount of 196.4 Billion Icelandic Kronur at the Beginning of this Year]. Report, February 12, 2012.

Sibert, Ann C. and Willem Buiter. "The Icelandic Banking Crisis and What to Do about It: The Lender of Last Resort Theory of Optimal Currency Areas." *CEPR Policy Insight* no. 26 (October 2008): 1–23. Accessed March 19, 2015. http://willembuiter.com/iceland.pdf.

Sigfúsdóttir, Vigdís Þóra. "Réttarstaða ráðherra sem sakborninga fyrir Landsómi í ljósi stjórnarskrár lýðveldisins Íslands og Mannréttindasáttmála Evrópu" [The Legal Position of Indicted Ministers before the Special Court *Landsdómur* in the Light of the Constitution of the Icelandic Republic and the European Convention on Human Rights]. ML thesis in Law, University of Bifröst, 2011.

"Skýrsla þingnefndar til að fjalla um skýrslu rannsóknarnefndar Alþingis" [Parliamentary Report on the Report by the Icelandic Investigative Commission] (September 2010). Accessed December 4, 2015. www.althingi.is/altext/138/s/1501.html.

Teitel, Ruti. *Transitional Justice*. Oxford: Oxford University Press, 2000.

"Tillaga til þingsályktunar um málshöfðun gegn ráðherrum" [Parliamentary Proposal on an Indictment against Ministers], September 11, 2010. Accessed December 4, 2015. www.althingi.is/altext/138/s/1502.html.

Toth, Mano. "The Myth of the Politics of Regret." *Millennium: Journal of International Studies* 42, no. 2 (2015): 551–566.

Valgreen, Carsten, Lars Christiansen, Peter Possing Andersen, and Rene Kallestrup. "Iceland: Geyser Crisis," March 21, 2006. Accessed December 4, 2015. www.mbl.is/media/98/398.pdf.

8 The strategy of redistribution

Iceland's way out of the crisis

Stefán Ólafsson

Introduction

The Icelandic financial collapse was a major event by international standards. The crisis that followed was multi-dimensional, featuring not just a banking collapse but also a stock market collapse, a currency collapse, an economic crisis, and a political crisis of lost trust in institutions as well as in politicians. The economic contraction was swift and deeper than had been seen at any previous time since the founding of the Icelandic Republic in 1944.

International Monetary Fund (IMF) researchers estimated that the Irish and Icelandic financial crises were among the 10 most costly financial crises in recent history, when assessed by direct fiscal cost, increased debt, and lost output.[1] Iceland is, thus, an interesting case for studying the advent of the crisis as well as its manifestations and the policy reactions to it. Given the enormity of the crisis, one might have expected that the consequences for standards of living would have been extensive and long lasting.

More than six years after the collapse, it appears that Iceland has done relatively well in dealing with, and ameliorating, many of the consequences of the crisis. It has been hailed by the IMF,[2] as well as by some renowned international economists, for its policy reactions and success in resurrecting the economy.[3] For some, Iceland is a case representing an alternative to the austerity policies that have prevailed in Europe in recent years. That description may, however, call for some qualifications, as we show in this chapter. For critics within Iceland, the government was seen as having failed to reinvigorate the economy by not sufficiently increasing growth-inducing investment, by not sufficiently easing excessive debt burdens, and by increasing taxation on businesses and society. Still, Iceland's growth rates from 2011 to date have been significantly higher than in most European economies, and by 2015, unemployment had come down again to one of the lowest levels in Europe.

In this chapter, we analyze Iceland's policy reactions to the crisis and their success. The stated aim of the incoming government in 2009 was to apply Nordic welfare policies, aiming to shelter the lower-income groups against the worst consequences of the crisis.[4] This meant softening the burden for these groups. That was, however, possible only by increasing the burden of the higher-income groups and by accumulating public debt. While the government was seriously restrained in applying welfare policies, due to an excessive public budget deficit by the end of 2008, it was able to redistribute expenditures and tax burdens to achieve its goals. Before mapping the developments of economy and society during the crisis and outlining the policy reactions, we start by putting the policy options into context with a brief survey of the international crisis policy debate.

The policy debate: stimulus, austerity, or a mixed approach?

The fundamentally opposed policy perspectives of Keynesian and Austrian political economics have been predominant in policy circles during the present financial crisis, as, indeed, they were during the Great Depression of the 1930s. Keynes' approach, emphasizing the virtues of governmentally induced stimulus to counter the fall of general demand in the economy in a crisis situation, has featured prominently as a cornerstone of policy reactions on one side of the debate.[5]

The US government and most European governments embarked, in fact, on an unprecedented level of Keynesian-style fiscal expansion in the form of stimulus packages at the start of the crisis, which included bank rescues. The Keynesian stimulus could come in the form of either a direct fiscal input or a tax cut, increasing the purchasing power of households and firms, and hence strengthening overall demand. Monetary policy was seen as not being sufficient on its own, but it could have a supporting role. These tenets were based on the lessons of the devastating consequences of the laissez-faire orientation and monetary contraction policy that were followed at the start of the Great Depression in the United States. That policy allowed the crisis to deepen nearly unhindered from 1929 for up to three years, that is, until the change of government in 1933.[6]

According to Keynesian analysts, the present Great Recession might have gone the same way as the Great Depression without the stimulus reactions, especially in the United States.[7] Thus, many thank the policy lessons of Keynesian political economics and the actual crisis lessons from the Great Depression for containing the present crisis within reasonable bounds, at least avoiding a more devastating collapse and depression for the world economy. On the other hand, some argue that the stimulus actions were not large enough to revitalize the respective economies fully; hence the ensuing slow growth to date, not least in Europe.[8] Others point to the restraints and dangers of high public debt levels.[9]

Following the typical early responses of generally successful government stimulus programs, the policy winds soon changed course, with a shift toward more emphasis on austerity measures, especially from 2010 onwards. That shift was, in most cases, driven by concern and worries about accumulating government debt. In addition, austerity policies tend to be more prominent in right-wing or neoliberal political circles.[10] They are based on a belief in the virtues of unrestrained markets and an ideological preference for small government. In the tradition of Austrian economics, they are based on the Hayekian and Schumpeterian conceptions of financial crises as being the result of financial excesses accumulated during the preceding boom, which need to be corrected by market forces during the inevitable depression.[11] Hence the Schumpeterian emphasis on a laissez-faire attitude to crises—the notion that crises could and should, fully and without interruptions, finish cleaning out the "rot" in the economic and financial system.

Governmental policy interference is seen from this perspective as a hindrance to the necessary crisis task of cleaning up by means of "creative destruction." The patient has to suffer for the sins committed during the boom for a healthy recovery to be possible.[12] Austrian economic theorists, therefore, emphasize that governments should not try to prevent the necessary reallocation process of the crisis effects, even though they may be painful. Keynesian-style stimulus programs and bailouts are seen as simply prolonging the unsustainable economic processes of the boom and delaying the recovery. Hence, the Austrian policy perspective advocates a withdrawal of government during the crisis and a reduction of spending and taxes. The last point accords well with the ideological preferences for small government of the neoliberally inclined Austrian economists. Hence, austerity policies can be seen as serving dual interests, as, indeed, can Keynesian-style policies from the opposite political perspective.

A particularly influential contemporary support for the case of austerity policy in crisis is the 2009 paper by Alberto F. Alesina and Sivia Ardagna,[13] which rejected the Keynesian proposition that cutting public spending during a recession further weakens the crisis economy. Instead, these authors argued that expenditure cuts would positively influence investor confidence, leading onwards to renewed growth. This contribution became a model for arguments about the virtues of austerity, formulated as the doctrine of "expansionary austerity," which runs counter to the mainstream Keynesian theory. A famous 2010 paper by Carmen R. Reinhart and Kenneth S. Rogoff[14] suggested that when governmental debt passed the level of 90% of gross domestic product (GDP), growth would be significantly negatively affected. These studies were later rejected by a more extensive study carried out at the IMF in 2011[15] and by researchers[16] who found flaws in Reinhart and Rogoff's methodology in that study.[17]

The bottom line seems to be clear. The Keynesian stimulus approach works, but the austerity position has an appeal due to concerns about excessive public debt levels after the costs of the banking crisis have been transferred to become public debts.[18] The neoliberal establishment also promotes austerity on the grounds of its laissez-faire and small-state ideological stance. Even though most states started their reactions to the crisis with successful Keynesian measures, many, not least the European ones, have, in turn, changed to austerity policies.[19] The turn toward austerity seems to be responsible for the sluggish recovery and significant cases of double-dip recessions.

The strategy of redistribution

Iceland was in dire straits after the collapse of the banks in October 2008. The public finances were devastated, with a budget deficit of almost 14% of GDP by the end of that year. The best part of the financial system was in total ruins, and emergency measures were required for keeping the daily economy functional and for new banks to be established, from the ruins of the old, as it turned out. The Central Bank also had to be refinanced with excessive sums. On top of that, the economy and the tax base were rapidly contracting, leading to large cuts in public revenues.

The Social Democratic/Left-Green coalition government that came to power in the spring of 2009 pledged to approach the crisis management in the spirit of Nordic welfare policies.[20] This involved the goal of sheltering households, in particular the lower-income ones, against the worst consequences of the crisis. This was easier said than done, considering the condition of public finances and unclear prospects about future debt levels for the government and the economy as a whole. It took, in fact, up to two years for the overall debt situation of the economy and future obligations of the state to become clear. Hence, the first steps of the new government were undertaken in a situation of great uncertainty.

Iceland was, thus, not in a position to save the banks with a massive injection of capital or to provide a large fiscal stimulus.[21] General government gross debt increased from some 25% of GDP before the crisis up to about 100% when it peaked in 2011. Still, the government managed to implement some stimulus policies. At the same time, it also implemented some measures better classified as austerity measures. This draws attention to the fact that governments can use a mixed approach. It is, indeed, not always clear in much of the economics or crisis policy literature what qualifies as stimulus and what as austerity policy in this context.[22]

Iceland increased its governmental expenditures greatly at the beginning of the crisis, at the same time as government revenues came down, as can be seen in Figure 8.1.

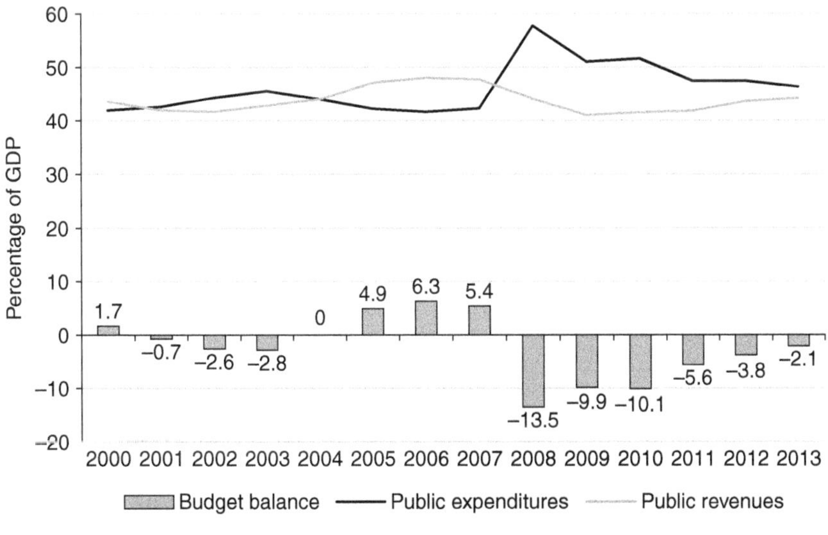

Figure 8.1 Contours of stimulus and austerity in Iceland. Development of public finances (expenditures, revenues, and budget balance), from 2000 to 2013 (figures in % of GDP) (source: Statistics Iceland, Data on Government Finance, accessed December 1, 2015, www.hagstofa.is).

Hence, the budget deficit became massive, as can also be seen in the figure, starting at 13.5% by end of 2008 and then gradually coming down to 2.1% in 2013. The deficit evened out in 2014. On the surface, this seems like a forceful Keynesian-style fiscal stimulus response. The government increases expenditures as the crisis hits, even though revenues collapse, thus leading to a large deficit and debt accumulation. And, indeed, we see that nearly all the European countries responded similarly, albeit to differing degrees. The countries hardest hit by the financial crisis accumulated the greatest government deficit during the crisis, from 2008 to 2012, as emerges from Figure 8.2. The deficit adds to the public debt level.

Here we see that the deep-crisis countries accumulated the greatest debt levels during the crisis. Ireland, which embarked on a great mission of saving banks, ranks highest, increasing the governmental debt by some 73 percentage points. Greece comes second, with Spain, Iceland, the United Kingdom, and Portugal

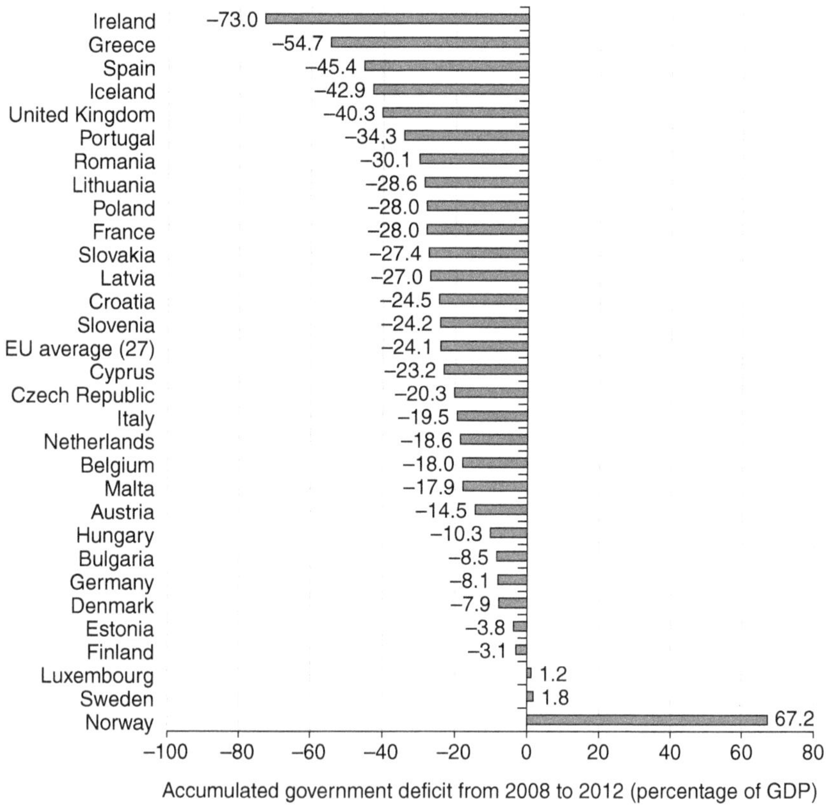

Figure 8.2 Total government accumulated deficit from 2008 to 2012 (in % of GDP) (source: Eurostat (EU-SILC data), Data on real disposable earnings, accessed December 1, 2015, http://ec.europa.eu/eurostat/web/income-and-living-conditions/data/database).

following suit. It is also interesting that some deep-crisis countries, such as Estonia, Hungary, and Cyprus, did not accumulate as much deficit as expected, given the size of the crisis in these countries. At the other extreme, we find Norway, which felt hardly any crisis effects, actually running a large positive balance, accumulating assets due to favorable oil revenues. The same applies to Sweden and Luxembourg, but at a much lower level.

In a way, these figures of budget deficits could be taken as indicators of stimulus measures, at least in relative terms. But when we look at the increase in government expenditures, including welfare expenditures, we see that Iceland did not set any records on that front. Some other European governments increased government expenditures to a greater extent than Iceland. Therefore, this was not the most important aspect of Iceland's crisis management strategy, even though it involved a huge budget deficit and a great accumulation of debt.

This is where the government's strategy of redistribution comes in. The aim of sheltering the lower-earning half or thereabouts of households from the worst of the consequences of the devaluation and contraction involved the implementation of some countervailing policies. The main characteristic was redistribution. This applied equally to taxation policy, minimum pensions, unemployment benefits, and debt relief measures, as well as to welfare expenditures in general. The overall strategy of redistribution, thus, involved channeling public expenditures to a greater extent to address the needs of lower-income households. In that sense, the strategy of redistribution was a strategy of equalization.

Welfare transfer expenditures were increased, but expenditures on welfare services and administration were cut. Expenditure cuts were directed more at education, health, and administration, while expenditure on welfare transfers increased. The welfare transfers were increasingly directed at lower-income groups than before and, at the same time, what had previously gone to higher-income groups was cut. The net effect was a higher level of overall welfare expenditures than ever before in the history of the Icelandic Republic. The consequence of this policy emphasis was a reversal in the previous trend toward increased income inequality, and the distribution becoming much more equal again, as can be seen in Figure 8.3.

Prior to the crisis, income inequality had been increasing rapidly in Iceland, in fact all the way from 1995 to a peak in 2007, just before the bubble burst. The Gini index of inequality for disposable earnings, with all taxable incomes counted, increased from 0.21 to 0.43 in 2007, an unprecedented speed of change in Organisation for Economic Co-operation and Development (OECD) countries. Then it came down again to about 0.25 in 2010–2011—also an unprecedented reversal of trends. If we look at the Gini coefficient for equivalized disposable earnings, excluding capital gains (which is data comparable to OECD and Eurostat data on income inequality), the index increased from about 0.19 in 1995 to about 0.29 in 2007–2008, before coming down again to 0.24.[23] A part of the reversal toward greater equality was due to a decline of financial earnings during the crisis, but a sizable effect was also due to the changed governmental policy on direct taxation and benefits.

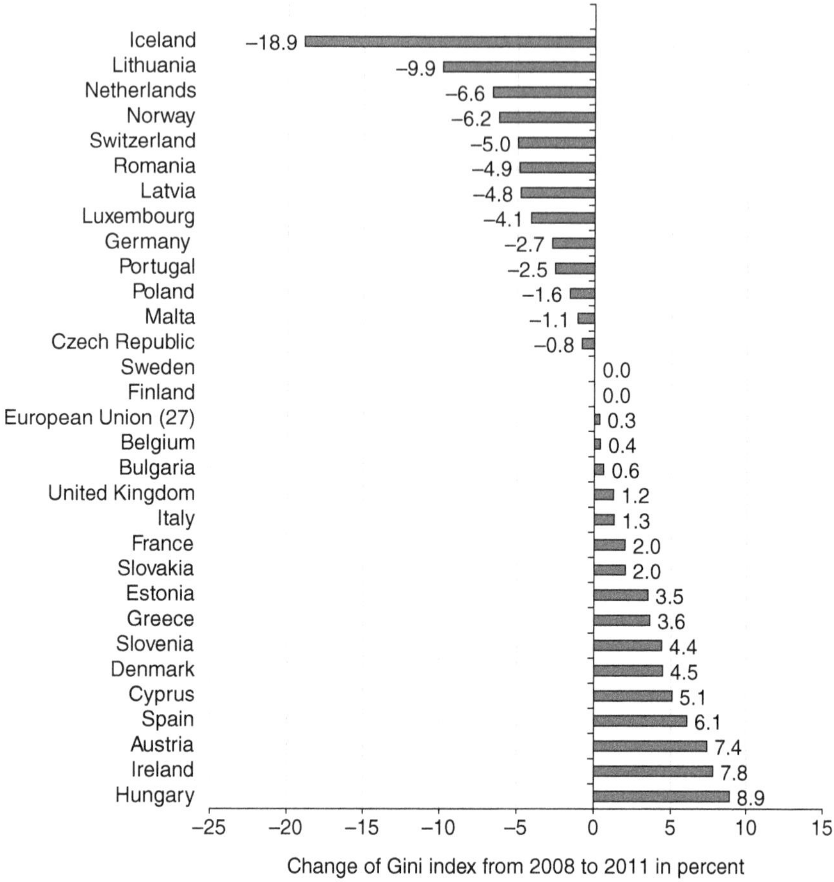

Figure 8.3 Development of income inequality during the crisis. Change of Gini Index from 2008 to 2011 (%)[24] (source: Eurostat (EU-SILC data), Data on real disposable earnings, accessed December 1, 2015, http://ec.europa.eu/eurostat/web/income-and-living-conditions/data/database).

As emerges from Figure 8.3, Iceland appears to have been in a class of its own as regards equalization during the height of the crisis. Thus, the Gini index for household equalized disposable earnings declined by 18.9% between 2008 and 2011, while it fell by 9.9% in the runner-up (Lithuania) and by about 6% in the Netherlands and Norway, which did not suffer a deep crisis.

It is also interesting that many of the deep-crisis countries increased inequality of income distribution during the crisis, a development that should be expected in a context of growing unemployment (which generally hits lower-class groups harder) and austerity policies (which also affect earnings of lower-income groups disproportionally). Thus, Croatia, Hungary, Ireland, Spain, Cyprus, and Greece all experienced increased inequality during the crisis. Exceptions to this trend among deep-crisis countries are Lithuania, Romania, Latvia, and Portugal, but these showed significantly lower inequality reduction than Iceland. Thus, these differing developments of inequality indicate differing crisis-management strategies. In Figure 8.4, we show how the real tax burden changed in Iceland during the height of the crisis. The strategy of redistribution is also evident, since the tax burden clearly increased for higher-income groups, while it was reduced among the lower-income groups.

The figure shows the share of total earnings paid in direct taxes (income tax, financial earnings tax) paid by each of the income decile groups and the top 1% of income earners, on the one hand in 2007 (gray columns) and then in 2010 (black columns). The figure shows clearly how the burden developed through the depth of the crisis. The tax burden was shifted from lower-income groups to the higher ones. In 2007, the net effective tax burden of the lowest-income decile was 3%, but in 2010 it had fallen to –3% (the negative figure is accounted for by child benefit and tax rebate for interest cost of mortgages, which are paid through the tax system). In the second-lowest-income group (group II in the figure), the burden was reduced from 10.5% to 7%, and so on up to group VI, where the change was minor, a lowering from 20.5% to 20.2%.

Thus, the real direct tax burden for the lowest-earning 60% of households was reduced, while it was increased for the top 40%: the higher up the income scale one looks, the greater the increase. The change was greatest for the top 1% of income earners, a shift from 13% direct tax burden up to 33.3%. The overall

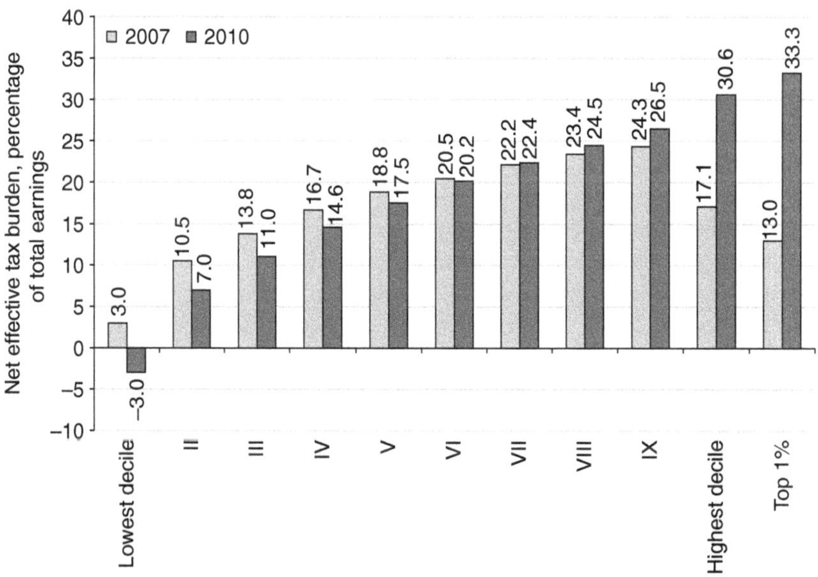

Figure 8.4 Net effective tax burden by income groups in 2007 and in 2010. Direct taxes paid as a proportion of total pre-tax earnings of households (source: public tax data).

change of the distribution of the direct tax burden was a major reversal of the trend that had prevailed for the 12 years prior to the crisis.[25] This change was implemented by raising the marginal tax rate on incomes; also, the flat tax rate on financial earnings was raised from 10% to 20%, and the taxation of businesses was also raised. The personal tax allowance was increased, along with other subtractions that specifically lowered the burden of the lower- and middle-income groups. In addition to these changes, a special temporary wealth tax was imposed on net wealth above a certain limit.

A strategy of redistribution and equalization is what best describes Iceland's crisis-management strategy, rather than the overall extent of a direct Keynesian-style stimulus program. The stimulus element was effective in these measures, since equalization harmonizes well with Keynesian policy strategy.[26] Everything that increases purchasing power or limits cuts in purchasing power disproportionally stimulates or contains private consumption, since the lower-income groups can be expected to spend all they have in the short term. The program of debt relief that the government implemented during the crisis was also important as a redistribution strategy, since it concentrated on helping the lower- and middle-income households, which were in greatest need.

Other aspects did, however, make a difference, such as the big devaluation of the national currency (Icelandic krona), which reduced real wage levels from their swollen height of the bubble years and thereby increased wage competitiveness, which facilitated a higher employment level through the crisis. In addition to the above-mentioned measures, strong policy efforts were directed at labor market activation and job creation, which turned out to be very successful.

In what follows, I first profile Iceland's progress through the crisis and the resurrection before describing the various policy measures of the strategy of redistribution in greater detail.

Iceland's progress through the crisis

The accumulated contraction of GDP from 2009 to 2010 was about 10%, the currency (the Icelandic krona) fell by some 50% altogether from beginning of 2008 through 2009, and unemployment increased from about 3% to 9% at the peak (in the second quarter of 2009), a level of unemployment not seen in Iceland since the 1930s. This raises the question of how Iceland fared through the reconstruction period.

As seen in Figure 8.5, the contraction of GDP was confined to 2009 and 2010; in fact, Iceland reached the bottom by mid-2010. From then on, the economy grew again, and with a persistently higher rate than the average for the Euro area from 2011 through 2013. Unlike the EU countries, Iceland remained growing, while the EU average went into contraction again with the double-dip crisis after 2011, as a result of the austerity policies in 2010–2011. Iceland's growth rate has, indeed, been among the very highest in the West since 2011. Growth of 4% in 2015 was significantly higher than the EU average, and the prognosis for 2016 is good too. Compared with some of the deep-crisis countries, it seems that

Iceland and the Baltic states were the fastest to rise again. On the lower diagram of Figure 8.5 is a more direct comparison of Iceland with Ireland, which experienced a bubble economy and financial collapse to a similar extent. Both countries experienced a deep recession, Ireland sinking somewhat faster, but climbing faster at first, in 2010. Then, from 2011, Ireland lagged decisively behind the growth rates of Iceland.

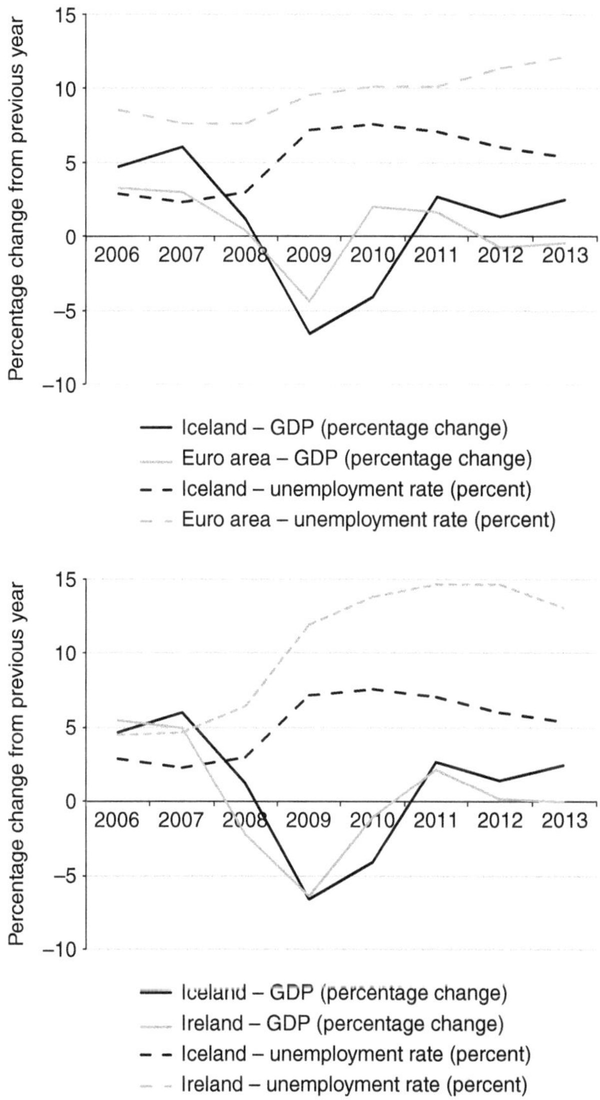

Figure 8.5 Economic growth and unemployment through the crisis (% change from previous year)—Iceland, Ireland, and the Euro area compared, 2006–2013 (source: Statistics Iceland and Eurostat).

The record on unemployment is even better for Iceland. Even though unemployment increased drastically with the onset of the crisis, this was from a very low level. At the depth of the crisis, the yearly average for Iceland never rose above the Euro area average. And while Iceland's unemployment rate came down from 2011 onwards, the Euro area rate kept rising through 2013, with only a minor decline, again, in the first months of 2014.

Ireland's unemployment rate climbed significantly faster and higher than Iceland's after the onset of the crisis, reaching about 15% in 2011–2012, before coming down a little in 2013 and early 2014. So, Ireland's crisis management was less successful than Iceland's in combatting unemployment and stimulating growth. By the end of 2013, Iceland had the fifth lowest unemployment rate in Europe, and by end of 2014, Iceland's unemployment rate was well below 5%. That may be considered a major achievement when the size of the financial collapse is kept in mind. All the countries that went deeply into crisis from 2008 had much higher unemployment levels through the crisis years. This applies most markedly to Spain, Greece, Croatia, Portugal, Cyprus, Ireland, Bulgaria, Italy, and the Baltic states.

Iceland's public debt level rose drastically until 2011, but has come down since then. Still, Iceland did not reach the highest debt level in Europe, since five EU countries had a higher government debt level than Iceland by the end of 2012. While Iceland's public debt is being reduced slowly, some of the other crisis countries are still increasing their debt levels, with significant budget deficits. Icelandic household debt levels have also come down significantly, and purchasing power is gradually rising. So, all things considered, the most common indicators of economic development tell a story of relatively successful resurrection from the ashes of the collapse in Iceland, stronger than in many of the countries that suffered the deepest contraction of their economies.

Paul Krugman, Nobel laureate in economics, has remarked in his *New York Times* column that Iceland did not need a stimulus program, since its currency was devalued by about 50%. That swiftly strengthened the wage competitiveness of the economy, facilitating a quick recovery based on export growth, which made possible a higher level of employment through the crisis. This, however, came at a great cost to the household sector, which suffered a drastic cut in its real earnings.

On average, the real disposable earnings of the household sector fell by some 20% due to the inflation that emerged from the devaluation (real wages fell by some 12%, but the rest of the real earnings decline was the result of lower work volumes and increased unemployment). Real private consumption contracted by more than 20% from 2007 to 2010. This represented a fall from a great height in 2007, when Iceland had a real earnings level among the very highest in Europe, due to an overrated currency and the bubble effect on consumption. Hence, there was some room for bearable cuts from that unsustainable level of affluence.

The strategy of redistribution ensured, however, that the average cut in real earnings for the household sector was softened by tax and benefit policies, so that the cut in living standards for the lower-income groups was significantly less than the average, while the highest-income group lost much more than the average.[27] This can be seen in Figure 8.6.

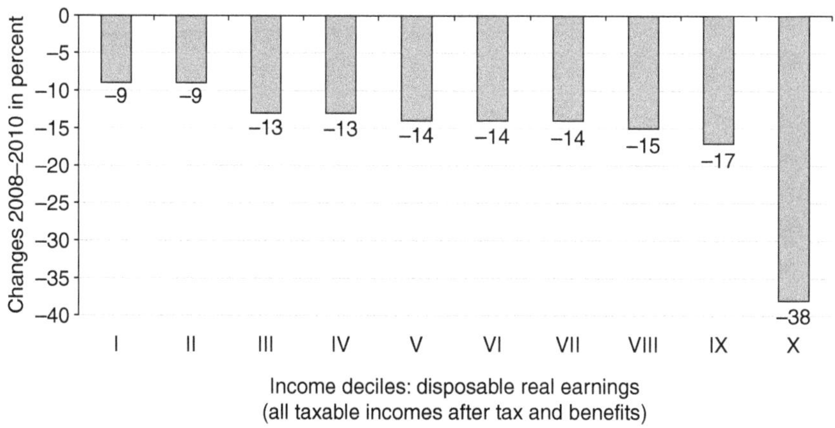

Figure 8.6 Change in real disposable earnings by income deciles, 2008–2010 (source: public tax data).

Thus, the real disposable earnings of the lowest two deciles (the lowest-earning 20% of households) fell by about 9%, while the median households lost 14% and the top decile lost 38% of the earnings they had had in 2008. This development was the opposite of what took place in the countries that increased inequality during the crisis, such as the United States, the United Kingdom, Ireland, Hungary, Spain, Cyprus, and Greece (see Figure 8.3).

While the overall setback for economic living standards was large by any standards, it was a fall from a great height; as it turned out, a fall from an inflated and unsustainably high earnings level. The real wage index started to increase again in the latter part of 2010, and more decisively in 2011 and 2012, as can be seen in Figure 8.7.

By 2014, the level of the real wage index was back to the level that had prevailed between 2004 and 2005. That is a significant achievement. Minimum wages have, in fact, increased faster than average wages during the crisis.[28] On the lower diagram of Figure 8.7, the development of real private consumption of households (volume index) is shown. It tells a similar story to the real wage index, even though the decline in private consumption is larger, due to the extra effect of lower work volumes and increased unemployment during the crisis.

On the whole, it can be stated that in comparison to the EU countries—and many other countries that were affected by the crisis—Iceland has climbed back up relatively quickly. The devaluation of the currency and the strategy of redistribution facilitated the recovery, along with strong activation and job creation measures as well as a relatively strong debt relief effort. One important benefit of the strategy of redistribution is that the overall need for austerity measures was reduced. It should also be mentioned that the currency devaluation facilitated a boom in tourism during the crisis years. This, as well as an increased catch of mackerel, provided a welcome addition to the economy in those lean years.

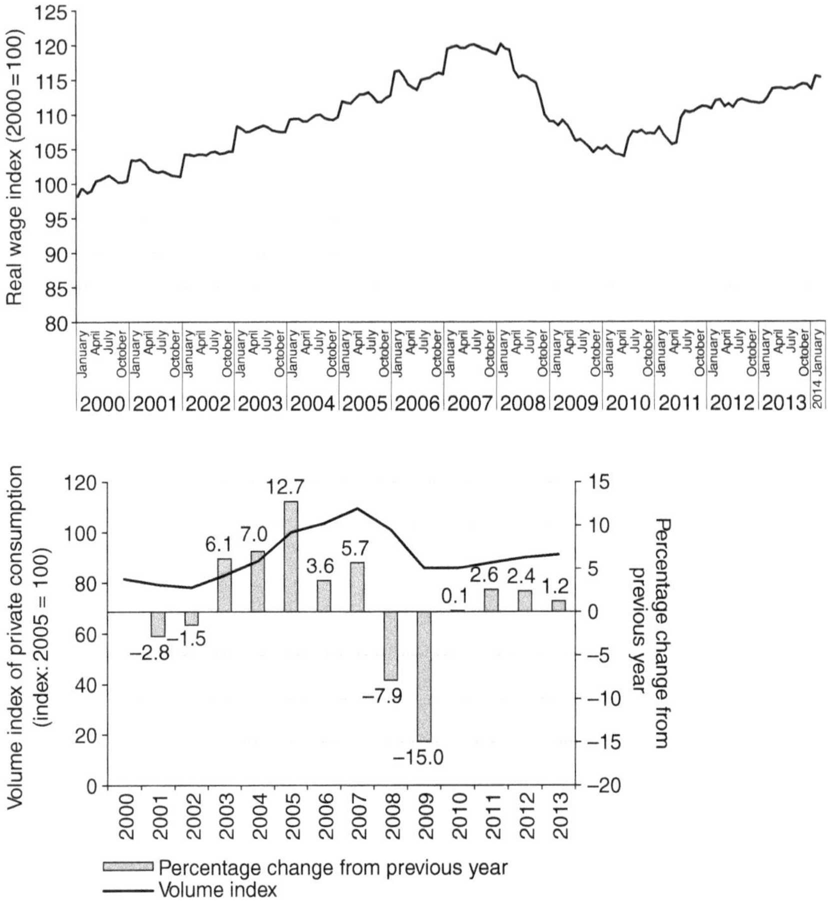

Figure 8.7 Development of the Real Wage Index (upper diagram) from 2000 through February 2014 and private consumption (lower diagram) from 2000 to 2013 (Volume Index) (source: Statistics Iceland, Data on real wage development, accessed December 21, 2015, www.hagstofa.is).

Policy profiles: how to cut and not cut welfare expenditures

Overall public expenditures increased greatly due to various costs of the collapse, as we have already shown. Thus, for example, the economic costs skyrocketed in 2008, covering the gigantic one-time costs of resurrecting the banking system and refinancing the Central Bank. Public expenditures in all main areas, other than social protection and economic affairs, fell significantly, including expenditures on health, recreation, and culture, as well as on education. Despite cuts in education, the enrolment of students, at both secondary and tertiary levels, significantly increased, since this was particularly promoted, for example, through activation programs. Thus, efficiency in education increased; that is, more students were accommodated despite reduced funding. It remains, however, to be seen whether this eroded standards. Expenditures on housing (debt relief) also increased greatly in 2010. Figure 8.8 shows the development of real value expenditures on social protection, health, and education during the crisis.

Thus, it was a mixed experience, with considerable increase in social protection transfers to households, while expenditures on health-care services and education were markedly cut in real terms. The main increase factors were unemployment benefits (due to increased numbers, extension of rights period, and a modest rise in the benefit), activation measures, housing cost subsidies, and minimum pension guarantees. The cuts in health were generally across that sector, except that disability pensioners enjoyed some increase. Hospitals, health care centers, and subsidies of medication costs and services were cut. In education, the cuts affected all levels, from primary to tertiary education. On the whole, the expenditures were targeted to a greater extent at lower- and middle-income households and were often cut for higher earners.

Hence, the minimum pension guarantee, for the elderly and disability pensioners, was raised on a par with price rises. Similarly, Social Assistance Allowance, the unemployment benefit, and minimum wages were also increased sizably, while average wages remained unchanged. These benefits targeted at the lowest-income groups were aimed to keep them above the poverty level through the crisis.

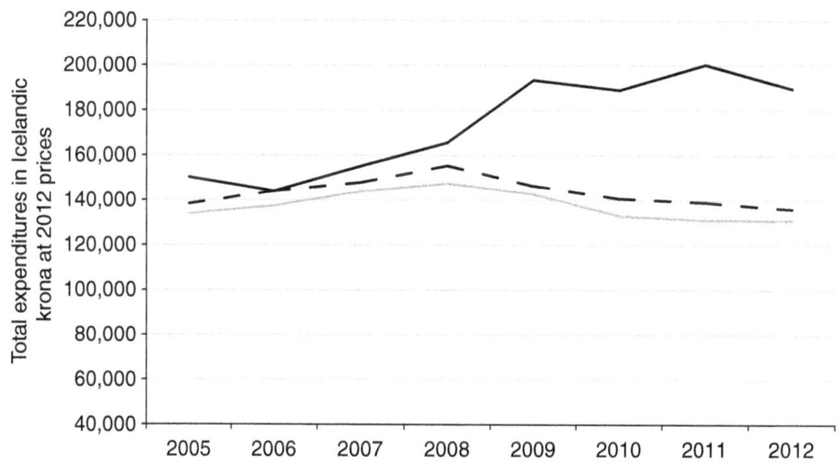

Figure 8.8 Development of main categories of public welfare expenditures from 2005 to 2012 (Icelandic krona at 2012 prices) (source: Statistics Iceland, Data on Government Finance, accessed December 1, 2015, www.hagstofa.is).

Thus, in the development of welfare expenditures, as well as in tax and benefits policy, there were significant measures aimed at redistribution and sheltering of the most vulnerable. This was also a good measure from a Keynesian economic perspective, that is, to give lower-income households some protection from cuts in living standards.[29] This is the case because it does not only relieve the burden on the backs of those who are weakest, but also helps to maintain relative consumer demand (even though most households experienced some cuts in living standards), since lower-income households spend most or all of what they have. The cuts were decisively directed more toward the higher-income-earning households.

Activation stepped up

Given the contraction in the number of available jobs in the wake of the collapse, it was bound to be difficult to make do with activation measures to combat unemployment. As shown in the upper diagram of Figure 8.9, the employment rate fell significantly, from in the region of 81% to about 74–75%. Working hours also fell, from 42–43 (for all employed, full-time and part-time together) to about 39–40. The employment rate increased again from April 2012, but modestly, and average working hours have fluctuated without a significant increase. So, the number of jobs has increased again without the overall volume of work having increased to the same extent.

Still, there was room for activation, since a sizable part of the population emigrated after the onset of the crisis. A number of immigrants returned to their countries of origin (about a fifth of those who had come to Iceland between 2004 and 2008), and native Icelanders moved in considerable numbers to Norway, where the employment situation continued to be good.

Altogether, about 1.7–2% of Icelanders went to Norway during the first five years of the crisis. This created better job opportunities for those who were on the unemployment register, as did some job creation schemes implemented by government. Activation measures were greatly stepped up during the crisis years. On the lower diagram of Figure 8.9, there is an indication of the overall increase in participation in active labor market measures (ALMPs) from 2008 to 2012.

It is quite clear from these data that the activation measures were drastically increased. Prior to the crisis, Iceland had for decades enjoyed very high employment participation rates and low unemployment. Hence, the need for active labor market policies was not greatly felt, and they remained modest. That situation is reflected in the numbers for 2008 in Figure 8.9. At that time, the primary activity consisted of short-term activation measures, short courses, and information provision.

Programs promoting educational participation were started as early as 2009, including long-term studies in secondary schools and special educational tracks. These increased in scope up to 2011, when the number of participants peaked. Other measures to spur employment were also implemented, with the use of a wage subsidy from the Unemployment Insurance Fund, and these peaked in 2012.

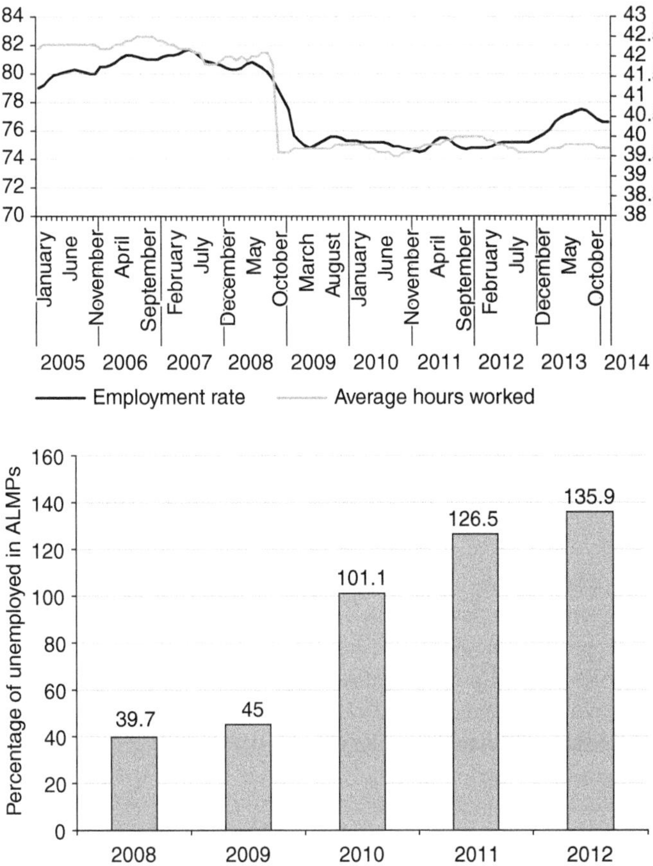

Figure 8.9 Development of the employment rate and average weekly working hours (upper diagram) and participation of unemployed individuals in ALMPs through the crisis (lower diagram) (source: Statistics Iceland and Directorate of Labor).

Of a similar character was a new program that was started in January 2013 (*Lið-sauki*), aimed specifically at long-term unemployed individuals who had fully utilized their four-year entitlement to unemployment benefits. This got off to a flying start in the first months of 2013, and the aim was to offer a job to everyone in that position, with the Unemployment Benefits Fund subsidizing the wage for the first six months. This program seems to have increased the number of participating individuals in employment. In-work or rehabilitation measures were also stepped up from 2009 onwards, including cooperation with the Rehabilitation Fund of the Labor Market (VIRK) and the Social Security Administration (TR).

The total number of participants in activation measures increased from about 40% of those on the unemployment register to 45% in 2009 and onwards, rising steeply to 136% in 2012. The proportion is more than 100% from 2010 to 2012 because some of the unemployed took part in more than one line of activity. As the activation efforts were increased, the unemployment rate was reduced from 8% to 6% in 2012, and it stayed below 5% during the summer of 2013. It was below 4% for the greatest part of 2015, and by January 2016 it is 2.8%. Immigrant laborers have experienced about twice the unemployment rate of native Icelanders, and it seems that activation measures have not reached them to the same extent.[30] They may also be disadvantaged by the fact that they have weaker social networks to help them back into the labor market.

An evaluation survey among those registered as unemployed from 2009 to November 2013 indicated that about 75% of those who took part in ALMPs were back in employment or education by December 2013.[31] On the whole, it seems clear that the activation measures and related labor market efforts have been quite successful in Iceland and greatly helped to alleviate the negative consequences of the crisis.

Poverty contained

What follows is an examination of the development of poverty indicators through the crisis. Given the already indicated success of the strategy of redistribution, the relative poverty level should have come down to some extent during the crisis, despite generally increased financial hardship of most households. This is, indeed, what happened, as indicated in Table 8.1.

The relative poverty rate of Iceland was fairly stable before the financial crisis, with about 10% of households having disposable earnings below 60% of median earnings. This was one of the lowest relative poverty rates among European nations, along with the other Nordic countries, Slovakia, the Czech Republic, and Holland. The more inclusive indicator of "at risk of poverty or social exclusion" was lowest in Iceland, according to Eurostat data for 2012. Thus, it is interesting to see how the poverty measures developed through the crisis.

From 2009 onwards (that is, 2010 in the table[32]), the relative poverty rate for all households gradually started to fall, and by 2011 (2012 in the table), it stood at 7.9%, lower than at any time since the start of these measures in 2003. This indicates that the disposable earnings of the low-income households declined less than those of median households. The low-income groups were, indeed, sheltered relative to higher-income groups.

Disaggregating this for different groups, we see that the percentage of employed people fell from about 6.5–8% before the crisis to 5.2% in 2011. The relative poverty rate in the category of those "not at work" was reduced even further, from in the region of 14–19% to 10.6% in 2011. The percentage of those categorized as unemployed fluctuated more through the period (this was a small group before the crisis, with a large margin of error in the survey data). It seems to have fallen from about 25–29% in the years immediately before the onset of the crisis to 20% in 2011.

Table 8.1 Poverty development through the crisis. Proportion under the 60% poverty line and those making ends meet with great difficulty

	2004	*2005*	*2006*	*2007*	*2008*	*2009*	*2010*	*2011*	*2012*
% under the 60% poverty line:									
Total	10	9.7	9.6	10.1	10.1	10.2	9.8	9.2	7.9
Employed	6.9	7.9	6.6	7	6.7	7.7	6.6	6.4	5.2
Not at work	16.1	14	16.2	17.2	18.9	17.4	13.6	12.3	10.6
Unemployed	27.1	26.1	13.8	20.6	25.1	29.3	25.5	21.8	20
Retired	11.3	10.2	13.5	18.8	17.9	14.8	6.3	4.6	3.8
Financial hardship (% of households): Make ends meet with great difficulty	9.7	6.9	5.8	5.6	5.9	8.2	13.7	13.1	11.5

Source: Statistics Iceland Data on poverty and financial hardship, accessed April 24, 2013, www.hagstofa.is.

But the most decisive change in relative poverty rates is found among retired individuals. They experienced poverty rates of about 18–19% in the last years before the crisis, but this fell to 4–5% in recent years. This big change was mainly due to the great increase in the minimum pension guarantee, which we mentioned in the previous section. A lower effective tax rate on lower incomes also helped to achieve this outcome. Hence, it appears not only that low-income pensioners were kept above the poverty rate through the crisis, but that the number of those below the poverty line was, in fact, greatly reduced. This is a telling example of the strategy of redistribution succeeding in action.

But relative poverty rates have a drawback, exactly by being "relative." They do not actually tell us whether the individuals or households in question suffered gains or losses of real disposable income. They only reveal the development of the incomes of the poor relative to the median household. Thus, the relative poverty rates show, in this case, that the lower-income groups lost less real income than the median household. And since most households lost some purchasing power due to rising inflation, particularly in the early crisis years, not many individuals would accept the message from relative poverty measures that poverty actually declined during the crisis. Most people felt rather strongly about their increased financial difficulties and hardships due to increased inflation and a rising debt burden. Real earnings were lowered across nearly all households, but less so among the lower-income groups, as shown in Figure 8.6.

Due to this ambiguity of relative poverty measures, we also present a more realistic measure of household financial hardship in the lower part of the table. This is the proportion of households finding it very difficult to make ends meet in their day-to-day living. There, we see a different picture. The proportion of households saying that they "make ends meet with great difficulty" rose from 5–6% immediately before the crisis to 13.7% when it peaked in 2010. It more than doubled. This is a fairly realistic indicator of the increased financial hardship experienced by households during the crisis. The proportion with great difficulties in making ends meet then came down a little in 2011 and 2012, ending at 11.5%.

Eurostat data on risk of poverty or social exclusion (combined index of relative monetary poverty, low work households, and experience of relative material deprivation) for 2011 and 2012 show that Iceland has retained its position as the country with the lowest combined rate during the crisis, as it was before the crisis. That is a significant achievement, given the enormity of the financial collapse.

On the whole, one can state that the strategy of redistribution, which increased equality in the distribution of living conditions after the onset of the crisis, managed to avoid increased relative poverty. The lower-income households were sheltered against the worst consequences of the financial crisis. Still, most households experienced increased financial strain.

Debt relief

Debt burden became one of the major issues after the crisis set in. Households, which generally had taken on increased debt during the boom years, found it much more difficult to carry the debt burden from 2009 onwards, due to rising inflation and reduced real earnings. The principals of the mortgages and consumer loans are tied to the consumer price index, and, therefore, they grew with rising inflation in 2008 and 2009. This—and the reduction in real earnings—created major difficulties for households, especially for lower-income households and those that had bought houses during the bubble years (2003–2007) at elevated prices, typically young families with children.[33]

The government had pledged to shelter the households and, therefore, had to provide some measures of debt relief. It made it possible to reschedule repayments or get a temporary freeze on repayments. Subsequently, more direct measures were introduced to cut the mortgage principals of the households that were in greatest difficulties. Two main programs were implemented. On the one hand, a general cut in housing debt for those with debt more than the value of their estate was enacted. The principal could be reduced to 110% of the value of the apartment or house, up to the cost of modest family housing. On the other, for those in gravest difficulties and with low earnings, there was the possibility of a special cut to 70% of the house value. Relatively few households had access to the latter measure, but the 110% approach was used by a considerable number of households.

Then, the governmental subsidy of the cost of interest of housing loans was increased greatly, or by some 108% from 2008 to 2011, while the interest cost increased by some 41% at the same time.[34] Figure 8.10 profiles the development of the household debt level prior to and after the collapse (upper diagram), as well as the changing subsidy of household interest cost (lower diagram).

The household debt level increased rapidly in Iceland, from about 90% of GDP in 2003 to about 125% in 2009. Then it came down to about 105% by 2013, a more extensive reduction than in any of the other countries in the figure. Ireland was, though, close to Iceland in that respect, with a reduction by 16.7 percentage points, as against 18.3 percentage points for Iceland, between 2009 and 2012. Taking the period from 2009 to 2013, Iceland's household debts came down by 23.4 percentage points. Denmark had the highest household debt level from 2006 onwards, and it fell only modestly from 2009. The same can be said about the UK level, which, however, was significantly lower. All the other countries in the figure kept increasing their household debt levels after the onset of the crisis. While Iceland had the second-highest debt level at the peak in 2009, it was down to the fifth highest by 2012.

The IMF surveyed the debt relief programs of some Western countries in its staff report on Iceland for 2012.[35] They found that the debt relief measures taken by the Icelandic government were more extensive than other measures taken during the crisis. The only program they found to be of comparable relative size to the Icelandic one was President Franklin D. Roosevelt's debt relief program during the Great Depression in the United States. No comparable measures were taken in the United States or the United Kingdom in the present crisis, or in Finland and Sweden when they were severely hit by financial crises in the early 1990s.

The other part of the debt relief programs was the increased subsidy for housing interest cost of mortgages. The lower diagram of Figure 8.10 shows how those were drastically increased during the crisis after having eroded gradually

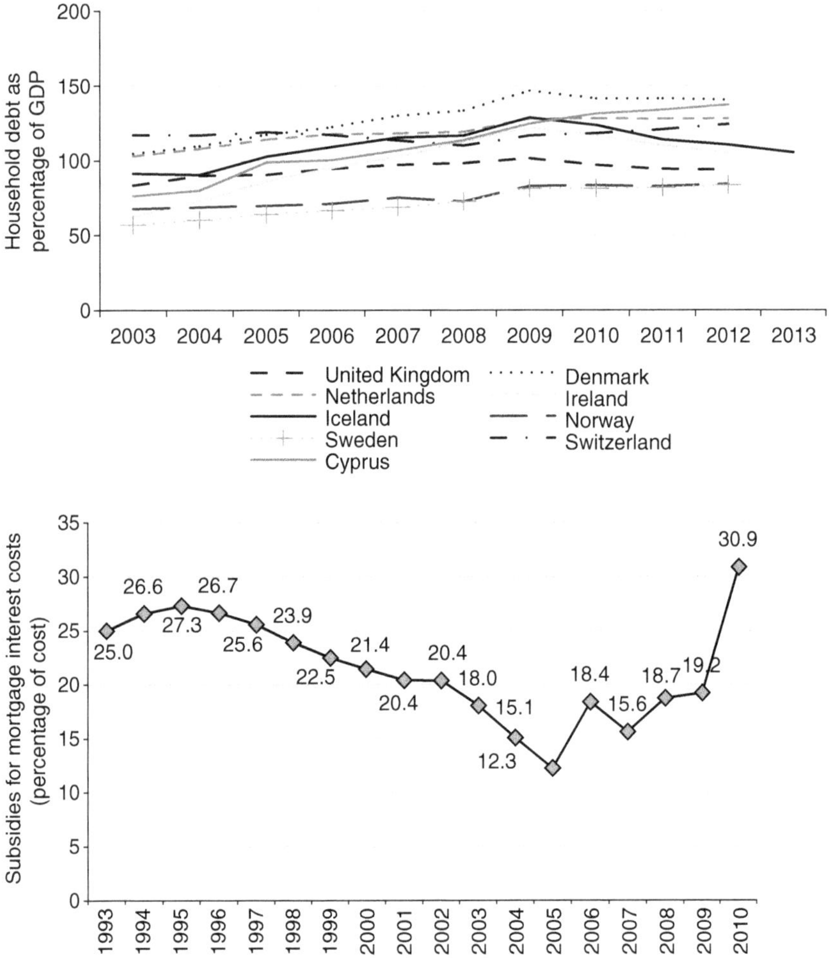

Figure 8.10 Household debt 2003–2013 in selected countries (as % of GDP) and subsidies of mortgage interest cost (the average subsidy as % of interest cost) in Iceland 1993–2010 (source: Central Bank of Iceland, Financial Stability Reports. Reykjavik: Central Bank of Iceland, 2012 and 2014 (available at www.sedlabanki.is); Ólafsson and Kristjánsson, "Umfang kreppunnar og afkoma ólíkra tekjuhópa," Report to the Ministry of Welfare, October, 2012, accessed February 5, 2015, http://thjodmalastofnun.hi.is/sites/thjodmalastofnun.hi.is/files/skrar/skyrsla_i-umfang_kreppunnar_og-afkoma_olikra_tekjuhopa–lokautgafa.pdf).

from 1995 to 2005. The share of the housing loan interest cost paid by government went from 15.6% in 2007, on average, to about 31% in 2010. This support was, however, well grounded in the redistribution strategy, giving more support to lower-income households than to the median and higher-income ones. Thus, the households with the lowest income (the lowest decile of income groups) had up to 44% of their housing interest cost paid by government in 2010, while the median household had about a third and the top income group (highest decile) had about 10% of their housing interest cost subsidized. Thus, the support for the lower-income groups was markedly greater, cementing the strategy of redistribution.

The debt relief measures of the former government were generally praised, including by the IMF, but many Icelanders wanted more support. Thus, when the parties of the former government (2009–2013) did not promise further significant relief measures during the election campaign of 2013, while the opposition parties promised to cut overall household debt further by some 20%, the voters went for the better offers. The left-wing parties, therefore, lost heavily in the election of 2013, despite having done a reasonably good job at resurrecting the economy and society after the collapse.

Thus, debt relief issues continued into the second election term after the financial collapse. The present government has introduced its plan for further relief, which will be spread out over a period between 2015 and 2017. It will be composed of a direct cut in principals of household housing debt and a tax benefit, which favors middle- and higher-income households more than the measures implemented by the former government. The new debt measures will be less redistributive than the measures of the former government. Still, we can expect the general level of household debts to fall further in the next few years, possibly by another 20% on average.

Conclusions

Despite suffering a major financial collapse and economic recession, Iceland appears to have done relatively well in its recovery phase. The crisis bottomed out by mid-year 2010, and from then on, growth was resumed. Economic growth was significantly above the EU average from 2011 onwards. The record in combatting unemployment is even better. Even though the unemployment rate increased drastically from a very low level before the crisis, it only surpassed the EU average for one quarter of 2009. Apart from that, it stayed below the European average. All the other countries that went into deep financial crisis (Ireland, Spain, Portugal, Greece, and the Baltic states) suffered considerably higher unemployment rates. The Icelandic unemployment rate also fell more quickly, and by the end of 2014 was already the fifth lowest among European nations.

In this chapter, we have analyzed Iceland's strategy for dealing with the consequences of the crisis in the context of policy debates about Keynesian-style stimulus and austerity measures. We then mapped the characteristics of the Icelandic approach and found that there were elements of both stimulus and austerity policies. The governmental finances were particularly difficult at the start of the crisis, but still the welfare system was strategically used to soften the worst consequences of the crisis for living standards. Welfare expenditures were, on the whole, increased for transfers to households but significantly cut on education and health-care services.

The main characteristic of the Icelandic crisis-management strategy is what we identify as a strategy of redistribution. This is exemplified by the fact that welfare expenditures were both increased and cut, but the primary emphasis was on redistribution. The approach ensured that the measures would benefit the lower-income groups to the greatest extent, at the expense of higher-income groups. Payments that primarily aided the lower-income groups were increased, such as the minimum pension guarantee, social assistance benefits, unemployment benefit, and minimum wages. Subsidies of the interest cost of mortgages were also greatly increased and directed primarily at lower- and middle-income groups. The net effective tax burden on the lowest 60% of households was lowered, while the burden on the highest 40% of income receivers was increased. A special wealth tax on large net assets was introduced.

These strategies of redistribution succeeded in softening the relative cuts in living standards of the lower-income groups, while cutting earnings in the higher-income groups, which also lost significant financial earnings that had increased greatly during the boom years prior to the crisis. Activation measures and job creation programs were greatly stepped up and also proved very successful in combatting unemployment. Relative poverty rates fell significantly during the crisis years, and the income distribution became decisively more equal, a major reversal of the trend from the pre-crisis years. No other Western country appears to have equalized its income distribution to the same extent as Iceland did during the crisis, according to Eurostat and OECD data.

The strategy of redistribution had a major role in achieving equalization. This strategy was also a good addition to Keynesian-style stimulus measures, since the lower-income groups give a better impetus to private consumption, by spending most of what they have, unlike the higher-income groups. This strategy thus facilitated a higher level of demand than otherwise would have prevailed. This, along with the devaluation of the currency, is likely to have helped in keeping the unemployment rate low and facilitated renewed growth.

The redistributive strategy is not just a more equitable way of dealing with deep crisis, by sheltering the more vulnerable in society to a greater extent than in most other deep-crisis countries. It is also a good complement to Keynesian economic crisis-management strategies.

Notes

1 Luc Laeven and Fabián Valencia, "Systemic Banking Crisis Database: An Update," IMF, Working Paper no. 12/163, 2012, accessed January 10, 2014, www.imf.org/external/pubs/ft/wp/2012/wp12163.pdf; same authors, "Resolution of Banking Crises: The Good, the Bad and the Ugly," IMF, Working Paper no. 10/146, 2010, accessed November 6, 2013, www.imf.org/external/pubs/ft/wp/2010/wp10146.pdf.

2 IMF, "Iceland: 2012 Article IV Consultation and First Post-program Monitoring Discussion," accessed November 14, 2014, www.imf.org/external/pubs/ft/scr/2012/cr1289.pdf.

3 Mark Blyth, *Austerity: The History of a Dangerous Idea* (Oxford: Oxford University Press, 2013).

4 Stefán Ólafsson and Arnaldur Sölvi Kristjánsson, "Umfang kreppunnar og afkoma ólíkra tekjuhópa," Report to the Ministry of Welfare. Social Research Centre, University of Iceland, April 2012, accessed February 5, 2015, http://thjodmalastofnun.hi.is/sites/thjodmalastofnun.hi.is/files/skrar/skyrsla_i-umfang_kreppunnar_og-afkoma_olikra_tekjuhopa–lokautgafa.pdf.

5 John M. Keynes, *The General Theory of Employment, Interest and Money* (New York: Harcourt, Brace and Company, 1936); see also Christina Romer, "Fiscal Policy in the Crisis: Lessons and Policy Implications," presented at the IMF Fiscal Forum, Washington, April 18, 2012, accessed March 15, 2014, http://eml.berkeley.edu/~cromer/Lessons%20for%20Fiscal%20Policy.pdf; J. Bradford DeLong and Lawrence H. Summers, "Fiscal Policy in a Depressed Economy," *Brookings Papers on Economic Activity* Spring (2012), accessed March 20, 2014, www.brookings.edu/about/projects/bpea/papers/2012/fiscal-policy-depressed-economy-delong.

6 John Kenneth Galbraith, *The Great Crash 1929* (Boston: Houghton Mifflin, 1988/1954); Paul Krugman, *The Return of Depression Economics* (New York: W. W. Norton and Company, 2009/1999).

7 Laurence S. Seidman, "Keynesian Stimulus versus Classical Austerity," *Review of Keynesian Economics*, Inaugural Issue, Autumn (2012): 77–92; Alan Blinder and Mark Zandi, "How the Great Recession Was Brought to an End," July 27, 2010, accessed March 21, 2014, www.economy.com/mark-zandi/documents/End-of-Great-Recession.pdf.

8 Paul Krugman, *End This Depression Now* (New York: W. W. Norton & Company, 2012); J. Bivens, "The Great Mistake: How Academic Economists and Policymakers Wrongly Abandoned Fiscal Policy," in *Restoring Shared Prosperity: A Policy Agenda from Leading Keynesian Economists*, eds. Thomas I. Palley and Gustav A. Horn (Creative Commons, 2013).

9 C. Rangarajan and Alok Steel, "Growth or Austerity: The Policy Dilemma," *ICRA Bulletin: Money and Finance* (February 2013), accessed March 5, 2014, http://eac.gov.in/-reports/speech_aust2005.pdf; IMF, "Reassessing the Role and Modalities of Fiscal Policy in Advanced Economies," IMF Policy Paper, September 17, 2013, accessed March 23, 2014, www.astrid-online.it/Governo-de/Studi–ric1/IMF_PP_Fiscal-Policy_09_2013.pdf.

10 Blyth, *Austerity*, chapters 1 and 6.

11 J. R. Crotti, "The Realism of Assumptions Does Matter: Why Keynes-Minsky Theory Must Replace Efficient Market Theory as the Guide to Financial Regulation Policy," in *The Oxford Handbook of the Political Economy of Financial Crises*, eds. Gerald Epstein and Martin Wolfson (New York: Oxford University Press, 2013).

12 Joseph A. Schumpeter, *Business Cycles, Vol. 1–2* (New York: McGraw-Hill, 1939); see also Blyth, *Austerity*, chapters 4 to 6.

13 Alberto F. Alesina and Silvia Ardagna, "Large Changes in Fiscal Policy: Taxes Versus Spending," NBER Working Paper No. 15438, October, 2009.

14 Carmen R. Reinhart and Kenneth S. Rogoff, "Growth in a Time of Debt," NBER Working Paper No. 15639, January 2010.

15 Jaime Guajardo et al., "Expansionary Austerity: New International Evidence," IMF Working Paper, WP/11/158.

16 Thomas Herndon et al., "Does High Public Debt Consistently Stifle Economic Growth? A Critique of Reinhart and Rogoff," WP 322, PERI, University of Massachusetts Amherst, April 2013, accessed April 3, 2014, www.peri.umass.edu-/fileadmin/pdf/working_papers/-working_papers_301–350/WP322.pdf.

17 Roberto Perotti, who was earlier a member of Alesina's team, admitted in a later paper that the IMF study was better founded in its methodology and conclusions (see Roberto Perotti, "The "Austerity Myth": Gain without Pain?" Working Papers No 362, Bank for International Settlements, December 2011, accessed February 5, 2015, www.bis.org/publ/work362.htm. See also Romer, "Fiscal Policy in the Crisis" and Krugman, *End This Depression Now*.

18 Carmen M. Reinhart and Kenneth S. Rogoff, *This Time Is Different: Eight Centuries of Financial Folly* (Princeton: Princeton University Press, 2009).

19 Romer, "Fiscal Policy in the Crisis"; also IMF, "Reassessing the Role and Modalities of Fiscal Policy in Advanced Economies."

20 The same government had served as an interim government from February until the spring, after the former government had been run out of power by protesting crowds in the streets of Reykjavík. The interim government started some emergency measures, including those laid down in the resurrection program negotiated with the IMF. See Stefán Ólafsson and Arnaldur Sölvi Kristjánsson, "Umfang kreppunnar og afkoma ólíkra tekjuhópa."

21 Guðrún Johnsen, *Bringing Down the Banking System: Lessons from Iceland*. (New York: Palgrave Macmillan, 2014).

22 Renee Haltom and Thomas A. Lubik, "Is Fiscal Austerity Good for the Economy?" Economic Brief EB13–09, Federal Reserve Bank of Richmont, September 2013, accessed March 10, 2014, www.richmondfed.org/publications/research/-economic_brief/2013/pdf/eb_13–09.pdf. See also Blyth, *Austerity*.

23 Stefán Ólafsson and Arnaldur Sölvi Kristjánsson, "Income Inequality through Boom and Bust: A Tale from Iceland's Bubble Economy," in *Income Inequality: Economic Disparities and the Middle Class in Affluent Countries*, eds. Janet Gornick and Markus Jäntti (Palo Alto: Stanford University Press, 2013); also Stefán Ólafsson and Arnaldur Sölvi Kristjánsson, "Þróun tekjuskiptingarinnar á Íslandi 1992 til 2010" [Income Distribution Development in Iceland 1992–2010], in *Stjórnmál og stjórnsýsla* 8, no. 1 (2012).

24 The income data in Figure 8.3 exclude capital gains. If they had been included, the decline of the Gini index would have been significantly larger, but at the same time that effect would to a greater extent have been due to declining capital gains rather than the government policy of equalization.

25 Ólafsson and Kristjánsson, "Income Inequality through Boom and Bust."

26 Cf. Hyman P. Minsky, *Stabilizing an Unstable Economy* (New York: McGraw-Hill, 2008/1986); Robert Skidelsky, *Keynes: The Return of the Master* (London: The Penguin Group, 2009); and Krugman, *End This Depression Now*.

27 Ólafsson and Kristjánsson, "Umfang kreppunnar og afkoma ólíkra tekjuhópa."

28 Katrín Ólafsdóttir and Stefán Ólafsson, *Economy, Politics and Welfare in Iceland: Booms, Busts and Challenges* (Oslo: Fafo Institute, 2014), accessed January 11, 2015, www.fafoarkiv.no/pub/rapp/20360/20360.pdf.

29 Krugman, *End This Depression Now*; also Skidelsky, *Keynes: The Return of the Master*.

30 Stefán Ólafsson, "Active Inclusion Developments in Iceland from 2008 to 2012," Report to the EU–Social Inclusion Network, autumn 2012; also Stefán Ólafsson, "Iceland's Way Out of the Crisis: Social Protection, Redistribution, Stimulus and Austerity," Report to the EU–Social Inclusion Network, spring 2012.

31 Maskína, "Fyrrum atvinnuleitendur Nóvember-desember 2013," Report for Directorate of Labour, accessed February 14, 2014, www.vinnumalastofnun.is/files/Konnun-VMST_764137556.pdf.

32 Note that the data on relative poverty rates in the table refer to incomes during the previous year, such that poverty figures for 2012 are actually for 2011. The data on difficulty making ends meet in the lower part of the table, on the other hand, refer to the noted calendar year. This is in accordance with Eurostat practice.

33 Þorvarður Tjörvi Ólafsson and Karen Áslaug Vignisdóttir, "Households' Position in the Financial Crisis in Iceland," Central Bank of Iceland, Working Paper No. 59, June 2012; also Stefán Ólafsson et al., "Áhrif mótvægisaðgerða gegn skuldavanda, fátækt og atvinnuleysi," Report of Social Research Centre, University of Iceland, to the Ministry of Welfare, September 2012, accessed February 5, 2015, http://thjodmalastofnun.hi.is/sites/thjodmalastofnun.hi.is/files/skrar/ahrif_motvaegisadgerda_a_skuldavanda_fataekt_og_atvinnu.pdf.
34 Cf. Ólafsson et al., "Áhrif mótvægisaðgerða gegn skuldavanda."
35 IMF, "Iceland: 2012 Article IV Consultation and First Post-program Monitoring Discussion."

References

Alesina, Alberto F. and Silvia Ardagna. "Large Changes in Fiscal Policy: Taxes versus Spending." NBER Working Paper No. 15438, October 2009. Accessed March 22, 2014. www.nber.org/papers/w15438.

Bivens, J. "The Great Mistake: How Academic Economists and Policymakers Wrongly Abandoned Fiscal Policy," in *Restoring Shared Prosperity: A Policy Agenda from Leading Keynesian Economists*, edited by Thomas I. Palley and Gustav A. Horn. Creative Commons, 2013.

Blinder, Alan and Mark Zandi. "How the Great Recession Was Brought to an End." July 27, 2010. Accessed March 21, 2014. www.economy.com/mark-zandi/documents/End-of-Great-Recession.pdf.

Blyth, Mark. *Austerity: The History of a Dangerous Idea*. Oxford: Oxford University Press, 2013.

Central Bank of Iceland. Financial Stability Reports. Reykjavík: Seðlabanki Islands, 2012 and 2014. Available at www.sedlabanki.is.

Crotti, J. R. "The Realism of Assumptions Does Matter: Why Keynes–Minsky Theory Must Replace Efficient Market Theory as the Guide to Financial Regulation Policy," in *The Oxford Handbook of the Political Economy of Financial Crises*, edited by Gerald Epstein and Martin Wolfson, 133–158. New York: Oxford University Press, 2013.

DeLong, J. Bradford and Summers, L. H. "Fiscal Policy in a Depressed Economy." Brookings Papers on Economic Activity, Spring (2012). Accessed March 20, 2014. www.brookings.edu/about/projects/bpea/papers/2012/fiscal-policy-depressed-economy-delong.

Eurostat (EU-SILC data). Data on real disposable earnings. Accessed April 19, 2014. http://ec.europa.eu/eurostat/web/income-and-living-conditions/data/database.

Galbraith, J. K. *The Great Crash 1929*. Boston: Houghton Mifflin,1988/1954.

Guajardo, Jaime, Daniel Leigh, and Andrea Pescatori. "Expansionary Austerity: New International Evidence." IMF Working Paper, WP/11/158. Accessed January 28, 2014. www.imf.org/-external/pubs/ft/wp/2011/wp11158.pdf.

Haltom, Renee and Thomas A. Lubik. "Is Fiscal Austerity Good for the Economy?" Economic Brief EB13–09, Federal Reserve Bank of Richmont, September 2013. Accessed March 10, 2014. https://www.richmondfed.org/publications/research/economic_brief/2013/pdf/eb_13-09.pdf.

Herndon, Thomas, Michael Ash, and Robert Pollin. "Does High Public Debt Consistently Stifle Economic Growth? A Critique of Reinhart and Rogoff." WP 322, PERI, University of Massachusetts Amherst, April 2013. Accessed April 3, 2014. www.peri.umass.edu/fileadmin/pdf/working_papers/-working_papers_301-350/WP322.pdf.

IMF. "Iceland: 2012 Article IV Consultation and First Post-program Monitoring Discussion." Accessed November 14, 2014. www.imf.org/external/pubs/ft/scr/2012/cr1289.pdf.

IMF. "Reassessing the Role and Modalities of Fiscal Policy in Advanced Economies." IMF Policy Paper, September 17, 2013. Accessed March 23, 2014. www.astrid-online.it/Governo-de/Studi-ric1/IMF_PP_Fiscal-Policy_09_2013.pdf.

Johnsen, Guðrún. *Bringing Down the Banking System: Lessons from Iceland*. New York: Palgrave Macmillan, 2014.

Keynes, John M. *The General Theory of Employment, Interest and Money*. New York: Harcourt, Brace and Company, 1936.

Krugman, Paul. *The Return of Depression Economics*. New York: W. W. Norton & Company, 2009/1999.

Krugman, Paul. *End This Depression Now*. New York: W. W. Norton & Company, 2012.

Laeven, Luc and Fabián Valencia. "Resolution of Banking Crises: The Good, the Bad and the Ugly". IMF, Working Paper no. 10/146. Accessed November 6, 2013. www.imf.org/external/pubs/ft/wp/2010/wp10146.pdf.

Laeven, Luc and Fabián Valencia. "Systemic Banking Crisis Database: An Update." IMF, Working Paper no. 12/163. Accessed January 10, 2014. https://www.imf.org/external/pubs/ft/wp/2012/wp12163.pdf.

Maskína. "Fyrrum atvinnuleitendur Nóvember-desember 2013." Report for Directorate of Labour. Accessed February 14, 2014. www.vinnumalastofnun.is/files/Konnun-VMST_764137556.pdf.

Minsky, Hyman Philip. *Stabilizing an Unstable Economy*. New York: McGraw-Hill, 2008/1986.

OECD. "Crisis Squeezes Income and Puts Pressure on Inequality and Poverty: Results from the OECD Income Distribution Database." May 2013. Accessed February 5, 2015. www.oecd.org/els/soc/OECD2013-Inequality-and-Poverty-8p.pdf.

Ólafsdóttir, Katrín and Stefán Ólafsson. *Economy, Politics and Welfare in Iceland: Booms, Busts and Challenges* (Oslo: Fafo Institute, 2014). Accessed January 11, 2015. www.fafoarkiv.no/pub/rapp/20360/20360.pdf.

Ólafsson, Stefán. "Active Inclusion Developments in Iceland from 2008 to 2012." Report to the EU-Social Inclusion Network, October 2012.

Ólafsson, Stefán. "Iceland's Way Out of the Crisis: Social Protection, Redistribution, Stimulus and Austerity." Report to the EU-Social Inclusion Network, May 2012.

Ólafsson, Stefán and Arnaldur Sölvi Kristjánsson. "Þróun tekjuskiptingarinnar á Íslandi 1992 til 2010" [Income Distribution Development in Iceland 1992–2010]. *Stjórnmál og stjórnsýsla* 8, no. 1 (2012): 39–71.

Ólafsson, Stefán and Arnaldur Sölvi Kristjánsson. "Umfang kreppunnar og afkoma ólíkra tekjuhópa." Report to the Ministry of Welfare, October 2012. Accessed February 5, 2015. http://thjodmalastofnun.hi.is/sites/thjodmalastofnun.hi.is/files/skrar/skyrsla_i-umfang_kreppunnar_og-afkoma_olikra_tekjuhopa--lokautgafa.pdf.

Ólafsson, Stefán and Arnaldur Sölvi Kristjánsson. "Income Inequality through Boom and Bust: A Tale from Iceland's Bubble Economy," in *Income Inequality: Economic Disparities and the Middle Class in Affluent Countries*, edited by Janet Gornick and Markus Jäntti, 416–438. Palo Alto: Stanford University Press, 2013.

Ólafsson, Stefán, Arnaldur Sölvi Kristjánsson, and Kolbeinn Stefánsson. "Áhrif mótvægisaðgerða á skuldavanda, fátækt og atvinnuleysi." Report to the Ministry of Welfare, September 2012. Accessed February 5, 2015. http://thjodmalastofnun.hi.is/sites/thjodmalastofnun.hi.is/files/skrar/ahrif_motvaegisadgerda_a_skuldavanda_fataekt_og_atvinnu.pdf.

Ólafsson, Þorvarður Tjörvi and Karen Áslaug Vignisdóttir. "Household's Position in the Financial Crisis in Iceland." Central Bank of Iceland, Working Paper No. 59, June

2012. Accessed February 15, 2014. www.cb.is/library/Skr%C3%A1arsafn-EN/Working-Papers/Working%20Paper%2059.pdf.

Perotti, Roberto (2011). "The Austerity Myth: Gain without Pain?" Working Papers No. 362, Bank for International Settlements, December 2011. Accessed February 5, 2015. www.bis.org/publ/work362.htm.

Rangarajan, C. and Alok Steel. "Growth or Austerity: The Policy Dilemma." *ICRA Bulletin: Money and Finance*. Accessed March 5, 2014. http://eac.gov.in/-reports/speech_aust2005.pdf.

Reinhart, Carmen R. and Kenneth S. Rogoff. "Growth in a Time of Debt." NBER Working Paper No. 15639, January 2010. Accessed April 2, 2014. www.nber.org/papers/w15639.

Romer, Christina. "Fiscal Policy in the Crisis: Lessons and Policy Implication." Presented at the IMF Fiscal Forum, Washington, April 18, 2012. Accessed March 15, 2014. http://eml.berkeley.edu/~cromer/Lessons%20for%20Fiscal%20Policy.pdf.

Schumpeter, J. A. *Business Cycles, Vol. 1–2*. New York: McGraw-Hill, 1939.

Seidman, Laurance S. (2012). "Keynesian Stimulus versus Classical Austerity." *Review of Keynesian Economics*, Inaugural Issue, Autumn (2012): 77–92.

Skidelsky, Robert. *Keynes: The Return of the Master*. London: The Penguin Group, 2009.

Social Security Administration. Staðtölur 2011 (Statistical Data). Available at www.tr.is.

Statistics Iceland. Data on Real Wage Development. Accessed April 20, 2013. www.hagstofa.is.

Statistics Iceland. Data on Employment and Unemployment. Accessed April 21, 2013. www.hagstofa.is.

Statistics Iceland. Data on Poverty and Financial Hardship. Accessed April 24, 2013. www.hagstofa.is.

Part III

The politics of Iceland's constitutional reform

9 Icelandic constitution-making in comparative perspective[1]

Jon Elster

The process of making a new constitution in Iceland is interesting in two ways. First, it had a number of very unusual features: a consultative National Forum, made up of citizens chosen at random; the mode of electing the members of the (exceptionally small) drafting body; the invalidation of the elections by the Supreme Court and the government's subsequent bypassing of this decision; the modus operandi of the Council, notably the much-cited "crowdsourcing"; and the two-track downstream approval procedures. Second, it failed, at least for the time being. There are precedents for such an outcome. In Canada, the Meech Lake Accords and the Charlottetown Accords both came to nothing: in the first case, because some states did not ratify the proposal, and in the second, because a referendum did not obtain the required majority.[2] In 12 referenda on state constitutions that were held in the United States between 1960 and 1980s, seven of the proposals were rejected, in two cases by a large margin: four to one in Rhode Island and three to one in New York State.[3] Other scattered examples could also be cited. Scholars of constitution-making have not, to my knowledge, systematically studied the causes of such failures.

It is impossible for scholars with no reading knowledge of the Icelandic language to study the process in the detail it deserves. Judging from my study of constitution-making in countries whose languages I read (French, English, Norwegian), the details are often decisive, both for understanding crucial junctures in the process and for suggesting generalizations. Although my ignorance constrains me to paint in broad strokes, I shall try to compensate by placing the work of the Council in a comparative perspective. Drawing on a variety of processes at different times and places, I shall distinguish between upstream, midstream, and downstream moments of constitution-making. In later sections, I apply this framework to the Icelandic process, to identify similarities with and differences from other episodes.

Upstream moments

Prior to the calling of a constituent assembly, there is usually a crisis of some kind. Constitution-triggers include revolution (France and Germany 1848); regime implosion (Eastern Europe 1989); fall of dictatorships (Southern

Europe and Latin America in the 1970s and 1980s); the aftermath of war (many countries after World Wars I and II); national independence (many English and French colonies in the 1960s); and financial crisis (the United States 1787; France 1789; and Hungary 2010). The element of crisis tends to confer an emotional, turbulent, and sometimes violent character on the constitution-making process, contrary to the cliché that "constitutions are written by Peter when sober to bind Peter when drunk." The link between constitution-making and crises is summarized in Table 9.1. In the overwhelming majority of cases (only a small sample is shown here), constitution-making occurs in the aftermath of a crisis.

In the absence of a crisis, constitution-making is very rare. Commenting on the failures of constitution-making in Canada, Russell wrote that it was

> clear that the present generation of Canadians will not try again to reach an accord on a broad package of constitutional changes designed to prevent a unity crisis. If in the near future, Canada plunges once again into the constitutional maelstrom, it will be because there is *an actual, not an apprehended crisis* [italics added] of national unity.[4]

Sweden is an exception. The abolition in 1969 of the Swedish bicameral system, followed by a thoroughgoing reform of the constitution in 1974, has been called "institutional change" rather than "constitutional change" because of the routine manner in which it was carried out. The fate of the Icelandic constitution-making process remains suspended. It may end up showing that crisis, while usually necessary for constitution-making, may not be sufficient.

For a crisis to bring about a constituent assembly, there must be a *convener*. The convener may be a reigning monarch (France 1789), an existing legislature (United States 1787), a provisional government (Italy 1946), an interim assembly (France 1945; South Africa 1993), an occupying power (Germany and Japan post-1945), an international body (Cambodia 1993), or a self-created one (Norway 1814; Germany 1848). The convener chooses the time and place for the meeting of the assembly and, crucially, imposes the rules for electing or selecting delegates to the assembly. Conveners may also try to shape the procedures of the assembly, notably by imposing a time limit, and the substance of the document they propose.

Table 9.1 Constitution-writing outcomes

	Crisis	*No crisis*
Successful constitution-making	United States 1787 France 1789, 1848, 1958 Norway 1814 Iceland 1944	Sweden 1976
Failed constitution-making	Iceland 2011	Canada 1990, 1992

Since the convener virtually never chooses the delegates, this task is left to *selectors*. In federal systems, delegates are often chosen by the state legislatures (United States 1787; Germany 1949). When they are chosen by popular elections, voters and deputies have in the past usually been subject to economic qualifications. Not infrequently, these qualifications have been less stringent than for elections to ordinary legislatures. Today, only age and residence are used to limit franchise and eligibility. Selectors, too, may try to shape the substance of the constitutional document, by the mechanism of "instructions" or imperative mandates.

Midstream moments

Once the selected delegates meet, they first have to verify their credentials. This is usually a routine matter, but proved crucial on one occasion. Deputies to the first French *Constituante* of 1789 were elected as representatives of their estates—the clergy, the nobility, and the commoners (the third estate). The last-mentioned wanted the verification of the credentials to be made by the assembly as a whole, so that, say, commoners could vote on the credentials of deputies for the clergy and the nobility. The privileged order strongly resisted this proposal, because it would give the numerically strong third estate the power to exclude reactionary deputies from the other orders and, more importantly, because it would set a precedent for voting by head rather than by estate in the assembly itself. The delay of six weeks caused by this quarrel was decisive in forging the unity of the third estate.

Next, the assembly has to adopt the rules of order for its proceedings. On a few occasions (Norway 1814), the convener has imposed these rules, but typically, constituent assemblies declare themselves to be sovereign in procedural no less than in substantive matters. With very few exceptions, they ignore imperative mandates that the selectors might try to impose on them as well as substantive orders or interdictions by which the convener might want to limit their freedom of action. The best-known exception may be the constraints that the interim constituent assembly of South Africa imposed on the main assembly, notably by requiring that the Constitutional Court approve the text.

Important procedural decisions concern the division of labor between committees and plenary sessions as well as the choice between secrecy and publicity in debates and votes. Some assemblies (United States 1787; Norway 1814; Germany 1949) have carried out their debates behind closed doors and used a mix of secret and public voting. Other assemblies (France and Germany 1848) have opened the doors to the public, often with dramatic consequences. A mixed system would allow sessions behind closed doors at critical or difficult junctures (South Africa 1996). If most of the work is done in committees, to which the public never has access, this issue is less relevant.

Many years after the Federal Convention, James Madison made a classic statement of the advantages of secrecy:

> Had the members committed themselves publicly at first, they would have afterwards supposed consistency required them to maintain their ground, whereas by secret discussion no man felt himself obliged to retain his opinions any longer than he was satisfied of their propriety and truth, and was open to the force of argument.[5]

In the French *Constituante* of 1789, the deputy Bouche made the opposite argument, when he proposed to transfer the locus of debate from closed committees to the plenary assembly, where "souls become strong and electrified, and where names, ranks, and distinctions count for nothing."[6]

Even in assemblies held behind closed doors, the deputies might want to receive information about external events (Norway 1814) and invite proposals from the public (South Africa 1995). These midstream variables might affect the downstream process. The failures of Canadian constitution-making may have owed much to the opaque and non-participatory nature of the processes. Whether popular participation can affect the substance of the constitution and not only its perceived legitimacy remains a controversial question.[7]

In some of the most dramatic episodes of constitution-making, assemblies or proto-constitutional bodies have been simultaneously subjected to the threat of military force and pressure from the street (France 1789; Eastern Europe 1989). In other cases, there has been pressure from crowds without a parallel pressure from the army (France and Germany 1848). The converse holds in cases of constitution-making in countries under foreign occupation (West Germany and Japan after 1945; Iraq 2005).

Downstream moments

A question that often arises in constitution-making is *when and how many times shall the people speak*? Often, the people speak only once, when electing delegates at the beginning of the process (France 1787; Norway 1814; France 1848; Germany 1919). Sometimes, they speak only at the end, when ratifying the constitution by referendum (France 1958) or by specially elected ratifying conventions (United States 1787). Sometimes the people speak twice, at the beginning *and* at the end (France 1946; most American state constitutions). When delegates are elected by the state legislatures in a federal system and these also ratify the constitution, the people do not speak at all (Germany 1949). Today, the "gold standard" seems to be that the people shall speak twice, and perhaps even a third time through their participatory midstream influence.

Generally speaking, an ordinary legislature should not serve as a constituent assembly or as a ratifying body. In either capacity, there is a risk that it might act in a self-serving manner by adopting excessively legislative-centric constitutions or by rejecting proposals that reduce the power of the legislature or of the current legislators. In 1787, the American framers were acutely aware of this problem, when they decided—contrary to their upstream instructions—to have the constitution ratified by specially elected ratifying assemblies rather than by the state legislatures. As the latter lost much of their power under the new constitution, they were unlikely to approve it. The case may be different if the legislature has been elected with an explicit mandate to also serve as a constituent assembly (France 1946) or as a ratifying body (no examples known to me).

Upstream moments in Iceland

The constitution-making process in Iceland was triggered by a financial *crisis*. Unlike the crises that many other countries experienced at the same time, the Icelandic crisis was due to—and widely perceived as being due to—the intimate connection between the financial and political elites. In the words of Thorvaldur Gylfason, "For more than a hundred years the banking system had comprised inept state bank institutions run by political operatives allocating subsidized credits and scarce foreign exchange to favored customers, paying scant attention to commercial profitability, risk, and economic health."[8] The crisis triggered a popular *anger* that was an important motive behind the Icelandic constitution-making process. In the words of one observer, "The public *outrage* [italics added], which after the economic collapse was directed at the government, converged on the issue of writing a new constitution."[9] To cite Gylfason,

> When countries crash, a natural thing for their inhabitants to do, *inter alia*, is inspect their legal and constitutional foundations to look for latent flaws and to fix them. This was, in fact, one of the demands of the "pots and pans revolution" that shook Iceland after the country's spectacular financial crash…[10]

Before I proceed to the other upstream moments, let me comment on the Icelandic response to the crisis. On the one hand, the anger induced a backward-looking demand for punishment of those held responsible for the crisis. Several banking officials have, in fact, been prosecuted, and some have been jailed. Politicians, though, have mostly been spared. On the other hand, as indicated by the statements just cited, the crisis caused a forward-looking demand to fix the system. The question, to which there is no obvious answer, is why the fix should take the form of a new constitution rather than of statutory regulation. Except for the requirement of an independent Central Bank, financial institutions are very rarely regulated by national constitutions (Gylfason cites examples from Bhutan and Ecuador),[11] no doubt because rigid constraints are thought to be undesirable.

In Iceland, a key constitutional demand concerned the management of natural resources, notably fish. The constitutional draft affirms that resources not owned by private individuals are the inalienable property of the nation, implying that they should be used for the public interest rather than, as in the past, for the benefit of private vessel owners who have been granted access to fishing grounds at virtually no cost. While this proposal seems justified, it is not clear how the mismanagement of natural resources was causally linked to the crisis and how an improved system might prevent future crises. Similarly, it is not clear why another key demand, the reform of the clearly unfair electoral system, would make crises more unlikely. It is possible that cheap access to natural resources, a skewed electoral system, unsound banking practices, and corrupt politicians were linked in an *engrenage* that could be broken by constitutional measures affecting some of the elements. I have, however, not seen a convincing argument to that effect. The anger seems to have triggered a demand to *do something*, rather than a careful reflection about what might work.[12] I am not saying that the work of the Constitutional Council was affected by anger, but perhaps its establishment was.

Anger, like most emotions, has a short half-life, unless it is continuously nourished. One reason why the constitution-making process, in the end, led nowhere may be that the popular anger abated as economic conditions improved *without* any reform of the constitution. Iceland managed to dump its debts on foreign creditors. "Where everyone else bailed out the bankers and made the public pay the price, Iceland let the banks go bust and actually expanded its social safety net," noted Paul Krugman. Iceland, he claimed, had demonstrated the "case for letting creditors of private banks gone wild eat the losses."[13] Conjecturally, the anger of the Icelanders was displaced toward Great Britain, which in an apparently absurd move used anti-terrorist legislation to freeze Icelandic assets. (Persistent rumors, however, claimed links between Icelandic banks and Russian money laundering.) That anger may also have sustained the repeated defeats in referenda over repayment schemes.

The *convener* of the drafting body, named the "Constitutional Council," was the Icelandic Parliament. Actually, Parliament convened *two* bodies: a National Forum and the Constitutional Council. The first body

> comprised about 1,000 individuals selected at random through stratified sampling from the national registry subject to certain constraints intended to secure equal representation of men and women of different age groups as well as of different parts of the country.[14]

To my knowledge, this was the first time since the creation of the Athenian *nomothetai* in the 4th century BC that randomization had been used to select agents of fundamental political change. Like the *nomothetai*, the National Forum was not a truly random sample of the population, since in both cases only willing participants were chosen. Unlike them, however, the National Forum had only a consultative status. The Constitutional Council was supposed to "take into consideration" the recommendations of the Forum, but was not constrained by this upstream body. Among its proposals were two reforms mentioned above: equal voting rights and national ownership of natural resources. The Forum may have had a causal influence on the Council, but I suspect that the latter would have made the same proposals in any case.

The Council had 25 members, probably the smallest constitution-making body in history. The Federal Convention had 55 members; the body that drafted the 1949 German constitution had 70 members. In a famous text, James Madison discussed the upper and lower bounds of assembly size:

> Sixty or seventy men may be more properly trusted with a given degree of power than six or seven. But it does not follow that six or seven hundred would be proportionably a better depositary. And if we carry on the supposition to six or seven thousand, the whole reasoning ought to be reversed. The truth is that in all cases a certain number at least seems to be necessary to secure the benefits of free consultation and discussion, and to guard against too easy a combination for improper purposes; as, on the other hand, the number ought at most to be kept within a certain limit, in order to avoid the confusion and intemperance of a multitude. In all very numerous assemblies, of whatever character composed, passion never fails to wrest the sceptre from reason.[15]

To the last comment, we may add that in very small assemblies, *interest* never fails to wrest the scepter from reason. Whereas the Council size obviously fell below the upper bound, it is not obvious that it exceeded the lower bound. There is no firm evidence for "combinations for improper purposes," but they may have occurred. Thus, one member of the Constitutional Council put it this way:

> [T]here was definitely a chance/possibility to swing votes with a very small number of people. Throughout the process, we worked on a consensus basis and this was not a problem, but in the end everybody was allowed to present their own proposals and these were then put to a vote without any discussions. Some (to my mind) very questionable proposals were submitted and were in a couple of instances passed, as people had negotiated before the votes started, even on issues that had been discussed and we had agreed to put to the side.[16]

The *selectors* were all citizens qualified to vote in parliamentary elections. They chose 25 delegates from among 523 candidates, not nominated by parties but by individuals. The mode of election was the single transferable vote. Turnout was 37%, a number that suggests a rather low political temperature. The turnout was lower in the countryside than in greater Reykjavík, where two-thirds of the population live. The occupations or professional situations of the delegates are shown in Table 9.2.

Thus, with the exception of one farmer, the make-up of the Council was entirely urban and heavily on the intellectual and academic side (two mathematicians!). Whereas the countryside was over-represented in Parliament—a flaw that the electoral reform was intended to abolish—it was under-represented on the Council (only three delegates came from outside Reykjavík). Whereas the National Forum was geographically balanced, nothing was done to ensure geographical balance on the Council. By contrast, the Council was representative along another dimension, since the Legislative Act ordered that at least 40% must be women. The media were strongly represented, suggesting that many delegates were chosen because of their visibility rather than for their competence. Of the three lawyers, one seems

Table 9.2 Constitutional assembly election results

Candidate	*Profession*	*First preference votes*
Thorvaldur Gylfason	University professor of Economics	7,192
Salvör Nordal	Director of the University of Iceland Ethics Institute	2,842
Ómar Þorfinnur Ragnarsson	Media presenter	2,440
Andrés Magnússon	Physician	2,175
Pétur Gunnlaugsson	Lawyer and radio presenter	1,989
Þorkell Helgason	Mathematician	1,930
Ari Teitsson	Farmer	1,686
Illugi Jökulsson	Journalist	1,593
Freyja Haraldsdóttir	Manager	1,089
Silja Bára Ómarsdóttir	Lecturer in International Politics	1,054
Örn Bárður Jónsson	Pastor	806
Eiríkur Bergmann Einarsson	Associate professor of Political Science	753
Dögg Harðardóttir	Manager at Reykjavik Art Museum	674
Vilhjálmur Þorsteinsson	Entrepreneur	672
Þórhildur Þorleifsdóttir	Theatre director	584
Pawel Bartoszek	Mathematician	584
Arnfríður Guðmundsdóttir	Professor of Theology	531
Erlingur Sigurðarson	Former museum director and teacher	526
Inga Lind Karlsdóttir	Media presenter and university student	493
Katrín Oddsdóttir	Lawyer	479
Guðmundur Gunnarsson	Trade union chairman	432
Katrín Fjeldsted	Physician	418
Ástrós Gunnlaugsdóttir	Political scientist and university student	396
Gísli Tryggvason	Lawyer and consumer spokesperson	348
Lýður Árnason	Filmmaker and physician	47

mainly to be a media presenter, whereas the two other work as a human rights lawyer and a consumers' spokesperson, respectively. Although three of the delegates were former members of parliament, the Legislative Act creating the Council made current MPs and cabinet members ineligible. Nothing prevented mayors or other local politicians from standing for election. Because of the near-absence of politicians and of lawyers, the institutional and constitutional expertise of the Council must have been low, compared with virtually all other constituent assemblies. Of the 55 delegates to the Federal Convention, for instance, 34 were lawyers, eight were judges, and all had some political experience from the state legislatures, the state constitutional conventions, or the Continental Congress. It should be added, however, that the Council and its members had access to and regularly consulted outside juridical expertise.

The elections were held in November 2010. Normally, the analysis of the upstream process would end here. In Iceland, however, two additional upstream events took place. After reviewing complaints, the Supreme Court decided in 2011 that the election was null and void, on the grounds that the secrecy of the vote had been jeopardized in five different ways. The decision was possibly politically motivated, and arguably technically flawed.[17] In a further upstream move, Parliament then *appointed* the 25 elected members to the Council. One delegate refused, and was replaced by the person who had come 26th in the elections.

As a concluding remark on the upstream part of the process, let me observe that the decisions by conveners and selectors can affect the perceived *legitimacy* of the assembly. The following factors may have had a negative impact: the low turnout, the skewed geographical distribution of the deputies, their lack of legal expertise, the cancellation of the election, and its replacement by a procedure with poorer democratic credentials.

Midstream moments in Iceland

As with any assembly, the Council began by choosing its President by secret ballot. The choice did not fall on the person who had received the highest number (by far) of first preferences, Thorvaldur Gylfason, Professor of Economics at the University of Iceland, but on the runner-up, the philosopher Salvör Nordal. Gylfason is known for his decided views and forceful character. The decision to elect another person as President may have reflected a desire for compromise and consensus. Next, the Council divided itself into three groups, where much of the actual debates took place. The weekly schedule was as follows: Monday and Tuesday: work in groups; Wednesday: group work presented for all members of council; Thursdays: open council meeting; Fridays: individual work—council meeting continued—group work. The Council worked from April 6 to July 28, 2011.

The Icelandic process was unique in the *midstream* influence on the delegates through crowdsourcing:

> The twenty-five members of the Council [...] regularly posted online, for the world to see and for the Icelandic people to read, the version of the draft they were working on. All in all, they posted twelve drafts, all at various stages of completion.[18]

In response, the Council

> received 323 formal proposals that the three committees of the Council discussed and answered. More than 3,600 written comments were posted on the [Council's] website by visitors; the Council representatives answered many if not most of them. The proposals and comments proved useful in one way or another, not only what was said, but also the things left unsaid. If no one objected to the provision articles posted on the website, then perhaps we were on the right track.[19]

In the best-known precedent, the making of the constitution of South Africa (1996), the impact of external comments on the text itself seems to have been slight, although its legitimacy may have been enhanced.[20] Above, I noted some upstream features that may have undermined the legitimacy of the constitution. By contrast, the crowdsourcing may have enhanced it.

In addition to receiving proposals *from* the public, the Council made its proceedings (somewhat) accessible *to* the public. Although the Legislative Act establishing the Council stated that "[s]essions shall be open to the public to the extent that constraints of space will permit,"[21] this practice does not seem to have been adopted. Instead, "the general 'open' meetings were filmed, recorded, and put out as PDF transcripts [several weeks later], in what is sometimes called 'time-lag transparency.' "[22] Committee meetings of the three subgroups of the council were closed unless otherwise decided for each meeting. In the words of one member of the Council, "the idea was to not lock people into a publicly stated view on any given issue, but create space for compromise and meeting of minds."[23]

Jón Ólafsson offers a glimpse into the relation between discussions in the subcommittees and plenary debates:

> In the subcommittees which were supposed to bring preliminary conclusions to the general council meetings, issues were often discussed and resolved, ending in a unanimous support for the one or the other result. Yet the members would not necessarily stick to their decisions in the subcommittees once the discussion resumed in the plenary sessions. According to one council member, the reasons for such a change were often strategic. Committee members would realize that they had a better chance in a plenary session to get something approved and therefore choose to abandon the issue in the subcommittee, knowing that they would have a chance to go through a new discussion of it later. But that basically undermined the deliberations meant to take place in the subcommittees. Instead of being the deliberative laboratories they were meant to be, preparing well-thought-out proposals to the plenary meetings, the

> discussion there would be in some cases like a first attempt to come to a conclusion and a chance to realize what kind of views were likely to emerge in the discussion of a particular issue. While this was not always the case, it often was, and in at least one of the subcommittees it did serious damage to the trust between individual council members. [24]

Although the details of this strategic behavior remain somewhat obscure, the general trust of the argument is clear enough. The subcommittee members, or some of them, did not argue sincerely, but instead misrepresented their views to gain an advantage in the plenary debates.

While the delegates lacked the relevant expertise, they were aided in several ways. Parliament had appointed a seven-member Constitutional Committee, comprising professionals from different directions, including law, literature, and science. The committee produced a 700-page report with detailed ideas concerning the composition of the new constitution. The Council could also draw on legal expertise during their proceedings. Nevertheless, constitutional experts have found flaws in the document. In the summary of a detailed critical analysis of the draft constitution, the European Commission for Democracy through Law (The Venice Commission) notes

> in particular that numerous provisions of the Bill have been formulated in too vague and broad terms, which, despite the clarifications that might be provided by the Explanatory Notes, may lead to serious difficulties of interpretation and application, including in the context of the adoption of the implementing laws. [...] The proposed institutional system is rather complex and marked by lack of consistency. This concerns both the powers granted to each of the main constitutional actors—parliament, government and President—and the balance between them and their inter-institutional relations, often too complicated, as well as the mechanisms of direct participation introduced by the Bill.[25]

Downstream moments

Article 79 of the Constitution of Iceland (1944) states that

> [p]roposals to amend or supplement this Constitution may be introduced at regular as well as extraordinary sessions of Althingi [Parliament]. If the proposal is adopted, Althingi shall immediately be dissolved and a general election held. If Althingi then passes the resolution unchanged, it shall be confirmed by the President of the Republic and come into force as constitutional law.[26]

This amendment procedure—which also regulates full replacement of the constitution—is unusual in not requiring any supermajority or even an absolute majority, but a simple majority of those present. (By contrast, Article 31 of the

Constitution states that changes in the electoral law require a two-thirds majority. This seems illogical, since a simple majority may amend the article itself.) The requirement of an election between the two votes may be interpreted either as providing for an appeal to the people or as a slowing-down device.

On normative grounds, it is, in general, undesirable to let an existing parliament have a central role in constitution-making, either in the role of drafter or in the role of ratifier, because of the obvious risk of institutional self-serving. In the case of Iceland, it was unlikely that a qualified majority of Parliament would approve a reform of the skewed electoral system to which many of the deputies owed their seats. Perhaps because it was aware of this fact, the government had promised, at the beginning of the process, that the constitution would also be subject to referendum. As the constitution allows for referenda only when the President refuses to sign a bill voted by Parliament, the referendum over the constitution could only be an advisory or consultative one. In many democratic societies, consultative referenda are de facto binding. Examples include the two Norwegian referenda on entry of the country into the EU in 1972 and 1994. Although the No vote obtained a bare majority on both occasions, it was accepted as definitive.

Thus, the Iceland process involved, unusually, *two* downstream ratifiers: the Parliament and the people. When I first visited Iceland in 2011, the *order* in which the two ratifications would take place was as yet unsettled. At the time, I assumed that Parliament would not dare reject the constitution if the people approved it. Events proved me wrong. The constitution was submitted to referendum in October 2012. In a most unusual procedure, the referendum included both an up-and-down vote (which means that the proposals cannot be amended) on the document as a whole and votes on five specific aspects of the constitution. The turnout for the referendum was 49%. The questions and the percentage of approving answers were as follows:

1 Do you want the proposals of the Constitutional Council to form the basis of a legislative bill for a new Constitution? 67% said Yes.
2 Would you want natural resources which are not in private ownership to be declared the property of the nation in a new Constitution? 83% said Yes.
3 Would you want a new Constitution to include provisions on a National Church of Iceland? 57% said Yes.
4 Would you want a new Constitution to permit personal elections to the Althing to a greater degree than permitted at present? 78% said Yes.
5 Would you want a new Constitution to include provisions to the effect that the votes of the electorate across the country should have the same force? 67% said Yes.
6 Would you want a new Constitution to include provisions to the effect that a specific proportion of the electorate could call for a national referendum on a specific matter? 73% said Yes.

The procedure is not entirely unprecedented. The constitutional convention that drafted the 1780 constitution of Massachusetts decided that:

> copies of the constitution would be sent to each town, discussed in town meetings, and all qualified voters (freemen 21 years or older) would vote on each clause. The towns would then send these voting records, including objections to each rejected clause, to the Convention for tabulation. Delegates would return to the Convention, entrusted with the power to either implement the constitution if all clauses obtained a two-thirds majority or alter the constitution to conform 'to the Sentiments of two-thirds of the Voters throughout the State' and then implement this revised version.[27]

Since there was no way of determining the "sentiments" of the voters without actually having them vote on the revised version, this procedure was obviously unworkable if some clauses failed to obtain a two-thirds majority, as did, indeed, happen. Although many clauses did not obtain a two-thirds majority, the committee that tabulated the results simply ignored negative votes to get the requisite majority.

The referendum on the Icelandic constitution might have given a positive answer to the first question, but negative answers to one or more of the others. This could have happened, for instance, if some voters approved of the constitution on the basis of the issues raised in the key questions (2) and (5), while disapproving of the draft on other issues about which they cared less. Although the referendum did not produce that kind of inconsistency, the relatively small majority on question (3) suggests that it might well have done so, in which case the very meaning of the referendum would have been unclear. Even worse, what I have called "the Poisson paradox,"[28] also known as the "doctrinal paradox" or "the discursive dilemma," shows that there is a theoretical possibility that the voters might have said Yes to the first question and No to *all* the others. The choice of this procedure indicates, to me at least, that the organizers of the referendum acted too hastily.

The 67% vote for electoral reform is highly suggestive. A breakdown of this vote in the six electoral districts shows that the reform was overwhelmingly accepted in the two urban districts, which had the most to gain from it, as well as in one of the two southern rural districts, essentially a suburb to Reykjavík. Although that district would lose from the reform in terms of its number of deputies, the population might have thought it would benefit from a stronger representation for Reykjavík. The reform was strongly rejected in the two northern rural districts, whereas the other southern rural district was split about evenly.

In the second downstream moment, the constitution was supposed to come before Parliament. Prior to the April 2013 elections, a majority of 32 MPs out of 63 declared in public and in writing that they supported the bill and wanted it passed before Parliament was dissolved, to enable the new Parliament to adopt the constitution definitively. Yet in a last-minute cliffhanger, the minority managed to prevent a vote. Since the details of what happened are controversial in Iceland, they are *a fortiori* beyond my competence. What is not controversial is that a *pouvoir constitué* such as the Parliament ought not to have the power to block decisions of the *pouvoir constituant*, especially when the people, as in

Iceland, had spoken twice, first in electing the members of the Constitutional Council and then in approving the constitutional draft.

The new elections produced a coalition of the two parties that many consider primarily responsible for the 2008 crisis. The government has shelved the issue of a new constitution. Although the Iceland constitution-making process may still rise from the ashes, I conjecture that the improved economic conditions have made the issue less salient. Although it may be perverse to hope for a new crisis, history suggests that this is what would be needed.

Notes

1 I am grateful to Thorvaldur Gylfason and the editors for helpful comments on earlier drafts.
2 Peter H. Russell, *Constitutional Odyssey* 2nd ed. (Toronto: University of Toronto Press, 1993).
3 Jeffrey Lenowitz, "Rejected by the People: Failed U.S. State Constitutional Conventions in the 1960s and 70s," Department of Political Science, Columbia University, 2007.
4 Russell, *Constitutional Odyssey*, 190.
5 Max Farrand, *Records of the Federal Convention*, vol. 3 (New Haven, CT: Yale University Press, 1966), 479.
6 *Archives Parlementaires*, Serie I: 1787–1799, vol. 8 (Paris, 1875–1888), 307.
7 See Hassen Ebrahim and Laurel E. Miller, "Creating the Birth Certificate of a New South Africa: Constitution Making after Apartheid," in *Framing the State in Times of Transition: Case Studies in Constitution Making*, ed. Laurel E. Miller (Washington, DC: United States Institute of Peace Press, 2010), 111–157.
8 Thorvaldur Gylfason, "Iceland: How Could This Happen?" CESifo Working Paper No. 4605, Center for Economic Studies & Ifo Institute, Ludwig-Maximilians University, Munich, 2014, 13.
9 Jón Ólafsson, "An Experiment in Iceland: Crowd-Sourcing a Constitution?" Unpublished paper, accessed October 31, 2015, www.yale.edu/polisci/conferences/epistemic_democracy/jOlafsson.pdf.
10 Thorvaldur Gylfason, "From Collapse to Constitution: The Case of Iceland," in *Public Debt, Global Governance and Economic Dynamism*, ed. Luigi Paganetto (Milan: Springer, 2013), 380.
11 Gylfason, "From Collapse to Constitution: The Case of Iceland."
12 Jon Elster, "Urgency," *Inquiry* 52 (2009): 399–411.
13 Paul Krugman, "The Path Not Taken," *New York Times*, October 28, 2011.
14 Gylfason, "From Collapse to Constitution: The Case of Iceland," 388.
15 James Madison, "The Total Number of the House of Representatives," *Federalist 55* (1788).
16 Information supplied by a member of the Constitutional Council, March 30, 2014.
17 Reynir Axelsson, "Comments on the Decision of the Supreme Court to Invalidate the Election to the Constitutional Assembly," accessed October 31, 2015, http://stjornarskrarfelagid.is/wp-content/uploads/2011/07/Article_by_Reynir_Axelsson.pdf.
18 Hélène Landemore, "Inclusive Constitution-Making: The Icelandic Experiment," *Journal of Political Philosophy* 23, no 2 (2015): 166–191.
19 Gylfason, "From Collapse to Constitution: The Case of Iceland."
20 Laurel E. Miller, "Designing Constitution-Making Processes," in *Framing the State in Times of Transition: Case Studies in Constitution Making*, 138.
21 Act on a Constitutional Assembly, accessed November 4, 2015, http://thjodfundur2010.is/other_files/2010/doc/Act-on-a-Constitutional-Assembly.pdf.

22 Landemore, "Inclusive Constitution-Making: The Icelandic Experiment."
23 Information supplied by a member of the Constitutional Council, March 30, 2014.
24 Jón Ólafsson, "An Experiment in Iceland: Crowd-Sourcing a Constitution?"
25 European Commission for Democracy through Law (Venice Commission), *Opinion on the Draft New Constitution.* March 11, 2013, CDL-AD(2013)010, www.althingi.is/pdf/venice.coe.pdf.
26 Constitution of the Republic of Iceland, accessed November 5, 2015, www.government.is/constitution.
27 Jeffrey Lenowitz, *Why Ratification?* Ph.D. diss. (Columbia University, 2013), 163.
28 Jon Elster, *Securities against Misrule* (Cambridge: Cambridge University Press, 2013), 62–63.

Bibliography

Act on a Constitutional Assembly. Accessed November 4, 2015. http://thjodfundur2010.is/other_files/2010/doc/Act-on-a-Constitutional-Assembly.pdf.

Archives Parlementaires, Serie I: 1787–1799. Vol. 8. Paris, 1875–1888.

Axelsson, Reynir. "Comments on the Decision of the Supreme Court to Invalidate the Election to the Constitutional Assembly." Accessed October 31, 2015. http://stjornarskrarfelagid.is/wp-content/uploads/2011/07/Article_by_Reynir_Axelsson.pdf.

Constitution of the Republic of Iceland. Accessed November 4, 2015. www.government.is/constitution.

Ebrahim, Hassen and Laurel E. Miller. "Creating the Birth Certificate of a New South Africa: Constitution Making after Apartheid." In *Framing the State in Times of Transition: Case Studies in Constitution Making*, edited by Laurel E. Miller, 111–157. Washington, DC: United States Institute of Peace Press, 2010.

Elster, Jon. "Urgency," *Inquiry* 52 (2009): 399–411.

Elster, Jon. *Securities against Misrule.* Cambridge: Cambridge University Press, 2013.

European Commission for Democracy through Law (Venice Commission). *Opinion on the Draft New Constitution.* March 11, 2013, CDL-AD(2013)010. www.althingi.is/pdf/venice.coe.pdf.

Farrand, Max. *Records of the Federal Convention.* 3 vols. New Haven, CT: Yale University Press, 1966.

Gylfason, Thorvaldur. "From Collapse to Constitution: The Case of Iceland." CESifo Working Paper No. 3770, Center for Economic Studies & Ifo Institute, Ludwig-Maximilians University, Munich, 2012.

Gylfason, Thorvaldur. "From Collapse to Constitution: The Case of Iceland." In *Public Debt, Global Governance and Economic Dynamism*, edited by Luigi Paganetto, 379–419. Milan: Springer, 2013.

Gylfason, Thorvaldur. "Iceland: How Could This Happen?" CESifo Working Paper No. 4605, Center for Economic Studies & Ifo Institute, Ludwig-Maximilians University, Munich, 2014.

Krugman, Paul. "The Path Not Taken." *New York Times*, October 28, 2011, A31.

Landemore, Hélène. "Inclusive Constitution-Making: The Icelandic Experiment." *Journal of Political Philosophy* 23, no. 2 (2015): 166–191.

Lenowitz, Jeffrey. "Rejected by the People: Failed U.S. State Constitutional Conventions in the 1960s and 70s." Department of Political Science, Columbia University, 2007.

Lenowitz, Jeffrey. *Why Ratification?* Ph.D. diss., Columbia University, 2013.

Madison, James. "The Total Number of the House of Representatives." *Federalist* 55 (1788).

Miller, Laurel E. "Designing Constitution Making Processes." In *Framing the State in Times of Transition: Case Studies in Constitution Making*, edited by Laurel E. Miller, 601–665. Washington, DC: United States Institute of Peace Press, 2010.

Ólafsson, Jón. "An Experiment in Iceland: Crowdsourcing a Constitution?" Unpublished paper. Accessed October 31, 2015. www.yale.edu/polisci/conferences/epistemic_democracy/jOlafsson.pdf.

Russell, Peter H. *Constitutional Odyssey*. 2nd ed. Toronto: University of Toronto Press, 1993.

10 Constitution on ice

Thorvaldur Gylfason

The purpose here is to review the making of Iceland's post-crash, partly crowd-sourced constitution. Following a brief historical introduction,[1] the chapter describes step by step how the bill was prepared and then put together by the Constitutional Council, how it was received, and how and why Parliament tried to prevent it from being adopted. Various criticisms leveled against the bill along the way will be addressed. It needs to be emphasized up front that these criticisms, whether well founded or not, may be considered irrelevant because Parliament held a national referendum in October 2012, in which the bill and its key individual provisions were accepted by an overwhelming majority of the voters. It will be argued that, if allowed to stand, Parliament's decision in 2013 to sidestep the outcome of the referendum and to quash the constitutional bill is fundamentally anti-democratic, because democracies do not permit the outcome of nationwide elections—in this case a constitutional referendum—to be fixed *ex post*.

Historical background

A key promise given by the post-crash government in early 2009 concerned the constitution, which, drawn up in haste at the time of Iceland's full separation from Denmark in 1944, Parliament had promised to revise ever since without being able or willing to keep its promise, partly because it was not impelled by crisis to do so.[2] In his New Year's address to the nation in 1949, Iceland's first President, Sveinn Björnsson, reminded the political parties of their failure to fix the constitution, saying that "…we still have a mended garment, originally made for another country, with other concerns, a hundred years ago."[3] The left-wing government that came to power in 2009 concluded that since the politicians had failed to revise the constitution for almost 70 years, it was time to bestow the task on a specially elected Constitutional Assembly. This promise constituted an admission of failure as well as an undeclared acknowledgement that a Constitutional Assembly elected in accordance with the principle of "one person, one vote" was better suited to the task than MPs elected on the basis of current electoral laws, granting rural voters on average twice as much say in parliamentary elections as voters in the Reykjavík area, where two-thirds of the population reside.

Emboldened by the first public opinion poll conducted in Iceland, Governor Sveinn Björnsson, soon to become President, managed to have two key novelties inserted into the provisional constitution of 1944, which was otherwise kept essentially unchanged from 1874. The novelties were that the President of the Republic would be elected by the people, not by Parliament as the parties wanted (this gave Iceland one of the first popularly elected presidents in Europe),[4] and that he/she could veto legislation from Parliament and refer it to a national referendum. This provision lay dormant for 60 years until it was activated for the first time in 2004 to block the government's plan to regulate media ownership in a way that could have forced Iceland's largest daily newspaper and the sole television station competing with state television to close down.

As even Iceland's own fairly uneventful, yet acrimonious, constitutional history shows, constitutions are by nature political declarations, outlining the rights and obligations of citizens, including the powers of the organized few versus the unorganized many.[5] Accordingly, constitutions are conducive to disagreements about individual provisions. Rights protected in constitutions entail obligations that may understandably meet resistance. Those who, like President Ólafur R. Grímsson,[6] claim that constitutional amendments must be approved by consensus are at odds with the historical evidence, but their position serves the interests of those opposed to constitutional reform.

The making of Iceland's post-crash constitution

The constitutional revision process launched by the government of the Social Democratic Alliance and Left-Green Movement in 2009 was, in many ways, exemplary.[7] To launch the process, Parliament appointed a seven-member Constitutional Committee, consisting mainly of academic experts from a range of fields (law, literature, natural science, and social science). The composition of the committee reflected Parliament's unspoken understanding that the constitution is not exclusively, and not even principally, a legal document, but primarily a social compact, a political declaration. Legal expertise, even if it can be helpful, is not really essential to writing a constitution, because the constitution supersedes ordinary legislation by virtue of the fact that the people are superior to Parliament.

The role of the Constitutional Committee was threefold: (a) to organize a National Assembly (or Forum) where citizens selected at random from the national register would, under expert supervision, convene for a day to define and discuss their views on the constitution´s contents; (b) to prepare a nationwide election of 25 representatives to a Constitutional Assembly, whose task would be to draft a new constitution reflecting as far as possible the views of the National Assembly; and (c) to prepare the ground for the Constitutional Assembly by offering analysis of the 1944 constitution, and gathering and making available in print, as well as on the internet, information about foreign constitutions and other material.

At first, there was reasonable harmony in Parliament, its members either encouraged or humbled by the results of the 2009 election that had produced

Iceland's first majority government without either the conservative Independence Party or the centrist and rural Progressive Party. Government and opposition collaborated on how to proceed. One key promise given by the Progressive Party before the 2009 election was a new constitution to be drafted by directly elected representatives of the people. To its credit, the Independence Party, also in opposition after the 2009 election, went along, proposing, or at least co-sponsoring, the idea of convening a National Assembly.[8] A similar national assembly had been elected and convened in Reykjavík in 1851 during the wave of revolutions then sweeping Europe, only to be unilaterally dissolved in mid-stream by the representative of the Danish King.

An experimental, privately organized National Assembly had been held in Iceland in 2009,[9] shortly after the crash, with foreign expert input based on the principle of collective intelligence, and this became the prototype of the National Assembly of 2010, to which 950 citizens from 18 to 91 years of age were selected at random from the national population register, subject to side conditions to ensure gender balance, fair representation of different regions, and so on. This means—and this point is the key to the democratic backbone of the project—that every Icelander 18 years or older had an equal chance of being invited to a seat in the National Assembly.

With the help of about 200 assistants, the National Assembly met for a day in early November 2010, at the end of which it issued a set of conclusions, stating that a new constitution was called for, and that it needed to contain certain provisions on national ownership of natural resources and equal voting rights and to foster accountability, decentralization of power, environmental protection, transparency, and other issues.[10] The resolution accorded well with the results of public opinion polls, which had consistently reported for many years that a majority of the voters did want national ownership of natural resources, equal voting rights, etc.[11] There were no inconsistencies or surprises. This is why criticisms of the way the National Assembly was organized and the short time it was given are beside the point in the Icelandic context, and also why the Assembly did so much to enhance the democratic legitimacy of the process.

Constitutional assembly elected

The next step was to elect the 25 representatives of the Constitutional Council in late November 2010 as laid down by the law, which stipulated, for example, that MPs were not eligible to run.[12] By that time, however, two years after the crash, reform fatigue had set in, partly, perhaps, because the economic rescue operation sponsored by the International Monetary Fund (IMF) already appeared likely to succeed, against serious odds. It emboldened those politicians and parties held primarily responsible for the crash in the Special Investigation Commission (SIC) report[13] to blame the crash on foreign conspirators[14] and to oppose the government's rescue effort, including the constitutional project. Some opposition politicians spoke of the "so-called crash," as if nothing had happened.[15] Even so, the months leading up to the November 2010 Constitutional Assembly election went by without fanfare. Until the deadline arrived for putting one's name forward as a candidate, it was impossible to know whether or not the election would prove to be a fiasco due to lack of interest. But after the deadline passed, about a month before the election, it became known that 522 individuals had stepped forward, each supported by between 30 and 50 signatures.

Thus, there were at least 15,660—and possibly as many as 26,100—signatures behind the 522 candidates, between 7% and 11% of eligible voters. On the other hand, political parties and interest groups showed little interest in the election, partly, perhaps, to underline that this was to be the people's constitution as opposed to the political elite's constitution, and they made no visible effort to encourage people to vote. The opposition parties had already turned their back on the project. Only the Independence Party sent lukewarm letters to their members with two slightly different lists of approved candidates. Even the governing coalition parties that had launched the project appeared listless. With one significant exception, the newspaper *DV*, the media showed little interest in presenting the views of the 522 candidates to the voters, except that each was given three to four minutes on public radio. There was no campaign to speak of, no competition for votes among the candidates, just chat among friends on social media and suchlike. Yet, 37% of the electorate turned out to vote.

The 25 candidates who got the most votes came from different walks of life. Perhaps the most striking feature of the group is that five of them were professors (economics, mathematics, medicine, political science, and theology) and three others were junior academics (mathematics, philosophy, and political science), a much higher proportion of Ph.D.s—six out of 25—than in Parliament. This, plus the uniformly high level of education and varied experience of the elected representatives, helped ensure access to outside expertise. After the election results were announced, the leaders of the opposition in Parliament went on the attack against the government, calling the election a failure on account of the 37% turnout (which, nonetheless, is comparable to earlier national referenda without direct political party involvement in Iceland,[16] or Switzerland, for that matter). It was, for them, one thing to have felt obliged, under pressure from protesters in the streets, to prepare for a directly elected constituent assembly, and quite another, 18 months later, to face a group of 25 elected members clearly beyond the control of the political parties used to behaving like a state within the state. Before the election, the answers given by 23 of the 25 elected representatives to questions concerning the constitution posed by *DV* were remarkably homogeneous. They showed that the vast majority of the representatives agreed with the conclusions of the National Assembly. For example, 19 out of 23 representatives favored changing the constitution; 22 favored national ownership of natural resources; 22 favored equal voting rights; and 21 favored more frequent national referenda.[17] Further, the answers given by a large majority of all 522 candidates showed a similar pattern, suggesting that a random drawing of representatives from the list of 522 candidates or from the population at large would also most likely have produced a constitutional bill containing these key provisions. Unmistakably, there was a broad and clear popular consensus in favor of substantive constitutional reform that would, among other things, aim to (a) sever what many saw as the corrupt relationship between the political class and parts of the business community, particularly the vessel owners, who had grown used to regarding Iceland's common-property fish resources as their private possession, and (b) reduce the power of political party leaders to surround themselves in Parliament with provincial MPs having few votes behind them.

The question can be raised whether this would have been possible had there been no crash. The 1944 constitution was not directly responsible for the crash, true, but it was clearly not able to prevent the crash either. The weak separation of powers between the three branches of government had led to executive overreach that produced, among other things, a poorly implemented privatization of the banks in 1998–2003, through which they were sold at modest prices to well-connected individuals, paving their way to the cliff in 2008.[18] In retrospect, it appears unlikely that the privatization of the banks as it was carried out would have been accepted in a national referendum. Unsurprisingly, therefore, many Icelanders, including the new majority in Parliament, thought it reasonable to take a close look at the constitution after the crash.

Enter the Supreme Court

Three technical complaints about the vote count and the shape of the voting booths were filed immediately after the Constitutional Assembly election by individuals with connections to the Independence Party. On the basis of these complaints, six Supreme Court justices out of nine—five of them Independence Party appointees—issued an unprecedented administrative decision to annul the election.

Never before had a national election in a democracy been invalidated *ex post*. Further, there is a strong case for arguing that there was no basis in law for the judges to make this decision, because the law permits such a decision to be made only if an elected representative can be shown to have been ineligible to run, or if fraudulent behavior can be shown to have influenced the election outcome, neither of which was claimed to have been the case. As a voter, one of the lawyers elected to the Assembly, Gísli Tryggvason, appealed to the Supreme Court to reconsider its decision or, at least, to permit a recount to address "significant deficiencies" alleged by the Court decision, but his appeal was dismissed by the Court.[19] The mathematician Reynir Axelsson[20] concludes his scathing analysis of the Supreme Court decision thus: "The only real and only significant deficiency in the election was that the Supreme Court spoiled it by a Decision which is demonstrably based on false reasoning and dubious sources of law."[21]

Parliament reacted to the Supreme Court's decision by offering the 25 elected Constitutional Assembly representatives appointment to a Constitutional Council. The opponents of constitutional reform were jubilant, reveling in the alleged lack of legitimacy of the Council and calling it an "irrelevant conference." Among other things, the 25 elected members were accused of dishonoring the 1944 constitution by accepting Parliament's appointment.[22] Council members did not take such charges seriously; nor did any of them, apart from Tryggvason's appeal, bother to consider mounting a legal challenge to the Supreme Court decision, which Parliament declared binding. The Council members had been summoned by the people and Parliament to draft a post-crash constitution, and this is what they set out to do.

First, a few informal meetings were held to prepare a set of operating rules, as allowed by the law on the Council. In preparation for my contribution to our joint work, I used my time to consult with colleagues at home and abroad, including one of the authors of the South African constitution from 1994 to 1996, and other constitutional experts abroad, as well as a number of local academics, lawyers, and others. Armed also with an excellent 700-page report from the Constitutional Committee plus other material, the Council came well prepared to the first formal meeting at the beginning of April 2011. After the group of representatives was divided into three subcommittees (A, B, and C), each charged with preparing initial drafts of about one-third of the bill, one of the first decisions that had to be made was whether to start the work with a clean slate or let it suffice to amend individual provisions of the 1944 constitution. Quickly, it became clear that there was a broad consensus in favor of drafting a new constitution *ab initio*, even if the old constitution would naturally serve as a point of departure. This consensus appeared to result from the widely held view that the financial collapse called for a general overhaul of the constitution rather than marginal amendments.

Another early decision concerned the extent to which the Council's work would be carried out in full view of the public. It was decided that transparency through crowdsourcing should be attempted, a decision that perhaps came especially easily to the Council members from academia, where peer review is a standard operating procedure. Thus, all General Assembly meetings were simulcast on the internet and, subsequently, posted on the Council website, whereas subcommittee meetings were held behind closed doors, except when the subcommittees invited the members of other subcommittees and expert witnesses to visit on occasion. The transcripts of all General Assembly meetings, as well as the minutes of all meetings, were posted on the Council website. As the work progressed, it became clear that transparency through crowdsourcing was a good thing, not only because of the quality and seriousness of the input received from members of the public who accepted the Council's invitation to review and react to its written text week by week, but also because it made it unnecessary to extend invitations to representatives of interest organizations—artists, farmers, fishermen, pensioners, teachers, and so on. This was in the spirit of the opening salvo of the preamble of the bill: "We, the people of Iceland, wish to create a just society with equal opportunities for everyone."[23] This marked a major departure from the *modus operandi* of Parliament, where it is common practice for strong interest organizations—for example, vessel owners—to be invited to single-handedly draft laws that concern them. Citizens from all walks of life offered their help, including artists and farmers. Few academics did, however, and even fewer lawyers—perhaps because they viewed the Constitutional Council as intruders on their traditional turf.[24]

The Constitutional Council went about its business in harmony. Naturally, though, there were some disagreements that needed to be addressed. For example, in view of the need for the new constitution to be approved by two successive parliaments in keeping with the 1944 constitution, some members thought it advisable to try to anticipate the will of Parliament by avoiding formulations considered likely to meet with its disapproval. Others thought it more important to stay true to the consensus reflected in the conclusions of the National Assembly in 2010, arguing that only in this way would a new constitution win approval in a national referendum, which Parliament could not permit itself to disregard.

Some members wanted to enact fairly radical changes through a direct strengthening of the role of the President or the direct national election of the Prime Minister. Others thought it enough to erect checks and balances between the three branches of government within the existing structure of government prescribed by the 1944 constitution, pointing out that the National Assembly had not asked for a strengthened role of the President. Some representatives felt that specific provisions—if such could be devised—were needed as precautions against another financial crash, while others thought that general provisions to strengthen checks and balances would suffice.[25] Some of the issues arising were settled by voting in subcommittees or in the General Assembly, which had the last word, while others were settled by compromise or consensus. For example, there was no need to take a vote on the natural resource clause in the A-subcommittee charged with drafting that provision, because consensus prevailed in full agreement with the National Assembly.

The debates in the General Assembly and, for the most part, in the subcommittees as well were marked by mutual respect. Otherwise, the work of the Council could hardly have been completed in the four months assigned to the task by Parliament, least of all with a unanimous acceptance of the bill in the end by 25 votes to zero, no abstentions.[26] Perhaps the main point here is that, even if Council members considered themselves bound only by their conscience, they produced a bill that was in nearly perfect harmony with the conclusions of the National Assembly. The sole substantive difference is that while the National Assembly called for a reduction in the number of MPs, the Constitutional Council decided to keep their number unchanged at 63 so as not to signal an apparent internal inconsistency in a bill aiming to strengthen the legislative and judicial branches of government vis-à-vis the executive branch.[27]

As the work of the Constitutional Council progressed, it became apparent to several Council members, especially to those with good contacts in Parliament, that parliamentary support for a new constitution was waning. When the bill was delivered to the Speaker of Parliament at a formal ceremony in July 2011, several Council members were struck by the Speaker's visible lack of enthusiasm. Parliament declined to have the bill translated into English to facilitate foreign reaction to the bill, so that an official translation had to be privately financed by the Constitutional Society, a non-governmental organization (NGO). Upon receiving the bill, Parliament sent it on to its Constitutional and

Supervisory Committee, which took several months to read and discuss the bill. In March 2012, nearly eight months after delivery, the former Council members were summoned on short notice to a four-day special meeting to respond to several written queries by the Constitutional and Supervisory Committee on behalf of Parliament.

Most but not quite all (21 of 25) former council members were able to attend that special meeting. As before, the Council's answers to Parliament's questions were unanimous. Perhaps the most significant query had to do with the natural resource clause, stipulating, among other things, that "[o]n the basis of law, government authorities may grant permits for the use or utilization of resources or other limited public goods against full consideration and for a reasonable period of time." Parliament asked if the formulation "full consideration" could be replaced by "fair consideration." The Council members' answer was a polite but resolute No, for two reasons. First, the replacement of "full" by "fair" might be interpreted as a constitutionally protected discount from full price to vessel owners, which was not intended. Second, because the article on the right of ownership, unchanged from 1944, stipulates "full compensation" for confiscation of property, internal consistency requires full price in both clauses so as not to introduce discrimination among different types of ownership.

Another question from Parliament led to a rewording of the electoral clause stipulating "one person, one vote" that reduced the number of words in the provision by a third without affecting its substance, a welcome change. In a few other cases, the former Council members responded to the Constitutional and Supervisory Committee's queries by suggesting alternative wording for clarification. The committee, or rather its majority of six of nine members, had declared that only changes in wording could be made, but no changes of substance.

National referendum

The government intended to hold a referendum on the bill at the time of the presidential election in June 2012 to encourage voter turnout, but the minority in Parliament, increasingly vociferous in its opposition to the bill, used filibustering to block this plan. Instead, the referendum was held on October 20, 2012. The governing parties holding the referendum, it turned out, did not explain the bill to the electorate before the referendum. This is why the Alliance for a New Constitution (SaNS) was founded, an advocacy group whose aim was, and remains, to secure the adoption of the constitutional bill.[28] The Alliance had no financial resources apart from a small amount supplied by the Movement, the smallest opposition party in Parliament, and the Constitutional Society. The government declined to provide financial support for the effort to promote the bill, as did both governing parties, the Social Democratic Alliance and the Left-Green Movement. SaNS was on its own; without it, the bill was an orphan. Even so, assisted by the Movement and its successor, Dawn, some meetings were held around the country to provide a modicum of visibility. A number of articles explaining the bill were published.

As had been the case before the Constitutional Assembly election, even the political parties who had laid the bill before the voters were mostly absent from the scene before the referendum. Nonetheless, 49% of eligible voters turned out, and 67% of them said Yes to the first question: "Do you want the proposals of the Constitutional Council to form the basis of a legislative bill for a new Constitution?" The formulation of this question could be seen to hold open the possibility that Parliament might turn against its original intention by trying to build something completely different on the basis of the bill. Parliament had, however, put five auxiliary questions on the ballot, including one on national ownership of natural resources (83% said Yes), another on equal voting rights, "one person, one vote" (67% said Yes), and yet another on more frequent use of national referenda (73% said Yes).[29] Thus, the majority in Parliament, including the Movement, could argue not only that an overwhelming majority of the voters supported the bill, but also that they accepted its key individual provisions. After the referendum, which they chose to refer to as an opinion poll because of its nonbinding nature, members of the opposition claimed that the absentees would have voted against the bill.

After the referendum, the Constitutional and Supervisory Committee asked a team of local lawyers, led by an official at the Prime Minister's Office, to go over the bill once more to suggest improved wording if needed from a legal and technical point of view, again with clear instructions to the effect that no changes in substance would be allowed. Hélène Landemore gives two examples of substantive changes for the worse suggested by the lawyers beyond their mandate.[30] Here is a third example. The lawyers suggested a redrafting of the natural resource provision that fundamentally changed its meaning—in favor of the vessel owners. To its credit, the Constitutional and Supervisory Committee restored the original formulation that had been proposed by the Constitutional Council and presented to the public before the referendum. The story does not end here, however, because at a later stage, the Constitutional and Supervisory Committee changed the natural resource clause by replacing the words "full consideration" with "normal consideration."

At the eleventh hour, in a surprise move, the Constitutional and Supervisory Committee asked the Venice Commission (VC) to review the bill, a proposal that members of the Constitutional Council had made to Parliament more than a year earlier without success.[31] Members of the VC visited Iceland in January 2013, and a month later delivered a provisional report,[32] the main points of which the Constitutional and Supervisory Committee found it easy to incorporate into the final version of the bill. In places, it must be said, the VC showed a lack of familiarity with Iceland's situation and history. In particular, the VC's thoughts on the nationally elected President and his or her constitutional authority to refer legislation from Parliament to a national referendum were arguably unhelpful but harmless. Some of the VC's more useful comments concerned changes of wording that the Constitutional and Supervisory Committee had introduced into the bill, changes that were easily reversible, as well as new formulations here and there that were easy to accept.

The most important substantive comment offered by the VC concerned the provisions on Parliament, provisions that neither MPs nor other observers had reacted against during the 18 months that the bill had been under scrutiny in Parliament, and that Parliament, accordingly, had not put on the ballot in the 2012 referendum. In particular, the VC speculated that the bill perhaps went too far in strengthening parliament vis-à-vis the executive branch, a point that the Constitutional and Supervisory Committee promptly rejected. Most importantly, however, the VC expressed its agreement with the key provisions of the bill on equal voting rights, personal elections to Parliament (as an alternative to party slates), direct democracy, freedom of information, and national ownership of natural resources. It took the Constitutional and Supervisory Committee only a short while to adjust the bill to the VC's comments.

Parliament's turn

As the parliamentary election of April 2013 drew closer, less and less time was left for Parliament to pass the amended bill in accordance with the results of the referendum the year before. To encourage MPs, members of the Constitutional Society opened a website inviting MPs to declare whether they favored passing the bill before Parliament adjourned. Gradually, and sometimes grudgingly, MPs submitted these declarations of support one after another, until there was a majority of 32 votes in favor of passing the bill. It seemed clear that not all of the remaining 31 MPs would vote against the bill. For comparison, the vote on holding the October 2012 referendum had been 35 in favor and 15 against with 13 abstentions. While MPs might have rejected the bill in a secret ballot, the point here is that in Parliament there is no such thing as a secret ballot.

When the new leaders of the governing parties (their older predecessors had stepped aside ahead of the approaching parliamentary election) presented a motion in Parliament aimed at defusing the constitutional debate, an MP for the Movement, Margrét Tryggvadóttir, presented an amendment to their proposal, an amendment comprising the constitutional bill *in toto*, which the Speaker of Parliament, in keeping with universal procedural rules, had to bring to a vote first. The proposed amendment was a last-minute attempt to bring the bill to a vote. It was long past midnight, the last day of Parliament before recess. The Speaker, in my view in violation of parliamentary procedure, did not bring the amendment—that is, the bill—to a vote. As a result, Parliament adjourned without voting on the bill that two-thirds of the voters had accepted the year before. The outgoing Prime Minister, Jóhanna Sigurðardóttir, whose Social Democratic Alliance would suffer the worst defeat in the history of parliamentary elections in Iceland a month later, said: "The past few weeks were the saddest period of my 35 years in Parliament."[33]

Why did the people not take to the streets banging their pots and pans in protest against these events? A likely explanation is that a parliamentary election was only a month away, and the opposition parties managed to steer the campaign toward short-term economic issues, promising instant debt relief to distressed households.

What went wrong?

Why did the bill fail to win acceptance in Parliament? As I see it, this outcome—which, for reasons laid out in what follows, I still view only as a temporary setback—had nothing to do with the alleged flaws of the bill. Rather, this occurred because the bill was designed to decentralize authority through redistribution of power from the political class to the people, in accordance with clear instructions from the National Assembly of 2010, and because MPs were in a position, granted them by the 1944 constitution, to block the bill. The fact that the referendum was advisory as opposed to legally binding can be seen as immaterial by virtue of the fact that the people are superior to Parliament.[34] The sole significant failure of the process was that the Speaker of Parliament could not be held accountable for not having a vote on the bill. In an open vote, MPs would probably not have dared kill the bill against the clear will of the people as expressed in the 2012 referendum. Had Parliament taken a vote, and, especially, had a second referendum been held at the time of the 2013 parliamentary election,[35] a new Parliament in 2013, however composed, would hardly have dared block the bill. Thus, one can argue that the process did not fail. A vocal minority in Parliament used filibustering, and the majority shied away from responding with the "nuclear option" of breaking it, fearing the consequences of such an extraordinary response.

Does the bill go too far?

In the constitutional referendum of 2012, the voters were for the first time invited to express their views on natural resource management, equal voting rights, and a few other key issues on a level playing field—one person, one vote—without interference from political parties. When the political parties began to comprehend the likely consequences of the constitutional reform process they had set in motion, they turned against themselves.[36]

There were other, less prominent provisions in the bill intended to protect and promote human rights, thus imposing obligations on others. The environmental protection clauses would restrain the freedom of polluters to continue spoiling nature as they had before; the freedom of information clauses would restrict the freedom of those used to operating with impunity under a veil of secrecy; and so on. Yet, no one stepped forward to declare opposition to these clauses, just as hardly anyone openly declared opposition even to the clauses on equal voting rights and national ownership of natural resources, apart from the aforementioned botched attempt by the government's lawyers to pull the teeth out of the natural resource provision. This was understandable, because the Constitutional Council's careful wording of the natural resource clause was consistent with and borrowed some of its language from official policy declarations of all the political parties—declarations that, it now appeared, they intended to remain empty words. This is why criticism of the bill that surfaced after the national referendum did not focus on any of the above-mentioned issues but on something completely different—that is, on issues that Parliament, correctly, had seen no reason to put before the voters in the 2012 referendum.

What happened next

Opponents of the bill behaved as if they hoped the 2012 referendum would sink the bill. Otherwise, they would have expressed their opposition to the bill before the referendum and warned the voters against accepting it. Three members of the seven-member Constitutional Committee, who had in unison prepared the ground for the Constitutional Council, now broke rank, raising individual objections to aspects of the bill—aspects that, based on analysis and debate on record,[37] the Constitutional Council had settled and the voters had accepted. Two of the former Constitutional Committee members even published an alternative bill—their personal constitution, as it were—leaving out both national ownership of natural resources and equal voting rights, as if no referendum had taken place. Having supplied more elected representatives to the Constitutional Council than any other single workplace, the University of Iceland, or rather, some of its departments, suddenly held a series of conferences, at which opponents of the bill, including the three minority members of the Constitutional Committee, aired their criticisms. As a rule, former members of the Constitutional Council were not invited to speak at these conferences,[38] but some of them tried from their seats in the audience afterward and on blogs to correct what they saw as falsehoods propagated by several speakers.

Professors were invited to give testimony to parliamentary committees. At one such parliamentary committee meeting, two economics professors testified that the adoption of the bill, especially the natural resource provision, would be ruinous, to the point of triggering a mass exodus from the country.[39] It needs to be added that many other academics not directly involved in the process supported the bill at the drafting stage and afterward, both as (mostly unofficial) advisors to (members of) the Constitutional Council and as external observers.

The criticisms of the constitutional bill did not really matter, because the people accepted it in a national referendum called by Parliament. Nothing has been presented to show that any provision of the bill contradicts the conclusions of the National Assembly of 2010. The sole significant source of opposition to the bill springs from the political class and the special interests, the usual suspects described by Jon Elster as an *engrenage* of "cheap access to natural resources, a skewed electoral system, unsound banking practices, and corrupt politicians."[40] The criticism has been political through and through, not legal, even if some lawyers have tried to dress it up in terms of legal jargon.

Some criticisms

Let me review a few of the criticisms directed against the bill and describe why I disagree with them. A member of the Constitutional and Supervisory Committee complained that the bill included a provision on the appointment of judges, an issue that 23 representatives, when asked by the newspaper *DV* before the Constitutional Assembly election, had said needed to be addressed in a new constitution. The Constitutional and Supervisory Committee member's complaint was that a new law had already been passed in the spirit of the constitutional provision proposed. The Council was, of course, aware of the new law, and inserted the provision into the bill simply to prevent the politicians from reverting to their old habits by retracting their recent reform of judicial appointments.[41]

Some observers have remarked that the Constitutional Council lacked legal expertise. This complaint is arguably misplaced. First, as stated earlier, a constitution is not a legal document but a political declaration of principle: in practice, a constitution can say whatever its framers want it to say. Second, there were four lawyers among the elected representatives on the Council, and still more on its staff and among its advisors, including the lawyers on the Constitutional Committee. Third, Eiríkur Tómasson, a respected law professor, now Supreme Court Justice, acted as the Council's official legal advisor during the last few weeks of our work. I consulted with several other law professors and judges throughout the process, as I am sure several of my Council colleagues did as well. Constitution-makers do not need to be experts in law, or anything else for that matter, just as MPs do not need to be experts. The key is to have democratically elected, competent, and well-intentioned representatives with good access to experts as well as to other citizens as needed. This the Council had, and this is an important reason why the Council succeeded and the voters accepted the bill.

Some have complained about the bill being drafted by a group of which most members reside in the Reykjavík area. This concern is not, however, borne out by the results of the 2012 referendum. All six questions, except the one on church and state, were answered in accordance with the bill in all six constituencies, with only two exceptions. The two rural northern constituency came out against "one person, one vote." The third rural constituencies—against its own interests, one might think—came out in favor of "one person, one vote," as did the three urban ones.[42] Accordingly, not too much should be made of the conflict between the rural voters and the rest in this case. In fact, most of the Council members residing in the Reykjavík area had strong roots in other parts of the country. Once again, the bill is fully consistent with the resolution of the National Assembly, where all regions had fair representation. The single most often heard criticism of the bill is that the "academic community" turned against it.[43] This is not true, for the simple reason that in a pluralistic, democratic society there is no such thing as an "academic community" as far as politics is concerned. Like other professions, academics can naturally disagree on politics.

Conclusion

As Elster has pointed out, "an ordinary legislature should not serve as a constituent assembly or as a ratifying body. In either capacity, there is risk that it might act in a self-serving manner…."[44] This problem is at the heart of Iceland's predicament. I have argued here that it is relevant to consider extra-constitutional means of respecting the popular will as expressed in the 2012 referendum, rather than giving in to politicians who thwart the will of the people. The next parliamentary election, to be held no later than 2017, will be held according to election laws that 67% of the voters rejected in the 2012 referendum by declaring their support for "one person, one vote." This prospect would have been averted had Parliament abided by the will of the people before and after the 2013 parliamentary election.

There is ample reason to view events like some of those described in this chapter—six Supreme Court judges annulling a national election on flimsy grounds, Parliament openly disrespecting the overwhelming result of a constitutional referendum—as deeply problematic. The constitution remains on ice, held hostage by a new parliamentary majority of the Independence Party and the Progressive Party, in government together again since mid-2013.

These events need to be viewed in context. Parliament's failure thus far to respect the outcome of the 2012 referendum stands in the way of a democratic resolution to several current controversies, not least concerning the government's pending plan to grant vessel owners exclusive rights to the fishing grounds for 20–25 years. This plan would have no chance of being adopted if the new constitution were already in place, for then 10% of the electorate could demand a referendum, in which the plan would surely be defeated in view of the overwhelming public support for national ownership of natural resources expressed in the 2012 referendum. Hence, the emphasis of the constitutional bill on checks and balances intended to reduce the risk of continued executive overreach by strengthening Parliament and the courts through the way MPs and judges are selected as well as through the right of the electorate to take certain issues out of the hands of the politicians.

Notes

1 For further background, see Thorvaldur Gylfason, "Constitution on Ice," CESifo Working Paper 5056, Munich, University of Munich, 2014.

2 Jon Elster, "Forces and Mechanisms in the Constitution-Making Process," *Duke Law Journal* 45 (1995): 364–396.

3 Sveinn Björnsson. "Nýársávarp forseta Íslands Sveins Björnssonar 1. janúar 1949" [New Year's Address of President Sveinn Björnsson January 1, 1949], accessed November 17, 2015, www.forseti.is/media/files/01.01.49.S.B.nyarsavarp.pdf.

4 Precedents include France in 1848 and Germany in 1919.

5 Ferdinand Lassalle, "On the Essence of Constitutions. Speech Delivered in Berlin, April 16, 1862," *Fourth International* 3 (1942): 25–31.

6 Ólafur R. Grímsson, "Nýársávarp forseta Íslands Ólafs Ragnars Grímssonar 1. janúar 2013" [New Year's Address of President Ólafur Ragnar Grímsson January 1, 2013], accessed November 17, 2015, www.forseti.is/media/PDF/01_01_2013_aramotaavarp.pdf.

7 Zachary Elkins et al., "A Review of Iceland's Draft Constitution," October 14, 2012, accessed December 17, 2015, http://comparativeconstitutionsproject.org/wp-content/uploads/CCP-Iceland-Report.pdf; Hélène Landemore, "Inclusive Constitution-Making: The Icelandic Experiment," *Journal of Political Philosophy* (2014): 1–30, accessed November 17, 2015, www.academia.edu/5289629/Inclusive_Constitution-Making_the_Icelandic_Experiment; A. C. M. Meuwese, "Popular Constitution-Making. The Case of Iceland," in *The Social and Political Foundations of Constitutions*, eds. Denis Galligan and Mila Versteeg (New York: Cambridge University Press, 2013), 469–496.

8 Law No. 90, June 25, 2010, accessed December 29, 2015, www.althingi.is/altext/138/s/1397.html.

9 Maurapúfan, "Þjóðfundur: Stefnumót við framtíðina" [National Assembly: Meeting with the Future], accessed September 25, 2015, www.thjodfundur2009.is/fraedsluefni/.

10 See "The Main Conclusions from the National Forum 2010," accessed December 29, 2015, www.thjodfundur2010.is/english/.

11 Thorvaldur Gylfason, *Hreint Borð* [Clean Slate] (Reykjavík: Gutti, 2012), 112–116.

12 Law No. 90, June 25, 2010, see footnote 6.

13 Rannsóknarnefnd Alþingis [Special Investigation Commission of the Icelandic parliament], *Aðdragandi og orsakir falls íslensku bankanna 2008 og tengdir atburðir* [The Causes and Effects of the Fall of the Icelandic Banks and Related Events] (Reykjavík: Icelandic Parliament, 2010).

14 Styrmir Gunnarsson, *Umsátrið* [*The Siege*] (Reykjavík: Veröld, 2009).

15 Former Prime Minister Geir Haarde told *The Guardian* on October 6, 2013 that "there were older people who didn't even realize there had been a crisis."

16 Thorvaldur Gylfason, "From Collapse to Constitution: The Case of Iceland," in *Public Debt, Global Governance and Economic Dynamism*, ed. Luigi Paganetto (Berlin: Springer, 2013), 379–417.

17 Gylfason, "From Collapse to Constitution: The Case of Iceland."

18 Gylfason, "From Collapse to Constitution: The Case of Iceland."

19 Gísli Tryggvason, "Beiðni um endurupptöku ákvörðunar Hæstaréttar vegna kosningar til stjórnlagaþings" [Appeal for Reconsideration of Supreme Court Decision concerning Election to Constitutional Assembly], February 8, 2011, accessed September 25, 2015, www.mbl.is/media/97/2597.pdf.

20 Reynir Axelsson, "Comments on the Decision of the Supreme Court to Invalidate the Election to the Constitutional Assembly," accessed August 17, 2015, http://stjornarskrarfelagid.is/wp-content/uploads/2011/07/Article_by_Reynir_Axelsson.pdf.

21 The Organization of Disabled in Iceland made an equivalent technical complaint about the 2012 presidential election, but the Supreme Court dismissed the complaint on the grounds that the alleged irregularities could not have affected the outcome of the election.

22 One elected representative declined to accept parliamentary appointment, and was replaced by the candidate next in line, a lawyer.

23 A literal translation of the original would replace "with equal opportunities for everyone" by "where everyone has a seat at the same table."

24 In a newspaper interview after the referendum in 2012, a political science professor who had kept silent throughout the process called the Council "completely illegitimate," adding that "a certain elite" should rewrite the constitution. Among the 25 Constitutional Council representatives, there were two political scientists, one of whom was shortly afterward promoted to a professorship.

25 Gylfason, "From Collapse to Constitution: The Case of Iceland."

26 Gylfason, "From Collapse to Constitution: The Case of Iceland."

27 This decision signals the Council's easy attitude toward Parliament. Had the Council wanted to make it more difficult in the eyes of the public for MPs to oppose the bill, it could have decided on a reduced number of seats in Parliament.

28 The establishment of SaNS was necessary because the articles of the Constitutional Society prescribed that society's neutrality concerning the content of the constitution. The two merged in 2014.

29 These numbers understate the level of support for the bill, because many voters said Yes to the first question without voting on the remaining questions. Specifically, at least twice as many passed on questions 2–6 as on question 1. This may be understood to impart a negative bias to the vote tally on questions 2–6, because if you vote for the bill as a whole, you are likely to approve of at least some of its main provisions listed in questions 2–6, even if you do not say so on your ballot. For more on the

results of the referendum, see Thorvaldur Gylfason, "Constitution-Making in Action: The case of Iceland," *VoxEU*, November 1, 2012; Þorkell Helgason, "Niðurstöður þjóðaratkvæðagreiðslu 20. október 2012 (leiðrétt)," [Results of National Referendum October 20, 2012 (corrected)], accessed August 17, 2015, http://thorkellhelgason.is/?tag=thjodaratkvaedagreidsla-2012.

30 Landemore, "Inclusive Constitution-Making: The Icelandic Experiment," 22–23.

31 In a comic turn of events, Parliament asked the Constitutional Society for permission to use the latter's privately financed English translation of the bill. The permission was gladly granted.

32 European Commission for Democracy through Law (Venice Commission), *Opinion on the Draft New Constitution*, March 11, 2013, CDL-AD(2013)010, accessed August 17, 2015, www.althingi.is/pdf/venice.coe.pdf.

33 "Daprasta tímabilið á mínum þingferli" [Saddest Period of my Parliamentary Career], *RÚV*, March 28, 2013, accessed September 12, 2015, www.ruv.is/frett/daprasta-timabilid-a-minum-thingferli.

34 This particular provision of the bill was approved by 73% of the voters in the 2012 referendum (Gylfason, "Constitution Making in Action").

35 By law, Parliament needed to decide three months in advance to hold a second referendum on the bill coinciding with the parliamentary election in April 2013, and let the deadline pass.

36 Gunnarsson, *Umsátrið* [*The Siege*], 206.

37 The minutes of Constitutional Council deliberations are available only in Icelandic.

38 An exception to the rule is the conference at which several of the chapters in this volume were presented (not including this chapter, however).

39 Thorvaldur Gylfason, "Tvöfalt líf: Þorvaldur Gylfason ræðir við Þráin Bertelsson" ("A Double Life: Thorvaldur Gylfason interviews Thráinn Bertelsson"), *Tímarit Máls og menningar* 4 (2014). Not long afterward, the two professors in question were appointed as chief economic advisors to the Independence Party Chairman and the Finance Minister.

40 Jon Elster, "Icelandic Constitution-Making in Comparative Perspective." In this volume.

41 In 2015, the Interior Minister presented to Parliament a bill retracting the recent reform.

42 Helgason, "Niðurstöður þjóðaratkvæðagreiðslu 20. október 2012 (leiðrétt)."

43 Grímsson, "Nýársávarp."

44 Elster, "Icelandic Constitution-Making in Comparative Perspective."

Bibliography

Axelsson, Reynir. "Comments on the Decision of the Supreme Court to Invalidate the Election to the Constitutional Assembly." Accessed August 17, 2015. http://stjornarskrarfelagid.is/wp-content/uploads/2011/07/Article_by_Reynir_Axelsson.pdf.

Björnsson, Sveinn. "Nýársávarp forseta Íslands Sveins Björnssonar 1. janúar 1949" [New Year's Address of President Sveinn Björnsson January 1, 1949]. Accessed November 17, 2015. www.forseti.is/media/files/01.01.49.S.B.nyarsavarp.pdf.

"Daprasta tímabilið á mínum þingferli" [Saddest Period of my Parliamentary Career)]. *RUV*, March 28, 2013. Accessed September 12, 2015. http://www.ruv.is/frett/daprasta-timabilid-a-minum-thingferli.

Elkins, Zachary, Tom Ginsburg, and James Melton. "A Review of Iceland's Draft Constitution." October 14, 2012. Accessed December 17, 2015. http://comparativeconstitutionsproject.org/wp-content/uploads/CCP-Iceland-Report.pdf.

Elster, Jon. "Forces and Mechanisms in the Constitution-Making Process." *Duke Law Journal* 45 (1995): 364–396.

Elster, Jon. "Icelandic Constitution-Making in Comparative Perspective." In this volume.

European Commission for Democracy through Law (Venice Commission). *Opinion on the Draft New Constitution.* March 11, 2013, CDL-AD(2013)010. Accessed August 17, 2015. www.althingi.is/pdf/venice.coe.pdf.

Grímsson, Ólafur R. "Nýársávarp forseta Íslands Ólafs Ragnars Grímssonar 1. janúar 2013" [New Year's Address of President Ólafur Ragnar Grímsson January 1, 2013]. Accessed November 17, 2015. www.forseti.is/media/PDF/01_01_2013_aramotaavarp.pdf.

Gunnarsson, Styrmir. *Umsátrið* [The Siege]. Reykjavík: Veröld, 2009.

Gylfason, Thorvaldur. "Iceland's Special Investigation: The Plot Thickens." *VoxEU.* April 30, 2010.

Gylfason, Thorvaldur. *Hreint borð* [Clean Slate]. Reykjavík: Gutti, 2012.

Gylfason, Thorvaldur. "Constitution-Making in Action: The Case of Iceland." *VoxEU.* November 1, 2012.

Gylfason, Thorvaldur. "From Collapse to Constitution: The Case of Iceland." In *Public Debt, Global Governance and Economic Dynamism*, edited by Luigi Paganetto, 379–417. Berlin: Springer, 2013.

Gylfason, Thorvaldur. "Constitution on Ice." CESifo Working Paper 5056, November 2014.

Gylfason, Thorvaldur. "Tvöfalt líf: Þorvaldur Gylfason ræðir við Þráin Bertelsson" [A Double Life: Thorvaldur Gylfason interviews Thráinn Bertelsson]. *Tímarit Máls og menningar* 4 (2014): 1–31.

Gylfason, Thorvaldur, Bengt Holmström, Sixten Korkman, Hans Tson Söderström, and Vesa Vihriala. *Nordics in Global Crisis.* Taloustieto Oy: The Research Institute of the Finnish Economy (ETLA), 2010.

Helgason, Þorkell. "Niðurstöður þjóðaratkvæðagreiðslu 20. október 2012 (leiðrétt)" [Results of National Referendum October 20, 2012 (Corrected)]. Accessed August 17, 2015. http://thorkellhelgason.is/?tag=thjodaratkvaedagreidsla-2012.

Kristjánsson, Svanur. "Frá nýsköpun lýðræðis til óhefts flokkavalds: Fjórir forsetar Íslands 1944–1996" [From the Creation of Democracy to Unfettered Political Party Power: Four Presidents of Iceland, 1944–1996]. *Skírnir* 186 (spring 2012): 50–97.

Landemore, Hélène. "Inclusive Constitution-Making: The Icelandic Experiment." *Journal of Political Philosophy* (2014): 1–30.

Lassalle, Ferdinand. "On the Essence of Constitutions. Speech Delivered in Berlin, April 16, 1862." *Fourth International* 3 (1942): 25–31.

Mauraþúfan. "Þjóðfundur: Stefnumót við framtíðina" [National Assembly: Meeting with the Future]. Accessed September 23, 2015. www.thjodfundur2009.is/fraedsluefni.

Meuwese, A. C. M. "Popular Constitution-Making: The Case of Iceland." In *The Social and Political Foundations of Constitutions*, edited by Denis Galligan and Mila Versteeg, 469–496. New York: Cambridge University Press, 2013.

Rannsóknarnefnd Alþingis [The Special Investigation Commission of the Icelandic Parliament]. *Aðdragandi og orsakir falls íslensku bankanna 2008 og tengdir atburðir* [The Causes and Effects of the Fall of the Icelandic Banks and Related Events]. Reykjavík: Icelandic Parliament, 2010.

Tryggvason, Gísli. "Beiðni um endurupptöku ákvörðunar Hæstaréttar vegna kosningar til stjórnlagaþings" [Appeal for Reconsideration of Supreme Court Decision concerning Election to Constitutional Assembly], February 8, 2011. Accessed September 25, 2015. www.mbl.is/media/97/2597.pdf.

11 Constitutional revision

A weak legislative framework compounded by political disputes

Salvör Nordal

Although the process of constitutional revision in Iceland was motivated by the financial crisis, it reflected a more ambitious agenda. It was about fundamental questions: whether a new constitution would safeguard against another banking collapse, and whether deep-seated changes of societal values and institutions were needed. Another aim was to engage the public in a dialogue on constitutional issues by according it a direct involvement in the experiment. After the crisis, trust in government and Parliament dropped dramatically. For some, inviting the public to participate in writing a new constitution was an important project to rebuild public trust. In spite of ambitious motivations, Parliament, which has the power to change the constitution, failed in the end to approve the bill in 2013 or to implement any of the suggested revisions drafted by the Constitutional Council.

The reasons for failure are many and complex. In this chapter, I deal with some of the weaknesses in the preparation of the constitutional project, paying special attention to the political debate over the 2010 Constitutional Assembly Law, the explanatory report accompanying the legislation, and the changes made by Parliament before it was passed.

Moreover, I explore the main disputes within the context of the interplay between political elites and the Constitutional Council. Despite the crowdsourcing novelty and the public participation, which has been examined by many scholars in relation to democratic theory,[1] I argue that, paradoxically, an effort that was originally meant to strengthen democracy may, in the end, have undermined democratic processes. I show that the project generated confusing ideas about democracy and, in some cases, contradictory notions about the aim of constitutional revisions. These weaknesses created tensions from the start—tensions that became more apparent after the Constitutional Council finished its work and Parliament started debating the bill.

The chapter is organized as follows. It begins with a general discussion of the rise of civil society or civil movement in relation to political protests. In the second part, some of the reasons for initiating the constitutional work in Iceland are explored. The third part deals with some key issues in the Icelandic constitutional reform effort, which were unclear from the very start. They had to do with defining the task of who was in control of the revision process and with the interaction between politicians and the representatives at the Constitutional Council. The fourth and final section presents a short discussion of the effects of a weak constitutional reform mandate on the outcome.

A unique task in unprecedented times: civil society and the crash

The reaction to the financial crisis included demands for new elections and a serious engagement with its systemic causes. The deep disappointment and distrust felt by the public stimulated civil society, and, in the first few months after the crash, there were not only public demonstrations and riots but also lively public debate. The fact that civil society became stronger in the wake of the financial crisis in Iceland manifested itself in different ways. It was, for example, reflected in a vibrant discussion in the traditional and social media—together with public demonstrations, open meetings, and a National Forum. This felt like a time of transformation, with many fostering the hope that changes in values would lead to a deeper understanding of democracy. It was in this political environment that the idea of a substantial revision of the constitution took shape. Yet, reliable information on what had actually occurred was scarce, notwithstanding sustained media attention. As a result, the causes of the crisis, and appropriate government reaction to it, were much contested.

The impact of civil society on social changes and social transformation has been debated for some time. John Keane contends that civil society—or the public sphere—is not only a place to show opposition to the state, but can also be an important stream for new ideas and social changes outside the political party system.[2] Grassroots organizations—for example, in the fields of environmental protection, women's rights, peace advocacy, or resistance against globalization—have put important issues on the political agenda through public protests, and, in some cases, have managed to exert deep influence on mainstream politics. While politically attractive, however, spontaneous and informal public actions do not automatically make civil society a source of real or permanent social change. Demonstrations frequently represent unorganized protests and political oppositional behavior, which do not necessarily lead to a "new beginning" or transformative politics.

The transnational reaction to the financial crisis is a case in point. The demonstrations in many countries, including those in Iceland, were first and foremost based on individual extra-parliamentary initiatives. They did not generally represent any novel thinking on politics or the financial system; they did not manage to transform the political sphere through the creation of party structures and organizations in any profound ways. Within the framework of democratic reform, this raises the questions of whether the strengthening of civil society is really desirable, or whether the emphasis should, rather, be on strong democratic institutions.

To illustrate this point, Krishan Kumar discusses the case of the Solidarity movement in Poland, where the power of the civil society was used to demand reforms but proved to be unfit to take the lead in transforming the state.[3] The implication is that it may be more important to have a well-functioning political society with institutionalized democratic practices. Although civil society gives voice to the public, one can question its democratic promise. It rarely manages to accommodate diverse viewpoints and demands within the public sphere, and does not speak for all groups.[4] There is no guarantee that demonstrations or protest movements represent majority views. On the contrary, the loudest ones may only represent a small group of people who have a personal interest in a different policy. Finally, it should be recognized that many grassroots movements and pressure groups are non-democratic, hierarchical organizations, whose practices are not subject to democratic accountability or transparency.[5]

Rationalizing constitutional change in Iceland

Two important questions arise about the relationship between the public and the constitutional revision process in Iceland. First, in what way did the public influence the decision to revise the constitution? And, second, to what degree was the process itself influenced by public participation? The left-wing government that came to power in February 2009 introduced its plan to elect a Constitutional Assembly, whose mandate was spelled out in a special bill on constitutional revisions. The initiative was clearly a reaction to the political protests that had been taking place in Iceland in the wake of the crash. The role of the Constitutional Assembly, as defined in the explanatory report that accompanied the bill, was to write *a new* constitution.[6] Furthermore, the purpose was to increase public involvement in constitutional changes. Referring to democratic societies in general, it was put as follows: "all power originates from the people and, therefore, constitutional law should be made by the representatives of the people."[7]

A look back at the reaction of civil society to the banking collapse shows that the demonstrators did not only demand the resignation of the government or the governors of the Central Bank and the director of the Financial Supervisory Authority. They also emphasized the need for a new start and social changes. At the beginning of 2009, a movement was launched under the heading "New Republic" with the agenda of electing a Constitutional Assembly to write a new constitution. In a short critical op-ed piece written by a professor emeritus at the University of Iceland, Njörður P. Njarðvík—one of the main figures in this movement—he argued that the solution to the country's troubles was the creation of a "new republic," because the existing one was "dead" and the crisis so deep that it would not be resolved "without revolutionary action and fundamental changes in Iceland's constitution."[8]

To be sure, not all subscribed to the radical idea of creating a new republic. But the view was widespread that there was a need for rethinking the social contract. Many felt that the nation had "lost contact" with its values during the boom years prior to the banking collapse. To discuss some of these issues, a private group organized the National Forum in Reykjavík in the fall of 2009,[9] where about a thousand individuals, randomly chosen, were invited to debate fundamental values.

The idea behind the meeting was based on "crowdsourcing," which was seen as a necessary tool because "big groups have intuition and wisdom that is more than individuals are conscious of."[10] Hence, the organizers called the initiative the Anthill. The National Forum was supposed to be an "initiative of the nation itself and owned by it."[11] While the gathering has been criticized on both theoretical and practical grounds, it was supposed to be a positive contribution to a national reconstruction process following the financial crisis. It also reflected the longing of many people to re-evaluate important features of Icelandic society and to build a stronger foundation for the future.

In the explanatory report attached to the bill for the Constitutional Assembly, no attempt is made to analyze different societal viewpoints and ideas; nor is there an analysis of the social demand for changes or their content. Instead, the main question was about whether the reform process should be guided by radical or moderate ideas. Similarly, the report fails to ask the fundamental question of whether the constitution caused or facilitated the financial crisis. In the report issued by the Special Investigation Commission (SIC), it was argued that Iceland's political system suffered from a lack of a clear enough division between legislative and executive powers.[12] The Working Group on Ethics (WGE), in its report, criticized the President and suggested that his role within the constitution needed to be revised. However, these ideas were not explored further in the auxiliary legislative report.[13]

Prior to the banking collapse, the question of whether to revise or write a new Icelandic constitution had been ongoing, though at intervals, from the founding of the Republic in 1944.[14] In the explanatory report attached to the bill, there is some discussion of prior attempts to revise the constitution. Before the Republic of Iceland was established, the government had to decide whether to write a new constitution from scratch or to revise the existing one. The latter option was chosen: to make only necessary changes at that point and to aim for a substantial revision later. Therefore, one could say that a revision of the constitution has been on the agenda since the 1940s. In the explanatory report of the constitutional bill, this background is discussed in some detail. Over the years, several attempts have been made to revise the constitution in a holistic manner, usually by constitutional committees appointed by Parliament. These attempts have led to revisions of some articles of the constitution without transforming the document itself. In 1953, a Constitutional Committee could not reach an agreement, but two of its members published their proposals for revision. In 1983, 30 years later, the then chair of the Constitutional Committee introduced another proposal for constitutional changes, but it was not discussed in Parliament. The third attempt was made from 2005 to 2007, when yet another committee was established with party political representatives, which failed to put forward any formal suggestions.

All these committees worked on the premise of revising the current constitution, not writing a new one. In a parliamentary bill introduced in 1983, which was based on proposals advanced by earlier committees, no substantial changes were suggested concerning the division of powers or the role of the President. The aim was, rather, to write into the constitution what was already being practiced or to update the wording. It is worth emphasizing that prior to 2013, changes or amendments to the constitution needed to be approved by two successive parliaments with parliamentary elections in-between. This means that broad consensus was required, as was the case when Parliament approved minimal changes of the constitution, such as the working procedures of Parliament in 1991, a new human rights chapter in 1995, and several changes in the electoral system. After the crisis, the history of failed revision by politicians was revisited to emphasize their incompetence to handle this task. The time had come to hand it over to the people.

Disputes over fundamental constitutional questions

The first bill on a Constitutional Assembly was introduced in Parliament in February 2009 by the minority government composed of the Social Democratic Alliance and the Left-Greens. After getting a majority mandate in the parliamentary election in April, the same parties put forward a revised bill in the fall, which, after long and contentious debate, was finally passed in June 2010. By the time the bill became law, it had been changed considerably.[15] The revisions had to do with several fundamental procedural questions, which were, actually, never clarified by Parliament before the bill was approved. This omission caused confusion later on. Here, I will only discuss three of these controversial issues: first, the question of whether the constitution should be revised or a new document created; second, whether the proposal of the Constitutional Assembly should be approved in a binding referendum before a parliamentary debate on the bill, or whether the Constitutional Assembly would merely be advisory for Parliament; and third, whether or what kind of a consultative mechanism or working relationship should be established between the Constitutional Assembly and Parliament, before, during, and after the Assembly's work.

When the Constitutional Assembly bill was first introduced, it was clearly stated by the government that the main aim was to write "a new constitution from scratch" on the grounds that such an idea enjoyed broad public support.[16] This claim was not supported by empirical evidence, only by a vague reference to an ongoing public debate. It is surprising how imprecise many parliamentarians were in the debate in their treatment of this issue. They used the terms "revision of the constitution" and "writing a new constitution" almost interchangeably, as if they had the same meaning. Writing a new constitution or forming a new republic is a major decision, and if that was the purpose, it would have required a thorough groundwork on the part of Parliament; it goes without saying that a revision of the constitution meant something far more modest.

Not making it clear from the beginning whether the existing constitution should be revised or a new one written caused a great deal of confusion and inconsistency throughout the process. The Constitutional Committee, whose role was to prepare the work of the Constitutional Council and which included some constitutional law specialists, introduced, in its report, two "ideas of a new constitution" without going into detail about what this meant.

Not only was the task of the project unclear, but also who should control the process. In the first draft of the bill on the Constitutional Assembly, the idea was to have some consultation between the Constitutional Assembly and Parliament. Once the Assembly had reached an agreement, the revisions or the new constitution, as the case might be, would be put to a binding referendum:

> "[T]he bill for a new constitution shall be presented to all eligible voters in the country in a secret vote for approval or rejection. Should the majority of the eligible voters approve the bill, at least 25% of all those eligible to vote, the President of Iceland shall confirm the vote and the proposed constitution shall be law."[17]

This was highly controversial because of the constitutional clause that stated that changes to the constitution needed to be approved by two successive parliaments with parliamentary elections in-between. Therefore, the power to change the constitution lies with Parliament, not directly with the voters. It was argued that having a binding referendum before the bill was debated in Parliament represented a violation of the present constitution. To address this problem, the government opted, in the revised bill submitted to Parliament in the fall of 2009, to change the status of the Constitutional Assembly to being consultative, "as the constitution does not allow for anything else."[18]

Unfortunately, other parts of the bill had not been changed accordingly in the revised version, which constituted a major flaw and illustrated how vaguely the interplay between Parliament and the Constitutional Assembly had been defined. First, the change affected the role of the Constitutional Assembly; without a binding referendum, its role was considerably weaker. According to many political theorists, consultative referenda are ineffective, since the result does not, in principle, have to be heeded by politicians. Citizens may also not be clear "as to whether they should take these referenda seriously."[19] The same goes for consultative committees or assemblies, unless the mandate is very clear, and the ways in which the result should be handled have been specified. What was lacking when the change was made was a thorough evaluation of how it affected the role and work of the Assembly. This question became even more pertinent when Parliament appointed the Constitutional Council after the invalidation of the Consultative Assembly elections by the Supreme Court on technical grounds.

Second, the original provision of having a binding referendum on a new constitutional bill composed by the Constitutional Assembly meant that Parliament could not debate the bill before the vote; hence, Parliament was de facto bypassed. Yet, the subsequent decision to make the referendum consultative guaranteed that Parliament regained full control of the constitutional process. This change would have required an explanation of how Parliament would handle the constitutional bill drafted by the Constitutional Assembly: whether or not, for example, a consultative referendum should be held on it. Instead, what ensued was a long debate about procedural steps, whether and when to have a referendum, whether to prioritize certain issues or whether to consult the public or other constitutional specialists. If this process had been spelled out in the law of the Constitutional Assembly or before the Constitutional Council was appointed, it would have saved Parliament much time. Once the debate started, it later became apparent that there was no majority in favor of writing a new constitution.

What this illustrates is how vaguely the relationship between Parliament and the Constitutional Assembly/Council was defined in the bill. Moreover, additional changes were made during the parliamentary debate, which further weakened the process, especially the decision to reduce the working time of the Constitutional Assembly. Originally, the Assembly was supposed to work for 18 months with an interval, but, in the end, the Constitutional Council was given less than four months to complete the task. Other changes were positive, such as the proposal to form a Constitutional Committee and to convene a National Forum attended by 1000 participants. Nevertheless, the fundamental aim of the exercise was not clear enough, and the mandate not adequately defined.

To judge from the confusing parliamentary debate, it was simply not possible to decipher the real aim of the constitution-writing project or its methodology. For example, the role of the National Forum was defined in this general and superficial way: to "find out the main views and ideas of the public on constitutional matters and its revision." Some argued that the National Forum served as a "national survey" on constitutional matters, showing which issues people were mostly interested in. Others saw it as a form of "crowdsourcing," whereby citizens were given a chance to decide on issues. But a national survey and crowdsourcing have different meanings. The former is based on a randomly chosen sample, as was the case for the National Forum, where the idea was to get general ideas from individuals. Crowdsourcing, on the other hand, aims at getting people together for problem-solving, most often through the internet.[20] It has also been argued that the meeting served as a deliberation forum on constitutional issues, but given its one-day time frame, there was little possibility of real discussion.

These are only a few examples showing how weak the legislative framework for the constitutional process was from the very beginning. All these issues led to endless quarrels about the process itself, which, again, turned the focus away from the real substance: the constitutional changes themselves.

Civil society and the constitutional process

Earlier, I discussed how the idea to revise the constitution can be seen as a reaction to public frustration and to demands for new social values. In this light, it is interesting to focus on the interaction between civil society and the Constitutional Council. Was the Council more like a consultative committee to Parliament, or was it closer to civil society or a public forum? After the Supreme Court invalidated the elections to the Constitutional Assembly in 2011, Parliament decided to appoint those who had been elected to a Constitutional Council. This can be interpreted as having moved the Constitutional Council closer to state power and away from the public or civil society. However, the issue is not that simple. The Constitutional Council was, rather, independent of party politics, and no formal dialogue took place between the members of the Council and political elites prior to—or during—the Council's work. Furthermore, the Council made an attempt to create a public forum by inviting the public to take part in a dialogue via the social media. This open environment and the National Forum moved the Council closer to civil society and away from the state.

Whether the process is seen as part of the political system or of civil society, it is clear that the dialogue between the public or the Council and politicians did not take place. Kumar argues that real changes need to affect the state and politics, and, therefore, it is more important to strengthen democratic institutions rather than civil society. Iceland's constitutional process was shaped, to a certain extent, by the public and took place, in part, within civil society. What was lacking, however, was a bridge between civil society and politics. No attempt was made to define how the work of the Assembly or the Council would be translated into the political sphere—how the dynamics of civil society could reach the political arena. This would have required political leadership and a vision of how public demands could transform politics. Instead, politicians were reluctant to take responsibility for a process they had themselves initiated. If this is a correct analysis of the constitutional work, it manifests the doubts some have about the capability of civil society to make real changes. The state is the legally authorized organization to make binding decisions for society,[21] and at the end of the day, Parliament has the power in Iceland to change the constitution.

Conclusion

The constitutional process was meant to strengthen democracy in Iceland. If by democracy is meant a broader public representation, the process succeeded—at least up to a point. It brought the public to the table, and almost 50% of the voters took part in the consultative referendum on the proposed constitutional bill. It also opened up a public debate over constitutional issues, a debate that had hitherto been limited to a small group of specialists and politicians. If, however, democracy refers to democratic institutions and abilities to make changes, the process was a manifestation of weaknesses. There was a lack of prior analysis of constitutional procedures and outcomes; the aims of the constitutional changes were explained in contradictory ways; and the constitutional bill was inadequately prepared.

These flaws were discussed by the SIC and analyzed by the WGE in their reports. It was argued that weak policy-making and legislative procedures were characteristic of Icelandic politics and civil administration. The shortcomings of the constitutional process echo this criticism. It created more procedural disputes than were necessary and an unproductive debate on its legitimacy. The constitutional process, which was meant to strengthen institutions and social foundations, suffered from similar democratic weaknesses to those it was meant to cure.

Does this mean that the constitutional experiment was doomed to fail? How this question is answered depends on how its main goal is defined. Some have argued that the process could only have succeeded if a new constitution had been passed by Parliament as the Constitutional Council presented it. This is an unrealistic view because of the contested nature of the exercise. If the original aim had been less ambitious—and geared toward amending the constitution—it could well have succeeded despite the procedural weaknesses. Parliament discussed quite extensively, for example, several parts of the Constitutional Council's proposal, including the idea of making it easier for the public to call for referenda on different issues and public ownership of natural resources, issues that also had been approved by the public in a referendum in 2012. These two changes alone would have been significant changes in Iceland's constitution if they had been approved by Parliament in the first months of 2013, shortly before the elections. Such an outcome would also have made it easier to continue the process immediately after the vote. To be sure, the fate of the constitutional experiment has still not been decided; it can still be revived in a different form. But, the flaws discussed above explain to a large extent why it did not succeed in the legislative period of 2009–2013, a period when public demands for societal changes were the greatest.

Notes

1 Hélène Landemore, "Inclusive Constitution-Making: The Icelandic Experiment," *Journal of Political Philosophy* (2014): 1–30; Jon Elster, *Securities against Misrule: Juries, Assemblies, Elections* (Cambridge: Cambridge University Press, 2013), 191–235.
2 John Keane in an interview available online, accessed March 19, 2015, http://sydney democracynetwork.org/video-middle-class-protest-and-democracy/.
3 Krishan Kumar, "Civil Society: An Inquiry into the Usefulness of a Historical Term," *British Journal of Sociology* 44 (1993): p. 387.
4 Jan Aart Scholte, "Civil Society and Democracy in Global Governance," *Global Governance* 8 (2002): p. 296.
5 Ibid.: p. 297–299.
6 Act on a Constitutional Assembly, no. 90/2010, accessed March 15, 2015, www.althingi.is/altext/136/s/0648.html.
7 Explanatory report following the Act on the Constitutional Assembly, no. 90/2010, accessed March 15, 2015, www.althingi.is/altext/138/s/0168.html.
8 Njörður Njarðvík, "Nýtt lýðveldi" [A New Republic], *Fréttablaðið*, January 14, 2009.
9 Þjóðfundur [National Forum], "Þjóðfundur um nýjan sáttmála" [National Forum on a New Social Contract], accessed October 1, 2015, www.thjodfundur2009.is/thjodfundur/um_thjodfundinn/.
10 Þjóðfundur [National Forum], "Þjóðfundur um nýjan sáttmála" [National Forum on a New Social Contract].
11 Þjóðfundur [National Forum], "Þjóðfundur um nýjan sáttmála" [National Forum on a New Social Contract].
12 Rannsóknarnefnd Alþingis [The Special Investigation Commission of the Icelandic Parliament], *Aðdragandi og orsakir falls íslensku bankanna 2008 og tengdir atburðir* [The Causes and Effects of the Fall of the Icelandic Banks and Related Events] (Reykjavík: Icelandic Parliament, 2010).
13 Vilhjálmur Árnason et al., "Siðferði og starfshættir í tengslum við fall íslensku bankanna 2008" [Morality and Working Practices in Relation to the Collapse of the Icelandic Banks 2008], in *Aðdragandi og orsakir falls íslensku bankanna 2008 og tengdir atburðir* [The Causes and Effects of the Fall of the Icelandic Banks and Related Events], vol. 8 (Reykjavík: Icelandic Parliament, 2010).
14 Explanatory report following the Act on the Constitutional Assembly, no. 90/2010.

15 See discussion on policy making in Iceland see Gunnar Helgi Kristinsson, "Bounded Rationality or Policy Fumble? Parliament and Executive in the Preparation of Public Policy," *Stjórnmál og stjórnsýsla* 9, no. 2 (2013): 257–277.
16 Explanatory report following the Act on the Constitutional Assembly, no. 90/2010, 3.
17 Act on a Constitutional Assembly, no. 90/2010, art. 4.
18 Explanatory report following the Act on the Constitutional Assembly, no. 90/2010, 9.
19 Maija Setälä, "On the Problems of Responsibility and Accountability in Referendums," *European Journal of Political Research* 45 (2006): 714.
20 Daren C. Brabham, *Crowdsourcing* (Cambridge, MA: MIT Press, 2013), xix.
21 John S. Dryzek, *Deliberative Democracy and Beyond. Liberals, Critics, Contestations* (Oxford: Oxford University Press, 2000), 82.

Bibliography

Act on a Constitutional Assembly, no. 90/2010. Accessed March 15, 2015. www.althingi.is/altext/136/s/0648.html.

Árnason, Vilhjálmur, Salvör Nordal, and Kristín Ástgeirsdóttir. "Siðferði og starfshættir í tengslum við fall íslensku bankanna 2008" [Morality and Working Practices in Relation to the Collapse of the Icelandic Banks 2008]. In *Aðdragandi og orsakir falls íslensku bankanna 2008 og tengdir atburðir* [The Causes and Effects of the Fall of the Icelandic Banks and Related Events]. Vol. 8. Reykjavík: Icelandic Parliament, 2010.

Brabham, Daren C. *Crowdsourcing*. Cambridge, MA: MIT Press, 2013.

Dryzek, John S. *Deliberative Democracy and Beyond: Liberals, Critics, Contestations*. Oxford: Oxford University Press, 2000.

Elster, Jon. *Securities against Misrule: Juries, Assemblies, Elections*. Cambridge: Cambridge University Press, 2013.

Explanatory report following the Act on a Constitutional Assembly, no. 90/2010. Accessed March 15, 2015. www.althingi.is/altext/138/s/0168.html.

Keane, John. Online interview. Accessed March 19, 2015. http://sydneydemocracynetwork.org/video-middle-class-protest-and-democracy/.

Kristinsson, Gunnar Helgi. "Bounded Rationality or Policy Fumble? Parliament and Executive in the Preparation of Public Policy." *Stjórnmál og stjórnsýsla* 9, no. 2 (2013): 257–277.

Kumar, Krishan. "Civil Society: An Inquiry into the Usefulness of an Historical Term." *British Journal of Sociology* 44 (1993): 375–395.

Landemore, Hélène. "Inclusive Constitution-Making: The Icelandic Experiment." *Journal of Political Philosophy* (2014): 1–30.

Njarðvík, Njörður P. "Nýtt lýðveldi" [A New Republic]. *Fréttablaðið*, January 14, 2009.

Rannsóknarnefnd Alþingis [The Special Investigation Commission of the Icelandic Parliament]. *Aðdragandi og orsakir falls íslensku bankanna 2008 og tengdir atburðir* [The Causes and Effects of the Fall of the Icelandic Banks and Related Events]. Reykjavík: Icelandic Parliament, 2010.

Setälä, Maija. "On the Problems of Responsibility and Accountability in Referendums." *European Journal of Political Research* 45 (2006): 699–721.

Scholte, Jan Aart. "Civil Society and Democracy in Global Governance." *Global Governance* 8 (2002): 281–304.

Þjóðfundur [National Forum]. "Þjóðfundur um nýjan sáttmála" [National Forum for New Social Contract]. Accessed October 1, 2015. www.thjodfundur2009.is/thjodfundur/um_thjodfundinn/.

12 Constituent power and authorization

Anatomy and failure of a constitution-making process

Pasquale Pasquino

Independently of its unsuccessful ending, and notably even before it, the recent attempt in Iceland to produce a constitution not only involved more citizen participation than is usually the case but also attracted much domestic and foreign attention. The general and unfortunate trend to discredit representative institutions—and the fashionable enthusiasm for deliberation and participation—is not the only reason for this interest. The popular involvement in the constitution-making process in Iceland pushes us to revisit the classical doctrine (or dogma) of the constituent power of the people. In this chapter, I will try to shed some light on this power, starting from the lesson that we can draw from the recent political experience of Iceland and its failure.

One must note from the outset that the Icelandic constitutional-making process was, from its inception, an ambiguous one. Born as a sort of (consultative) constituent assembly, the organ in charge of working on the constitutional revision lost part of its (*ex ante* expected) popular legitimacy both because of low turnout in the election for its members and because of the nullification of the electoral results by the Supreme Court. The ensuing establishment of the Constitutional Council by a politically divided Parliament (the center-right/conservative parties were clearly hostile to the experience) transformed this body into a creature of the political class, rather than a direct expression of popular choice. Another peculiarity of the process was that the creature of the political class—I mean the decision by the majority of Parliament to appoint the Constitutional Council—was made up of candidates external to the political class. These circumstances gave the Council a peculiar identity: it became an implicit antagonist vis-à-vis the official/elected representatives, and this position made its task far more difficult.

The Constitutional Council, thus, possessed a kind of inherent haziness in terms of its role and function. It was at the same time a consultative body, entrusted with the task of presenting a project of constitutional *reform* to the Althingi, and a body claiming a *special relationship* with the people and, hence, embodying and expressing the people's constituent power, independently and beyond the will of an allegedly disqualified parliamentary elite. The President of the Council, Salvör Nordal, was wise to reduce this innate tension. As far as I can judge, after having spoken with members of the Council, she was able to avoid open conflicts with the political actors in Parliament and to keep together the Council, which was eventually able to speak with one voice. Nevertheless, the tension remained latent during the entire process of writing the project of the new constitution, a process that was clearly controversial among politicians and that ended up being supported by only a minority of citizens, and after (and perhaps even before) the last political elections by the minority of the representatives.

Theoretical approaches to constitution-making

Much has been written about the unconventional, possibly unique character of the Icelandic constitution-making process (although there were precedents in Poland (1952)[1] and more recently in Mali (1991)).[2] It may be worth considering this assumed uniqueness more closely, since such scrutiny might teach us some interesting lessons. One crucial element seems to lie at the very starting point of the Icelandic experience: the financial and economic crisis that hit in 2008 produced a profound collapse of *trust*, which had traditionally characterized the relationship between the citizens and their government. Hence, the idea of creating an elected body, made up of non-professional politicians working on constitutional reform, seemed, at least to part of the political class, like an opportunity to cool down, and perhaps defuse, some of the popular anger generated by the discovery of political co-responsibility in the financial crisis.[3] It was at the same time an opportunity to put on the agenda the old question in Iceland of constitutional revision. One might recall here that it was a big financial crisis that triggered the summoning of the Estates General in France in 1789, a decision that became the starting point of modern constitutional history on the European Continent. The difference between these two cases is, nonetheless, crucial, since there were no evident signs suggesting that there might be a reason in Iceland for a deep legal break with the existent *constitutional* order. In that sense, the idea of writing an entirely new constitution was not clearly justified, and the reasons for bypassing the rules of a "rigid"[4] constitution—like the Icelandic one—to introduce constitutional reform were not persuasive.

It was quite apparent, though possibly disappointing, to the members of the Constitutional Council that constitutional reform in Iceland had to go through the long process of regulating amendments to the constitution as spelled out in Article 79, a legal provision that only a constitutional coup would have been able to sidestep:

> Proposals to amend or supplement this Constitution may be introduced at regular as well as extraordinary sessions of *Althingi* [the House of Representatives]. If the proposal is adopted, *Althingi* shall immediately be dissolved and a general election held. If [the new] *Althingi* then passes the resolution unchanged, it shall be confirmed by the President of the Republic and come into force as constitutional law.[5]

The second significant dimension of the constitution-making process I am discussing is its supposed "popular" character. Since the French Revolution, and notably in the theoretical work of the abbé Sieyes, what we now call a liberal-democratic constitution has/ought to have its origin in the so-called "*pouvoir constituant du peuple*" [constituent power of the people].[6] This doctrine,[7] beginning with the constitutional theory of the French Revolution, and systematized by Carl Schmitt during the Weimar Republic,[8] pretends that "the people" are the only legitimate *source* of power that may establish a constitution. One might think also of the opening words of the US constitution: "We the People of the United States [...] do ordain and establish this Constitution for the United States of America."

It is worth analyzing more precisely what we understand here by the "source" of the constitution. Sieyes, like Schmitt after him, explicitly emphasizes that only representatives can exercise the constituent power of the people. Schmitt, notably, is very clear on this point both in his *Verfassungslehre*[9] and in a very important text entitled *Volksentscheid und Volksbegehren.*[10] And in his *Third Estate*, Sieyes suggested the necessity to elect a representative assembly with the extraordinary and specialized mandate to write a constitution.[11]

A serious fallacy plagues the general understanding of this doctrine; it lies in conflating two different concepts: *authorship* and *authorization.* In my opinion, the only non-rhetorical version of the theory of constituent power of the people consists in asserting that the constitution (in the modern sense of a text establishing fundamental rights, their guarantee, and the basic rules for governing a given country) has to be freely approved/authorized and endorsed by a large majority of the citizens. Historically, this authorization has generally taken two forms: *ex ante*, through the election of a *representative* assembly exercising the constituent power of the people, or *ex post*, through popular ratification. An instance of the first case is the Italian constitution of 1947, written and enacted—after two years of intense debate, culminating in a large consensus among the major political parties—by the *Assemblea Costituente*, which was itself popularly elected and given an explicit mandate (at the same time, there was a popular referendum through which the voters chose a republican versus the monarchical political regime). Instances of the second modality are, among others, the French Constitutions of the 4th and 5th Republic.[12] The Icelandic constitution of 1944 was ratified by Parliament (Althingi) after a popular referendum that approved the choice for the republican form of government and the end of the Act of Union (*Sambandslög*) of 1918 with the Kingdom of Denmark.[13]

The "people," more precisely the citizen-voters, thus do not write the constitution, which is largely prepared by legal experts[14] and decided by political actors. In party states (*Parteienstaaten*), the old or new political parties control the constitution-making process. The "people," then, are not the authors; rather, they authorize, in different ways, their representatives to formulate their "will" in the form of a constitution. The role of the legal experts must not be underestimated. The negative reaction of legal experts, both in Iceland and abroad, to the text prepared by the Constitutional Council undoubtedly contributed to its eventual demise. Moreover, it is very difficult, in the absence of dramatic circumstances, such as the collapse of an entire regime, to expropriate the (old) political parties from being in command of the original or derivate constituent power (that is, the power of constitution-making or constitutional revision). Of course, none of this prevents citizens from being asked to offer input either before (as was the case in the French Revolution, thanks to the *Cahiers de doléance*) or during the constitution-making process. However, this input must be systematized and made coherent by legal experts, and it must have the explicit approval of representatives. Neglecting these conditions, in the absence of a deep social revolution, which normally produces new representatives, condemns the process to failure.

The concept of constituent power of the people, therefore, refers much more to the notion of authorization. I need first to restate that conflating the two terms—authorship and authorization—is a way to reproduce the questionable Hobbesian doctrine of representation. Hobbes reduced to a unity the presumed "author" (the members of the political community) and the "actor" (the representative/Leviathan). The assimilation of the two concepts suggests—if we replace the metaphor of the social contract with the vote—that the mechanism of the elections of the constituent assembly or, alternatively, the ratification referendum gives to this *reductio ad unum* some appearance of plausibility. Concerning the constituent power, such an argument de facto denies the existence of an "agency problem." I speak of denial, since in reality, the author of the constitution (the representatives) and the subject of the authorization (the citizen-voters) are not one and the same agent. This distinction is important even if, as I said above, some input can come from "below" to the real authors of the constitution.

Once this clarification is made, however, it is worth stressing that the doctrine of the constituent power of the people is not based solely on a fiction. If, following on from a specific point within Schmitt's conceptualization,[15] we take into account the *Gegenbegriff*, the antonym of a constitution authorized by the citizens, that is, the *constitutions octroyées* [constitutions granted to the subjects] by the Kings (on the basis of the *monarchisches Prinzip* [monarchical principle]),[16] we realize that a liberal-democratic constitution is based not on the popular authorship of the text, but actually on the legal principle of *equality*. By this term, I mean here the presupposition of equal *political* rights for all the citizens, which characterizes this type of constitution and takes the concrete legal form of the popular authorization through the vote. Unlike Schmitt, I would stress that the major difference between those modern constitutions based on the so-called *pouvoir constituant du peuple* and the old pre-eighteenth-century constitutions is that the latter, being forms of mixed government,[17] considered the "people" to be only one element of the constitutional order (the others being the king and the nobility—as was, until the nineteenth century, the case with the English customary constitution). Hence, the "people" were simply a partial source of legitimate political authority, and not the only one, since the concept of legal/political equality was foreign and even inimical to societies of that type, and to their understanding of political life. So, popular authorization becomes a *conditio sine qua non* of the existence and legitimacy of a democratic constitution.[18] The citizen-voters, who cannot write a constitution, nevertheless have a veto power on its enactment, and, in this limited sense, they are somehow co-authors, or, at least, responsible for it. The constitution, notably if ratified *ex post*, is their constitution, not because they themselves made it, but because they accepted the text written by their representatives, giving to it a sort of popular imprimatur.

More generally, authorization is the specific function of the citizen-voters in representative democracies. The ordinary mechanism is the one that Sieyes called *pouvoir commettant*, the electoral power that allows the citizens to vote their representatives (at the end of the mandate) in and out. In addition, in this case, it is in a way deceptive to say that the citizens make their laws, since in reality (with the rare exception of legislative referenda), what they do is to choose the people who will make the laws. The expression of self-government is, thus, either naïve or rhetorical. Modern democracy is, at its best, an authorized oligarchy based on competitive elections. The rule of authorization through elections (typical of contemporary representative democracies) is the same as that exercised by the citizen-voters to endorse a set of rules (the constitution) that they have not written. Furthermore, the people authorizing the constitution are themselves a *constituted power*. Some authority has to decide who is a member of "the people" and decide on those who are excluded (during the French Revolution, the aristocrats, the women, and the servants; nowadays, generally, immigrants) and those who are included (now women, and in some countries, for instance, inmates, in others, not). Still, without explicit popular authorization, the constitution cannot be enacted in a democracy (with the famous exception of the United Kingdom, which has no written text called a constitution).

Authorship and authorization: the case of Iceland

I need to return now to the distinction between authorship and authorization. In the Icelandic experience, the weak popular authorization (36% turnout in the election of the Constituent Assembly) was eventually replaced by an even weaker parliamentary authorization/appointment (after the nullification of the election results by the Supreme Court). The creature was, as such, not strong enough to impose its will on its original creator, the Althingi, notwithstanding the popular input of the Forum of November 2010. The Constitutional Council needed increased popular involvement, which extended beyond the "cancelled" election. One might speculate that this was attempted, in the end, by opening up the Council's debates to the public via the new social media, in the hope that this could give more credibility to the legitimacy of the Council.[19]

Moreover, as many members of the Constitutional Council soon understood, a popular referendum would have been a useful mechanism of authorization *ex post* for the constitutional draft produced by the Council if one takes into consideration the weak authorization *ex ante* of the entire project, authorization that the political class did not seem eager to endorse. Eventually, a popular referendum on the bill took place in October 2012, with positive results: 67% of the electorate declared their support for the bill; however, the voters' turnout was just 49%. We must remember that it was legally arduous to bypass the ordinary amendment procedure established by Article 79. The Althingi, as is well known, refused to vote on the constitutional bill before the end of the legislature, and the April 2013 election gave the majority in the new Parliament to the political parties hostile to the constitutional revision.

The Constitutional Council was, from its inception, trapped by a difficult challenge. It is, in a sense, remarkable that its members were able to accomplish their task, producing a document that, in any event, is undeniably a useful contribution to future constitutional debates. I can explain the challenge and its difficulty more clearly in Figure 12.1.

This figure describes a major dilemma in the constitution-making process. Had the Constitutional Council taken authorization by the Althingi most seriously (a), it would have been in a position of subordination vis-à-vis the politicians, and this, in turn, would have made the Council weak and discredited it in the eyes of (its) voters (that is, the *people*, putative antagonists of the "untrustworthy" representatives). Had the Council insisted instead only on (b), popular legitimacy (within a context of hostility vis-à-vis the official political elites), its position of contrast, and its identity as an *alternative* representative body would have put it in opposition to the Althingi, itself a fully legitimate representative body of the citizens, since it had been legitimately elected after the economic/financial crisis. So the Council was right to keep its distance from the official politicians, without taking the radical position as a counter-representative body, at least up to a point. The Council was able to produce a draft of a new constitution without making any *major* strategic mistakes. The legal quality of the text, however, raised doubts both inside and outside Iceland.

Only a large and sustained surge of popular support could have given this attempt to revise the constitution a lasting future. This popular support was difficult to anticipate and did not materialize.

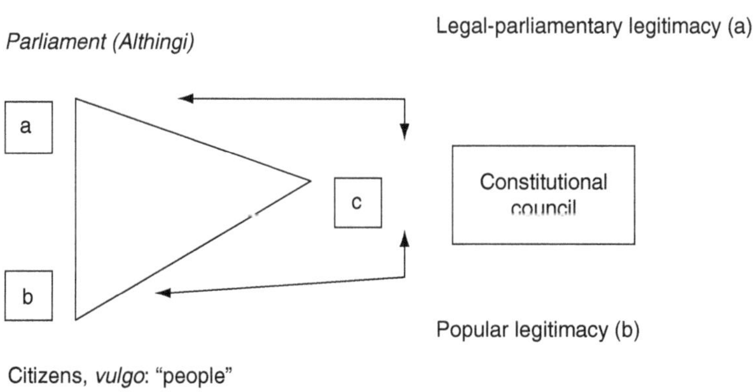

Figure 12.1 The constitution-writing process.

Conclusion

It is not easy to draw a general lesson from the Icelandic constitutional experience. Contingencies and circumstances are always different in different historical situations, and only a robust statistical sample might, perhaps, tell us what to expect in similar circumstances. Still, history seems to suggest that any constitution-making process that aims to produce a stable (non-oppressive) political order has to include all the relevant political forces within the country—the US constitution and, even more, the post-World War II constitutions of Germany and Italy are examples of this type of constitutional agreement. A stable constitution cannot originate in a *constitutional coup*, in a political order imposed by one section of the society over the others. While it is true that a constitution is a political decision, it must be decided by all who have to live under it. If a new or revised constitution has any hope for survival, it must be authorized (though not authored) by the relevant political forces among the citizens and their representatives.

Notes

1 See Adam Przeworski, "Ruling against Rules," in *Constitutions in Authoritarian Regimes*, eds. Tom Ginsburg and Alberto Simpser (Cambridge: Cambridge University Press, 2013), 21–35.

2 The National Conference took place as foreseen from July 29 through August 12, 1991. It gathered together 36 parties and 1070 [*sic!*] associations and adopted a project of Constitution. See Susana Wing, *Constructing Democracy in Transitioning Societies of Africa: Constitution and Deliberation in Mali* (New York: Palgrave Macmillan, 2008); see also Cheick Oumar Diarrah, *Le défi démocratique au Mali* (Paris, L'harmattan, 1996).

3 *Ex post*, we can say that this strategy, combined with the economic recovery of the country, was successful, if not in accomplishing a constitutional reform, at least in defusing the popular anger and resentment vis-à-vis the political elite.

4 By the term "rigid," the European constitutional doctrine means a constitution that cannot be modified following the procedures used to pass a statute law (mostly majority rule), but requires more complex procedures: either supermajority or some form of popular participation in the amendment process.

5 The rule for amending the Icelandic constitution is reminiscent of the mechanism originally introduced by the first French constitution of 1791.

6 I presented my interpretation of Sieyes' doctrine in "Constitution et pouvoir constituant: Le double corps du peuple," in *Figures de Sieyes*, ed. Y. Quivigier (Paris: Publications de la Sorbonne, 2008), 13–23.

7 On its origins, see E. Zweig, *Die Lehre Vom Pouvoir Constituant. Ein Beitrag Zum Staatsrecht Der Französischen Revolution* (Tübingen, J. C. B. Mohr, 1909). On the precedents in the United States, see my chapter "Le pouvoir constituant, le gouvernement limité et ses origines dans le Nouveau Monde," in *Le pouvoir constituant et l'Europe*, eds. O. Cayla and P. Pasquino (Paris, Dalloz, 2011), 49–60.

8 Carl Schmitt, *Constitutional Theory* (Durham and London: Duke University Press, 2008), 125–146.

9 "The people as bearer of the constitution-making power are not a stable, organized organ." Schmitt, *Constitutional Theory*, 131.

10 Carl Schmitt, *Volksentscheid und Volksbegehren* (Berlin: de Gruyter, 1927).

11 The *ordinary* representatives of a nation are charged with the exercise, under the constitution, of that portion of the common will which is necessary to maintain a good social administration. Their power is confined to governmental affairs. *Extra-ordinary* representatives will have whatever new powers the nation chooses to give them. Since a large nation cannot physically assemble when extraordinary circumstances make this necessary, it must entrust extraordinary representatives with the necessary powers on such occasions. If it could meet and express its will before your eyes, would you dare to dispute it on the ground that it did so by one procedure rather than another? Here reality is everything, the form is nothing. A body of extraordinary representatives takes the place of the assembly of the nation. It does not, of course, need to be in charge of the *whole* of the national will; it needs only special powers, and those only in rare cases; but it is in the same position as the nation itself in respect of *independence* from any constitutional forms.

E. J. Sieyes, *The Essential Political Writings*, eds. O. W. Lembcke and F. Weber (Leiden: Brill, 2014), 92

12 In the last case, the constitution—which should have been a revision of the chart of the 4th Republic—was written by the government of Charles de Gaulle, not by a constituent assembly.

13 There have also been a few cases when there was popular authorization both *ex ante* and *ex post*.

14 Among many examples, we can think of the role of lawyers such as Alexander Hamilton in Philadelphia, Jacques-Gauillaume Thouret and Antoine Barnave in Versailles/Paris, and of constitutional law experts such as Hugo Preuss for the Weimar Constitution, Costantino Mortati for the Italian Constitution of 1948, and Carlo Schmid (a Social Democrat) and Hans Nawiasky, among others, for the West German Basic Law (*Grundgesetz*).

15 Schmitt, *Constitutional Theory*, 126 ff.

16 Concerning this doctrine, see Otto Brunner, *Neue Wege der Verfassungs- und Sozialgeschichte* (Göttingen: Vandenhoeck & Ruprecht, 1968).

17 Important exceptions are the so-called absolutist regimes, like the one established in Denmark by the *Lex regia*, 1665, one of the few European absolutist written constitutions.

18 The first constitution of the French 4th Republic was rejected by a popular referendum held on May 5, 1946, since 53% of the voters did not approve the text.

19 Notice that this experience of popular participation was not unprecedented. A similar model was used at the Convention for the Future of Europe, which aimed to give the EU a constitution (an attempt paralyzed by the French popular referendum, which denied authorization to that endeavor).

Bibliography

Brunner, Otto. *Neue Wege der Verfassungs- und Sozialgeschichte*. Göttingen: Vandenhoecku & Ruprecht, 1968.

Diarrah, Cheick Oumar. *Le défi démocratique au Mali*. Paris: L'harmattan, 1996.

Lembcke, Oliver W. and Florian Weber eds. *E.J. Sieyès: The Essential Political Writings*. Leiden: Brill, 2014.

Pasquino, Pasquale. "Constitution et pouvoir constituant: Le double corps du people." In *Figures de Sieyes*, edited by Pierre-Yves Quivigier, 13–23. Paris: Publications de la Sorbonne, 2008.

Pasquino, Pasquale. "Le pouvoir constituant, le gouvernement limité et ses origines dans le Nouveau Monde." In *Le pouvoir constituant et l'Europe*, edited by Olivier Cayla and Pasquale Pasquino, 49–60. Paris: Dalloz, 2011.

Przeworski, Adam. "Ruling against Rules." In *Constitutions in Authoritarian Regimes*, edited by Tom Ginsburg and Alberto Simpser, 21–35. Cambridge: Cambridge University Press, 2013.

Schmitt, Carl. *Constitutional Theory*. Durham: Duke University Press, 2008.

Sieyès, Emmanuel Joseph. *Qu'est-ce que le Tiers état?* Paris: Éditions du Boucher, 2002. Accessed November 5, 2015. www.leboucher.com/pdf/sieyes/tiers.pdf.

Wing, Susana. *Constructing Democracy in Transitioning Societies of Africa: Constitution and Deliberation in Mali.* New York: Palgrave Macmillan, 2008.

Zweig, Egon. *Die Lehre Vom Pouvoir Constituant. Ein Beitrag Zum Staatsrecht Der Französischen Revolution*. Tübingen: J. C. B. Mohr, 1909.

13 The Constitutional Council

Objectives and shortcomings of an innovative process

Björg Thorarensen

The process of constitutional rewriting in Iceland was an innovative transitional mechanism to introduce political and democratic reforms in response to the banking collapse. The aim was to involve the citizens in the making of a new constitution through a specially elected consultative Constitutional Assembly. Therefore, the political parties, whose credibility had suffered a major blow as a result of the crash, were excluded from the preparation and drafting stages of the new constitution. Their absence, however, was bound to affect the legitimacy of the process, because constitutional changes cannot be made without two consecutive parliamentary assemblies having approved them, with a general election taking place in-between. While the constitutional experiment has received considerable domestic and foreign attention, there has been no consensus on how to interpret it. Some scholars have characterized it as being "tremendously innovative and participatory."[1] Others, including many Icelandic political scientists and legal scholars, have expressed skepticism or criticism of the quality of the draft constitution and its proposal for a new political system, which many saw as complex and marked by a lack of consistency.[2]

The constitution-writing process was undermined by early setbacks and controversies. First, there were flaws in the election of the Constitutional Assembly, resulting in the annulment of the election by the Supreme Court of Iceland in January 2011. This cast doubt on the legitimacy of the Constitutional Council appointed by Parliament, Althingi, to complete the task. After the Council eventually submitted its draft of a new constitution to Althingi in July 2011, Parliament did not act on it for more than a year. In October 2012, an advisory referendum was held on the question of whether the draft should be used as the basis for a new constitution. Five other questions on certain issues were also added to the ballot. The outcome sparked controversy over how to interpret the responses to the open questions and whether the draft should be considered binding upon the legislature. Eventually, Althingi blocked a bill on a new constitution before the 2013 parliamentary elections.

In this chapter, the topic is approached from a constitutional law perspective. I explore the objective behind the process, which was strongly inspired by the idea that constituent power derives from the people. I show how this principle emerged in Icelandic constitutional theory and practice and how the innovative procedure proved to be self-contradictory in the context of constitutional democracy. Furthermore, the question of why the momentum for constitutional reform was not sustained and its idealist aims not achieved will be addressed. Finally, I examine some of the problems associated with advisory referenda, including how and why the Icelandic constitution itself prevents the circumvention of its own provisions on the procedure for constitutional amendments, even if these were to be effected though democratic processes and with strong public support.

Motives for constitutional revision

After the banking collapse, the view was widespread that some of the blame could be pinned on the Icelandic constitution; after all, it could hardly be denied that some aspects of the existing constitution, which was adopted in 1944, were outdated. When Iceland decided to break off the union with Denmark and establish a republic, only minimal amendments were made to the previous constitution initially adopted in 1874 because of the special circumstances that prevailed during World War II. The main purpose was to complete the transformation from constitutional monarchy to a republican form of government by putting in provisions for a directly elected President. The decision was made to postpone any comprehensive revision until later. The Constitution of the Republic of Iceland took effect in 1944 following a referendum, in which it was approved with approximately 95% of the vote.

Large parts of the Icelandic constitution, especially regarding the executive and its relation to Althingi, and the provisions on the judiciary, have remained intact since Iceland received its first constitution from the King of Denmark in 1874, with subsequent additions made in the second constitution of 1920.[3] Thus, important provisions of the constitution do not reflect current realities regarding the executive and the work of the government, or the role of Althingi in supervising the executive. It does not mention key concepts, such as "democracy," "nation," "parliamentary rule," or even "government." However, some important constitutional amendments have been made, for example, regarding the organization of Althingi in 1991, the human rights chapter in 1995, and the electoral system in 1984 and 1999, respectively. It is certainly a great simplification to argue that the causes of the bank collapse can be traced to the flaws of the constitution. Yet, there were, nevertheless, direct links between the economic crisis and the public demand for constitutional reform. Not only was the debate on the need for modernizing the constitutional structures revived; the economic crisis also aroused deep public anger toward the government and state institutions for their lack of control and failure to take action against the unsustainable expansion of the banking system.[4] The collapse, furthermore, resulted in a call for a certain degree of reassessment of values and a need for some form of reckoning with the past. Undoubtedly, one of the consequences of the crisis was an unprecedented lack of confidence, both in the political parties and in the ability of the elected representatives in Althingi to make decisions on important public affairs. Finding a way to restore this confidence was in itself a separate matter for concern.

Since politicians had failed to carry out the long-awaited revision of the constitution, many believed that now was an opportunity to adopt a constitution, a covenant on the organization of the state and the position of its citizens, deriving from the nation itself. The resignation of the government and the general elections of 2009 paved the way for such ideas. These, in a nutshell, were the underlying reasons and the circumstances in which the new coalition government, consisting of the Social Democratic Alliance and the Left-Green Movement, gave particular priority to the project of revising the constitution.

Constitutional reforms: aims—and setbacks

The new approach taken in 2009 was to involve the nation directly in the reform process in a way that was unprecedented in constitutional history. It was inspired by the view that the nation, as the constituent power, should have a direct impact on its contents and the values it was to reflect. Thus, political parties were, as noted, excluded in the initial stages. In June 2010, Althingi passed an Act establishing a consultative Constitutional Assembly, with the task of revising the constitution.[5] It provided for election on an individual basis to the Constitutional Assembly in order to select 25 delegates, who were given the role of reviewing the constitution and submitting to Althingi a proposal for a new constitution.

The Act also provided for a new means of seeking input from the public concerning the structure of the country's government and its constitution. A special body, the Constitutional Commission, prepared a National Forum, which was held and completed in a single day in November 2010. The main conclusions from the National Forum were divided into broadly framed themes, grouping together the viewpoints of the participants and reflecting some basic values, which they wished to see form the basis of Iceland's new constitution.

In the election to the Constitutional Assembly in November 2010, 25 individuals were elected from 522 candidates. This unexpectedly large number of candidates caused difficulties with regard to both publicity and the organization of the vote. It was a cause for disappointment, however, that voter turnout was far lower than expected, with only about 37% of the electorate casting their ballot. This was considerably short of the normal turnout in elections to Althingi, which generally exceeds 80%. One plausible explanation offered was that the large number of candidates made it difficult for voters to pick candidates from the great number of people. Since the candidates had no direct connections with political parties and acted solely in their own personal capacity, their stance on various issues was not clear.

The election to the Constitutional Assembly was disputed on the grounds of various alleged flaws in its execution. Following the invalidation of the election by the Supreme Court of Iceland in early 2011, Althingi responded in March by appointing the 25 candidates who had been elected to take a seat in a new body, the Constitutional Council, which was given the same consultative role as the Constitutional Assembly had been intended to perform. The decision by Althingi was severely criticized, mostly by the opposition parties, on the grounds that it constituted a circumvention of the decision of the Supreme Court. It was clear that there was little consensus on the direction that the matter had taken, which was likely to weaken the outcome of the whole project, as the initial idea had been that specially elected representatives of the nation should be given the task of writing a new constitution.

The Constitutional Council was finally convened in early April 2011. It faced an extremely difficult task. It was working in an environment of heated political argument; its legitimacy had been questioned, and, hence, the credibility of its work. However, in the short space of time accorded to the Council, less than four months, it succeeded in organizing its work well. Also, all its proceedings were open and transparent. The Council gave great priority to maintaining open communication with the public, and its work was accessible on social media, such as Facebook, YouTube, and Flickr. Its proposals were unanimously approved by all members and submitted to the Althingi at the end of July 2011.

The response of the government coalition parties in Parliament was somewhat vague, and it seemed unclear what procedural steps should be taken next. The main opposition party, the center-right Independence Party, which had been against the appointment of the Council from the outset, sharply criticized the substance of the proposals. Instead of a bill on constitutional amendments being introduced in Althingi, as initially planned, it was referred to one of the parliamentary standing committees, the Constitutional Committee. For more than a year, nothing really happened. This entailed the loss of valuable time. If Althingi were to be able to approve the draft constitution, it would have to do so by the spring of 2013, because a general election had been scheduled for April that year.

Political disputes continued regarding the process, but eventually Parliament—that is, a majority of MPs in the governing coalition parties—decided to hold an advisory referendum on the original proposals in October 2012. The main question was whether the Council's proposals should form the basis of a bill for a new constitution.[6] The 49% turnout in the referendum was considerably lower than that in parliamentary elections, but 64% of those who voted on the question voted in favor of the main question. After a team of legal experts appointed by Althingi submitted its report, with some technical amendments, in the middle of November 2012, the majority of the Constitutional Committee finally introduced a bill to Althingi, based on the council's constitutional proposals. By this time, only four months remained of the parliamentary term.

The proposals of the Constitutional Council

The Constitutional Council's proposals entailed a number of changes to the existing constitution.[7] Among notable features was the presentation of various fundamental concepts regarding the constitutional structure aimed at enhancing the image of the constitution as a national covenant. There were also numerous improvements in the proposals from the present system, in particular a strengthening of the role of Parliament and its supervisory control over the executive;

the clarification of the duties of ministers toward parliament; and new provisions designed to increase the independence of the courts.[8]

Even though the proposals did not involve fundamental changes of the Icelandic system of governance, they were radical in many respects, for instance, with regard to the institutional structures of the political system. Furthermore, drawing inspiration from constitutions around the world, they included new provisions on referenda and popular initiatives. The proposals bore the marks of having been prepared in a very short time, not all of them carefully considered, and with a lack of harmonization. Great emphasis was placed on human rights provisions, with a new human rights chapter inspired by various constitutions and international human rights instruments. Yet, the revision of the human rights chapter was not included in the main tasks of the revisions as defined in the initial Act on the Constitutional Assembly. This part of the current constitution had only recently been revised and updated, partly to bring it into line with Iceland's international obligations, such as those under the European Convention on Human Rights.

From the outset, there was much criticism of the quality of the proposals, their goals, and possible unforeseeable consequences. When the bill was eventually introduced in Parliament in November 2012, the Constitutional Committee sought the formal opinion of a number of experts and stakeholders. Comments were also invited from anyone interested in the matter. Many comments were received. While many welcomed the proposals, particularly in view of the broad democratic participation in their preparation, most of the more detailed comments were highly critical, both of their substance and of the short time allowed for bringing the matter to a conclusion.

In this connection, reference should be made to the comments by the Venice Commission, which visited Iceland in January 2013 and met representatives of the Constitutional Council, MPs, academics, and representatives of non-governmental organizations (NGOs) and other interested parties.[9] The Venice Commission's report expressed serious doubts about the proposals. Among other things, it described the proposed constitutional order as being associated with a complex set of mechanisms aimed at enabling increased direct participation of citizens in decision-making. While drawing on the existing system, this involved the introduction of a series of changes and innovations, most of which were intended to concretize the option of a strong parliamentary regime that underlined the proposed system. While, in itself, such a model might be deemed suitable to the specific context in Iceland, its translation into legal and constitutional terms raised a number of issues of concern.

Similarly, the Commission found that the mechanisms of direct participation introduced by the bill raised concerns. The many possibilities for intervention in decision-making by the people through referenda were welcomed in principle, but these decision-making mechanisms, as expressed in the constitutional provisions, were found to be too convoluted, requiring a review from both legal and political perspectives. Overall, the Venice Commission saw a risk of political obstruction and instability, which could seriously hamper good governance.[10] As regards the human rights provisions, the Venice Commission expressed its concern over the lack of clarity in the delineation of rights. Most of the provisions were worded in very general terms, failing to provide clear answers as to whether concrete rights and obligations could be derived from them, and, if so, what these would be. It was considered a substantial risk that the public would take them as promises to ensure high living conditions.[11]

The Parliamentary Ombudsman of Iceland also submitted a detailed opinion on the bill, expressing concerns regarding its proposals. The Ombudsman pointed to the lack of a comprehensive assessment of the aims and effects of the proposed constitutional changes. Various innovations seemed to have been modeled on the constitutions of dissimilar states without attention being given to their original contexts, including a consideration of the effectiveness of the judiciary in applying constitutional provisions.[12]

It was evident that the very short time remaining before the dissolution of Althingi in March 2013 was insufficient to enable it to examine the extensive amendments involved in the proposals and to make the necessary adjustments to take account of the criticisms and comments that had been received. It would have been possible to force the proposals through Parliament with a narrow majority of the MPs of the governing parties. But, according to the rules applying to constitutional amendments, the bill could not take effect unless it was approved without amendment by the new parliament following the forthcoming elections.

In the closing days of the parliamentary session at the end of March 2013, the leader of one of the governing parties, the Social Democratic Alliance, introduced another bill. It allowed for the addition of an interim provision to the existing constitution, stipulating a new mechanism for amendments. It was proposed that until April 30, 2017, it would be possible to amend the constitution if, after being passed with the support of at least two-thirds of MPs, amendments were then approved by at least 40% of the electorate in a national referendum. This bill was passed, and was also approved by the new parliament that convened after the general elections of 2013, in which the two left-wing parties sustained heavy electoral losses. The new center-right government appointed a new committee with representatives from all the political parties to propose amendments to the constitution. It remains to be seen what will come out of the work of this committee. Most likely, some amendments will be suggested, but it seems clear that the idea of writing a new constitution has been shelved.

Exercising the constituent power by drafting a constitution: an assessment

The unique process that the Icelandic government decided to set in motion in order to revise the constitution in 2009 is without parallel, and was characterized by extensive consultation with the electorate on the contents of the proposed constitution. This new method of creating a constitution attracted attention and admiration in many parts of the world. Three foreign academics who commented on the project stated that the draft constitution proposed by the Constitutional Council reflected significant input from the public and would mark an important symbolic break with the past.[13]

Those who supported the project with the most enthusiasm in public debates, including some who had been representatives of the Constitutional Council, regarded the outcome of the advisory referendum in October 2012 as imposing a binding requirement on Parliament, that is, that it was Althingi's democratic duty to comply with the will of the electorate and to approve the draft constitution. They argued that Althingi had waived its right to discuss the substance of the constitution any further, including as regards its legal and political implications, after the bill was introduced in Parliament in November 2012. Public discussion of the fate of the bill became very heated at times, with allegations such as "in spite of popular support, Iceland's new crowd-sourced constitution was killed by politicians."[14]

Such arguments contain intrinsic contradictions. One of the cornerstones of Iceland's constitutional structure, ever since democratic processes were introduced and the country received its first constitution, has been the concept of popular sovereignty, and even that the people are the constituent power.[15] Iceland's 1944 constitution reflects this view: the people approved it in a referendum following the examination and passing of a bill on a draft constitution by Althingi. The people's decision was, legally, the final word, in accordance with the rules laid down in the constitution itself, and, thus, the electorate set its seal of approval on the work done by its elected representatives. The purpose of this procedure is to make it likely that the representative decision-makers will strive to fulfill the demands of the people, whose approval of the outcome is necessary, and at the same time to give legitimacy to the final document in a decisive referendum. The constitution contains built-in rules calling for a particularly exacting procedure for making amendments, and making them considerably more difficult than amendments to ordinary legislation. As in other states based on constitutional democracy, these principles in Icelandic constitutional law are intended to ensure that the constitution reflects certain fundamental values that underpin society and are unaffected by short-term political trends and the power wielded by a narrow parliamentary majority at any given time.[16] Thus, a barrier is in place to prevent pressure from interest groups in society, resulting in constitutional changes being forced through via channels other than those prescribed in the constitution itself.

Prevention of opportunistic amendments or revisions can be ensured either by demanding that changes to the existing constitution be supported by a qualified majority of MPs or by accepting the support of an ordinary majority but then demanding that Parliament be dissolved, elections held, and then that the new parliament approve the measure taken. To accommodate the fundamental view that the nation is the entity that grants the constitution, it is necessary to find a mechanism to ensure that the electorate will be involved, directly or indirectly, in the process of amendment. The procedure laid down in the second paragraph of Article 79 of the Icelandic constitution, with approval by two parliaments with a general election in-between, combines these two aims, that is, ensuring broad parliamentary support over and above a simple majority in one parliament and also granting the people indirect involvement in the process. The electorate is given a chance to declare its position on the amendment by either supporting or rejecting political parties in the general election following the first approval of the bill.

While provisions on referenda as part of the process of constitutional change differ from one European state to another, they usually have one feature in common: the people, as the constituent power, have a clear role to play in the process, either by giving their approval to the measure taken by Parliament or by rejecting it in a legally binding manner. The decision by the governing parties to hold an advisory referendum on the proposals by the Constitutional Council, before Althingi had examined the bill, was, therefore, ill advised. Even though such a referendum might, to some extent, have raised the legitimacy of the product from the Constitutional Council, since its appointment and mandate were contested, it created more confusion. Not only did it arouse false expectations regarding the legal value of the outcome vis-à-vis the Althingi; also, answers given to the questions presented in the referendum were open to a variety of interpretations and disputes as to what answers had, in fact, been given.

The value of advisory referenda has been called in question from the point of view of constitutional legal theory.[17] The phenomenon has been criticized because this particular form of referendum is so loosely regulated and fits so poorly into the constitutional and political system of a country that it may cause various problems. One is the question of how advisory referenda are to be reconciled with the principle of the free mandate of members of parliament, which is enshrined in most democratic constitutions. Both the timing and the choice of issues suitable for putting to a referendum are important.[18] It is crucial that the question put forward relates to a concrete issue with clear choices. This has been the case in such referenda in Sweden, Finland, and Norway on the accession to the EU, where it was understood by both the political class and the electorate that the result would be heeded.

It can be maintained that the advisory referendum on the Constitutional Council's proposals combined, in a nutshell, all the shortcomings of such referenda. The questions were imprecise; the timing was unfortunate; and, most importantly, it gave the impression that Althingi had been deprived of its competence to discuss and amend the material proposals in the bill. This created a clash with the principle of free mandate as stipulated in Article 48 of the Icelandic Constitution, which states that the members of Althingi are bound solely by their conviction and not by any instructions from their constituents. Due to the relatively low turnout in the referendum and the varying interpretations of its conclusions, political pressure to continue the exercise was clearly reduced.

In the light of these events, it came, perhaps, as no surprise, but all the same as a deep disappointment, that no substantive proposals made in the bill on a new constitution were enacted before the end of the parliamentary term in spring

2013. However, it was clear from the outcome of the general election that the electorate was not much interested in the issue at that time, and did not regard it as a priority.[19] This was underscored by the fact that the winners of the elections, the Independence Party and the Progressive Party, had been most vigorous in their opposition to a new constitution on the basis of the proposals from the Constitutional Council. It should also be noted that the revision of the constitution was not among the main election issues, and probably accounted only for a small part of the massive loss of support by the outgoing government parties.

Conclusion

As a method of revising the constitution, the creation of the Constitutional Assembly, and later the Constitutional Council, was a radical innovation with noble aims, including the restoration of public faith in political institutions. The reasons for the failure of the exercise are manifold, and involve a number of factors, both political and legal. First, the idea of shifting the task of constitution-making from the political forum to a consultative body raised questions of whether it is possible, in a constitutional democracy, to circumvent elected parliamentary representatives in this way by defining "the people" as a special source of power in clear contradistinction to political entities.

The involvement of the citizens at the initial stages, through the method of crowdsourcing, to reflect their will in the preparation and drafting of a new constitution was, indeed, a positive step, introducing innovative political and democratic processes. It might eventually have strengthened the democratic foundations and legitimacy of a new constitution and even created greater consensus regarding it. However, as the project developed, with the emergence of claims that the Council's role was to draft a comprehensive and complete document, it proved to be an unrealistic approach on the part of those who most enthusiastically supported the initiative. Accordingly, defining constitution-making as a non-political issue and excluding it entirely from the political forum was bound to end in failure. At the end of the day, parliamentary intervention was inevitable, with the political parties needing to take a stance on the substance of a new constitution before its final adoption.

The exercise was never intended to replace the legitimate processes provided for in the constitution; this would have been in clear defiance of the principles of constitutional democracy. Only some kind of a constitutional coup could justify setting aside such constitutional processes, a situation that did not evolve in Iceland in the aftermath of the bank collapse. This, perhaps, reflects both the strengths and weaknesses of constitutionalism. By making constitutional changes difficult through special procedures, democratic stability is guaranteed. What is more, fundamental values and core democratic institutions cannot be easily abolished in a wave of popular support. But the price to be paid is that even the most liberal constitutions are not characterized by heightened opportunities for popular participation to develop the constitutional system. In short, they prevent the future exercises of constituent power, such as initiating radical changes, from taking place.[20]

Second, there is a necessity to distinguish between the involvement of the people in preparing a constitution and influencing its substance, on the one hand, and adopting a constitution, on the other. That a group of individuals with little or no experience of legislative work (and, indeed, they had been chosen for the task precisely because of their non-involvement in politics) managed to produce a comprehensive document was a great achievement. But, even though the framework and main components of their proposals were intended as the basis for processing by the legislature, the task needed to be continued in Althingi. The material quality of the document had to be improved. A thorough assessment of the suggested innovative institutional framework was needed for the sake of harmonization. The alternative would have been to risk political obstructionism and instability, with a potentially harmful impact on governance.

Finally, the government parties in Parliament failed to react promptly to the proposals when the Council submitted them in July 2011. This resulted in hesitation on how to proceed and how to introduce and handle a bill for a new constitution, a situation that ended a year later in the controversial decision to hold the advisory referendum. This time should have been used to elaborate on the Council's proposals via the parliamentary process, assess their probable impact, and address their material shortcomings.

Finally, from early on, it became unlikely that the consensus aimed at with the initial establishment of the Constitutional Assembly would be achieved. This was partly due to the extremely low turnout in the election to the Constitutional Assembly in 2010, but primarily due to the invalidation of the election by the Supreme Court. The inevitable consequence of this was that the Constitutional Council, which replaced the Assembly on the basis of a parliamentary resolution, lost the popular legitimacy that the Assembly was able to claim in its first days before the election was annulled. From then on, the staunch political resistance by the largest opposition party in Althingi to any continuation of the revision process undercut the credibility of the Council, exposing it to severe criticism and dividing voters into two groups in their attitudes toward the task.

In spite of all this, it is, at least, safe to assert that the new paths chosen to revise the Icelandic constitution had a powerful impact on public awareness in Iceland regarding the significance of the constitution and its core principles, which, in itself, is a positive development. The great amount of attention that this new experiment in constitutional revision in Iceland attracted outside the country is also likely to make both citizens and governments in other countries think about whether, and if so how, greater consultation of the electorate can be achieved concerning the substance and aims of constitutions. Thus, much can be learned from this experiment regarding means and ends, the advantages and drawbacks of various methods, and, not least, the limitations imposed by constitutions themselves on innovations in the revision of the foundations on which democratic states are built.

Notes

1 Zachary Elkins et al., "A Review of Iceland's Draft Constitution," *The Comparative Constitutions Project*, October 14, 2012, accessed March 19, 2015, http://comparativeconstitutionsproject.org/wp-content/uploads/CCP-Iceland-Report.pdf.

2 European Commission for Democracy through Law (Venice Commission), *Opinion on the Draft New Constitution.* Council of Europe, March 11, 2013, CDL-AD(2013)010, para. 182 accessed January 4, 2016, www.althingi.is/pdf/venice.coe.pdf.

3 The Constitution of the Kingdom of Iceland, No. 9/1920, was adopted after Iceland was granted sovereignty in 1918 and recognition of its equal status in a union with Denmark under a joint monarchy.

4 This was confirmed in an extensive report issued in April 2010 by the Special Investigation Commission elected by Althingi at the end of 2008, to investigate the events that led to the collapse of the three main banks in Iceland and seek to answer what caused their failure. When the banks collapsed in October 2008, the size of Iceland's financial system was nine times the gross domestic product of the country. Rannsóknarnefnd Alþingis [The Special Investigation Commission of the Icelandic Parliament], *Aðdragandi og orsakir falls íslensku bankanna 2008 og tengdir atburðir* [The Causes and Effects of the Fall of the Icelandic Banks and Related Events], vol. 1 (Reykjavík: Icelandic Parliament, 2010), 31; see also Mark J. Flannery, "Appendix 8: The Importance of Government Supervision in Producing Financial Services," in *Aðdragandi og orsakir falls íslensku bankanna 2008 og tengdir atburðir* [The Causes and Effects of the Fall of the Icelandic Banks and Related Events] (Reykjavík: Icelandic Parliament, 2010); and Eyvindur G. Gunnarsson, "The Icelandic Regulatory Responses to the Financial Crisis," *European Business Organization Law Review* 12 (2011): 2.

5 The Act No. 90/2010 is accessible in English translation at thjodfundur2010.is/other_files/2010/doc/Act-on-a-Constitutional-Assembly.pdf, accessed January 4, 2016. For a more detailed description of the Act and the revision process, see Björg Thorarensen, "The Impact of the Financial Crisis on Icelandic Constitutional Law: Legislative Reforms, Judicial Review and Revision of the Constitution," in *Constitutions in the Global Financial Crisis. A Comparative Analysis*, ed. Xenophon Contiades (Farnham: Ashgate, 2013), 273–275.

6 The referendum included five further questions, as follows:

- In the new Constitution, do you want natural resources that are not privately owned to be declared national property? (74% voted yes).
- Would you like to see provisions in the new Constitution on a national church in Iceland? (51% voted yes).
- Would you like to see the new Constitution authorize the election of particular individuals to the Althingi more than is the case at present? (69% voted yes).
- Would you like to see a provision in the new Constitution giving equal weight to votes cast in all parts of the country? (58% voted yes).
- Would you like to see a provision in the new Constitution stating that a certain proportion of the electorate is able to demand to have issues put to a referendum? (63% voted yes).

(Source: *National Election Commission. Advertisement of the Result of 23 October, 2012*)

7 An English translation is accessible at http://stjornlagathing.is/other_files/stjornlagarad/Frumvarp-enska.pdf, accessed January 4, 2016.

8 Thorarensen, "The Impact of the Financial Crisis on Icelandic Constitutional Law: Legislative Reforms, Judicial Review and Revision of the Constitution," 280.

9 The European Commission for Democracy through Law (Venice Commission) acts as the Council of Europe's advisory body on constitutional matters and is composed

of constitutional and international law experts and members of the judiciary or national parliaments in Member States of the Council of Europe.

10 The European Commission for Democracy through Law (Venice Commission), *Opinion on the Draft New Constitution*, paras. 179–182, accessed January 4, 2016, www.althingi.is/pdf/venice.coe.pdf.

11 The European Commission for Democracy through Law (Venice Commission), *Opinion on the Draft New Constitution*, para. 32, accessed January 4, 2016, www.althingi.is/pdf/venice.coe.pdf.

12 Letter of the Parliamentary Ombudsman to the Constitutional Committee of the Althing, January 21, 2013, 4.

13 Elkins et al., "A Review of Iceland's Draft Constitution," 11.

14 Thorvaldur Gylfason: "Democracy on Ice: A Post-Mortem of the Icelandic Constitution," openDemocracy, June 19, 2013, accessed March 19, 2015, www.opendemocracy.net/can-europe-make-it/thorvaldur-gylfason/democracy-on-ice-post-mortem-of-icelandic-constitution.

15 Iceland's constitution of 1944 makes no distinction (as is done in some states) between piecemeal amendments and a comprehensive revision or the enactment of a completely new constitution. There are certain arguments in favor of having particular rules on the enactment of a new constitution, on the one hand, and subsequent amendments to it, on the other. See Eivind Smith, *Konstitusjonelt demokrati. Statsforfatningsretten i prinsipielt og komparativt lys* 2nd ed. (Bergen: Fagbokforlaget, 2012), 96.

16 On the purpose of special procedure and methods for amending the Icelandic constitution, see Björg Thorarensen, *Stjórnskipunarréttur*. Handhafar ríkisvalds [Constitutional Law. Foundations and the State Powers], (Reykjavik: Codex Publishing, 2015), 212.

17 Advisory referenda have more frequently been held in the Nordic states, where, traditionally, national constitutions do not provide for referenda as part of the legally binding decision-making procedures. Questions on the accession of Sweden (1994), Finland (1994), and Norway (1972 and 1994) to the European Union were put to referenda, and in all instances the political decisions taken on accession were in line with the outcomes.

18 Markku Suksi, "The Advisory Referendum in Finland," *European Public Law* 5, no. 4 (1999): 551.

19 It should be mentioned that a new political party, the Democratic Watch (*Lýðræðisvaktin*), fielded candidates in the election, including some who had sat as representatives on the Constitutional Council. The party's main election platform was to continue with the revision of the Constitution and to respect the outcome of the 2012 referendum. The party received very little support, receiving only about 2.5% of the vote and failing to gain any seats in Parliament.

20 Joel I. Colón-Ríos, *Weak Constitutionalism. Democratic Legitimacy and the Question of Constituent Power* (Abingdon: Routledge, 2012), 21.

Bibliography

The Althing Ombudsman. "Bréf til stjórnskipunar- og eftirlitsnefndar" [A Letter to the Constitutional and Supervisory Committee]. January 21, 2013.

Colón-Ríos, Joel I. *Weak Constitutionalism. Democratic Legitimacy and the Question of Constituent Power*. Abingdon: Routledge, 2012.

Elkins, Zachary, Tom Ginsburg, and James Melton. "A Review of Iceland's Draft Constitution." *The Comparative Constitutions Project*. October 14, 2012. Accessed March 19, 2015. http://comparativeconstitutionsproject.org/wp-content/uploads/CCP-Iceland-Report.pdf.

European Commission for Democracy through Law (Venice Commission). *Opinion on the Draft New Constitution.* March 11, 2013, CDL-AD(2013)010. Accessed January 4, 2016. www.althingi.is/pdf/venice.coe.pdf.

Flannery, Mark J. "Appendix 8: The Importance of Government Supervision in Producing Financial Services." In *Aðdragandi og orsakir falls íslensku bankanna 2008 og tengdir atburðir* [The Causes and Effects of the Fall of the Icelandic Banks and Related Events]. Reykjavík: Icelandic Parliament, 2010.

Gunnarsson, Eyvindur G. "The Icelandic Regulatory Responses to the Financial Crisis." *European Business Organization Law Review* 12 (2011): 1–39.

Gylfason, Thorvaldur. "Democracy on Ice: A Post-Mortem of the Icelandic Constitution." OpenDemocracy, June 19, 2013. Accessed March 19, 2015. www.opendemocracy.net/can-europe-make-it/thorvaldur-gylfason/democracy-on-ice-post-mortem-of-icelandic-constitution.

Rannsóknarnefnd Alþingis [The Special Investigation Commission of the Icelandic Parliament]. *Aðdragandi og orsakir falls íslensku bankanna 2008 og tengdir atburðir* [The Causes and Effects of the Fall of the Icelandic Banks and Related Events]. Reykjavík: Icelandic Parliament, 2010.

Smith, Eivind. *Konstitusjonelt demokrati. Statsforfatningsretten i prinsipielt og komparativt lys.* 2nd ed. Bergen: Fagbokforlaget, 2012.

Suksi, Markku. "The Advisory Referendum in Finland." *European Public Law* 5, no. 4 (1999): 535–556.

Thorarensen, Björg. "The Impact of the Financial Crisis on Icelandic Constitutional Law: Legislative Reforms, Judicial Review and Revision of the Constitution." In *Constitutions in the Global Financial Crisis. A Comparative Analysis*, edited by Xenophon Contiades, 263–285. Farnham: Ashgate, 2013.

Thorarensen, Björg. *Stjórnskipunarréttur. Handhafar ríkisvalds* [Constitutional Law. Foundations and the State Powers], Reykjavik: Codex Publishing, 2015.

14 The Constituent Assembly

A study in failure

Jón Ólafsson

The idea of electing a constituent assembly was not born with the left-wing government that took power in early 2009 after days of barricaded protest on the streets of Reykjavík. But circumstances had certainly transformed this rather fantastic idea into a realistic proposal. Less than two years later, an assembly existed with 25 individually elected representatives who were to begin rewriting—or revising—the Icelandic constitution in early 2011. Then came the backlash: the Supreme Court, whose role was to evaluate complaints about the elections, decided that due to a number of technical flaws in how the elections were conducted, the results would have to be annulled.[1] This decision was fateful for the process. Parliament voted to reappoint the elected members of the Constitutional Assembly, since in spite of the conclusion that the elections had not been ideally carried out, no suspicion of fraud ever arose.[2] But the process was already tainted, and the legitimacy of the reappointed Constitutional Assembly (CA) as a Constitutional Council (CC) was contested. The CC basically had the status of a parliamentary commission appointed by resolution; the status of its members was strangely undefined.[3] Most of them continued to see themselves as elected representatives of the people. Yet, critics certainly had a point when they argued that an appointed council must be seen as such and that by accepting appointment, the CC members had not resurrected their roles as representatives of the public, but, rather, had just agreed to serve on a parliamentary commission.[4]

There is no single reason that explains why the draft constitution, which the CC submitted to Parliament in 2011, failed to become the basis for a new constitution. A few central issues can be identified. Weaknesses in the design of the process help understand the deeper flaws that eventually drove supporters of the constitutional bill into a blind alley. The time frame to consider is approximately two and a half years, from the beginning of the campaign before the elections to the CA in November 2010, and until massive criticism of the draft constitution effectively killed it in the spring of 2013.

During this time, the process suffered a number of crucial setbacks, each of which upset the hopes of those who had believed that a new and improved constitution would result from the work of the CC. Setbacks are, of course, to be expected in any process. Arguably, however, confusion about the status as well as the task of the CC prevented an effective response to setbacks. Moreover, political disagreement about the CA and subsequently about appointing the CC was never directly addressed by Parliament. As I will show here, disagreement and discontent, together with the confusion about status and tasks, served to increase the distrust between the CC and political elites. The consequences were serious, since the CC needed the support of political elites in order that the constitutional bill could be passed.[5]

This chapter is a study of the constitution-making as a failed process. I will focus on one step made by the CC, which, in my view, had the most fateful consequences, and which must be understood in connection with, on the one hand, Parliament/Council relations and, on the other, activism of prominent Council members. This was the decision to write a new constitution rather than revise the old one. My reason for discussing only this part of the process is twofold. First, it is a topic that needs to be treated at length, and second, even if not the only reason for the defeat, it is clearly the most serious one, since it was a decision made by the Council itself, which obviously increased the risk of failure greatly in comparison with simply revising the current constitution. Had the CC chosen the path of revision, it would most probably have been able to accomplish something. Yet, the Council does not seem to have debated the pros and cons of its choice in any systematic manner. I will explore the discussion (or lack of discussion) in the CC about this decision and suggest some explanations.

Since I think that it was unfortunate that the Council decided to rewrite without sufficiently exploring what that meant, I also question the motivations behind it: whether, for example, some of the Council members may have seen it as a bigger sacrifice to agree to a compromise than to fail in writing a new constitution. I also partially lay out the consequences of the decision. I conclude that what it shows is that if a deliberative body that, like the CC, is given a specific task must also work under instructions specific enough to avoid a situation in which it must itself make controversial policy decisions. The CA/CC should have been asked either to write a new constitution (in which case four months would have been insufficient) or to revise the constitution or some important parts of it.

Public against Parliament: the activist face of the Constitutional Council

The CC was conceived as an independent body with the specific task of submitting a bill to Parliament. The Council's members took very seriously and quite literally their independence of governmental institutions. Not only was there no communication with Parliament at all; the more vocal CC members argued that Parliament was morally obligated to pass the bill with, at most, cosmetic changes and, thus, had no right to debate the draft as such.[6] This activist stance and the lack of communication further exacerbated conflicts between the CC and political and administrative elites. Although opinions differed within the CC on how Parliament should treat the draft constitution once it had been submitted, the most vocal and active members of the Council continued to confront Parliament and demand that it accept the bill as expressing the will of the people by simply organizing a referendum on it with a clear commitment to abide by the results.[7]

This position was somewhat supported by opinion polls, which showed a majority in favor of the new constitution. The most active proponents, however, vastly overstated the case, since public opinion seemed to favor "basing" a new constitution on the draft rather than simply accepting the draft.[8] When it was finally put to national referendum in 2012, that was also the question asked: should the new constitution be based on the draft? The last and the most serious wave of attacks on the draft began after the 2012 referendum, when a number of prominent legal specialists and political scientists delivered reports and openly criticized the draft itself as well as the whole constitutional process. At this point, supporters of the bill had run out of political capital, due, at least in part, to the strained relations between the Council and Parliament.[9]

The clash between the "political" and the "civic" is, in my view, another central issue for the work of the CC. It is too simple to understand the hostile reaction of many members of different "establishments" as a display of elite maneuvers to neutralize a non-traditional civic body. Opinion pieces written by some of the CC members as well as a number of public statements showed a desire to identify with grassroots movements against political elites.[10] Yet, some of the CC members saw their work in the Council as a prologue to more direct political involvement. They participated in founding a new political party, Dawn, with other activists. Subsequently, CC members led in the formation of two other parties, which also put up candidates in the parliamentary elections in 2013. The creation of the parties suggests that, for at least some of the individuals elected to the CA, the experience of campaigning to be elected and then participating in writing a constitution proved a politically formative experience.

Given the seemingly favorable reception of the draft constitution by the general public, the assumption was not unreasonable that a new party, having grown out of this novel experience in civic participation, would appeal to a considerable number of voters. But general support of the draft did not translate into meaningful support of any single new political force derived from the Constitutional Council. Dawn got less than 3.0% of the vote in the parliamentary elections and not a single MP elected; the other two parties, the Iceland Democratic Party and the Households Party, also received around 3% of the vote.[11] Many—even most—CC members probably never intended to translate their civic experience into direct politics, but saw their involvement in writing a constitution as just that: an important exercise in civic participation.[12] A split can, therefore, be seen in the Council between those for whom the CC, in the end, became an instrument of political resistance against established elites—"the political class," as one CC member put it—and another group for whom the CC remained a civic forum, in an important way detached from everyday politics. Since activists of a political bent, however, presented a much more visible face of the CC, their views tended to dominate public discussion about the constitutional process.[13]

It is clear that the process failed, in the sense of failing to produce a constitutional text that could get the necessary support to be passed by Parliament. I do not think, however, that the exercise as a whole was worthless. It provided an extremely important experience both for the democratic process in Iceland and, more importantly, for the idea of constitutional reform in general.[14] The experience showed that a short and well-organized campaign could bring interesting results. It is quite impressive how much a group of people, most of whom had no legislative experience, were able to accomplish in a few months. The draft, in spite of all its flaws, presents a more or less complete constitutional structure. But it also showed how carefully such a process must be managed and how easily it can be compromised.

By appointing a Council with an open mandate, the government apparently meant to ensure that it could do its work without political interference or meddling. At the same time, it left crucial decisions in the hands of the Council itself.[15] The Council, of course, could have made a wise choice. And yet, given the high spirits surrounding it, and the revolutionary rather than reformist agenda of many of the CC members, it should not be seen as surprising that its initial—and critical—choices were neither wise nor strategically well thought out.

From clean slate to consensus: methodological weaknesses

The CC met for the first time on April 6, 2011. The first meetings were spent on discussing organizational and procedural issues. Rules of procedure, as the parliamentary resolution on the Council instructed, were quickly designed to ensure the quality and constructive spirit of the Council's work. One of the main principles stated at the beginning of the document was that the Council would aim to "use judicious discussion and objective criticism to achieve a consensus rather than force of vote."[16] This principle may have been partly inspired by the atmosphere of consensus that had characterized the 2010 National Forum, which had ranked core values and objectives and whose results the CC was expected to take into account.[17] No available evidence suggests that anyone questioned this goal. It seems to have been taken for granted that discussion and criticism, if done in the right way, would support the objective of reaching consensus.[18]

While consensus may be valuable as such, deliberation in assemblies—the invitation to comment, criticize, and discuss—should produce better and more informed conditions of decision-making and may help in generating higher-order principles to govern conflict, but will not necessarily create a consensus.[19] The emphasis on consensus, which can be seen in the rules of procedure, was also expressed in many of the comments made by CC members in the Council's first meetings. The idea seems to have been generally accepted that a sufficiently informed and intelligent group of people must be able to develop a common vision on what constitutes the public interest, and that deliberation will lead to convergence.[20] But, as the overly general and vague proposals put forward by the National Forum had already shown, loss of precision is the cost of consensus. The consensus orientation, arguably, led to a tendency to avoid debating the more contentious issues, and to seek instead less definitive formulations, allowing different interpretations.[21] The "happy ending" of the National Forum is easily explained by the absence of trade-offs. Participants were invited to brainstorm together and then commonly rank values and objectives. No discussion took place on the consequences of the priority rankings.[22]

The eventual consensus on the final draft, which was supported by all CC members, can be explained in a similar way. The consensus did not mean that all CC members actually agreed on how the constitution should be. The consensus, rather, showed that they could all see the document and the vote itself as allowing the interpretation they favored.[23] But, as was later pointed out, insufficient attention had been given to excluding interpretations. Once legal scholars and constitutional experts began to scrutinize the text, they could point out a number of articles that were either too vague or could be interpreted in a number of different ways from a legal standpoint.[24] This suggests that the consensus objective worked against deeper deliberation. It may also have increased the tendency to strategic behavior, in some cases, and a willingness to leave open the interpretation of individual articles rather than face trade-offs.[25]

The Council's third meeting on April 13, 2011 appointed a committee of five people to make proposals on the division of labor between working groups and on a "basic document" to work with.[26] This was quite a relevant issue, since, of course, there existed an "old" constitution, and Parliament had not made it clear whether it expected the CC to revise it, write a new constitution, or simply make a number of proposals for each article of a new constitution, which would then be submitted to a referendum.[27] The original law on the CA describes the task as a "revision" of the constitution (the English translation of the CC's rules of procedure uses the even weaker term "review").[28] However, the law also describes how the Assembly was to prepare a "constitutional bill" without specifying whether such a bill should propose changes in the current constitution or a whole new constitution.[29] The parliamentary resolution by which the elected CA members were reappointed to the CC used a slightly different formulation, according to which the Council was to make proposals on revisions of the constitution and these proposals should be "submitted to the parliament in the form of a constitutional bill."[30] The commentary accompanying the bill on the CA submitted to Parliament on November 4, 2009 also referred to revisions and proposals to be made in a way that would leave it open for the Assembly to write a new constitution.[31]

Thus, the task of the CA/CC was never fully clarified. The very idea of electing a CA seems to imply that a new constitution is to be written rather than revised. CC members understood suggestions made by the Constitutional Committee as pointing in the same direction.[32] The Constitutional Committee appointed by the government to prepare the ground for the CA—a task that included the convening of the 2010 National Forum—had prepared guidelines for the CC. Its report contained expert analysis on some of the central issues that the CC was to discuss, as well as a summary of the results of the National Forum. It also contained two ready-made constitutions variants to be used in part or as a whole.[33]

The question of where exactly the work of the CC should begin was not really brought to the table until after the committee on working groups and the "basic document" had been adopted.[34] In the committee, perhaps predictably, two opposing views immediately emerged: whether the current constitution should be treated as a "basic document" and the CC would then propose changes to its text and structure, or whether the CC should start with a "clean slate."[35] After what the committee members described as a "long discussion," a compromise was reached, according to which the CC would compose a new text, but it would keep the "old" constitution at the side, regarding the new text as an alternative to the current constitution rather than as proposals to change it. Thus, the CC would, indeed, write a new constitution rather than just change the current one, but it would not entirely throw away the old constitution.[36]

This formula, a compromise between two groups of Council members, seems quite confusing. To make matters even more complicated, as some Council members pointed out in the discussion, the variants prepared by the Constitutional Committee needed to be taken into account. If Council members were to focus on the existing constitution and the proposals made by legal experts, the danger was that their mission, to both genuinely represent the public and change the political culture in Iceland, would be unsuccessful. During a short and rather confused discussion of the different kinds of approaches, one Council member expressed such frustration quite strongly. He said:

> I am totally against somehow basing the work on the current constitution, even if it is only considered a working document. I think we are all here to write a new constitution, not to improve the old one, which is as we all know, deeply flawed. And I think it will give a completely wrong message to society if we seem to be patching up this old, unusable document.... We should start with a table of contents, nothing else.[37]

The compromise suggested by the committee seemed difficult to grasp for some Council members. One who spoke a little later admitted that she did not understand what the discussion was about: "I don't know what we are debating. Sorry, I just have to admit I don't really understand it."[38]

The main issue concerned the general approach. Those who favored using the current constitution as a basic document and defining their work as a revision of that document—whereby deviating from it needed to be argued for—were described as conservatives, and those who wanted a clean slate as radicals. Some Council members openly protested such labels, but the division seems to have lasted for the whole four-month period.[39] The difference between the radicals, on the one hand, and the conservatives, on the other, emerged not only when debating the question about whether or not to use the current constitution as a basis but also with respect to the more general vision of the task itself.[40]

The radicals (and not only the radicals) tended to be aware of restrictions and instructions from the authorities, and emphasized the freedom of the CC to organize its work and determine its task in any way it saw fit.[41] For them, the

CA/CC was a direct consequence of the crisis of 2008, and the new constitution should be conceived of as a break with the past. Some wanted to treat the framework provided by the Constitutional Committee simply as suggestions to be taken into consideration as a part of the Council's working documents.[42] During the work of the CC, one group even conferred to work on ideas about how to include backward-looking articles in the draft, that is, articles that would serve to prevent or, at least, minimize the chance that social, financial, and political developments could be similar to what had happened prior to the 2008 crisis, to the extent of even allowing retroactive legislation to deal with the perceived perpetrators of the economic collapse.[43]

While clearly not sharing this vision, the "conservatives" also had doubts about the Council's chance within the given time frame of rewriting—successfully—the constitution in a way that would secure its backing by parliament.[44] One of them pointed out that there were strong arguments in favor of revising rather than rewriting, even for the more radically minded among Council members:

> It was my personal view that the most promising way to go in light of what has happened—given the low participation in the elections and the perhaps contestable method to appoint us, it was at least controversial in the parliament and many other things—that it would in many ways be more suitable to begin with the current constitution, it was just more likely that such an approach could to lead to success in the end.[45]

Yet, the discussion in the Council about this crucial step was very limited. According to one appraisal, the approach finally taken was in a way natural. Given the differences, and the very strong opposition to basing the work on the current constitution, the compromise simply seemed a perfectly reasonable solution.[46] Those in favor of a different approach realized that they were a minority and, therefore, seem also to have thought that the compromise (not throwing out the old constitution entirely) was about as good a solution as they could expect. Some of the more radically minded had suspicions about the compromise proposal to begin with, but then also admitted that it was sufficient:

> [B]ecause I may have put it in rather strong terms before, it seems to me, as things have been explained better, that I put it too strongly and that the empty sheet may very well have the respect it should have there. So I will not oppose this proposal, but will abstain.[47]

So it was decided to work on the compromise principle suggested by the committee, according to which the task was essentially to write a new constitution, using the current constitution and the two variants provided by the Constitutional Committee as proposals or alternatives that could be used, but were not to be seen as basic in any way.[48] The rather obvious worry that this might prove impossible seems not to have entered the discussion except in the general remark quoted above that revision might be less risky than embarking on writing a new constitution. A greater worry seems to have been that the CC would be engaged in patching up an old document rather than creating something new, and that existing documents might put illegitimate restraints on CC members. As one of them put it:

> [I] must say that I don't think it is appropriate to put the old constitution in [the evolving draft] because … it is a basic document. Certainly it is. But we should not allow that basic or provisional document to influence this too much. We should write the material. It's a quilt that's being discussed, but I want a whole blanket.[49]

Many concerns about the current constitution no doubt contributed to the view that it would be a mistake to try to continue to build on that document. It had not only retained the basic character of nineteenth-century thinking: it really was a kind of patchwork, formed by successive attempts to write new political realities into a textual construct that, as a whole, conveyed an archaic spirit. One of the points made by participants in the National Forum was that a constitutional text should be very lucid and easy to understand for the general public.[50] The argument was sometimes made that a child should be able to understand it—its meaning so crisp that no legal interpretation was really necessary to grasp at once what the constitution said and what it meant.[51] In less idealistic terms, it was also argued that some of the more complicated articles dealing with how power was vested in the President, who then transferred it to ministers, needed to be made simpler and to reflect more accurately the fact that the role of the President was first and foremost ceremonial.[52]

However, none of these concerns were formally or systematically addressed in the Council, since it never discussed its prioritization in terms of what were the most important tasks. One Council member later argued that "one of the main challenges of the CC was the fact that the mechanics of the existing constitution … no longer mirrored the democratic governmental system in the country."[53] Unfortunately, no recordings or verbatim reports exist of the committee meetings, but judging from the verbatim reports of Council meetings, Committee B—which was responsible for the role of the executive and legislative branches of government, including the presidency—did not, at least not to begin with, see this as the main problem. According to the first report of Committee B to the Council, its initial discussion was about changing—fundamentally—the constitutional order, for example, by electing the executive directly.[54] Committee B seems at the beginning to have been more concerned with the question of whether or not to propose radical changes than with problematic aspects of archaic formulations in the constitution. Eventually, however, the task became to write a new text that made the constitutional order clearer and simpler without essentially changing it.[55]

To be sure, substantial issues emerged in the discussion, where differences were also addressed and, to some extent, dealt with. But any methodological discussion—or a common decision about priorities—was conspicuously missing. There is even evidence that such discussion was treated with impatience by Council members who wanted to get on to substance rather than spend time on "procedures and methods."[56] In his book *Iceland and the International Financial Crisis*, Eiríkur Bergmann, a Council member, explains that "rather than developing the document in a traditional linear fashion, the Council decided to apply the agile method often used in software development gradually completing the holistic document in several rounds."[57]

This approach certainly facilitated the use of input from the public, since everyone could comment on the document on every stage. But while CC members apparently were genuinely interested in eliciting public participation, their work lacked the clear vision necessary to focus on public input as well as a formal means of filtering and dealing with commentary, criticisms, and proposals from the wider audience that ideally should be monitoring and, to some extent, participating in the work of the Council. Adopting a procedure for moving back and forth between submitting drafts and admitting proposals and commentary from the public is not establishing a method in that sense. Since relatively few members of the public actually were active in engaging CC members in Facebook discussion, submitting formal and informal proposals or demanding attention from Council members in other ways, this aspect of the work never became a big problem. But it certainly would have become very difficult to do justice to real widespread interest.[58]

The Council's lack of methodology explains, at least partly, how severely constitutional scholars and political scientists later attacked the draft. Without clear priorities and real trade-offs, many of the provisions proposed could only be superficially addressed. As a result, the question most frequently asked after the draft was submitted was simply: What does this or that article actually mean? How can its consequences be assessed? Many critics immediately complained that the new constitution would need to be tested for "stress"—that, for example, some of the new rights could not be adopted unless it was clear that they did not impose too heavy obligations on the government.[59] One must conclude that the apparent inability of the CC to make methodological decisions, as well as the vague instructions its mandate was based on, left the Council in a very weak position to address, convincingly, the basic questions of how to plan its work and establish methodological and substantial priorities to guide it.

We—the people: the public again

Many critics of the plan to convene a CA argued that it was not right to change or rewrite the constitution at a time when emotions were high and many people, feeling that it was important to punish those responsible for the disastrous pre-crisis policies in Iceland, were moved to activism.[60] The argument most often put forward to support this criticism was simply that since the constitution could not be seen as having caused the Icelandic crisis, there was no hurry to rush to rewrite it as a consequence of it. Although no one (to my knowledge) argued that the constitution had directly caused the crash by somehow allowing or even leading to the decisions and reactions of the government prior to the crisis, now seen as vastly inadequate, activists argued that a better constitution could have prevented some of the excesses during the boom years.[61] Awkward responses to public criticisms from leading politicians showed how unprepared they were to be openly accused of total failure.

Just a few weeks after the collapse of the banking system, a town hall meeting was held in Reykjavík, by an informal group of citizens who had organized themselves after the crisis struck. The meeting was held in the biggest cinema hall in Reykjavík. Around 1500 people filled the hall and formed a crowd outside, where the meeting could be followed on a wide screen. The meeting was one in a series of gatherings held during this period, but the occasion was special because all MPs had been invited, including all government ministers.[62] During the meeting, there was a lot of shouting and arguing, and the slogan "We are the people" was often seen and heard, creating a symbolic reference to the 1989 collapse of Communist governments in Eastern and Central Europe.[63] Toward the end of the meeting, a crowd shouting various slogans constantly interrupted Ingibjörg Sólrún Gísladóttir, the Minister of Foreign Affairs and leader of the Social Democratic Alliance, in her final remarks. She finally lost her patience and pointed out that the people who happened to be present at the meeting could hardly claim that they represented the whole nation. Rather, she wanted to see them as a group of individuals, using their right to free speech to express their personal opinions. The immediate effect of these words was only increased booing and shouting as the discussion continued.[64] Its long-term echoes, however, were quite interesting. Over the next months and years, the remark would be quoted and repeated as an example of how a political leader loses touch with political realities that have become radicalized.

This small example illustrates the problem as grassroots activists perceived it: the political establishment was unable to develop a meaningful dialogue with the public. While the more conservatively minded among the public pointed out that the political system had not collapsed in spite of the financial collapse, the more activist-minded argued that the disappearance of trust amounted to political collapse. The Icelandic crisis was, thus, interesting not least because of the strong and general sentiment that there was more behind it than a series of catastrophic events in the international financial system, as Icelandic governmental ministers and officials tried at first to argue.[65] The overwhelming sentiment in the country was that the international crisis only partly revealed the reasons for the financial disaster in Iceland. The failure of the Icelandic government to respond properly to the crisis was frequently explained by two different approaches. First, the public administration had failed because of its incompetence, caused partly during years of corrupt hiring policies, through which ties to the governing Independence Party consistently played a bigger role than professional ability, education, and experience.[66] Second, a deep and long-standing corruption among top members of the political elite meant that some of the privatizations for which

Iceland had been lauded internationally constituted the handing out of public property to favored individuals and groups who had then become too strong for the government to control.[67]

A widespread view was that the only effective reaction to such incompetence and corruption would be a complete overhaul of the political system and the introduction of new practices within the government and in the public sector in general. A new government should be committed to improving politics through systemic reforms, within both the political and administrative spheres. Gradually, the groups that emphasized a social contract and the need for a clean-up of political practices in Iceland converged on the constitutional project, especially after the parliamentary elections of 2009 and the formation of the left-wing government. Constitutional reform was now widely seen as the most promising sphere for achieving wide-ranging social and political reform. As a consequence, many, if not all, Council members seem to have honestly believed in the possibility of creating a document that would lead to palpable changes in the country's political structures and traditions.

The cooperative spirit reflected in public statements by CC members and in the emphasis on unanimity about the final document suggests that eventually a relative consensus on public priorities emerged in spite of the persisting divide between conservatives and radicals. Discussion in the Council seems to have been agonistic rather than antagonistic, thus creating a suitable environment for debating priorities, consulting specialists and politicians who, in the end, would be instrumental in the success of the draft.[68] But, for some reason, the Council never took such steps, and it can be argued that its isolation grew as its work progressed. Transparency may also have had contradictory results. Since it was well exposed through its own website and social media, no Icelandic newspaper or broadcast media provided a regular coverage of its work. Reports would appear only around something "newsworthy," such as a disagreement about some principal issue, radical proposals, or evidence of split within the Council.[69] This may also partly explain why CC members eventually felt that if they really wanted to reach their goal of transforming Icelandic politics, they would have to do more than just submit a constitutional bill to a corrupt parliament. They would actually have to take the further step of forming their own political party to transform the political culture.[70]

Transitional solidarity

If there was any overarching demand that unified the civic activists and grassroots movements of the 2008 crisis, it was the demand for an improved—even a radically new—political culture. But, like the overly general "values" expressed by the National Forums in 2009 and 2010, this demand was somewhat unspecified. For some, the culture change consisted primarily in the move from bargaining strategies to reasoning—which implied preferring deliberative rather than aggregative conceptions of policy- and decision-making; for others, however, it meant direct public control of political representatives.[71]

These two conceptions of political culture (deliberation and public control) are not opposed, but they tend toward different ideals of political organization. While deliberation acknowledges moral disagreement and takes it as a fact that political decision-making must be based on accepting and working with difference, the idea of public control rests on the idea that the public shares interests and goals—even comprehensive views or doctrines—and that in a representative democracy it is most important to ensure that politics serves public rather than special interest.

The National Forums were based on the belief that Icelandic society, since it is small and relatively homogeneous, could express values that were not only common but also comprehensive. As such, it should guide the government as well as the CC in making choices that reflected a shared Icelandic worldview. It follows that moral disagreement was treated as either absent or irrelevant. The CC, to a large extent, adopted this basic view, which may explain the emphasis on final consensus and on seeing the Council as representing the uncorrupt public in contrast to the argumentative and corrupt Parliament, where special interest would always, in the end, come out stronger than the public interest. In this description, the CC did not engage in deliberative democracy in the sense in which this concept is usually understood.[72] There was no clear distinction drawn between a political role (discussing, clarifying, and even reaching an agreement about constitutional provisions given moral disagreement) and moral leadership (showing how a diverse group of people could find ways of creating a constitutional framework that would prevent moral failure of government). But ignoring moral disagreement is to leave out a central part of pluralistic politics, since it requires the acceptance of one or more comprehensive doctrines as the basis for political culture.[73]

Activists, and later on many CC members, shared the desire to restore integrity to political life by forging a new social contract. But instead of emphasizing the deliberative part of that enterprise, the most visible members of the group argued that the main goal would be achieved not by ensuring better deliberative practices, but, rather, by excluding politicians and interest groups bypassing the supposedly corrupt former elites.[74] In the discussions and debates in and around the CC, ideas about solidarity, common values, and consensus thus dominated the scene, rather than questions about trade-offs, diversity, and consequences.[75]

The belief in solidarity may have blinded CC members not only to actual political disagreements but also to the inevitable moral disagreement in a pluralistic society. Since the CC was working toward one document on which agreement was to be reached, its members acted as if the Council could serve as a vehicle of national consensus. This created an idea of moral superiority, which was shared by many or most CC members, who also expected Parliament to acknowledge it by accepting as a moral obligation that no obstacles should be put in the way of the eventual constitutional bill, and submitting it unchanged to a national referendum. Thus, they expected that even though neither the Council's proposals nor the result of a referendum could be legally binding for Parliament, it would accept both as morally binding.[76] The consensus outlook, of course, may have corresponded to the post-crisis mood that had dominated political discussion in Icelandic society after the publication of the damning reports by the Special Investigative Committee and the special Working Group on Ethics.[77] Icelandic officials and political leaders certainly had all the information they needed to draw the right conclusions, yet failed to do so until it was too late.[78]

Given the unusual circumstances in Icelandic society due to the financial crisis and the resulting demand for transformative changes, the emphasis on solidarity was both easy to understand and to justify to a large part of the public. But solidarity inevitably excludes. It can either be formed around very basic issues or be the solidarity of a very distinct group. A third kind of solidarity can be formed around views or proposals formulated very generally or in terms that allow for several interpretations. Such solidarity is not worth much once a clear understanding is needed, and in that sense the solidarity so greatly emphasized by the CC may have prevented, rather than facilitated, a more favorable reaction from Parliament. Although it must remain speculative, the possibility cannot be excluded that a more diverse product, such as a bundle of proposals that would have given Parliament a considerable choice of alternatives, accompanied by a rich discussion on pros and cons, explanation of trade-offs, and some assessment of consequences, would have had more impact than the ready-made constitution submitted to Parliament with the expectation of swift approval.

Conclusion

I have focused here on the constitutional process and avoided discussion of the proposal itself made by the CC. There is no doubt that the process was a great experiment, but as with all great experiments, what is most important is not any particular success, but what can be learned from it. One general lesson should be clear by now: it is unfortunate if a body elected, or put together in other ways, is given an open or unclear task and mandate. It means that the body must itself make policy decisions, which will (since they are controversial) undermine its legitimacy and general appeal. I believe that the main flaws in the constitutional process may be summarized in the following way: the CC was given too little time. It was insufficient for both the proper attention to detail that would be necessary and for adequately working with Parliament, which in the end would have to pass the bill not once but twice. The CC was not equipped to make the decisions necessary to ensure that the approach toward writing the new constitution would be sufficiently methodic and built on a deliberated prioritization whereby actual substantive differences had been dealt with and resolved. More time, especially if a draft constitution could have gone through critical assessment by specialists before the CC was supposed to have finished its work, would have helped considerably.[79]

The CC overestimated the political significance of unanimity and underestimated the ability of constitutional scholars and political scientists to undermine the project by pointing out textual obscurities and structural weaknesses. It also failed to see how unanimity may serve to conceal differences to the extent of preventing compromise. The problem is that a common expression of basic values or fundamental preferences needs both common instrumental preferences, that is, a common understanding of the means to promote the fundamental preferences, and a common interpretation of the fundamental preferences. The CC, just like the earlier National Forums, provided an excellent platform to reaffirm a common commitment to building a society of equality, transparency, freedom, and integrity. But the interpretation of concepts like these was kept open, and instrumental preferences, the ranking that could reflect the means that would be required, were also kept open, and that means unresolved.[80]

Although the constitutional bill did not survive opposition from political and academic elites, theoretically it can still be used as the basis for a new Icelandic constitution by any future government that chooses to do so. If this happens, its novelty should not be underestimated. Even if changes are made in individual chapters and articles, the fact remains that the draft submitted to the Icelandic Parliament by the CC was the result of audacious and original thinking, which should inspire and influence the way we think about constitutions and how they should be written.

Notes

1 Ákvörðun Hæstaréttar [Supreme Court Decision], January 25, 2011, accessed 5 December, 2015, www.haestirettur.is/control/index?pid=1109.

2 Of the elected 25 CA members, 24 accepted the reappointment. The person who had been number 26 was appointed to replace the only elected member who declined to be reappointed. Many of the elected members, however, although they accepted reappointment, were openly critical of how Parliament had dealt with the situation (see, for example, Salvör Nordal, "Opið bréf til Alþingis," *Fréttablaðið*, March 30, 2011).

3 "Þingsályktun nr. 19/139 um skipun stjórnlagaráðs" [Parliamentary Resolution 19/139 on the Appointment of the Constitutional Council], 549. mál, þskj. 1120. Alþingi 2010–2011, 139. Löggjafarþing, accessed December 5, 2015, www.althingi.is/altext/139/s/1120.html.

4 "Nefndarálit um tillögu til þingsályktunar um skipun stjórnlagaráðs" [A Committee Report on a Proposed Parliament Resolution on the Appointment of the Constitutional Council]. 549. mál, þskj. 1028, Alþingi 2010–2011, 139. löggjafarþing, accessed December 5, 2015, www.althingi.is/altext/139/s/1028.html. It is made clear in the commentary that the Parliament did not regard Council members as representatives of the public:

> In light of the Supreme Court decision to annul the elections, those individuals who were elected to the Constitutional Assembly do not any more get their mandate from the people. The parliamentary resolution means that Parliament appoints a constitutional council and that its members get their mandate from the Parliament, i.e., from its nationally elected representatives.

See per contra Thorvaldur Gylfason, "From Collapse to Constitution," in *Public Debt, Global Governance and Economic Dynamism*, ed. L. Paganetto (Milano: Springer Milan, 2013), 392.

5 A simple majority was sufficient to pass the bill. Before the 2013 elections, the government would probably have been able to have Parliament accept the constitutional bill. But since two consecutive parliaments were needed to pass changes of the constitution, and it was improbable that the majority would survive elections, passing it, without broad support, could even have proved counterproductive.

6 Thorvaldur Gylfason, *Hreint borð. Greinasafn um frumvarp Stjórnlagaráðs til nýrrar stjórnarskrár* (Reykjavík: Gutti, 2012), 59–60. Gylfason pointed out that in the case that MPs were opposed to the draft constitution as submitted by the CC, Parliament could propose an alternative and ask voters to choose between the Council's version and its own. See also personal blog of Council member Illugi Jökulsson ("Vesalings fíflin í Stjórnlagaráði," accessed December 5, 2015, http://blog.pressan.is/illugi/2011/08/03/vesalings-fiflin-i-stjornlagaradi/).

7 Thorvaldur Gylfason, *Hreint borð*, 65. Among MPs, there were supporters of making the people decide in a referendum whether to adopt the new constitution, leaving Parliament out of it (see Guðmundur Steingrímsson, "Fín stjórnarskrá," personal blog, accessed December 5, 2015, http://blog.pressan.is/gummisteingrims/2011/08/12/fin-stjornarskra/). Valgerður Bjarnadóttir, who chaired the Constitutional and Supervisory Committee, was quick to point out that "Parliament has the last word" (Valgerður Bjarnadóttir, "Stjórnlagaráð—hvað næst?" *Fréttablaðið*, August 9, 2011).

8 According to an opinion poll by the Icelandic survey company Market and Media Research (MMR) in April 2012, 66.1% of voters supported "basing a new constitution on the CC's proposals" (see Market and Media Research, "Tveir þriðju styðja tillögur Stjórnlagaráðs," accessed December 5, 2015, www.mmr.is/frettir/birtar-nieurstoeeur/249-tveir-trieju-styeja-tilloegur-stjornlagaraes). According to a poll in September 2011, 75.3% supported an immediate national referendum, but supporters were divided as to whether the referendum should be binding (47.7% in favor, 27.6% against; see Market and Media Research, "Vilja þjóðaratkvæðagreiðslu um Stjórnlagaráðsfrumvarp," accessed December 5, 2015, www.mmr.is/frettir/birtar-nieurstoeeur/223-vilja-tjoearat kvaeeagreieslu-um-stjornlagaraesfrumvarp). A third poll just a few weeks after the constitutional bill was submitted to Parliament suggested that a majority (57.6%) still thought that Parliament should "thoroughly discuss" the CC proposal, while 42.6% thought that Parliament should not have much to do with finalizing the bill (see Market and Media Research, "Skiptar skoðanir á aðkomu Alþingis að stjórnlagafrumvarpi," 2011, accessed December 5, 2015, www.mmr.is/frettir/birtar-nieurstoeeur/220-skiptar-skoeanir-a-aekomu-altingis-ae-stjornlagafrumvarpi).

9 The draft, and indeed much of the work of the CC, was fiercely attacked in a series of meetings organized by Law Departments of four Icelandic universities and held between November 2012 and February 2013. See Stofnun stjórnsýslufræða og stjórnmála, "Fundaröð um stjórnarskrána," accessed December 5, 2015, http://stjornsyslustofnun.hi.is/node/494.

10 See, for example, Eiríkur Bergmann's piece in the daily *DV*. He discusses the critical reception of the constitutional bill by an academic, a former prime minister, and a specialist on public administration, claiming that their critical comments simply represented feeble attempts to defend the interests of political and academic elites. "Stjórnlaga hvað?" *DV*, August 8, 2011, accessed December 5, 2015, www.dv.is/blogg/eirikur-bergmann/2011/8/8/stjornlaga-hvad/.

11 See official election results as reported by the National Electoral Commission: Landskjörstjórn, "Apportionment of Seats to the Althingi, the Parliament of Iceland: Results of the Elections on April 27, 2013," accessed December 5, 2015, www.landskjor.is/media/frettir/ElectionsResults_April27_2013.pdf. It is ironic, of course, that the new parties had considerable combined support. Their solidarity in backing the draft constitution was clearly not enough to trump their political differences about other issues.

12 The Ministry of Justice and Human Rights published a booklet with short introductions to all CA candidates. These introductions in some cases contain concrete policy issues or views, but in most cases personal motivation is in the foreground, where the desire to participate as a citizen is emphasized. See the website providing information about the elections, accessed December 5, 2015, www.kosning.is/stjornlagathing/, and the booklet "Kynning á frambjóðendum og kosningum til stjórnlagaþings 27.

nóvember 2010," accessed December 5, 2015, http://issuu.com/athygli/docs/stjornlagathing?e=2270875/5699599.

13 Thorvaldur Gylfason, "Democracy on Ice: a Post-Mortem of the Icelandic Constitution," openDemocracy, June 19, 2013, accessed December 5, 2015, www.opendemocracy.net/can-europe-make-it/thorvaldur-gylfason/democracy-on-ice-post-mortem-of-icelandic-constitution.

14 See Hélène Landemore, "Inclusive Constitution-Making: The Icelandic Experiment," *Journal of Political Philosophy* 23, no. 2 (2015): 166–191.

15 Parliamentary Resolution 19/139 specified eight basic issues that the Council was to discuss, but stated also that it could decide to discuss other things it wanted to include in its eventual constitutional bill.

16 See an English translation of the rules available on the Council's website, accessed December 5, 2015, http://stjornlagarad.is/english/rules-of-procedure/.

17 *Skýrsla stjórnlaganefndar*, vol. 1 (Reykjavík: Constitutional Council, 2011), 21–22.

18 This was not understood, of course, as consensus on every level, and there was a lot of voting both in committee meetings and in the Council sessions. But the goal was to create a document that would be passed by consensus, and that goal was achieved.

19 See Amy Gutmann and Dennis Thompson, *Why Deliberative Democracy?* (Princeton: Princeton University Press, 2004), 64–65.

20 Toward the end of the Council's work, the pressure increased on working to reach consensus. But the spirit of cooperation was cultivated from the very beginning, which can be seen, for example, by the frequent use of the address "dear friends" in the proceedings.

21 This kind of compromise could be seen clearly in how the questions about the constitution and some key issues in the 2012 referendum were formulated. They could be understood in different ways, and therefore the results were of limited help to policymakers. See Jón Ólafsson, "Rökræðulýðræði verður stofnanalýðræði: Er hættulegt að færa vald til almennings? Athugasemdir við grein Vilhjálms Árnasonar 'Valdið fært til fólksins?'" *Tímarit um stjórnmál og stjórnsýslu* 10, no. 1 (2014): 119–142.

22 James Fishkin, "Rökræðulýðræði og lýðvistaða stjórnarskráin. Tilraunastarfsemin verður að halda áfram," in *Lýðræðistilraunir. Ísland í hruni og endurreisn*, ed. Jón Ólafsson (Reykjavík: University of Iceland Press, 2014), 23–32, 27; Jón Ólafsson, "Rökræðulýðræði verður stofnanalýðræði: Er hættulegt að færa vald til almennings?" 133–134; Vilhjálmur Árnason, "Valdið fært til fólksins? Veikleikar og verkefni íslensks lýðræðis í aðdraganda og eftirmála hrunsins," *Skírnir* 187 (2013): 11–54.

23 One curious episode resulting from remarks made by the President of Iceland, Ólafur Ragnar Grímsson, in a speech given to Parliament at its opening session two months after the constitutional bill was submitted illustrates the situation. The President claimed that the Council had proposed increasing the power of the President. CC member Eiríkur Bergmann reacted in a radio interview, arguing that the President had completely misunderstood the draft. That same evening, another CC member, Lýður Árnason, on his regular blog, contradicted Bergmann, saying that on his understanding the President's interpretation made perfect sense (see "Address by the President of Iceland Ólafur Ragnar Grímsson at the Opening of the Althingi October 1, 2011," accessed December 5, 2015, www.forseti.is/media/PDF/2011_10_01_Thingsetning_English.pdf; Lýður Árnason, "Túlkun forseta á tillögum Stjórnlagaráðs", personal blog, accessed December 5, 2015, www.dv.is/blogg/lydur-arnason/2011/10/1/tulkun-forseta-tillogum-stjornlagarads/). A third CC member partly supported Eiríkur Bergmann, pointing out that the President's interpretation showed the importance of public discussion in which CC members would have a chance to further explain and justify their proposals (Vilhjálmur Þorsteinsson, "Forsetinn og nýja stjórnarskráin," personal blog, accessed December 5, 2015, http://blog.pressan.is/vthorsteinsson/2011/10/02/forsetinn-og-nyja-stjornarskrain/).

24 This criticism was made and challenged in numerous seminars and public meetings in 2011 and 2012. See, for example, Kristrún Heimisdóttir, "Comment on the CC proposals," unpublished talk, Reykjavík University, November 16, 2012. She argued that to adopt the draft constitution without substantial changes could lead to a "constitutional paralysis."

25 Gunnar Helgi Kristinsson, "Ráðskast með stjórnarskrá," *Tímarit um stjórnmál og stjórnsýslu* 8, no. 2 (2012): 565–569 (The Constitutional Council chose to organize its work in such a way that the result was a wish list of changes to be made rather than a sober exploration of strengths and weaknesses of individual ideas or their inner coherence) 568.

26 *Stjórnlagaráðstíðindi 2a: Umræður á ráðsfundum* (Reykjavík: Constitutional Council, 2011), 33. In the original law on the CA, three working groups were supposed to work on different issues. The CC was not required to abide by instructions in the CA law, since it was established on the basis of a parliamentary resolution. The Council had much more freedom to organize its work according to what Council members felt was best.

27 Discussion in the CC on this issue revealed the uncertainty about the actual task (see *Stjórnlagaráðstíðindi* 2a, 23 (Lýður Árnason)). According to the exact instructions given by Parliament in its decision to appoint a Constitutional Council, the CC should prepare "a bill on constitutional law." In the early discussion in the CC, at least some of the members seem to have understood this as a bill containing a complete constitution to be adopted or rejected. But this is an incorrect, albeit not illogical, understanding of the formulation (see *Stjórnlagaráðstíðindi* 2, 31 (Gísli Tryggvason)).

28 *Lög um stjórnlagaþing* [Act on a Constitutional Assembly], nr. 90/2010, art. 1. An English translation of the Act is available. Accessed December 5, 2015. http://thjodfundur2010.is/other_files/2010/doc/Act-on-a-Constitutional-Assembly.pdf.

29 *Lög um stjórnlagaþing* nr. 90/2010, art. 26.

30 Parliamentary Resolution 19/139 on the Appointment of the Constitutional Council.

31 *Frumvarp til laga um stjórnlagaþing*, 152. mál, þskj. 168. Alþingi 2009–2010, 138. löggjafarþing, 17, 20. [Bill No. 152 from 2010 on the Constitutional Assembly].

32 Salvör Nordal, interview, May 6, 2014. See also Salvör Nordal, "Þátttaka borgara í ákvarðanatöku og ábyrgð stjórnvalda. Lærdómar af stjórnarskrármáli," *Skírnir* 189, no. 1 (2015): 119–141.

33 See *Skýrsla stjórnlaganefndar*, vol. 1, 182–214.

34 *Stjórnlagaráðstíðindi* 2a, 33.

35 *Stjórnlagaráðstíðindi* 1, 34.

36 *Stjórnlagaráðstíðindi* 2a, 35.

37 *Stjórnlagaráðstíðindi* 2a, 35 (Illugi Jökulsson).

38 *Stjórnlagaráðstíðindi* 2a, 38 (Þórhildur Þorleifsdóttir).

39 *Stjórnlagaráðstíðindi* 2a, 36–38.

40 Pawel Bartoszek, interview, September 9, 2011.

41 *Stjórnlagaráðstíðindi* 2a, 231 (Andrés Magnússon), 252 (Pétur Gunnlaugsson).

42 *Stjórnlagaráðstíðindi* 2a, 37 (Eiríkur Bergmann). Although dissatisfaction was not expressed at Council meetings, some of the more radically minded CC members felt that the proposals made by the Constitutional Committee were too narrow and limited the scope for new thinking in the Council. Björg Thorarensen, who was a key member of the Constitutional Committee, had, according to one CC member, simply expected her proposals to flow smoothly into a new constitution, but that was not acceptable for the CC (Thorvaldur Gylfason, interview, September 6, 2011). The verbatim reports of Council meetings, however, clearly show that once the Council got down to discussing proposals to put into its evolving draft, members were constantly in dialogue with the Constitutional Committee proposals, comparing them with their own or, in some cases, adopting them.

43 *Stjórnlagaráðstíðindi* 2a, 76 (Andrés Magnússon). See also *Stjórnlagaráðstíðindi* 2b, 606 (Andrés Magnússon), 611 (Íris Lind Sæmundsdóttir), 660 (Andrés Magnússon).

44 There were "radicals" who had argued before the CC was convened that it would be more practical not to embark on writing a new constitution right away but, rather, begin with amendments to the old one. Thorvaldur Gylfason was among those arguing in this vein before the CA elections (see Thorvaldur Gylfason, *Hreint borð*, 119). He did not continue this argument in the CC, but accepted the compromise solution.

45 *Stjórnlagaráðstíðindi* 2a, 34 (Pawel Bartoszek).

46 Thorvaldur Gylfason, interview, September 6, 2011.

47 *Stjórnlagaráðstíðindi* 2a, 40 (Illugi Jökulsson).

48 When possible, proposals made by the CC subcommittees was discussed in connection with a corresponding proposal in the Constitutional Committee's report (or in connection with the lack of such a proposal). Salvör Nordal also points out that the report was a very important document for the CC's work. Interview, May 6, 2014.

49 *Stjórnlagaráðstíðindi* 2a, 40 (Erlingur Sigurðarson).

50 See statements of this sort in the list of sentences made by participating groups expressing visions of future social, political, and economic arrangements in the forum, accessible from its site thjodfundur2010.is, accessed December 5, 2015.

51 The demand for simplicity and lucidity was frequently heard from candidates in the CA elections in 2010; see, for example, Valgarður Guðjónson's web page with his campaign program, accessed December 5, 2015, www.valgardur.com/frambod.htm.

52 The point is emphasized in the CC's commentary to the constitutional bill, which clearly states that according to the draft, the President will no longer have an active legislative role. See *Frumvarp stjórnlagaráðs*, 35.

53 Eiríkur Bergmann, *Iceland and the International Financial Crisis*: *Boom, Bust and Recovery* (London: Palgrave Macmillan, 2014), 180.

54 After a short report describing the discussion in one of the first meetings of Committee B, one council member (Lýður Árnason) urged the committee members to discuss urgently "whether the executive should be elected by the public or the parliament" (*Stjórnlagaráðstíðindi 2a*, 81). The committee members pointed out that this was one of the questions under discussion, and that proposals could be made in that direction (81–82). Subsequent discussion, however, shows that the committee was treating the question as completely open, that is, as regards the role of the President under a new constitution as well as the possibility of electing the prime minister directly. Yet, by the committee's second meeting, it seems clear that its members did not consider abandoning parliamentary democracy a real option (68), although such changes certainly continued to be discussed.

55 Some discussion arose on this issue after the publication of the draft with extensive commentary in August 2011, where numerous changes are explained as attempts to clarify meaning rather than actually change the constitutional order. See, for example, *Frumvarp stjórnlagaráðs með skýringum*, 50, 76, 195; see also Eiríkur Bergmann "Of flókið fyrir þjóðina?" February 21, 2012, accessed December 5, 2015, www.dv.is/blogg/eirikur-bergmann/2012/2/21/of-flokid-fyrir-thjodina/.

56 See, for example, a remark made by Erlingur Sigurðarson during discussion on the basic document: "I don't like this discussion now, how we are talking about procedures and methods, but not the issues," *Stjórnlagaráðstíðindi* 2a, 40.

57 Eiríkur Bergmann, *Iceland and the International Financial Crisis*, 179.

58 Eiríkur Bergmann even suggests in his assessment of the process that the CC's handling of the comments and proposals it did get was not satisfactory. See *Iceland and the International Financial Crisis*, 179.

59 See "Gagnrýnir óvissuferð stjórnvalda," *mbl.is*, December 13, 2012, accessed December 5, 2015, www.mbl.is/frettir/innlent/2012/12/13/gagnrynir_ovissuferd_stjornlagarads/. In this newspaper article, Gunnar Helgi Kristinsson, Professor of Political Science at the University of Iceland, argues that the draft constitution would have

uncertain consequences if it were adopted. The old constitution, on the other hand, he pointed out, had been tested many times in various judicial proceedings.

60 See, for example, Pétur Blöndal, "Stjórnlagaþingið," *Morgunblaðið*, December 6, 2010. Some candidates in the CA elections even declared their intention, if elected, to defend the old constitution from "agitators." See, for example, Þorsteinn Arnalds, "Skemmum ekki stjórnarskrána," *Morgunblaðið*, November 20, 2010.

61 See *Stjórnlagaráðstíðindi*, vol. 2b, 312 (Thorvaldur Gylfason).

62 "Um 1500 manns voru á borgarafundi," *Fréttablaðið*, November 25, 2008. Government ministers are as a rule also MPs in Iceland.

63 The most visible movement at the time was the newly formed "Borgarahreyfingin" [The Citizens' Movement], whose members often mentioned the Civic Forum during the Czech Velvet Revolution as their model.

64 An amateur recording of the remarks is available on youtube.com, "Púað á Ingibjörgu Sólrúnu," www.youtube.com/watch?v=LVq9nA3DIg0. The meeting took place on November 24, 2008. Her exact words were (my translation): "I am not sure that those in the audience can necessarily claim to be talking on behalf of the nation, or have the right to … [booing and shouting from the audience] … that's it."

65 Geir Haarde, "Address to the Nation by H. E. Geir H. Haarde, Prime Minister of Iceland," October 6, 2008, accessed December 5, 2015, http://eng.forsaetisraduneyti.is/news-and-articles/nr/3035. See also Ingimundur Fridriksson, "The Banking Crisis in Iceland in 2008," February 6, 2009, 11, www.sedlabanki.is/lisalib/getfile.aspx?itemid=6795; Heather Horn, "Iceland Is Wrong to Blame Its Leaders for the Financial Crisis, and So Are We," *The Atlantic Monthly*, March 6, 2012, accessed December 5, 2015, www.theatlantic.com/international/archive/2012/03/iceland-is-wrong-to-blame-its-leaders-for-the-financial-crisis-and-so-are-we/254039/.

66 This claim is made in part in a report on the causes of the collapse of the Icelandic banks written by a special parliamentary commission. See Rannsóknarnefnd Alþingis [The Special Investigation Commission of the Icelandic Parliament], *Aðdragandi og orsakir falls íslensku bankanna 2008 og tengdir atburðir*, 9 vols. (Reykjavík: Icelandic Parliament, 2010). See also Thorvaldur Gylfason, *Hreint borð*, 28.

67 Thorvaldur Gylfason, *Hreint borð*, 15–16.

68 For a discussion on agonism, see Chantal Mouffe, *The Democratic Paradox* (London: Verso, 2000), 80–108.

69 During June 2011, as most of the main ideas supported by the CC took shape, the daily *Fréttablaðið* (the most widely read newspaper in Iceland) only twice reported on the CC. In both cases, the news stories were superficial, without any attempt at analysis or explanation, and published in a somewhat sensational way. The first ("Dregið verði verulega úr hlutverki forsetans," *Fréttablaðið*, June 6, 2011) stated that the CC intended to greatly limit the role of the Icelandic President, the second ("Stjórnlagaráð leggur til að kosningakerfinu verði bylt," *Fréttablaðið*, June 11, 2011, 12) that changes to the election system proposed by the CC would be revolutionary. At the same time, some of the CC members published opinion articles in the paper about some aspects of the CC's work.

70 See the party statutes "Lög Dögunar," accessed December 5, 2015, www.xdogun.is/index.php?page=loeg-doegunar, and central policy statements "Kjarnastefna," accessed December 5, 2015, www.xdogun.is/index.php?page=kjarnastefna.

71 Discussion on various systems and e-platforms that could be used to channel the views and wishes of citizens directly to politicians, who would then be required to react in some way to such information, was frequent in the immediate aftermath of the crisis. The idea of directly controlling delegates still exists within movements such as the Pirates, who won three seats in the 2014 parliamentary elections 2013. See information on the Pirate Party policy platform on its website, accessed December 5, 2015, www.piratar.is/policies/?lang=en.

72 Gutmann and Thompson, *Why Deliberative Democracy?* 3–7.

73 Amy Gutmann and Dennis Thompson, *Democracy and Disagreement* (Cambridge, MA: Harvard University Press, 1996), 26.
74 It is a little difficult to cite direct textual evidence to support this, since no one argued explicitly against deliberation. The idea that central political institutions in Iceland were deeply corrupt and should not be consulted was frequently heard in debates about the constitution. A memorable event during which the idea of consulting with MPs was discussed was a seminar with Pasquale Pasquino and a few CC members, organized by the EDDA—Center of Excellence, May 30, 2011. Pasquino encouraged active consultations with MPs to create a friendlier atmosphere around the CC's work. The CC members present, however, argued vehemently and at length against this idea. The main argument was that the CC's integrity would suffer from such connections.
75 The draft was passed unanimously in the CC on July 29, 2011, as many of the Council members had hoped, since they thought that consensus would increase moral pressure on Parliament to accept it. See "Íslendingar verði hreyknir af nýrri stjórnarskrá sinni," *Morgunblaðið*, July 30, 2012; Thorvaldur Gylfason, "Við lýsum eftir stuðningi," *Fréttablaðið*, July 28, 2011.
76 See Thorvaldur Gylfason's blog, in which he argues, citing Jon Elster, that from a moral perspective Parliament must adopt the draft as fit for a referendum and, depending on its outcome, approval or rejection, accessed December 5, 2015, www.dv.is/blogg/thorvaldur-gylfason/2012/5/15/thetta-sagdi-jon-elster/.
77 Vilhjálmur Árnason, "Moral Analysis of an Economic Collapse—An Exercise in Practical Ethics," *Nordic Journal of Applied Ethics* 4, no. 1 (2010), 109–115.
78 Special Investigation Commission, *Causes and Effects of the Fall of the Icelandic Banks*, vol. 8, 179–180.
79 In its report, the Venice Commission, which had been asked to evaluate the constitution bill, developed a number of criticisms, emphasizing shortcomings that clearly reflected lack of time and organization. See European Commission for Democracy through Law (Venice Commission), *Opinion on the Draft New Constitution*, March 11, 2013, CDL-AD(2013)010.
80 See Scott Page, *The Difference: How the Power of Diversity Creates Better Firms, Schools and Societies* (Princeton: Princeton University Press, 2007), 240.

Bibliography

Árnason, Vilhjálmur. "Moral Analysis of an Economic Collapse—An Exercise in Practical Ethics." *Nordic Journal of Applied Ethics* 4, no. 1 (2010): 101–123.

Árnason, Vilhjálmur. "Valdið fært til fólksins? Veikleikar og verkefni íslensks lýðræðis í aðdraganda og eftirmála hrunsins." [Power Given to the People? Weaknesses and Problems of Icelandic Democracy before and after the Collapse] *Skírnir* 187, no. 1 (2013): 11–54.

Árnason, Vilhjálmur, Salvör Nordal, and Kristín Ástgeirsdóttir. "Siðferði og starfshættir í tengslum við fall íslensku bankanna 2008" [Morality and Working Practices in Relation to the Collapse of the Icelandic Banks 2008]. In *Aðdragandi og orsakir falls íslensku bankanna 2008 og tengdir atburðir* [The Causes and Effects of the Fall of the Icelandic Banks and Related Events]. Vol. 8. Reykjavík: Icelandic Parliament, 2010.

Bergmann, Eiríkur. *Iceland and the International Financial Crisis: Boom, Bust and Recovery*. London: Palgrave Macmillan, 2014.

European Commission for Democracy through Law (Venice Commission). *Opinion on the Draft New Constitution*. March 11, 2013, CDL-AD(2013)010.

Fishkin, James. "Rökræðulýðræði og lýðvistaða stjórnarskráin. Tilraunastarfsemin verður að halda áfram." [Deliberative Democracy and the Crowdsourced Constitution. The

Experimentation Must Go On]. In *Lýðræðistilraunir. Ísland í hruni og endurreisn* [Democratic Experiments: Iceland in Collapse and Resurrection], edited by Jón Ólafsson, 23–32. Reykjavík: University of Iceland Press, 2014.

Gutmann, Amy and Dennis Thompson. *Democracy and Disagreement*. Cambridge, MA: Harvard University Press, 1996.

Gutmann, Amy and Dennis Thompson. *Why Deliberative Democracy?* Princeton: Princeton University Press, 2004.

Gylfason, Thorvaldur. *Hreint borð. Greinasafn um frumvarp Stjórnlagaráðs til nýrrar stjórnarskrár* [A Clean Slate. Collection of Articles on the Constitutional Bill Proposed by the Constitutional Council]. Reykjavík: Gutti, 2012.

Gylfason, Thorvaldur. "From Collapse to Constitution." In *Public Debt, Global Governance and Economic Dynamism*, edited by L. Paganetto, 379–417. Milano: Springer Milan, 2013.

Kristinsson, Gunnar Helgi. "Ráðskast með stjórnarskrá" [Pushing the Constitution Around]. *Tímarit um stjórnmál og stjórnsýslu* 8, no. 2 (2012): 565–569.

Landemore, Hélène. "Inclusive Constitution-Making: The Icelandic Experiment." *Journal of Political Philosophy* 23, no. 2 (2015): 166–191.

Mouffe, Chantal. *The Democratic Paradox*. London: Verso, 2000.

Nordal, Salvör. "Þátttaka borgara í ákvarðanatöku og ábyrgð stjórnvalda. Lærdómar af stjórnarskrármáli" [Citizen Participation in Decision-Making and Government Responsibility]. *Skírnir* 189, no. 1 (2015): 119–141.

Ólafsson, Jón. "Rökræðulýðræði verður stofnanalýðræði: Er hættulegt að færa vald til almennings? Athugasemdir við grein Vilhjálms Árnasonar 'Valdið fært til fólksins?'" [Deliberative Democracy becomes Institutional Democracy: Is It Dangerous to Give Power to the People? Comments on Vilhjálmur Árnason's Article "Power to the People?"] *Tímarit um stjórnmál og stjórnsýslu* 10, no. 1 (2014): 119–142.

Page, Scott. *The Difference. How the Power of Diversity Creates Better Firms, Schools and Societies*. Princeton: Princeton University Press, 2007.

Rannsóknarnefnd Alþingis [The Special Investigation Commission of the Icelandic parliament], *Aðdragandi og orsakir falls íslensku bankanna 2008 og tengdir atburðir* [The Causes and Effects of the Fall of the Icelandic Banks and Related Events]. 9 vols. Reykjavík: Icelandic Parliament, 2010.

Skýrsla stjórnlaganefndar [Report of the Constitutional Committee]. Vol. 1. Reykjavík: Constitutional Committee, 2011.

Stjórnlagaráðstíðindi [Constitutional Council News] 1. Fundargerðir, aðdragandi og starfið [Constitutional Council Reports vol. 1, Meeting Minutes, Preparations and Progress]. Reykjavík: Constitutional Council, 2011.

Stjórnlagaráðstíðindi [Constitutional Council News] 2a, 2b. Umræður á ráðsfundum [Constitutional Council Reports vol. 2a: Verbatim Reports of Plenary Sessions]. Reykjavík: Constitutional Council, 2011.

Index

Page numbers in *italics* denote tables, those in **bold** denote figures.

For Product Safety Concerns and Information please contact our EU representative GPSR@taylorandfrancis.com
Taylor & Francis Verlag GmbH, Kaufingerstraße 24, 80331 München, Germany

www.ingramcontent.com/pod-product-compliance
Ingram Content Group UK Ltd.
Pitfield, Milton Keynes, MK11 3LW, UK
UKHW020015200926
475702UK00014B/1894
9781138598423